ENGLISH METRICAL PSALMS

During the sixteenth century the Book of Psalms was considered to be a uniquely authoritative and universally applicable collection of religious poems. Whereas the Bible in general taught what God said to man, the Psalms, it was felt, taught man how to speak to God. From the 1530s people of many different religious and intellectual persuasions discovered that the poetry of the Psalms lent itself to memorable English translation, and a substantial and varied range of imitations of the Psalms began to appear. Dr Zim's book is the first full-scale study of this important poetic genre to be published in this century.

After a brief examination of sixteenth-century perceptions of the Psalms and renaissance views of imitation, there are separate chapters on psalms by Wyatt, Surrey, Sternhold, Sidney, and the Countess of Pembroke with discussion of many minor figures' work; a guide to ninety 'English Psalm Versions Printed 1530–1601' is included as an appendix. In challenging a number of current critical orthodoxies and illuminating the expressive qualities of these poems, Dr Zim has produced a major contribution to our understanding of Tudor literary culture.

ENGLISH METRICAL PSALMS

POETRY AS PRAISE AND PRAYER
1535–1601

RIVKAH ZIM

Fellow of Pembroke College
Cambridge

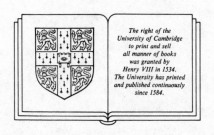

The right of the
University of Cambridge
to print and sell
all manner of books
was granted by
Henry VIII in 1534.
The University has printed
and published continuously
since 1584.

CAMBRIDGE UNIVERSITY PRESS

CAMBRIDGE

LONDON   NEW YORK   NEW ROCHELLE

MELBOURNE   SYDNEY

Published by the Press Syndicate of the University of Cambridge
The Pitt Building, Trumpington Street, Cambridge CB2 1RP
32 East 57th Street, New York, NY 10022, USA
10 Stamford Road, Oakleigh, Melbourne 3166, Australia

First published 1987

Printed in Great Britain at
the University Press, Cambridge

British Library cataloguing in publication data
Zim, Rivkah
English metrical psalms: poetry as praise and prayer 1535–1601.
1. Bible. O.T. Psalms – Paraphrases, English – History and criticism
2. Christian poetry, English – Early modern, 1500–1700 –
History and criticism
1. Title
821'.309'382   PR535.C65

Library of Congress cataloguing in publication data
Zim, Rivkah.
English metrical psalms.
Bibliography.
Includes index.
1. Bible. O.T. Psalms – Paraphrases, English – History and criticism.
1. Title.
BS1440.A1Z55   1987   223'.205201   87–24425

ISBN 0 521 33302 4

CE

FOR MY PARENTS AND TEACHERS

CONTENTS

vii

PREFACE

The Book of Psalms contains 150 short lyrics. Psalms are vehicles for the expression of human feeling – excitement, anger, fear, doubt, tenderness – as well as earnest personal prayer and jubilant adoration. Hence the psalmists' relationships with God are lively, direct and invigorating; their attitudes and tones in addressing the Almighty are not consistently pious. The psalmists assume not only that God listens, and sometimes hears, but also that God can be argued with and given orders. The spiritual realities of these relationships are powerfully imagined in terms of the realities experienced within nature and human society.

It is scarcely possible to over-estimate the significance which these texts, employing formulaic expressions, parallelisms, personal forms of address and symbolic metaphors, had on innumerable lives. Whether or not they were personally religious, people lived in familiar ease with the ideas and images from the Psalms, which became ingrained habits of mind. For generations, literacy was determined by a test of knowledge of psalm texts. The peculiar value of the Psalms was their capacity to articulate in moving, poetic language, the spiritual experience of mankind. Psalms have always been regarded as poetic prayers and praises by and of the people. Whereas the rest of the Bible taught man the Word of God, the Book of Psalms not only taught man how to speak to God but also encapsulated the teaching of the entire Bible.

As memorable poetry which lends itself to memorable translation psalms captured the imagination of countless writers. There have been many English translations: thirteen manuscripts of Latin psalters survive with continuous interlinear glosses in Old English; Middle English translations include the Surtees Psalter, Richard Rolle's psalms (written for Margaret Kirkby), the West Midlands psalter and versions of the seven penitential psalms by Richard Maydestone and by Thomas Brampton. In the seventeenth and eighteenth centuries psalms in old and new translations provided models for devotional poetry and for hymns. Later, Romantic poets responded to the psalmist's literary realization of God's immanence in nature and the clarity of his direct apprehension of the sublime by writing Hebrew Melodies, Odes to the West Wind, and Songs of Innocence and Experience.

But in the sixteenth century, English writers, including some of the best lyric poets, imitated a wider range of psalm themes, tones and applications by engaging directly with the biblical models, and produced varied and enthusiastic responses to the poetry of the Psalms as praise and prayer in scores of new metrical paraphrases.

This book started life as a doctoral dissertation in 1975. Over the years I have benefited from the advice, encouragement, criticism and intellectual stimulus of many scholars and pupils (too many to mention separately) in the Universities of Leeds, London, Oxford and Cambridge. However, some special acknowledgements are due and gratefully given.

Among those who have very kindly either given advice on specific matters, or, read all, or part, of this book in various drafts, offering many helpful suggestions are: Dr H. V. Baron, Dr J. A. Caldwell, Professor R. E. Clements, Mrs E. E. Duncan-Jones, Professor I-S. Ewbank, Mr A. S. Hollis, Dr L. A. Jardine, Professor E. L. Jones, Mr D. Lindley, Dr R. Luckett, Mr W. D. McGaw, Dr A. J. Minnis, Professor J. Rees and Mr S. Wall. Professor J. R. H. Horden and Dr D. M. Rogers taught me the rudiments of research and encouraged my first explorations into the Bodleian Library's collections of early printed books. I thank them all most warmly.

My debts to individual scholars' printed works are recorded in the end notes. Unless otherwise acknowledged all the opinions expressed in this book are my own and I am solely responsible for any errors which may lurk within.

I am grateful to the Trustees of the Caroline Spurgeon Research Fellowship for financial support during work towards this book in 1978–9.

I should also like to express my gratitude to Mrs F. J. Templeton who has cheerfully typed innumerable drafts from appalling manuscript copy, and to the assistant library staff in the Bodleian Library, the University Library, Cambridge, and the British Library.

My greatest single debt is to Dr M. B. Parkes who gave me substantial help and encouragement at all stages in the writing of this book. The benefits of Dr Parkes's wide academic experience, formidable example and selfless generosity can best be fully appreciated by the many scholars and pupils who have been privileged to receive his criticism and guidance.

Finally, it is a great pleasure to thank my parents, Dr and Mrs M. H. Zim, for teaching me most of the best lessons of my life, both personal and academic, in their wisdom, patience and love.

Pembroke College
Cambridge

CONVENTIONS AND ABBREVIATIONS

The word 'Psalms' as a singular form is used to refer to the Book of Psalms in the Bible. When referring to individual psalms I use the Hebrew numbers, as in the English Protestant Bibles from 1539 onwards. In references to the Vulgate text, or versions which use the Vulgate numbers, the Hebrew number follows in square brackets: for example, 'Ps. 54[55]'. When, for the reader's convenience, I have compared extracts from metrical psalm versions with the biblical text, I have quoted that translation (of an appropriate date) which happens to be closest to the metrical version under discussion. In some instances I have offered comparisons between an English version and the Hebrew original or the Latin Vulgate translation.

Quotations from the Psalms in Hebrew are taken without further acknowledgement from, *The Psalms: Hebrew Text & English Translation*, ed. A. Cohen, Soncino Books of the Bible (London and Bournemouth, 1950).

Quotations from the Vulgate Psalms are from the Gallican version in *Quincuplex Psalterium Gallicum. Rhomanum. Hebraicum. Vetus. Conciliatum*, 2nd edn (Paris, 1513), facsimile edn Travaux d'Humanisme et Renaissance, clxx (Geneva, 1979).

Quotations from the Psalms in Coverdale's English Bibles (1535 and 1539), the Geneva Bible (1560) and the Bishops' Bible (1568) are taken from *The Hexaplar Psalter being the Book of Psalms in Six English Versions*, ed. W. A. Wright (Cambridge, 1911, repr. in *Anglistica & Americana: A Series of Reprints*, lv, Hildesheim and New York, 1969).

In all quotations from sixteenth-century texts I have endeavoured to preserve the spelling and punctuation of the copies or facsimiles I have used. However, I have expanded silently all contracted forms no longer in modern use, abandoned such typographical conventions as 'y^e' and 'y^t' in favour of 'the' and 'that', and adapted the variant forms of i j u v w to conform to modern usage.

In the end notes the first reference to a work in each chapter is given in full, thereafter repeat references are by short title in the case of a book, and by abbreviation of the title of the journal in the case of an article.

Citations include such references as fol. (folio), sig. (signature) (in which cases superscript r or v indicate the recto or verso of the leaf), p. (page), col. (column), pref. (preface), ded. (dedicated/dedication), ch. (chapter), edn (edition), tr. (translator), MS(S) (manuscript(s)), Ps.(s.) (Psalm(s)).

BCP	Book of Common Prayer
B. Lib.	British Library, London
Bodl.	Bodleian Library, Oxford
CUL	Cambridge University Library
D & M	T. H. Darlow and H. F. Moule, rev. A. S. Herbert, *Historical Catalogue of Printed Editions of the English Bible 1525–1961* (London and New York, 1968)
DNB	*Dictionary of National Biography*
H & L³	Halkett and Laing, *A Dictionary of Anonymous and Pseudonymous Publications in the English Language*, 3rd edn 1475–1640, ed. J. Horden (Harlow and London, 1980)
OED	*Oxford English Dictionary*
SR	*A Transcript of the Registers of the Company of Stationers of London 1554–1640*, ed. E. Arber, 5 vols. (London, 1875)
STC²	A. W. Pollard and G. R. Redgrave, *A Short Title Catalogue of Books Printed in England,*

Scotland, & Ireland And of English Books Printed Abroad 1475–1640, 2nd edn, revised and enlarged by W. A. Jackson, F. S. Ferguson and K. F. Pantzer, vol. 1 (London, 1986), vol. 2 (London, 1976)

The illustration is from the heading to the Psalms from the Matthew Bible (1537). It shows David with Uriah and Bathsheba before Jerusalem, the battle, and David's penitence. (Reproduced by permission of the Bodleian Library)

1

AN INTRODUCTION

IMITATIO AND THE PSALMS IN SIXTEENTH-CENTURY ENGLAND

The Book of Psalms is a treasury of memorable, lyrical expression, which has been especially valued as a mirror of mankind's spiritual experience. The poetic qualities of the Psalms had been recognized and assessed by the early Church Fathers and by medieval commentators. The views of the Fathers were transmitted to sixteenth-century readers by contemporary translators and commentators. Throughout the sixteenth century the Psalms were regarded as authoritative and eloquent texts, and were used to enrich the spiritual life of all Christians. These traditional attitudes to the Psalms and their intrinsic affective appeal ensured their continued application for devotional purposes by Catholics and by Protestants of all denominations. To a priest and poet such as John Donne the Psalms embodied 'the highest matter in the noblest forme'.[1]

In the sixteenth century a powerful stimulus to new translations and imitations of the Psalms was provided by humanist studies of the Hebrew Bible:[2] the new opportunities for scholarly reassessment of the text coincided with traditional motives for interest in the Psalms. In 1530, George Joye was the first Englishman to offer his countrymen a printed text of 'the trowth of the Psalmes' translated into English from 'the Ebrue verite/ in the which tonge David/ with the other syngers of the Psalmes firste sunge them'.[3] Joye omitted to mention that he knew no Hebrew

1

himself, but he did acknowledge his dependence on the new Latin translation from Hebrew by the continental scholar Martin Bucer (1491–1551).[4] In his dedication Joye asked 'the gostly lerned in the holy tonge' (i.e. Hebrew) to judge whether or not his version was 'faithfully & purely translated: which ye may not mesure and Juge aftir the comen texte'[5] (i.e. the Latin Vulgate).

More than seventy different, new versions in English were printed during the seventy-year period from the publication of Joye's psalter until the end of the century. These printed versions include scholarly, devotional and literary versions of various kinds. In addition, numerous versions survive in contemporary manuscripts.[6]

English metrical psalm versions may be regarded as a particular 'kind' of literature. Each different literary version is related to all the others in that they all share the same model – the Book of Psalms. They are also related to each other in that they are products of a particular historical period and hence of the culture of that period. I have selected for discussion those metrical versions which seem to be representative of the various treatments and applications of psalms during the sixteenth century. Each example embodies contemporary views of what was thought to be proper to the nature of a psalm. An examination of metrical psalms as instances of a literary kind, rather than as the works of individual authors, can show how different authors exploited the shared, contemporary resources of that kind. Such an examination is also a way of restoring copious opportunities for assessing the originality of different writers in their responses to the same biblical model. I am concerned with those literary qualities of the Psalms which were translatable, and with the opportunities in this period, which these model texts afforded for writing poetry, rather than with the place of the Psalms in theological debate.

Sixteenth-century readers of metrical psalms (and probably a large proportion of their non-literate audience too) had an intimate knowledge of the biblical models. They had inherited an educational tradition in which the Book of Psalms was regarded as a vehicle for basic moral and religious instruction.[7] They had also inherited a devotional tradition in which the Psalms provided a nucleus for the private prayers of the laity and this tradition persisted among Catholics and Protestants alike.[8] I have assumed that sixteenth-century readers' attitudes to the Psalms would have conditioned their responses to the various sixteenth-century English metrical versions.

However, for most of us the Psalms no longer feature prominently in our daily lives and are unfamiliar texts. In so far as this may be so, we have lost the knowledge and cultural contexts which enable us to evaluate the character and quality of these poetic paraphrases. A significant part of the intellectual pleasure to be gained from reading these paraphrases was derived from instantaneous comparisons with their models. Nevertheless there have been notable studies of psalm versions by influential scholars such as Hallett Smith, Lily B. Campbell and Barbara Lewalski; in addition, H. A. Mason, Kenneth Muir and Patricia Thomson have made prominent contributions to the study of Wyatt's psalms, while Theodore Spencer, Louis Martz and Coburn Freer, for example, have focussed attention on Sidney's psalms.[9]

I have questioned three of the various assumptions made about sixteenth-century psalmists' motives and premises. The first of these derives from the general application of an argument based on only part of the available material: that the creation of a Christian literature based on the Bible was 'a means of combating the influence of the revival of classical learning and the developing taste for pagan and secular story and song'.[10]

This assumption receives some support from the titles and dedications of psalm versions by such zealous moral reformers as Miles Coverdale, Thomas Becon and John Hall (all Protestants), and the Catholic writer and publisher, Richard Verstegan.[11] Becon, for example, expressed the pious hope that 'all Mynstrels in the world', and all sorts of persons 'both olde & yonge, woulde . . . leave theyr lascivious, wanton & unclene balades, & syng such godly & vertuous songes, as David techeth them'.[12] He would also have liked 'all Scholemasters & teachers of youth' to 'teach these verses of David . . . in stede of Virgile, Ovide, Horas, Catullus, Tibullus, Propertius, &c.'.[13] Nevertheless, a general application of Becon's words cannot explain why some of the best English poets of the period – including Wyatt, Surrey, Sidney and Spenser[14] – should have imitated psalms. These poets did not repudiate their amatory and classical verse in order to write imitations of biblical verse.

Far from being a puritanical reaction to advances in scholarly textual and literary studies, the vogue for biblical literature, especially for metrical psalm versions, during the sixteenth century was a direct consequence of these humanist trends. We no longer regard the cultural history of the Renaissance as a battle between the old learning and the new 'pagan' learning. There were ancient precedents for co-existence: 'as a man and a citizen, one [was] a Christian; as a rhetor, a pagan'.[15] In northern Europe especially, the revival of ancient learning was largely the work of theologians and clerics. Humanist scholars such as Reuchlin, Erasmus, Colet and Vives were devout men who dedicated themselves with pious and moral intentions to the textual study of the Bible.[16] They were also immediately concerned with the refinement of contemporary Latin style by the imitation of classical and patristic authors. Juan Luis Vives wrote in his *De tradendis disciplinis* (1531):

No subject matter, no knowledge is, of itself, contrary to piety . . . For subjects of study are taken from things which the good God has made, and for that reason they are good

(Pietati nulla est ex se materies contraria, nulla cognitio . . . Materiae namque ex rebus sumuntur, quas omnes condidit bonus Deus, ideo bonas)[17]

4

Vives insisted on a positive moral utility for all studies: whether or not they were intrinsically good was not the only consideration, they must also be of use to us, 'since we do not learn arts and disciplines for their own sakes, but for our good'.

(Sed quamvis nulla eruditio, & peritia pietati non serviat ex se, non hoc tamen est consyderandum [sic] unum, sed quid nobis conducit: quando quidem artes ac disciplinas non propter ipsas discimus, sed propter nos)[18]

Moreover, sixteenth-century English authors and readers had comprehensive tastes, and approached literary texts in many different ways. Arthur Golding was the translator of both Ovid's *Metamorphoses* and Calvin's commentaries on the Psalms. The title page of Golding's *Metamorphosis translated oute of Latin into Englishe meter* advises the reader that it is 'A woorke very pleasaunt and delectable', but also warns that

With skill, heede, and judgement, thys woorke must bee red,
For els too the reader it stands in small stead[19]

Such warnings were usually aimed at the common reader by scholars who believed that literature had the power to influence men's lives directly. Their prime concern was with the moral standards of unsophisticated readers for whose benefit they translated 'piththy and grounded matter' without the 'rhetorical inlarging of painted sentences'.[20] Golding explained in the dedication which he added to his translation of Calvin's commentaries that he had 'sincerely performed the dutie of a faithfull Interpreter', and laid 'foorth things plainlye ... to the understanding of many', rather than 'too the pleasing of a fewe. For in this and suche other workes, the rude and ignorant have more interest, than the learned and skilful'.[21] Golding was a much respected gentleman scholar with pronounced puritan opinions in religious matters, but in the sixteenth century his literary reputation was based both on his translation of Calvin and on his translation of Ovid. To regard sixteenth-century metrical psalms as part of a general determined effort to displace love poetry is misleading.

An examination of the activities of sixteenth-century metrical psalmists such as Wyatt, Surrey and Sidney can help to illuminate our understanding of the culture of renaissance humanism, and the place of literary studies within that culture. Each wrote poetry by exploiting the resources of several literary kinds, both religious and secular. Modern studies of renaissance culture and of all the poetry (not only metrical psalms) of the period should seek to restore a balance between religious and secular kinds.

The arts of reading and writing were connected with the whole experience of the whole man. Literature and wisdom were not considered ends in themselves, but means to induce some morally well-directed action. According to Christian humanist criteria there were several ways and means to achieve worthy ends. The resources of Christian literature, especially the Bible, and of pagan literature were employed in parallel. By the end of the sixteenth century English literary theorists were able to defend 'poesie', and the authority of verse, by citing biblical and pagan poets as ancient, excellent exponents of the art.[22] Sir John Harington, for example, allowed 'Heroicall Poesie' a fit training for the appreciation of 'true divinitie'[23] in the Bible, and cited the examples of Moses and Daniel brought up in the secular learning of their early pagan cultural environments before coming to their higher vocations. The Renaissance valued both sources of wisdom and eloquence.

The second assumption (found especially in interpretations of Wyatt's penitential psalms), is that the expressions of feeling found in sixteenth-century psalm versions represent the personal experiences and feelings of the individual poet. As a result autobiographical reference and personal 'sincerity' have been inferred in works which are successful and persuasive imitations of model texts by other writers.

6

In the Psalms the personal expression of deep feeling is proper to the biblical texts. It was these expressive qualities which made the Psalms appropriate vehicles of personal devotion. Nevertheless, when dealing with such moving (i.e. affective) and lyrical subjects as psalms critics may be unconsciously influenced by Romantic conceptions of poetry as 'the spontaneous overflow of powerful feelings', and of the poet as 'a nightingale who sits in darkness and sings to cheer its own solitude'.[24]

The third assumption is that translation or imitation is an inferior, non-creative activity. The argument that metrical psalm versions cannot be considered new or original works because 'the act of translation is a species of submission'[25] is based on a misunderstanding of the significance of imitation for a humanist poet, and of the literary processes of imitation themselves.

In the sixteenth century, the art of poetry was considered an art of imitation. Sidney's definition of 'Poesie', for example, is a digest of the *loci* of ancient and humanist literary theory:

Poesie therefore, is an Art of Imitation: for so Aristotle termeth it in the word [*mimesis*], that is to say, a representing, counterfeiting, or figuring forth[26]

The poet was commonly regarded as a 'maker', inventively representing or 'figuring forth' in words, the images within his mind in order to imitate.[27]

The misunderstanding of imitation and translation may be related to Puttenham's remark that the translator who follows 'any foreine copie or example . . . may well be sayd a versifier, but not a Poet'.[28] However, Puttenham also stated in the same chapter, 'Of Poets and Poesie', that 'a Poet may in some sort be said a follower or imitator, because he can express the true and lively of every thing is set before him'.[29] Although he is here discussing the imitation of nature, or Aristotelian *mimesis*, the notion of imitation had wider and more diverse implications for sixteenth-century writers.

7

Interpretation is necessarily transient and historical, but I regard it as axiomatic that when a renaissance author chose a particular genre that choice was appropriate to his specific purpose in writing. As Alastair Fowler has argued, an author's expectations of the literary kind he chooses enable (rather than disable) his creativity.[30] The generic model determines an interpretative horizon of prior instances of works to which the author must respond or react in some way. The particular relevance of such an approach to sixteenth-century poetry was recognized by Hallett Smith more than thirty years ago: 'in the sixteenth century . . . the appropriate context for poetry is a series of ideals, values, commonplaces, or conventions'.[31] It is necessary therefore to examine the values and conventions which determined the sixteenth-century psalmists' perceptions of their models. However, we must look first at some of the concepts and premises of these psalmists in relation to the processes of literary imitation.

All the sixteenth-century imitators of the Psalms were engaged in an activity that in one way or another underlay the greater part of renaissance literature: the differences between poems, according to J. C. Scaliger, himself influenced by Aristotle, lay in 'quae imitamur, quibus imitamur, & quomodo imitamur'.[32] I have selected from the range of contemporary discussions of imitation a limited number which can best illuminate those aspects of imitation with which sixteenth-century psalmists were most concerned. The whole system of imitation – the what, with what, and how – offered a way of talking about style, as well as a way of learning to write.

Vives had asserted that imitation was the fashioning of a certain thing in accordance with a proposed model:

Imitatio . . . effictio est rei alicuius ad exemplar propositum[33]

The imitator, he said, studied the proposed model most attentively, not only interpreting it but also considering the art or procedure by which the author accomplished it:

in order that he himself with a similar artifice may achieve that which he intends by the will

(Proposito autem ante oculos exemplari attentissime aemulator contempletur, ac consyderet, qua tandem arte, ac ratione ab autore id putet confectum ut simili artificio & ipse quod animo destinarit, perficiat)[34]

Since the imitator sought to accomplish his own willed intention (*quod animo destinarit*) in his own work, an imitation was a new work. The process of imitation promoted originality in the literary expression of traditional materials and values.

Translation and paraphrase were both processes of imitation *ad exemplar propositum*, but an important distinction between them turns on the imitator's intentions with respect to the original author's meaning. The object of a translation was to provide a faithful transposition of the original author's meaning in a form which allowed synonymity. This objective gave rise to a method of interpretation which paid scrupulous attention to the words and style of the author. As Thomas Norton, who translated Calvin's *Institutes*, observed:

they that wote what it is to translate well and faithfully . . . do know that not only the grammaticall construction of words suffiseth, but the very buildinge and order to observe all advantages of vehemence or grace, by placing or accent of wordes, maketh much to the true setting foorth of a wryters minde[35]

The 'fit translater' was required to show proper concern for the original author's style – 'a certaine resembling and shadowing out of the forme of his style and the maner of his speaking' in the imitation.[36]

Fidelity to the words and style of the original was particularly important in a 'matter of faith and religion', where, as Norton believed, it was 'perillous . . . to erre'.[37] Norton complained that Calvin's terse and precise style, and his difficult but important subject matter, 'encombred' the translator 'with great doutfulnesse for the whole order & frame' of the translation.[38] Norton's principal anxiety was that he might misrepresent the original. He realized that it was not possible to transpose his author's 'meaning in Latine' by simply using English equivalents of the individual Latin words:

> If I should follow the words, I saw that of necessity the hardnesse in the translation must nedes be greater than was in the tonge wherin it was originally wrytten[39]

The interpretative value of such a translation would be negligible. On the other hand, Norton explained,

> If I should leave the course of wordes, and graunt my selfe liberty after the naturall maner of my owne tonge, to say that in English which I conceaved to be his meaning in Latine, I plainly perceived how hardly I might escape errour ... For I durst not presume to warrant my selfe to have his meaninge without his wordes[40]

Norton's problem was to accommodate the meaning of his words in English with Calvin's in Latin and thus to make available the work which he considered 'sound truth'[41] in a form comprehensible to English readers. He realized that the style of the original revealed the writer's mind and, therefore, after careful consideration of the difficulties of translation, he chose a method which allowed him to achieve a degree of synonymity: 'to followe the wordes so neere as the phrase of the Englishe tonge would suffer me'.[42]

Norton's scruples indicate that matters of religion raised problems of an exceptional nature for scholarly translators. The actual words of the Bible required the most exacting scrutiny when scholars translated texts which were intended to carry the authority of the Word of God. In the 1530s Coverdale had condemned the irresponsibility of too 'rash wryters' who did not give 'so greate diligence, as is due in the holy scripture,' and left out '& sometyme altered some word or wordes ...'[43] Coverdale's epistle to the reader in his *newe testament* expresses his sense of duty to the 'pure and very originall texte' of 'the worde of God', and asserts his intention to interpret 'the meanynge of the holy goost' whom he considered to be 'the authoure' of the text.[44] But when commenting on the doctrinal disputes which had arisen from his choice between such English words as 'penance' or 'repentance', he wrote:

I am indifferent to call it aswell with the one terme as with the other, so longe as I know that it is no prejudice nor injury to the meanynge of the holy goost: Neverthelesse I am very scrupulous to go from the vocable of the text[45]

Coverdale's belief in the 'lyke worthynesse and authorite' of the 'worde of God', 'in what language so ever the holy goost speaketh it',[46] is a measure of his confidence in the scrupulous translator's ability to achieve a high degree of synonymity with the letter of the text:

And therefore am I, and wyl be whyle I lyve . . . alwaye wyllynge and ready to do my best aswell in one translation, as in another[47]

In such a spirit of optimism new translations of the Bible were undertaken, and were constantly revised, throughout the sixteenth century.[48]

Although fear of compromising the integrity of the sense of the Word of God raised exceptional problems for translators of the Bible, in practice, sixteenth-century translators of other works rarely aimed at strict literal translation.[49] As Coverdale and Norton recognized, a translation, however viable, was always a provisional representation of the meaning of the original author. The primary requirement of any translation was fidelity to the sense of the original. Nicholas Grimald was adamant that if a translation

yelde not the meaning of the author: but eyther folowing fansie, or misledde by errour, forsakes the true pattern: it cannot be approved for a faithfull, & sure interpretacion: which ought to be taken for the greatest praise of all[50]

Although the conscientious translator's aim was synonymity with his model, a translation or 'interpretacion' was nevertheless acknowledged as a new work. Grimald wrote of his translation of Cicero's *De officiis* (1558):

I have made this latin writer, english: & . . . have caused an auncient writing to becomme in a maner, new againe[51]

He regarded himself as having 'now brought into light' the 'auncient writing' which was 'so long . . . hidden' from 'our unlatined people'; and he called his new book 'mine, as Plautus, and Terence called the comedies theyrs, which they made out of Greeke'.[52]

By contrast, the object of a paraphrase was to provide a 'plain declaracion, exposicion or glose'[53] of the original author's meaning in new words and as briefly as possible. This objective gave rise to a method of interpretation by emulation, 'by speaking alongside the model as it were', *quasi iuxta loquens*.[54] When Quintilian had recommended poetic paraphrase to the young orator in search of eloquence, he had said that it should strive and contend with the original to express the same meaning, and not be restricted to a bare transposition of the model:

Neque ego paraphrasim esse interpretationem tantum volo, sed circa eosdem sensus certamen atque aemulationem[55]

However, since the paraphrast was not obliged to preserve the author's meaning in the author's words, a paraphrase could not carry that degree of authority which was held by the best translation or literal interpretation. By adopting paraphrase as his method of imitation a writer acknowledged that he was not presenting the original text, nor claiming to reproduce it. Coverdale, for example, was careful to explain that a paraphrase 'be not the texte' itself.[56] Anthony Gilby, translator of Theodore Beza's psalm paraphrases, pointed out the relationship between *paraphrasis* and commentary: 'there be two special kinds of explaning the Scriptures, one in long Commentaries, another by Paraphrasis, that is giving the ful sense and meaning . . . in other words, as briefelie as may be'.[57]

In scholarly paraphrases emulation was subordinated to elucidation. However, although some humanists wanted the art of paraphrase reserved for the best scholars,[58] not all paraphrases were the works of scholarly interpreters. When a poet paraphrased an admired model, and aimed at emulation rather than elucidation, he was free to use a more inventive method. Roger Ascham declared: 'if ye alter also, the composition, forme, and order' of a model text, as well as the 'wordes', 'than that is not *Paraphrasis*, but *Imitatio*'.[59] Ascham's definition of *imitatio* by contrast with *paraphrasis* raises a major problem in connexion with sixteenth-century discussions of creative writing, where a wide range of literary activities was often subsumed under the same term: *imitatio*.[60]

The term *imitatio* could be applied equally to the translation exercises of schoolboys and to the creative methods of great poets. It could refer to the imitation of a complete text or any part of it, to the imitation of special local features of style associated either with a model author, such as Cicero, or with a genre, such as epic. *Imitatio* could also refer to the exploitation of catch phrases, verse forms, or to the slightest allusion to an image, or to a proper noun associated with a particular model.[61] Although it sometimes seems that each author understood something different by the term, all their meanings would have fallen within Vives's general definition of *imitatio* as the fashioning of a certain thing *ad exemplar propositum*.

Ascham defined 'Imitation' as 'a facultie to expresse livelie and perfitelie that example: which ye go about to folow', and observed that 'of it selfe it is large and wide: for all the workes of nature, in a maner be examples for arte to folow'.[62] He went on to distinguish 'three kindes of it in matters of learning': imitation 'of the life of everie degree of man', imitation of 'the best authors', and thirdly 'to know perfitlie' how to imitate a chosen model and how to evaluate that imitation, or 'trewelie [to] discern, whether ye folow rightlie or no'.[63] Such '*Imitatio is dissimilis materiei*

13

similis tractatio: and also, *similis materiei dissimilis tractatio*, as Virgill folowed Homer'.[64] Ascham set out six points to observe when comparing a Roman author's imitation with its Greek model. The last point was to note how the imitator 'altereth and changeth' his model to suit his own 'present purpose' in writing:

either, in proprietie of wordes, in forme of sentence, in substance of the matter, or in one, or other convenient circumstance of the authors present purpose[65]

He continued his account of *imitatio* by citing and summarizing the debates among the ancients and his contemporaries on the nature and value of 'Imitation'.[66]

Erasmus, Vives, Scaliger and Ascham used the word *imitatio* when discussing the imitation of texts, but Sidney used an Aristotelian term, *mimesis*, when he glossed the conventional definition of poetry as an art of imitation. In the *Poetics*, Aristotle had advised young Greek writers to ensure that their representations of nature, especially human nature in the drama, were credible and typical.[67]

However, when Sidney used the Artistotelian term he invested it with a neo-Platonic significance: Sidney was not advocating the imitation of nature as such, but rather an ideal perception of a kind of pre-lapsarian world, which was generated imaginatively by the aspiring mind, or 'erected wit', of a 'right' poet.[68]

In the present discussion, where *imitatio* denotes the literary imitation of texts, this term may be understood to include and assume the effects of Aristotelian *mimesis*, in so far as the model text and its imitation would both have been composed with respect to the credible representation of types occurring in nature, or, as Ascham observed, imitation of 'the life of everie degree of man'.

Since there was confusion and contradiction in the use of descriptive terms in renaissance debates, I have attempted to concentrate on those aspects of imitation which seem to be common to all its major varieties. In the first place, successful imitation of any kind required the exercise of a mature critical judgement by the imitator. Secondly, it was important that any imitator's studious consideration and evaluation of his model, *ut simili artificio ... perficiat,*[69] should be matched by an independent capacity to apply the products of his attentive critical reading to his 'present purpose', or that *quod animo destinarit* in writing.

Any imitator was free to exploit the resources of his model inventively. The relationship between the model and the new work could be as close or as distant as the imitator wished. However, an interpretative imitation, such as a paraphrase, was a new work in which the imitator tried to respect and elucidate the original author's meaning as the imitator had understood it. In such cases the relationship between the model and the imitation was well developed, and a close one, because the imitator expected the meaning of his new work to overlap with the original author's meaning. He therefore used his individual voice to 'speak alongside' that of the original author, representing his understanding of the sense of the *exemplar propositum* in his own words.

Since every imitation embodies the imitator's meaning, whether or not this overlaps with the original author's meaning, every imitation is a new work: a re-creation or a transposition, but never a reproduction, because every imitator is an individual. It was an ancient truism that every individual's style was peculiar to him. Vives, following Quintilian, wrote

Certain of those [things] which are proposed for imitation, can never be completely reproduced, because of the sort of thing which is natural to mankind

(Eorum quae imitatione sunt proposita, quaedam nunquam possis ad perfectum referre, quod genus sunt homini naturalia)

He continued that the imitator must nevertheless try to follow the models 'since it is not granted to equal them'; it would be madness, he considered, to hope to do that:

ea vero semper sunt sequenda, quoniam aequare non est concessum: furoris est enim hoc sperare[70]

The differences between models and their imitations were as inevitable as the differences between individual human beings, because, ultimately, every individual's style was peculiar to him. It could never be copied exactly by anyone else and there would therefore be as many different imitations of a particular model as there were imitators.

However, this did not preclude what was commonly referred to as a family resemblance between the model and the imitation, such as that which exists between a father and his son. Petrarch had explained in a letter to Boccaccio that 'an imitator must see to it that what he writes is similar, but not the very same' as his model; this similarity 'should be not like that of an image of the person represented . . . but rather like that of a son to a father' who has a totally independent identity:

Curandum imitatori, ut quod scribit simile non idem sit, eamque similitudinem talem esse oportere, non qualis est imaginis ad eum cuius imago est . . . sed qualis filii ad patrem[71]

Vives also took up this *topos* which seems to have originated in Seneca's moral epistle 84.[72] Vives, however, stressed the moral influence of the parental model:

A son is said to be like his father, not so much in that he recalls his features, his face and form, but because he shows to us his father's manners, his mode of thinking, his conversation, his gait, his movements, and, as it were, the very life which issues forth in his actions as he goes abroad, from the dwelling-place of the soul within, and shows itself to us

(Filius non tam dicitur patri similis, si lineamenta, si figuram & formam referat, quam si mores, ingenium, sermonem, incessum, motum, & illam quasi vitam, quae ex interiore animae sede foras, per actiones emicat, & se nobis ostendit)[73]

The analogy from life also occurs in those descriptions of imitation which are couched in terms of natural metaphors drawn from anabolic processes, such as the bees' manufacture of honey, or the digestion and assimilation of food. It was recognized that in such processes the raw materials are transformed into new substances. Petrarch and Erasmus both took over these anabolic metaphors which had been developed in Seneca's epistle. Petrarch advised: we must write just as the bees make honey, not keeping the flowers but turning them into a sweetness of our own.[74] Erasmus's Bulephorus echoed Quintilian's imitation of Seneca in stressing the personal lively qualities of successful imitation:

What you have consumed (*devoraris*) in varied and prolonged reading has to be digested, and transferred by a process of reflection (*meditatione*) into the grain of the mind (*in vaenas animi*) rather than into your memory or your notebook (*indicem*), so that your natural talent (*ingenium*), gorged on all kinds of foods, will of itself bring forth a discourse which will be redolent ... of the character and feelings of your own heart

(Concoquendum est, quod varia diutinaque lectione devoraris, meditatione traiiciendum in vaenas animi, potius quam in memoriam aut indicem, ut omni pabulorum genere saginatum ingenium ex sese gignat orationem, quae ... redoleat ... indolem affectusque pectoris tui)[75]

The individual was characterized by his mind as reflected in his style of utterance: *oratio speculum mentis*.[76] Puttenham wrote:

Stile [is] the image of man, *mentis character*; for man is but his minde, and as his minde is tempered and qualified, so are his speeches and language at large[77]

Since the writer's mind is reflected in his personal style, his imitation of a literary model (which is only achieved by the anabolic, transforming processes of his own mind) must also reflect his *mentis character* and the norms (both literary and moral) which he held as an individual. Like style in general, eloquence or the 'bewtifull habite of language or stile', was considered either as 'naturall to the writer', or as 'his peculier by election and arte' and a product of his careful study of literary or eloquent models and much practice.[78] Since the personal qualities of an individual's style of expression can never be reproduced exactly, and his style is as peculiar to him as his finger prints, the measure of a literary personality is eloquence. Learning and wisdom might account for a poet's critical faculties as an interpreter and judge, but it was his eloquence which accounted for his capacity as an imitator to communicate with 'efficacie' and 'perswasiveness'.[79]

Erasmus knew that readers relished the differences between individuals mirrored in their voices on the page as in life

this is what delights the reader in the first place – to come to know from the utterance of a writer, the feelings, character, the meaning, and the peculiarity of his talent

(quod in primis delectat lectorem, ex oratione scriptoris affectus, indolem, sensum, ingeniumque cognoscere)[80]

When renaissance theorists adopted the view of poetry as an art of imitation, they also raised questions as to whether the poet, considered as a maker, could, or should imitate by such methods as translation or paraphrase. Humanist views of poetic imitation were themselves often imitations of those found in ancient rhetorical guides and literary criticism. In his *Ars poetica* Horace had assured the young poet that he would be able to transform the common stock of traditional subjects into his own new work, provided that he took care to avoid certain pitfalls. Horace developed the idea in a legal metaphor: the poet could make public property his own by assuming private rights over it. But he warned that slavish imitation was like jumping into a narrow space which would stifle creativity.

publica materies privati iuris erit, si
non circa vilem patulumque moraberis orbem,
nec verbo verbum curabis reddere fidus
interpres, nec desilies imitator in artum,
unde pedem proferre pudor vetet aut operis lex
(lines 131–5)

common matter thou thine own maist make,
If thou the vile, broad-troden ring forsake,

For, being a Poet, thou maist feigne, create,
Not care, as thou wouldst faithfully translate,
To render word for word: nor with thy sleight
Of imitation, leape into a streight,
From whence thy Modestie, or Poemes law
Forbids thee forth againe thy foot to draw[81]

Humanist writers recognized that imitation was an important part of the poet's craft, which required much more than close attention to the surface detail of a model text. Scaliger adopted Horace's precepts by stating that the basis of all poetry was imitation (*tota in imitatione sita fuit*).[82] Imitation however was only a means to the end of poetry, which was teaching with delighting (*Hic enim finis est medius ad illum ultimum, qui est docendi cum delectatione*).[83] Whatever emphasis individual poets might choose to give either to teaching or to delighting, poetry was considered *utile et dulce* because it gave instruction in pleasurable form. The poet's imitation could be of an actual or an ideal model, since poetry – unlike history – was not restricted to fact. The poet was free to add a fictitious element to historical fact and to imitate truth by fiction. Poems differ, said Scaliger, in what we imitate, the means we use, and the manner in which we imitate.

The poet was a maker because he was obliged to transform the constituent elements of his actual or ideal model into his own new work. In the mid sixteenth century Joachim Du Bellay distinguished between the 'cold' and constrained diction of translation and that of lively imitation. Like Horace, Du Bellay warned the young poet that in observing

la loy de traduire, qui est, n'espacier point hors des limites de l'aucteur, vostre diction sera contrainte, froide, & de mauvaise grace[84]

However, following that humanist tradition based on Seneca and Quintilian, he also depicted imitation as an anabolic process of transforming digested material into new tissue: of devouring the works of the best authors, '& apres

les avoir bien digerez, les convertissant en sang, & nourri-
ture'.[85] He acknowledged that it was not easy to imitate a
model author, and 'quasi comme se transformer en luy' by
penetrating 'aux plus cachees, & interieures parties de
l'auteur', but, this penetration was considered necessary in
order not to lose 'la force des choses' and the essence of the
model.[86]

In England in the 1580s Sidney described the imitation
or transformation of model authors' texts in terms of the
same anabolic metaphor. In his discussion of English
poetic diction towards the end of the *Defence of Poesie*,
Sidney wrote:

> I could wish ... the diligent Imitators of *Tully* & *Demosthenes*, most
> worthie to be imitated, did not so much keepe *Nizolian* paper
> bookes, of their figures and phrases, as by attentive translation, as it
> were, devour them whole, and make them wholly theirs[87]

Such 'attentive translation' was legitimate poetic imitation
or a means of acquiring private rights over the common
legacy of the past.[88]

Sidney followed Scaliger and defined poet-makers as
those

> which most properly do imitate to teach & delight: and to imitate,
> borrow nothing of what is, hath bin, or shall be, but range onely
> reined with learned discretion, into the divine consideration of what
> may be and should be[89]

A 'right poet' disdained the brazen world of nature, since,
'lifted up with the vigor of his own invention', and 'faining
notable images of vertues, vices, or what els', he figured
forth or delivered instead a superior 'golden' imitation of
what he imagined 'nature might have done'.[90]

This inventive process might seem to preclude the imitation of another author's work, where the text is a model
which exists in substance: 'what is'. But Sidney emphasized that

> the skill of ech Artificer standeth in that *Idea*, or fore conceit of the
> worke, and not in the worke it selfe[91]

20

The imitator of another artist's text attempted to reconsti-
tute that artist's preconception of his work. This implies a
process of deep penetration, such as Du Bellay had
described, rather than a representation of the surface
product 'in the worke it selfe'.

Imaginative invention did not exclude the interpretation
and dynamic transformation (or imitation) of model texts,
nor did interpretation of a model text preclude invention.
The title page of George Gascoigne's poetic miscellany, for
example, acknowledges the fertility of both methods of
creative writing:

A Hundreth sundrie Flowres bounde up in one small Poesie.
Gathered *partely (by translation)* in the fyne outlandish Gardins of
Euripides, Ovid, Petrarke, Ariosto, and others: and *partly by inven-
tion*, out of our owne fruitfull Orchardes in Englande[92]

However, various sixteenth-century critics expressed
different opinions as to whether a 'translator' could claim
to be a 'poet'. Thomas Sebillet wrote in his *L'Art poétique
françoys* (1548):

la version ou traduction est aujourd'huy le Poëme plus frequent &
mieux receu des estimés Poetes & des doctes lecteurs . . . la version
n'est rien qu'une imitation[93]

Jacques Peletier, in his *L'Art poetique* (1555) agreed that
'La plus vręę espęcę d'Imitacion, c'ęt dę traduirę',[94] but he
disparaged such imitation which he associated with the
constraints operating on Horace's *fidus interpres*. Like
Quintilian and Vives, Peletier knew that ultimately such
imitation was impossible: 'car la naturę des chosęs nę
soufrę jamęs pęrfeccion dę ręssamblancę'.[95]

When such critics refused to allow that translation was a
proper activity for a poet, they had in mind the scrupulous
process of translation as an attempt at synonymity, which
impeded the development of private rights over *publica
materies*. Du Bellay, for example, when discussing the
utility of prose translations, distinguished between the
activities of the learned translator and paraphrast on the

one hand, and the 'fidèle traducteur' on the other. Although they shared a common interpretative purpose, he observed that their approaches to their work were different, since 'le sçavant translateur fist plus tost l'office de Paraphraste, que de traducteur'.[96] A positive moral quality attaches to the phrase *le sçavant translateur*, but by the balance inherent in a contrast and by a play on words, Du Bellay damned *le traducteur* as ignorant and unworthy: 'mieux dignes d'estre appellez traditeurs, que traducteurs'.[97]

There was a similar debate on the literary merits of translation in England at the end of the sixteenth century. Puttenham's list of 'writers in our English poesie' at the end of Book 1 of his *Arte of English Poesie* (1589) implies a division between translators and inventors or makers, since the works of 'some appeare to be but bare translations, other some matters of their owne invention and very commendable'.[98] It is clear where his own preference lay. However, his distinctions between the different activities of the translator and the maker were blurred by the examples he cited. On the one hand he gave unstinted praise to Wyatt and Surrey as 'courtly makers'

in all imitating very naturally and studiously their Maister Francis Petrarcha[99]

On the other hand he regarded Chaucer's 'bookes of *Troilus* and *Cresseid*' as 'but bare translations ... yet ... wel handled'.[100]

Sir John Harington defended all such 'translators' by using Puttenham's argument in praise of Wyatt and Surrey against him. In the *Briefe Apologie of Poetrie, and of the Author and Translator* (1591), which Harington wrote as a preface to his verse imitation of Ariosto's *Orlando Furioso*, he wrote (somewhat provocatively):

I would wish to be called rather one of the worst translators then one of the meaner makers, specially sith the Earle of Surrey and Sir Thomas Wiat, that are yet called the first refiners of the English tong, were both translators out of Italian[101]

Harington himself assumed the title 'poet' by virtue of the fact that his activity as a 'translator' of Ariosto was the same as Chaucer's and Wyatt's and Surrey's in their 'translations'. Harington did not disparage 'invention or fiction'; he described the 'principal part of Poetrie' as 'fiction and imitation'.[102] The art of poetry was an art of imitation, and both translation and invention were methods of poetic imitation. Harington saw himself as a kind of paraphrast or poet-interpreter, and when answering his critics denied that it was his duty to 'observe' Ariosto's 'phrase so strictly' as a scholarly 'interpreter'[103] or *fidus interpres*.

Such imitators as Chaucer, Wyatt, Surrey and Harington were thought to merit the title poet because their processes of interpretative imitation of other writers' 'fore conceits', and their inventiveness in effecting imitations of the models or of their own 'fore conceits', generated wholly new poetic works. Their private rights to the common stock of traditional subjects depended on a combination of personal qualities in their activities as readers or critics, and their expressive originality as writers.

Renaissance discussions of imitation indicate that an imitator's choice of literary process reflected different degrees of respect for the original author's meaning. That choice also reflected the degree of proximity to the style of the original that the imitator sought to achieve. A scholarly translator sought to transpose the meaning of his original by paying close attention to words and style, in order to achieve as high a degree of synonymity as possible. A paraphrast was not restricted to transposition of the sense of the model. While a scholarly paraphrast attempted to elucidate the meaning of the original text by 'speaking alongside' the model, other paraphrasts and imitators were free to emulate the original author's meaning and style to suit their own purposes. The flexibility of renaissance attitudes to imitation allowed any individual writer to combine inventive freedom with the interpretative scruples of a scholarly paraphrast or 'sçavant translateur', even within the same work.

In the case of the metrical psalmists a special sense of decorum prevailed because, as Norton suggested, where matters of faith and religion were involved it might be 'perillous . . . to erre'. Thus, in their imitations of biblical models, the interpretative scruples of the sixteenth-century psalmists are often more apparent than their inventive freedom or latitude. Nevertheless, where an imitator was striving and contending with the model psalm for the same meaning, 'inventive' qualities in his style, and in his treatment of the model psalm, did not necessarily compromise his 'interpretative' purpose. In so far as interpretation is historical, an accomplished scholarly poet's inventive freedom in his imitation may have enhanced a contemporary reader's understanding and appreciation of the model.

Since there are as many imitations of a model as there are imitators, the proper context for an assessment of the imitator's personal eloquence, is comparison with a normative text of the original. In England before the late 1530s this was the Vulgate, the *Psalterium gallicum* attributed to Jerome (d. 420).[104] Sixteenth-century English Catholics continued to use this Latin translation in the liturgy and in their private devotion, as the standard text authorized by the Church. However, for the majority of Englishmen, after the Reformation the normative text of the Psalms may be identified with Coverdale's English translation in the Great Bible of 1539, which was disseminated widely as a result of its association with the Book of Common Prayer from 1549.

Humanists regarded the imitation of ancient writers as a process whereby they could discover and re-discover the cultural legacy of Antiquity, which, they thought, had been lost or neglected during the 'Middle Ages', in order to enrich their own culture. In his study of 'Imitation and Discovery' in renaissance poetry, Thomas M. Greene emphasizes the function of literary imitation in 'bridging a rupture' between different cultures or 'mundi significantes'.[105] He discusses mainly the relationship of Italian and French renaissance poets with Antiquity, symbolized by their efforts to re-kindle the flickering light from the ruins of Troy, which had illuminated the cultural development of Europe. Greene discussed *imitatio* 'in terms of otherness and discontinuity'[106] because he considers only the relationship between the Renaissance and pagan Antiquity: for example, Petrarch's anxieties and frustrations in his attempt to resuscitate the literary personality of Cicero; and the renaissance awareness of the 'rupture' between the culture of either the *trecento* or the sixteenth century, and that of Augustan Rome, evident in Petrarch's imitations of Virgil, or in Du Bellay's attempt to 'disinter' the 'Antiquitez de Rome'.[107]

A different situation pertains in the case of those authors of metrical psalm versions, who worked within the context of a long, stable tradition of attitudes to the Psalms, which had persisted into the sixteenth century and which was very much alive. Almost the only features which these versions have in common with the imitations discussed by Greene are the processes of imitation itself, and their coincidence with contemporary studies of an inherited text. However, humanist scholars had no need to disinter the *Hebraica veritas* of the Old Testament from the ruins of time, because they were able to turn to a parallel live tradition of Jewish scholarship. The Hebrew Bible and a large body of Hebrew scholarship were readily available to Christian scholars from the ghettoes of Italy and Germany in the form of carefully preserved texts both in manuscript and in printed books; Jewish teachers, including some converts to Christianity, were also available to expound the Hebrew text. Moreover, Christian scholars in the Middle Ages had already had recourse to this parallel tradition, and their contributions to biblical studies had helped to mould the traditions which the sixteenth century had inherited.[108]

By contrast with the exploitation of the rediscovery and resuscitation of ancient pagan literature, access to the Hebrew verity of the Psalms served to nourish existing, live literary and devotional traditions. Some of the sixteenth-century psalmists showed themselves to be aware of their responsibilities in working within such traditions: Matthew Parker, archbishop, scholar and antiquary, admonished readers of his metrical psalm versions:

> Require not heere great difference,
>   In wordes so ofte the same:
> Although to feele great violence,
>   I might not chaunge the name.
>
> Conceyve in hart, no griefe to sore,
>   wordes olde, so ofte to vewe.
> Thy gayne therby is wrought the more,
>   though wordes be never newe[109]

He argued that the spiritual power of his psalter to comfort readers was enhanced because he had not felt free to change old, familiar words. However, even though Parker's 'wordes be never newe', his psalter is different from other versions in so far as it reflects the image of his mind. Whereas Greene stresses the importance of 'otherness and discontinuity' in renaissance imitations of classical texts, in the case of psalm versions we should emphasize rather familiarity and continuity-in-change. Despite the doctrinal upheavals of the period sixteenth-century readers and writers continued to participate in a long and relatively stable tradition of Christian devotion. The Psalms occupied a unique position within the literature of this devotional tradition. Although contemporary imitations of the Psalms were new works, they nevertheless retained a special relationship to the store of traditional views of those biblical models. By considering this tradition within which sixteenth-century readers' perceptions and expectations of the Psalms were fashioned we can appreciate what sixteenth-century writers saw in the Psalms, and we can thereby identify and, to some extent, assess those contributions which derive from the writers' own religious and literary sensibilities.

The biblical Psalms were regarded as providing models for self-examination and as the source of spiritual comfort. Since the fourth century, at least, Christian commentators had regarded the Book of Psalms as applicable to all the conditions of mankind's spiritual and emotional experience. Matthew Parker cited Athanasius (296–373) as a patristic authority for the statement that the Psalms contained 'the alterations of every mans hart and conscience described and lively paynted to his owne sight'.[110] The range of their themes, and affective, lyric styles, made them 'moste present remedies against all tentations, and troubles of minde and conscience',[111] and ready for 'any griefe or disease incident into the soule of man'.[112]

Calvin regarded the Psalms as an 'Anatomy of all the partes of the Soule, inasmuch as a man shalnot find any affection in himselfe, wherof the Image appeereth not in this glasse'.[113] The examples of 'the Prophets themselves talking with God' in the Psalms provoked an individual to spiritual self examination 'bycause they discover all the inner thoughtes', and thus 'do call or drawe every one of us to the peculiar examination of himself'.[114] In the words of the psalmist 'I call to remembraunce my songe: and in the nyght I commune with myne awne hert, and search out my spretes' (Great Bible, Ps. 77:6).

Sixteenth-century commentators, such as Thomas Wilcox, emphasized that the variety of themes and styles in the Psalms reflected their original authors' needs and attitudes:

As they were divers Writers, so they comprehended divers matters: some are full of instruction touching both fayth and maners ... Othersome containe confession of sinnes, and prayer for repentaunce ... Othersome are Prayers agaynst the enemies of the Church ... Some containe the histories of the olde Testament ... Some are commendations of Gods lawes ... Some descriptions of Gods wonderfull power ... Some are particuler prayers of particular persons, in particular greefes eyther of body or soule ...

27

Othersome are prayers of a number of godly and faithfull people . . .
To be shorte, there is such diversitye of matter, that a man can
hardlye devide aright; yea one and the selfe same Psalme sometimes
shall comprehende the most of these thinges[115]

Amid this 'diversitye of matter' Wilcox identified two
main applications for Psalms: as prayers (including 'confession' and praise or 'commendations'), and as a medium
of instruction.

The value of the Psalms as prayers and meditations had
not been diminished by the Protestant Reformation. The
prologue to the Bishops' Bible Psalms contains a description of the Psalms by Basil the Great (d. 379) as 'A booke of
contemplations or secrete meditations, whereby the godly
speaketh solitarily and alone to almightie God'.[116]
Anthony Gilby characterized the special value of the
Psalms as follows:

whereas al other scriptures do teach us what God saith unto us,
these praiers . . . do teach us, what we shall saie unto God

They were, therefore, 'dailie to be used with great rever-
ence and humilitie'.[117] In the words of the psalmist,
'Kynges of the earth and all people, Princes and all judges
of the worlde. Yonge men and maydens, olde men and
chyldren: prayse the name of the Lorde' (Great Bible, Ps.
148:11–12). The first-person singular form which pre-
dominates in the Psalms allowed an individual to identify
with the psalmists' words in the liturgy, and invited him to
apply the words to himself in his personal devotions. The
simultaneous dual application of psalms to participants in
the liturgy had been described by Basil in the fourth
century, and this was repeated by Bishop John Jewel in the
mid sixteenth century.

Tanquam ab uno ore et uno corde confessionis psalmum offerunt
Domino et verba poenitentiae eorum quisque proprie ascribit sibi:
As it were from one mouth and from one heart they offer up unto
the Lord the psalm of confession and the words of repentance every
of them applieth particularly unto himself[118]

Before the Reformation the Psalms had been used regularly in all Christian liturgies. The entire Psalter was sung or read through in weekly or monthly cycles, and several groups of psalms, such as the seven penitential psalms (Pss. 6, 32, 38, 51, 102, 130, 143) or the gradual psalms (Pss. 120–34), acquired special devotional or liturgical functions. Throughout the sixteenth century Christians of all denominations continued to use the Psalms in private devotion and communal worship.

The liveliness of the devotional tradition centred on the Psalms can be seen in the numerous sixteenth-century volumes of new prayers and meditations modelled upon them. An anonymous devotional manual, entitled *Psalmes or prayers taken out of holye scripture*, compiled primarily from verses from different psalms, was printed in at least thirteen editions between 1544 and 1608;[119] the original compilation, first published in Latin, has been attributed to John Fisher. In anonymous English translations the prayers of this Catholic bishop, scholar and martyr proved popular with Protestants. Another devotional manual, *A Golden Chaine, taken out of the rich Treasurehouse the Psalmes of King David* (1579), contains new occasional prayers called 'lynks', which were also composed from individual verses taken from different psalms.[120] The author, Thomas Rogers, dedicated his book to Queen Elizabeth, and explained the purpose of the 'chaine', 'in which any may see, both what dutie they owe unto God, and what unto man; be they of what calling, or condition soever'.[121] Henry Bull's *Christian Praiers and holie Meditations, as wel for Private as Publique exercise* contains a text described as 'A Psalme of thanksgivinge for deliveraunce from the Plague, or any other kind of sicknes, trouble or affliction', likewise compiled from verses taken from different psalms.[122] By contrast, Sir Anthony Cope in his *A godly meditacion upon .xx. select and chosen Psalmes of the prophet David* (1547) used the Psalms in a different way when formulating his prayers: twenty free variations on, or 'expositions' of complete psalms, 'reduced' to 'the kynde or fashion of prayers and contemplatife meditations'.[123] Cope saw the Psalms as providing perfect models for praise and prayer: 'Who so wyll learne to geve to God dewe honoure and prayses: maye in them take a perfecte patron' [i.e. pattern].[124] His book was dedicated to the Queen, Catherine Parr, who had herself acquired a reputation for writing such prayers and meditations.[125]

The Book of Psalms provided not only models for prayer but also a treasury of moral and religious instruction. The translators of the Geneva Bible described the Psalms as

a moste precious treasure, wherein all things are conteined that apperteine to true felicitie: aswel in this life present as in the life to come. For the riches of true knowledge, and heavenlie wisdome are here set open for us, to take thereof most abundantly[126]

Traditionally the Psalms had been regarded as a microcosm of the whole Bible. Some psalms, such as Ps. 78, were at the literal level rehearsals of great events in the earlier history of the children of Israel. However, according to the typological interpretations of patristic and medieval exegetes, David was seen as a figure of Christ. Sixteenth-century commentators, such as Jacques Lefèvre d'Etaples and the translators of the Geneva Bible, also followed these spiritual interpretations:

If we wolde knowe wherein standeth our salvation, and how to atteine to life everlasting, here is Christ our onely redemer, and mediator moste evidently described[127]

The comprehensiveness of the Psalms' teaching was reasserted in similar terms throughout the sixteenth century. Thomas Becon's enthusiasm for the Psalms led him to believe apparently 'that even this one boke alone of Davids songes had ben sufficient truly to instructe a man in the ryghteousnes of God but that the goodnes of God woulde that ... [we] shoulde be holpen with mo scriptures'.[128] Becon proclaimed:

Certes, the Psalmody of David maye well be called the Treasure house of the holye Scripture. For it contaynethe what so ever is necessary for a christen man to know[129]

Cope was equally confident that 'there is nothynge necessarie for any christian to do, thynke, or saye, but in them as in a myrroure he maye beholde the perfecte image therof'.[130] Fifty years later Richard Hooker asked: 'What is there necessarie for man to know which the Psalmes are not able to teach?'[131] He considered that the Psalms were of equal value in all stages of instruction:

They are to beginners an easie and familiar introduction, a mightie augmentation of all vertue and knowledge in such as are entered before, a strong confirmation to the most perfect amongst others[132]

Such attitudes to the Psalms had made them especially appropriate as a means to instill the foundations of Christian teaching, and to enrich the life of the individual. The use of the Psalms in Latin as a first reader for children had been established by the eighth century.[133] Later in the Middle Ages the Primer, in which texts of psalms predominated, came to serve a dual function as a devotional manual and as a school text.[134] In 1539 Bishop Hilsey suggested that the Primer was so called 'bycause ... it is the fyrst boke that the tender youth was instructed in'.[135]

Many sixteenth-century English books intended as elementary teaching aids retained connexions with the form and function of such devotional books for the laity. The editor of William Lily's Grammar (1542) advised English school masters to give to their pupils psalms and such biblical wisdom literature as Proverbs and Ecclesiasticus as set texts for daily Latin translation exercises.[136] Psalm paraphrases, in various Latin metres, by the poet and scholar George Buchanan were used in humanist schools in Germany and Scotland to promote, simultaneously, 'true piety' and 'purity of Latin style' (*veram pietatem & linguae Romanae puritatem*).[137] Sixteenth-century Christians (like their precursors) were brought up on the Psalms as a book of elementary instruction and were therefore familiar with the texts from early childhood.

The Book of Psalms retained its traditional function in sixteenth-century curricula, because humanist school-masters, such as Richard Mulcaster of the Merchant Taylors' School, believed that 'goodnesse and vertew of matter is most fit for the young childe in the first seasoning of his tender minde'.[138] John Colet would have only 'suych auctours that hathe with wisdome joyned the pure chaste eloquence' taught at St Paul's School.[139] Thomas Wilson, in his *Arte of Rhetorique*, pointed out that 'before we use either to write, or speake eloquently, wee must dedicate our myndes wholy, to followe the most wise and learned men'.[140] The choice of models to study and imitate was important, because, as Wilson said, 'we can not but in time appere somewhat like them'; thus, he argued, 'by com-panying with the wise, a man shall learne wisdome'.[141]

Moreover, psalms were thought to contain not only good 'matter' but also eloquent expression of that matter. Arthur Golding offered his readers a considered literary appreciation of the unique qualities of the Psalms; 'The thing that is peculiar to it, is the maner of the handling of the matters wherof it treateth'.[142] He compared the narra-tive style of 'other partes of holy writ' with the poetic and lyric qualities of psalms, which made them complex and rhetorical, and 'every man . . . a bewrayer of the secretes of his owne hart':[143]

For whereas other partes of holy writ . . . do commonly set down their treatizes in open and plaine declarations: this parte consisting of them all, wrappeth up things in types & figures, describing them under borowed personages, & oftentimes winding in matters by prevention, speaking of thinges too come as if they were past or present, and of things past as if they were in dooing, and every man is made a bewrayer of the secretes of his owne hart

Cope also remarked on the 'lyvely' images of Christian teaching 'in colours set forth before oure eyes, wyth so many tropes, figures and allegories'.[144]

At the end of the dedication to the reader in his translation of psalm paraphrases by Johannes Campensis, Coverdale prayed that 'the lorde of al truth'

gyve thee grace so for to turne these songes of David, so to tempre them in thy understandyng & so to [n]ote them in thyne harte that thou also mayest be made a new David: a man accordynge unto the wyll of God[145]

The figure of David, and David's psalms, could provide humanist schoolmasters with ideal models for their pupils to imitate. Ascham repeated John Cheke's views about the essential curriculum necessary to promote both learning and spiritual values:

he that will dwell in these few bookes onelie: first in Gods holie Bible, and than joyne with it *Tullie* in *Latin, Plato, Aristotle: Xenophon: Isocrates:* and *Demosthenes* in *Greke:* must nedes prove an excellent man[146]

Learning was not an end in itself, but a means to promote religion and virtue. In a letter to Edward Denny, Sidney outlined an elementary programme of study. He began by urging the young man *se ipsum noscere* and to do so primarily by following the guidance of the holy Scriptures whose pre-eminence was based on revelation:

The knowledge of our selves no doubte ought to be most pretious unto us; and therein the holy scriptures, if not the only, are certainly the incomperable Lanterne in this fleshy darkness of ours.[147]

Since the Book of Psalms in particular was considered an anatomy of the soul, containing 'the alterations of every mans hart and conscience described and lively paynted to his owne sight',[148] it was inevitable that in reading and interpreting the Psalms any man studied an image of himself. The vogue for metrical psalms is also part of the popular response to a humanist belief in man's capacity to fashion his own character. Even Calvinists encouraged individuals to search for signs of their election and to fashion themselves – for this earthly existence at least – in the shape of God's elect.[149] Self-fashioning and moral improvement entailed first, self-knowledge and secondly, the imitation of good models selected not only from life but also from literature.

Psalms were regarded as peculiarly efficacious and delightful texts for moral instruction because of their intrinsic poetic qualities, and their association, as David's 'songs', with music. David was regarded as a 'celestial Orpheus' in that he 'hath so sette forth his songes that they have strength and force to cause men which be carnall and beastly, to become spiritual and heavenly'.[150] Cope explained this analogy by alluding to the 'poetes' story 'that Orpheus made so pleasaunt harmonie on his harpe that he caused the beastes and stones dauncing, to folow hym'.[151] Similarly, Cope refers his patroness to the 'chapter of the boke of Kynges, where David by playinge on his harpe and syngynge' psalms 'expelled from Kynge Saule ... the wycked spirite which ... sore tourmented hym': such was 'the power of the noble Psalmes that he sange'.[152] Becon thought that the musical qualities of the Psalms accounted for 'the wonderful & mervelous strength ... the great and excedyng vertu of Davids songes'.[153] Coverdale emphasized a moral purpose in singing the Psalms, and explained

the very ryght use wherfore Psalmes shulde be songe: Namely, to conforte a mans herte in God, to make hym thankfull, & to exercyse hym in his worde, to corage hym in the waye of godlynesse, and to provoke other men unto the same[154]

In this spirit Thomas Sternhold dedicated his own metrical versions of psalms to Edward VI as 'holye songes of veritie'.[155]

The reputation of the Psalms as poetry was enhanced by the fact that many of the features of the Hebrew poetry – the metaphors, similes, apostrophes and parallelisms of the Hebrew poetic text – lend themselves to memorable translations: not only the Vulgate but also the new Latin translations by Christian Hebraists, such as Sebastian Münster, and through these into vernacular translations, such as Coverdale's in his Great Bible.[156] In Coverdale's English the psalmist was moved to exclaim in awed humility 'what is man, that thou art myndfull of him?'. Some of the best remembered phrases from sixteenth-century English versions of the Psalms describe the human predicament which is imagined as just a little 'lower then the aungels', but scattered like chaff before the wind, or labouring under 'the yocke of the ungodly' for the space of 'thre score yeares and ten'.[157] Some Hebraic idioms survive the processes of translation, as in the following expressions of time: 'from the rysyng up of the sonne, unto the goynge downe therof' (Ps. 50:1), 'the dayes of thy servaunt' (Ps. 119:84), both of which preserve the Hebrew construct form;[158] and 'for ever and ever' (Ps.9:5). There are also metaphors and similes like 'the wynges of the wynde' (Ps.18:10), and more 'then the heeres of my head' (Ps. 40:12). Many of the metaphors and similes of the Psalms are drawn from nature, a feature which contributes to their relevance and appeal beyond a particular time or place. In such phrases as

Our soule is escaped, even as a byrde out of the snare of the fouler: the snare is broken, and we are delyvered (Ps. 124:7)

O that I had winges like a dove, for then wold I flye awaye and be at rest[159] (Ps. 55:6)

the image of the bird became symbolic of man's spiritual vulnerability, and the power of God to relieve and save was realized in a physical image. The psalmist's desire for God is represented as a thirst:

Like as the hert desyreth the water brookes, so longeth my soule after the (O God). My soule is a thurste for God[160] (Ps. 42: 1–2)

The tone of the psalmist can also be ecstatic, marvelling at the mysterious beauty and majesty of God in nature:

The heavens declare the glory of God . . . There is nether speach ner language, but their voyces are herde among them (Ps. 19:1, 3)

The speechless 'voyces' of the heavens are not only heard but transmitted by the poet, whose imagination also has the power to 'see' the invisible:

O Lord my God ... thou art clothed with majesty and honoure. Thou deckest thy selfe wyth lyght, as it were wyth a garment, and spredest out the heavens lyke a curtayne   (Ps. 104:1–2)

Some of the psalmist's metaphorical verses, like 'They that sowe in teares, shall reape in joye',[161] have a proverbial quality: the symmetry of ideas is matched by the balanced phrases, lending a sense of aphoristic wisdom to this comment on time, human endeavour and suffering. Other Hebraic features transmitted easily in translation are the short, often terse phrases linked by simple conjunctions, especially 'and':

stonde in awe, and synne not: comen wyth youre awne herte, and in youre chambre, and be styll   (Ps. 4:4)

Simple cause and effect constructions, like 'he maketh the storme to ceasse, so that the waves therof are styll' (Ps. 107:29), or inverted, 'That thy beloved maye be delyvered: let thy ryght hande save them' (Ps. 108:6), could also be translated literally. Such poetic Hebrew parallelisms retain their poetic effect when translated into English prose, sometimes with the force of a metaphor as:

Thy worde is a lanterne unto my fete, and a lyght unto my pathes   (Ps. 119:105)

The poet and critic Sir Philip Sidney was moved by such imaginative qualities to say that the psalmist's 'handling his prophecie', 'the often and free chaunging of persons' and rhetorical figures, were no less than 'a heavenly poesie', and he described 'holy Davids Psalms' as 'a divine Poeme'.[162]

Any translation of the Psalms completed in a given short period, and especially one made by an individual, is likely to have a greater stylistic homogeneity than the original Hebrew poems which are the work of various authors over a period of several centuries. Coverdale's Great Bible Book of Psalms has a stylistic and scholarly integrity which indicates conscientious study of contemporary Latin and German translations derived from the Hebrew. Coverdale's first English translation of the Psalms for the 1535 Bible was revised in accordance with Münster's *Hebraica Biblia* (1534–5) for the Great Bible Psalms (1539).[163] It is unlikely that Coverdale ever knew enough Hebrew to translate independently.

However, in spite of its scholarly sources, the language of Coverdale's Psalms also closely resembles spoken language, a feature of style which may have been determined by a wish that his translation would be appropriate for use in the liturgy. Some of his more colloquial English turns of phrase may have their origins in German translations: Luther's 'Augenblick' in Ps. 30:5 was the source for Coverdale's description of God's wrath enduring 'but the twincling of an eye'.[164] In other psalms, the 'Heithen' may 'make moch a doo' crying 'fye on thee, fye on thee' and threaten to 'make havoke' of the godly, but Coverdale's psalmist urges 'Up Lorde, and let not man have the upper hande.'[165] The godly man asserts confidently that he has 'an eye unto all' God's laws; his heart therefore 'daunseth for joye' because he knows 'The Lord is on my syde' and 'taketh my parte'.[166] Although the distressed may be 'at their wittes end', they also know that God 'shall stande by' all those who put their trust in Him even when trouble 'is harde at hande', whereas, 'they that runne after another God, shall have great trouble' and the Lord 'shall laugh them to scorne'.[167]

Coverdale also introduced small details into his translations, such as the occasional figurative use of a verb. In Ps. 86:11, the psalmist prays, 'O *knytt* my hert unto thee'; in Ps. 119:102, he exclaims, 'I have not *shryncked* from thy judgementes.'[168] When the wicked prosper, the people '*fall* unto them' and the wicked '*sucke* no small advauntage' (Ps. 73:10).[169] The enduring qualities of the Great Bible Psalms are due to its being a scholarly translation by a man who combined learned judgement with 'no small advantage' in literary flair. Coverdale's responses to the Psalms were determined by a single predominant ideal. This was to give all his countrymen easy access to the poetic Word of God in clear, relatively simple language which could be comprehended and used by any of them.

The memorable features of the Book of Psalms, preserved by a memorable and widely used translation, helped to stimulate interest in its inherent poetic qualities. One of the best witnesses to renewed interest in this aspect of the tradition is the proliferation of metrical versions written during the sixteenth century. Occasionally authors of metrical psalm versions show themselves to be conscious of working within a live literary tradition. William Hunnis and William Forrest, for example, each explained their selection of particular psalms on the grounds that no other metrical psalmist had as yet attempted them.[170] Robert Crowley and Francis Seagar invited their readers and others to correct and continue their works.[171]

Moreover, appropriate psalm images were also incorporated into secular verse. An anonymous contributor to the popular anthology *A Gorgeous Gallery of Gallant Inventions* (1578) draws on the imagery of a sleepless penitent from Ps. 6 in order to describe the physical effects on a lover's health of impassioned devotion to an obdurate, unresponsive lady:

> In mourning weed, so spend I tyme
>   Lamentinge mine estate.
> The night renewes my cares
>   When weary limmes would rest,
> And dreadfull dreames abandon slepe
>   Which had my greefes represt.
> I drench my couch with teares
>   Which flow from gushing eyes[172]

Compare:

I fainted in my *mourning*: I cause my bed every night to swimme, & watter *my couche with my teares*   (Geneva Bible Ps. 6:6; my italics)

The opening of Daniel's 'Complaint of Rosamund' (1592) – 'Out from the horror of infernall deepes' – may carry an allusion to the well-known first verse of the penitential psalm *De profundis* Ps. 130.[173]

Shakespeare's characters frequently allude to verses of the Psalms, mostly from Coverdale's translation in the Book of Common Prayer.[174] In *As You Like It* Adam, offering his life's savings to Orlando, says

> he that doth the Ravens feede,
> Yea providently caters for the Sparrow,
> Be comfort to my age
> (II, iii, 43–5; First Folio, lines 747–9)

The form of the parallelism is that found in the Psalms, and the idea of the feeding of the ravens is from Ps. 147:9 ('. . . and fedeth the yong ravens that call hym'). As Henry VI dismisses Gloucester he says

> Henry will to himselfe Protector be,
> And God shall be my hope, my stay, my guide,
> And Lanthorne to my feete
> (*2 Henry VI*, II, iii, 23–5; First Folio, lines 1078–80)

Compare:

trulye my hope is even in the [Lorde]   (Great Bible, Ps. 39:7)

Thy worde is a lanterne unto my fete[175]   (Great Bible, Ps. 119:105)

Hamlet asks

What a piece of worke is a man! . . . in Action, how like an Angel? in apprehension, how like a God?[176]
> (*Hamlet* II, ii, 303–6; First Folio, lines 1350 & 1352–3)

Claudius, contemplating his 'cursed hand', asks

> Is there not Raine enough in the sweet Heavens
> To wash it white as snow?
> (*Hamlet* III, iii, 45–6; First Folio, lines 2321–2)

Compare:

thou shalt wash me and I shalbe whiter then snowe
> (Great Bible, Ps. 51:7)

In other plays Shakespeare used the Psalms even more inventively. Antony, in his anger and despair, rails at Cleopatra's lust and mocks himself as a champion cuckold:

> O that I were
> Upon the hill of Basan, to out-roare
> The horned Heard
> (*Antony & Cleopatra*, III, xiii, 126–8; First Folio, lines 2304–6)

Compare:

Greate oxen are come about me, fatt bulles of Basan close me in on every syde (Great Bible, Ps. 22:12; cf. Ps. 68:15)

Macbeth, arguing with himself against the murder of Duncan, envisages

> Pitty, like a naked New-borne-Babe,
> Striding the blast, or Heavens Cherubin, hors'd
> Upon the sightlesse Curriors of the Ayre
> (*Macbeth* I, vii, 21–3; First Folio, lines 495–7)

Compare:

He rode upon the Cherubins and dyd flye: he came flyenge with the wynges of the wynde[177] (Great Bible, Ps. 18:10)

Old Seward, on hearing that his son died bravely, exclaims

> Had I as many Sonnes, as I have haires,
> I would not wish them to a fairer death
> (*Macbeth* V, ix, 14–15; First Folio, lines 2496–7)

Compare:

my synnes ... are mo in nombre then the heeres of my head (Great Bible, Ps. 40:12)

Seward echoes the psalmist: Shakespeare turned 'sins' into 'sons' and made an English pun on 'heirs'.

In the late sixteenth century the word 'Psalm' could be applied as a generic term in relation to poetry. The title of William Byrd's song-book, *Psalmes, Sonets, & songs of sadnes and pietie* (1588), ranks metrical psalms as a literary kind of lyric comparable with 'sonets & songs'.[178] Michael Drayton used the word 'Psalmes' as the generic term for religious songs of praise in *The Harmonie of the Church* (1591), although the work does not contain any text derived directly from the Book of Psalms.[179]

As Wilcox explained, the biblical psalmists 'were divers Writers, so they comprehended divers matters', but it is possible to detect a consensus of opinion among sixteenth-century commentators as to both the nature of the Psalms and their applications. The Book of Psalms was regarded as divinely inspired poetry which combined essential doctrine with necessary comfort for the Christian reader; it was recognized that some psalms take the form of private prayers or meditations; and the long tradition of singing psalms had served to emphasize their inherent lyrical qualities.

Such views of the Psalms are also manifested in sixteenth-century metrical imitations of the biblical models, since writers responded to their models initially in accordance with these contemporary opinions, and subsequently in accordance with their own priorities and individual capacities. Thus among the new imitations we can discern certain groups. There are those imitations which were recognized as capable of teaching and delighting by providing poetic vehicles for a doctrine of comfort for the Christian reader. Secondly, there are those imitations which reflect the adaptation of selected psalms to articulate what Wilcox described as the 'particuler prayers of particular persons, in particular greefes eyther of body or soule'. Thirdly, there are those imitations where the inherent lyrical qualities of the biblical models were realized by musical settings as, in Sternhold's words, 'holye songes of veritie'; but, finally, these qualities were also imitated as devotional poetry of 'that Lyricall kind' whose effects were independent of musical settings.

We may regard these as four groupings within the single literary 'kind' of 'metrical psalm',[180] but these are four overlapping groups which should not be regarded as mutually exclusive. As Wilcox realized 'one and the selfe

41

same Psalme sometimes shall comprehende the most of these', and this is true also of the metrical versions by virtue of their being imitations of the biblical poetry of praise and prayer. Nevertheless, these groupings are offered as aids to the interpretation and evaluation of the new psalm versions, in that they indicate the relative emphasis – crucial to meaning – which was placed on the variety of expectations of the biblical models by sixteenth-century psalmists.

2
'HOLY DAVIDS DIVINE POEME'

SIR THOMAS WYATT'S IMITATION OF DAVID'S PENITENTIAL PSALMS, AND SIR THOMAS SMITH'S 'OTHER PSALME'

Some sixteenth-century readers and authors perceived the Psalms as 'holy Davids divine Poeme'; they responded to generic expectations of the Psalms as poetry, and to traditional views of David as the divinely inspired poet. Wyatt, Surrey and Sidney among others, regarded the Psalms as poetic models which stimulated and enabled their own poetic imitations by challenging their creative powers of interpretation and expression. However, each responded to different aspects of the literary and historical figure of David, and selected which psalms to imitate, and in what manner, according to different criteria. Wyatt selected a traditional image of the poet David as a lover and a sinner for his imitation of the seven penitential psalms:

he was a synner as we be[1]   (John Fisher)

The narrative structure of Wyatt's sequence of seven prologues and seven penitential psalms derives from the Italian prose version of Pietro Aretino printed in Venice, 1534.[2] Wyatt followed Aretino in exploiting the dramatic potential inherent in the progress from contrition and confession to full penitence, which is contained in these psalms, and was enhanced by their association with the story of David and Bathsheba.[3] This association had developed during the later Middle Ages, when illustrations of David watching Bathsheba bathing became increasingly common in late-fifteenth-century Books of Hours.[4] Similar illustrations appear in woodcuts in English books published during Wyatt's lifetime.[5]

Wyatt's use of Aretino's text, and several other contemporary sources which are mainly theological paraphrases and commentaries, has been extensively studied by
H. A. Mason, Kenneth Muir and Patricia Thomson, R. G.
Twombly, R. A. Rebholz and Helen Baron.[6] Mason and
Twombly, in particular, have discussed the theological
implications of Wyatt's use of Aretino, of the psalm paraphrases by Campensis and Zwingli published together in
1534, and of John Fisher's sermons or *Treatyse concernynge
the fruytfull saynges of Davyd . . . in the seven penytencyall
psalmes* (London, 1509).[7] Helen Baron has also demonstrated that Wyatt used Cardinal Cajetan's translations and
commentary on the Psalms.[8] All these scholars are agreed
that Wyatt's dependence on Aretino is more apparent in
the earlier parts of the sequence, especially in the long first
prologue and the shorter narrative links between the first
three penitential psalms. The holograph manuscript shows
that Wyatt revised his text in order to draw out the features
of David's spiritual predicament, leaving aside the most
fulsome detail of Aretino's visual imagery. Thus even
where he is closest to Aretino's text Wyatt maintains an
independent emphasis reflecting his own sensibilities and
purpose.[9]

While there is agreement that Wyatt's dependence on
Aretino diminished as his own version developed, and that
he became more eclectic in his use of other sources, there is
less unanimity in the different interpretations of Wyatt's
purpose in the poem.

Hallett Smith suggested that Wyatt saw his poem as a
kind of *de remedia amoris*, but within the poem David's sin
is presented as pride rather than as lechery.[10] H. A. Mason
not only made an invaluable contribution to the study of
Wyatt's texts and their sources but also revived modern
critical interest in Wyatt's psalms. In *Humanism and Poetry
in the Early Tudor Period* Mason restored Wyatt's standing
as a humanist poet:

The Wyatt we should attend to is the author of poems that stand in a
significant relation to the work of the Humanists . . . His character-

istic verse, the verse on which his reputation should rest, is 'moral-reflective' rather than lyrical

Mason argued that Wyatt's various translations (including those from Seneca and Petrarch) were 'an attempt to create a vehicle for conveying strong private feelings in a public form'.[11] Mason regarded Wyatt's penitential psalms as occasional poems which refer to the poet's own circumstances as a prisoner in the Tower of London in 1536, and he identified the persona of David with that of a Protestant Wyatt. Raymond Southall, D. M. Friedman, and R. G. Twombly (amongst others) have all based their discussions of Wyatt's psalms on the assumption that the persona of David within the poem is the literary persona of Wyatt himself.[12] In his *Life and Letters of Sir Thomas Wyatt* Kenneth Muir expressed doubt that the psalms were 'completely adapted to the poet's inner needs' (as Mason had claimed), but stated nevertheless that Wyatt 'contrives ... to express with an individual voice his own religious feelings'.[13]

R. A. Rebholz, following Mason's discussion, regarded Wyatt's departures from Aretino as reflecting his intention to make David the type of 'Reformed Christian' who is justified by faith in God's grace.[14] Twombly stressed the continuous cycle of hope and fear in the experience of David. He is seen as an individual 'working out', in an undisciplined 'dramatic' form, his 'emotional and intellectual dilemma'.[15] However, it would appear from Twombly's discussion that he had under-estimated the contribution to the poem of the biblical models, since these psalms present both the conflicting emotions and the progress of a penitent in the form of a direct address to God. As Stephen Greenblatt points out, 'the inwardness of these psalms can in no way be conceived as Wyatt's private affair'.[16] The interpretations by Twombly, Rebholz and Mason focus on Wyatt's handling of Ps. 51 which, they agree, is associated with the Apostle Paul's analysis of justification in the Epistle to the Romans. Whereas Rebholz and Twombly emphasized the Protestant theological implications of Wyatt's version of Ps. 51, Mason frankly acknowledged that 'much of Wyatt's faith as expressed in these Psalms would have been as acceptable to "reformists" inside the Catholic Church as 50 "reformers" outside it'.[17]

Both Twombly and Mason drew attention to the dramatic qualities of Wyatt's psalms, and praised the poet for having created 'a living voice'. Twombly located the dramatic element of the poem in the conflict within the mind of David. He observed that Wyatt's psalms 'appear as separate poems with no continuity except the outward one'. He saw the prologues as 'a kind of novel', and dismissed them as 'dramatically superfluous'. He concluded that Wyatt was not in control of his work, and 'hence' that 'the poems are not didactic'. Twombly considered that the psalms, although discrete, were 'a vehicle for the display of piety in the first person', which piety is vicariously the author's.[18] By contrast, Mason located the dramatic element in the sequence of psalms itself, which presents a fully-worked-out drama of penitence, with the prologues providing a functional dramatic situation; the unifying principle of the poem is repentance. Barbara Lewalski has followed Mason in describing Wyatt's psalms as 'a Protestant cycle of spiritual regeneration' probably 'composed while he was expecting arrest and trial', in which 'Wyatt's voice and situation' is merged with the psalmist's.[19] According to Greenblatt the poet's imprisonment became 'a metaphor for the state of grace' as David finally affirms that he is God's 'servant ay most bownd'.[20]

These assertions that the work is not didactic, and that it was a vehicle for the expression of Wyatt's personal anxieties, need more careful consideration. There is no external evidence to suggest either that Wyatt wrote this poem in prison, or that he intended his imitation of these psalms to articulate his personal prayers on any other occasion. The emotional tensions made evident in David's meditations, and the prevailing sense of personal anxiety and struggle in his expressions, are proper to the biblical models. Indeed, it was the themes and styles of these psalms which had made them seem especially appropriate for Christian penitential exercises. To over-emphasize the potential for personal significance in each of the seven psalms is to underestimate larger patterns of meaning and significance in the sequence as a whole.

There are two personae in Wyatt's poem: David, the psalmist, and a narrator (or, as in Harington's edition of 1549, the 'Auctor').[21] Psalmist and narrator each have their proper styles of expression: David's prayers and meditations are in the first person and *terza rima*, the narrative is largely in the third person, and in stanzaic *ottava rima*. From the outset the reader is distanced from David by the presence of this second persona who introduces David to the reader, and comments authoritatively in each of the seven prologues on David's meditations and on his progress towards true repentance. The Narrator sets the scene before and after each of David's lyrical outbursts in which he either addresses God in prayer, or meditates in soliloquy. The rôle of this narrator who addresses only the reader, not David, is to act as a guide to the reader, 'speaking alongside', or paraphrasing and expounding the psalmist's self-expression. There is no need to identify Wyatt with either of these figures; Wyatt fashioned both speakers and controls both forms of discourse from an invisible, external position.

In its juxtaposition of prologues and psalms, the structure of Wyatt's poem resembles a sermon on selected texts. This structure aids the poem's function as a whole by showing the reader how the psalms could be read. The spiritual progress of Wyatt's David to the restoration of his soul's health is not straightforward. He is depicted as a proud, emotionally unstable man who deludes himself. He can neither understand the nature of repentance nor the concept of divine grace. Eventually, David does learn how to make 'holsome penaunce', but inevitably at the cost of much suffering and soul-searching. He is characterized as an articulate and eloquent backslider, but his laments and pleas are full of specious argument, self-pity and moral confusion. By themselves, David's soliloquies and monologues convey little sense of continuity or stability, in spite of their representing the voice of a single persona. David's confusion is confusing. However, this representation of David's infirmity and pride typifies the effect of his sins as much as it characterizes David as the sinner. Moreover, it is in the nature of the personal and religious crises which sustain the reader's interest throughout the poem, that there should be some action or change. David's character is seen to develop as he learns from his spiritual suffering; he achieves a stable viewpoint only at the end of the sequence. By contrast, the Narrator's privileged commentary describing and analyzing David's repentance, provides not only a stable framework for the whole poem but also a doctrine of comfort for the reader.

There are relatively few metaphors in the prologues and these few are derived either from Aretino or from the biblical models. David's harp is made the instrument of his confession, his unhealthy spiritual condition is represented as a physical sickness, and his shameful situation in the darkness of a cave, mirrors his comfortless spiritual state when he feels bereft of the light of the world. However, there are slight variations in these recurrent stock images, which signal David's spiritual change and development. Wyatt's and Aretino's David takes up his harp for the first penitential psalm and 'synges' 'with tendre hert';[22] but before the second psalm Wyatt's Narrator states that David 'cryth' 'with straynid voyce', implying a more emotional tone; the third psalm David 'with sobre voyce did say'; but for the fourth 'his voyce he strains' so that Wyatt's Narrator cannot say 'wyther he crys or singes', which indicates a crisis. At the fifth psalm Wyatt's David simply 'begynth his song'; at the sixth, 'his song agayne thus did begynn'; and with the seventh psalm David successfully renews what Wyatt (departing from Aretino's text) calls 'the suyt off his pretence' or plea to God. This sequence of variants introducing the different psalms outlines the spiritual progress of the protagonist. David is depicted as proud and over-confident in his first psalm, and his spiritual condition deteriorates until he reaches his lowest point in the fourth psalm. Thereafter he comes to a new understanding of his situation and of divine grace, so there is a turning point in his spiritual progress, 'he begynth', and his renewal culminates in a vision of Christian redemption.

At the beginning

> Love to gyve law unto his subject hertes
> stode in the Iyes off barsabe the bryght   (lines 1–2)

David is seen as an unfortunate victim sacrificed by the tyrant Love whose real purpose is the widespread subjection of human hearts.[23] He is thus made representative of humanity and helpless in his conflict with Love. At the climax of Love's conquest,

> And when he saw that kendlid was the flame
> the moyst poyson in his hert he launcyd
> so that the sowle did tremble with the same
>   (lines 9–11)

the grammatical subject changes, and David's soul becomes the focus of interest for the rest of the poem. The soul trembles because, although Love's attack is physical, affecting David's 'sensis' and 'bonis' with 'creping fyre' (lines 7–8), once the flame of lust is kindled, the effect of the physical wound is immediately evident in David's moral confusion:

> the forme that love had prentyd in his brest
> he honorth it as thing off thinges best   (lines 15–16)

Wyatt's juxtaposition of 'honorth' with the ambiguous circumlocution 'thing off thinges best' in practice gives a pathetic irony to the couplet describing David's lustful rapture. The mutual dependence of body and soul emerges as a dominant theme throughout the poem in which we see David attempting to assert the power of his wit or reason in order to repair the damage caused by the attack on his will. David's senses have been poisoned, but it is his soul which is imperilled.

In the next two stanzas David's 'wisdom and fore cast', or prudence, are forgotten, and the suggestion of idolatry implicit in lines 15 and 16 is made explicit. Wyatt's David, 'forgettyng ... goddes majestie ... and his own', conspires to make Uriah ('his Idolles mak'), 'a redy pray' 'for enmys swordes',

> Wherby he may enjoy her owt of dowte
> whom more then god or hymsellff he myndyth

(lines 25–6)

(Aretino had specified that David would become her 'husband' and that David 'loved' her more than God or himself.) Wyatt's holograph manuscript shows him revising these lines away from Aretino's text: 'myndyth' stresses the impact on David's reason and his perverted moral judgement. Wyatt's phrase 'owt of dowte' means simply 'in security or certainty' but it also suggests the hesitation caused by moral doubt; Wyatt originally wrote 'all alone' which does not convey the implication of public accountability inherent in the king's search for security.

David, whose physical and moral perception has been dazed by Love, thinking everyone similarly blinded, is 'all amasid' and 'woofull' when Nathan reveals his treachery. As in Aretino's version David's reaction causes 'his hete his lust/ and plesur' to 'consume and wast', but Wyatt introduced a second set of triple parallelisms: 'offence outrage & Injurye' and amplified Aretino's 'ingiuria' in order to suggest a sequence of cause and effect. In lines 18 and 28–30, the Narrator describes the detrimental effects for 'Kyndomes & cytes' when 'lust' undermines authority and order by causing the king to forget his public duty and responsibilities. Wyatt's David is not depicted as an heroic character when he tries to hide from the light of truth in an underground cave which is likened to a 'pryson or grave' (lines 60–2).

The haste with which David begins his song 'with owt prolonging or delay', undermines the value of his appeal to God, which is prompted by fear of divine retribution rather than by genuine contrition or inner sorrow. However, in this first psalm David begins confidently with flattery (and emphatic English alliteration):

> O Lord sins in my mowght thy myghty name
>   sufferth it sellf/ my lord to name and call
>   here hath my hert hope taken   (lines 73–5)

He then acknowledges the gravity of his sins:

>   chastyse me not for my deserving
>   acordying to thy just conceyvid Ire   (lines 81–2)

But his panic and fear of punishment soon become evident in the apparently extempore repetitions, and the rhythm of the short, paradoxical phrases which follow:

>   O lord I dred/ and that I did not dred
>   I me repent/ and evermore desyre
> the the to dred/ I open here & spred
>   my fawte to the/ but thou for thi goodnes
>   mesure it not in largenes nor in bred   (lines 83–7)

Wyatt's David argues his need for divine assistance in combating the physical frailty which has endangered his soul: since he is weak and 'clene with owt defence' he has more need of 'remede'. He points out to God that the doctor does not tend the healthy. Wyatt derived this traditional image of sin as sickness from Fisher's *Treatyse*,[24] but introduced his own parallel: his David claims attention because, as he says, the shepherd only seeks 'the shepe that strayth':

> I lord ame strayd/ I sek with owt recure
>   fele al my lyms that have rebelld/ for fere
>   shake in dispayre onles thou me assure   (lines 97–9)

David's pride leads him to suggest that, in presenting himself as a candidate for God's mercy, he is really doing God a favour: 'Here hath thi mercie matier for the nonis' (line 126).

David's character is further illustrated by the evidence he presents to God of his attempts at mortification of the flesh:

> How oft have I cald up with diligence
>   This slouthful fleshe long afore the day
>   For to confesse his fault and negligence?
> That to the dounc for ought that I could say
>   Hath stil returnd to shroude it self from cold
>   Wherby it sufferth nowe for such delay   (lines 142–7)

Wyatt's David like Aretino's has no will-power to get out of a warm bed on cold mornings; he repudiates his 'slouthful fleshe' by contrasting 'I' with 'it'. (He has already referred to his flesh and his soul in the third person as 'the wretche' and 'the caytif' respectively (lines 120 and 124).) However, the fact that he has repeatedly 'cald up' his 'slouthful fleshe' undermines the value of David's 'diligence' which is subsequently associated with 'negligence' by means of the rhyme in line 144. Wyatt's choice of language gives the reader a sense of superiority over David who has been detected in an undignified situation attempting to evade his personal responsibility.

By the end of this first psalm David has diagnosed his ailment, but shown himself as yet unready to take responsibility for his remedy. He wants God to 'reconsile' the war within him (line 119). The vehemence of David's reaction against the temptation of his senses belies the apparent confidence of his statement that God pities him and

> shall do mak my sensis by constraint
> Obbey the rule that reson shall expres   (lines 174–5)

Wyatt's David is perhaps shrewder than he imagines in requiring that his treacherous instincts 'to hurt my helthe no more assay'. Readers may doubt whether any new onslaught at this stage would be successfully repulsed. The final emphasis on divine protection is an important part of Wyatt's interpretative imitation of the biblical verse.

In the prologue to the second psalm the Narrator elicits the reader's sympathy for 'sorowfull David' with a descriptive simile (imitated from Aretino) of a sick man's fainting sighs 'in his fevour' (line 185). David lays down his harp, described as the 'faythfull record of all his sorows sharp' (line 192), and weeps. Such 'terys of penitence' (line 207) were traditionally regarded as a sign of the heart's compunction – the pain of which recalled the attention of the sinful soul to God – and of a state of contrition.[25] Wyatt's Narrator describes how David's tears and his will to seek forgiveness mitigate his temptation to despair:

> It semid now that of his fawt the horrour
> did mak aferd no more his hope of grace
> the thretes whereoff in horrible errour
> did hold his hert as in dispaire a space
> till he had willd to seke for his socour,
> hym selff accusing/beknowyng his cace   (lines 193–8)

However, he is careful to state that the crisis is not yet resolved: David is 'esd not yet held he felith his disese' (line 200).

A surer sign of progress is that, before David picks up his harp to address God and himself in the second psalm, Wyatt's Narrator indicates that he stops to think 'a while', 'gadryng his sprites that where dismayd for fere' (line 211). In the psalm which follows, David 'with straynid voyce' considers the happiness of those

> that have forgiffnes gott
> off theire offence/ (not by theire penitence
> as by meryt wych recompensyth not
> Altho that yet pardone hath non offence
> withowte the same/) but by the goodnes
> off hym that hath perfect intelligens
> Off hert contrite/ and coverth the grettnes
> off syn within a marcifull discharge   (lines 217–24)

In this extended paraphrase of Ps. 32:1 Wyatt followed Aretino in providing a full and complex explanation of traditional Christian doctrine on penitence: the grace of God is discharged freely to those whose hearts are genuinely contrite, regardless of their individual merits (always assumed to be negligible), even though no offence is pardoned without the sinner's initiative in seeking forgiveness.

After this general statement by David, Wyatt, still following Aretino, developed the biblical theme – 'Beati quorum remisse sunt' – yet further by applying it to David's situation in the immediate historical context:

> and happy ar they that have the willfullnes
> Off lust restraynd/ afore it went at large
> provokyd by the dred of goddes furour   (lines 225–7)

David's principal reason for regretting his wilfulness of lust is that it has made him an exemplum of 'errour', and has caused others to sin; the burden of this charge is a grievous pain. Those who succeed in restraining their will

> have not on theyre bakes the charge
> of others fawte to suffer the dolour
> for that theire fawte was never execute
> in opyn syght/ example of errour   (lines 228–31)

The theme of this psalm is a recommendation of confession:

> And happi is he to whom god doth impute
> nomore his faute by knoleging his syn   (lines 232–3)

(The verbs 'impute' and 'knoleging' indicate the influence of Coverdale's Bibles.) In Aretino's version David explains at length that he had thought his rank and status would have protected him from censure, that it would even have allowed him to sin. Wyatt turned this idea into a compressed parenthetical comment: 'thynking by state in fawte to be preferd' (line 238). In the following verse the biblical psalmist and Wyatt's David describe the pressure of God's 'hevy hand':

> thy hevy hand on me was so encrest
> both day and nyght/ and held my hert in presse

with priking thowghtes byreving me my rest
   that wytherd is my lustynes away
   as somer hettes that hath the grene oprest   (lines 245–9)

(Thy hande was so hevy upon me both daye and night, my moysture was like the drouth in Sommer)
                          (1535 Bible, Ps. 31[32]:4)

In response to the biblical image Wyatt extended his
David's use of an emblematic metaphor of the 'hert in
presse', and, where he first wrote 'restles' (line 247),
revised his text to enforce the physical effects of compunction by substituting 'priking'.

These changes show Wyatt's literary sensibilities
rejecting the verbosity of Aretino in order to focus on the
terse and vivid biblical metaphor. Although Wyatt imitated the substance of Aretino's extended variations on the
biblical source, nevertheless, the holograph manuscript
shows that, by reducing the quantity of Aretino's metaphors, Wyatt sustained a pattern of revision in favour of
more abstract forms of expression. For the last part of line
224, for example, Wyatt originally wrote 'under the
mantell off mercy', following Aretino's 'col lembo [i.e.
hem] de la misericordia',[26] but introducing a related
English image which gave him the opportunity for alliteration. He subsequently revised this idea to 'within a mar-
cifull discharge', which in the context of 'offence' and
'pardone' strengthens the underlying theme of a judicial
process. One effect of this kind of revision is to focus
attention on to fewer, but therefore more dominant,
metaphors, such as the traditional equation of sin with
sickness: a bad conscience with dis-ease.[27]

Wyatt's David makes up his mind 'to opin in thi
syght', or to confess 'my fawt/ my fere/ my filthines . . . '
(lines 251–2). The triple parallelism here is an imitation of
biblical style, but Wyatt's punctuation and English alliteration also enhance the impact of the rhetorical figure
which reflects David's restored integrity in his use of
'my'. It then occurs to Wyatt's David (as it did to the bib-

lical psalmist) that his experience may encourage others who

> At me shall take example . . .
> and pray and seke in tyme for tyme of grace
>
> (lines 259–60)

In this way he can expiate his previous 'example of errour'; the king and prophet recognizes his moral duty to teach by example. David's reflexion on his exemplary status is a significant feature of Wyatt's imitation as he interpreted the biblical verse:

Pro hac orabit ad te omnis sanctus in tempore oportuno

(For this shal every saynte make his prayer unto the in due season)
(Ps. 31[32]:6, Coverdale, 1535 Bible)

Wyatt's David is 'esd' because he has found the beginning of his way back to grace, but 'not yet held' and made whole because he is only starting the course of his penitence. He finds comfort in interpreting God's personal promise to him to

> tech and gyve understondyng
> and poynt to the what way thou shalt resort
> for thi adresse to kepe the from wandryng   (lines 272–4)

There is a note of self-conscious realism in David's conclusion of this second psalm:

> Oh dyverse ar the chastysinges off syn . . .
>
> that never soffer rest unto the mynd
> filld with offence/ that new & new begyn
> with thowsand feris the hert to strayne & bynd
>
> (lines 281–6)

This is tempered by his new-found hope which he proclaims in terms of general admonition:

> but for all this he that in god doth trust
> with mercy shall hym sellff defendid fynd.
> Joy & rejoyse I say ye that be just   (lines 287–9)

David has learnt that man's spiritual condition is his own responsibility, since both sin and repentance arise from within himself; a strong and sincere effort to control both will and mind, coupled with faith or trust in God, are thus recommended as necessary to maintain the soul's health. By the end of this second psalm the Narrator reports that David is at peace:

> pees that did rejoyce
> the sowle with mercy/ that mercy so did Crye
> and fownd mercy at mercyes plentifull hand
> never denid but where it was withstand   (lines 297–300)

The word play in Wyatt's imitation of Aretino signifies that mercy is not only a divine attribute and synonym for God but also the cry of the penitent sinner, and that sinner's reward for confessing his sin.

The narrative of David's spiritual progress continues in the second half of the prologue to the third psalm. A brilliant light signifying divine grace,[28] emanating from 'that sonne the wych was never clowd cowd hide' (line 310), pierces the cave, and, gliding over the 'cordes' of David's harp, shines into his eyes and infuses his heart. David is 'surprised with Joye/by penance off the hert' (line 316), and 'inflamd' with divine rather than profane love as he simultaneously takes up his harp and 'sure hope of helth' (line 322). The action of the light indicates that the 'harme' originally caused by the similar action of profane love, is repaired by confession.

In the third psalm David immediately draws attention to his change of heart by contrasting divine immutability (emphasized by Aretino) with human mutability (emphasized by Wyatt):

> O Lord as I the have both prayd & pray
>   (altho in the be no alteration
>   but that we men/ lik as our sellffes we say
> mesuryng thy Justice by our Mutation)
>   Chastice me not o lord in thi furour   (lines 325–9)

In Wyatt's version this theme of human mutability dominates the first part of the psalm. His David reveals

> that in my fleshe for terrour of thy yre
> Is not on poynt of ferme stabilite
> nor in my bonis there is no stedfastnes   (lines 336–8)

(There is no whole parte in my body, because of thy displeasure:
there is no rest in my bones, by reason of my synnes)
                                      (1535 Bible, Ps. 37[38]:3)

(The words 'fleshe' and 'yre' were suggested by the Vulgate's 'in carne' and 'irae'.) Wyatt subsequently revised his
poem in order to emphasize David's consciousness of his
infirmity or instability. (He may have been influenced by
Campensis whose close paraphrase of this verse is 'nihil
integrum est *in toto* corpore meo', but the search for integrity and 'stedfastnes' is also a characteristic theme of
Wyatt's secular verse.)[29] Following the Vulgate he first
wrote 'helth' (cf. 'sanitas') in line 337, which he later
revised to 'ferme'. This is part of a general pattern of
revision to represent David's overwrought consciousness:
Wyatt originally wrote 'fere' for both 'dred' (line 336) and
'terrour' (line 339).

Wyatt's David has no confidence that his resolve to resist
temptation will endure:

> such is my drede of mutabilite
> For that I know my frailefull wykednes   (lines 339–40)

His remorse is depicted as 'gruging off the worme within',
'fedyng the harme that hath my welth oprest' (line 354). In
imitation of Ps. 38:5 and Fisher's *Treatyse*, the pain of
remorse

> ech not well curyd wound
> That festred is by foly and neclegens   (lines 345–6)

becomes a horrible physical suffering

(the woundes of our synnes waxe rawe agayne ... roten ... by our
folysshenes and neclygence)[30]   (Fisher, Ps. 37[38]:5)

By contrast, Wyatt's David imagines his virtues as 'frendes most sure wherein I sett most trust' (line 365), which then failed him when they were most needed. Similarly, David's 'reson and witt' are 'kyn unkynd' because they allowed him to err when they should have protected him. (Such word play on 'kyn' and 'kynd' is also a feature of Wyatt's secular verse.) These simple, commonplace images of the family and gnawing remorse enhance David's status within Wyatt's poem as a human type.

Another function of such imagery is to promote and increase the reader's sympathetic understanding of David's situation without particularizing it: sin is imagined as tyranny, and temptations as fraudulent, provoking foes. Readers of Wyatt's poem, as of other works on sin and confession, would have wanted to know what contrition should feel like, in order to recognize the often contradictory signs of their own 'penaunce off the herte'.[31] Simple and strong metaphors were likely to be most expressive. The frustration of Wyatt's David who laments his lack of stability is made evident by his being 'plongid up/ as horse owt of the myre' by the prick of conscience, and simultaneously held back in his 'good pursuyte off grace' by the 'hevi wheyght' of sin.[32] At the mid point of Wyatt's poem, David reminds God of his instability in the hope that he will not be left to 'the tyranny off sin'[33] too long:

> Lo now my god that seist my hole Intent
> My lord/ I ame thow knowst well in what case
> Forsak me not/ be not farre from me gone
> hast to my help hast lord and hast apace
> O lord the lord off all my helth alone   (lines 390–4)

God's haste is required to counteract the irresolution of Wyatt's David.

In the prologue to the fourth psalm the reader is offered an impression of a pause before a climax. David is sighing and weeping, but so absorbed in his misery that he fingers his harp's 'sonour cordes . . . withowt herying or Jugement off the sownd' (lines 403–4). Such detachment from the

59

world of sin and selfhood was a recognizable sign of compunction.[34] When 'the pilgryme' rests, he turns aside from his holy path and 'viage end'. Similarly when Wyatt's David rests 'under such shaad as sorow hath assynd' (line 400), he turns aside from his holy purpose even though he does not forget it. David's excessive tears and 'wofull plaint', which cannot 'expresse' (or expel) the 'inward restraintes' of his heart, do not advance his penitential course, in fact they cause a relapse. It seemed to David

> that the shade
> off his offence/ agayne his force assays
> by violence dispaire on hym to lade   (lines 421–3)

The path to true penitence is not straightforward. However, many of Wyatt's readers would have recognized that, according to traditional Christian teaching on the psychology of the spiritual life, such temptation to despair was part of the cure for pride. According to Gregory the Great, the sinner's fear and hope are like two millstones: one stone without the other cannot grind the grain. As Fisher expounded Gregory's simile:[35]

Lyke wyse it is with synners whan hope is myxed with drede and drede with hope, so that by overmoche hope of forgyvenes the mynde be not lyft up in to presumpcyon, and by overmoche fere it be not put downe in to dyspayre

When these two stones – hope and fear – operate together, sin is 'broken in to many small partes and in conclusyon utterly done away'.

Wyatt's David begins his fourth psalm, oppressed by the consciousness of his need for God's grace and of the enormity 'off his offence'. The crisis is marked by the Narrator's reaction to David's emotion:

> stertyng like hym whom sodeyne fere dismays
> his voyce he strains and from his hert owt brynges
> this song that I not wyther he crys or singes   (lines 424–6)

David pleads in all humility for pity and for God's infinite mercies which

> much more then man can synn
> do way my synns that so thy grace offend
>
> (lines 435–6)

This emphasis on 'grace' is Wyatt's.[36] Whereas the biblical psalmist had anticipated that God would act, Wyatt's David begs repeatedly

> Agayne washe me but washe me well within
> and from my synn that thus makth me affrayd
> make thou me clene/ as ay thy wont hath byn
>
> (lines 436–8)

assuring God that

> I/ beknow my Fawt my neclegence
> & in my syght my synn is fixid fast
> theroff to have more perfett penitence   (lines 442–4)

Nevertheless, David's sense of personal integrity is a measure of his progress towards 'perfett penitence'. When Wyatt's David plainly acknowledges 'my Fawte my neclegence . . . my syght my synn' as a whole man, repetition of the pronoun makes another emphatic contrast with the third person forms by which he had earlier attempted to evade responsibility for his 'slouthful fleshe' (lines 142–4). At this point David is genuinely contrite. He confesses fully and affirms his 'fydelite' (lines 461–2), praying for spiritual enlightenment,

> tech me the hydden wisdome off thy lore
> sins that my fayth doth not yet dekay   (lines 467–8)

and anticipating the purgation of his sin,

> thow shalt me wash/ & more then snow therfore
> I shall be whight. how fowle my fawt hath bene
>
> (lines 471–2)

Like the biblical psalmist, Wyatt's David promises, in return to teach other sinners to seek God:

> rendre to me/ Joye off thy help and rest
> my will conferme with spryte off stedfastnesse.
> And by this shall thes goodly thinges ensue

61

> sinners I shall in to thy ways adresse
> they shall retorne to the and thy grace sue   (lines 483–7)

(Redde mihi leticiam salutaris tui: et spiritu principali confirma me.
Docebo iniquos vias tuas: et impii ad te convertentur)
                                              (Ps. 50[51]:12–13)

David also acknowledges that he must humble himself to
the will of God before he can be purged and justified:

> The sacryfice/ that the lord lykyth most/
> is spryte contrite/ low hert in humble wyse
> thow dost accept   (lines 500–2)

(Sacrificium deo spiritus contribulatus: cor contritum et humilia-
tum deus non despicies)   (Vulgate, Ps. 50[51]:18)

He therefore prays:

> make Syon lord acordyng to thy will
> inward syon/ the syon of the ghost
> off hertes Hierusalem strength the walles still
>   (lines 503–5)[37]

After this fourth psalm the Narrator elaborates on the
mysteries of divine grace and mercy 'that gratis . . . to men
doth depert' (line 524). He reports that David is overwhelmed by the greatness of 'diepe secretes . . . off mercy
off fayth off frailte off grace' (lines 509–10), and that he
meditates silently on these mysteries

> in his hert he tornith and paysith
> ech word that erst/ his lypps myght forth aford.
> he poyntes/ he pawsith/ he wonders/ he praysyth
>   (lines 518–20)

David's calm deliberations contrast with his earlier panic-
stricken outbursts, and as a result of his meditation David
has

> confort when he doth mesure
> mesureles marcys to mesureles fawte
> to prodigall sinners infinite tresure
> tresure termeles that never shall defawte (lines 525–8)

62

This comfort marks a turning point in David's spiritual experience. He begins the fifth psalm boldly 'Lord here ...', but soon reminds God (and the reader) of his particular difficulty:

> do not from me torne thy mercyfull fase
> Unto my sellff leving my government   (lines 543–4)

(Hyde not thy face fro me in the tyme of my trouble)
                                        (1535 Bible, Ps. 101[102]:2)

He acknowledges that his heart and mind are 'wytherd up like haye' because he has forgotten to take his 'brede off lyff/ the word off trowth'.[38] The following lines remind the reader of the cause of David's fall from grace and its effects:

> And for my plaintfull syghes and my drede
>   my bonis my strenght my very force of mynde
>   cleved to the flesh/ and from thi spryte were flede
> as dispairate thy mercy for to fynd   (lines 556–9)

(I was so dried up with my sorowfull and lowde syghes: that my bones cleved to my scynne)   (Joye, *Psalter* (1530), Ps. 102:5)

The 'flesh' here has a dual function, as an image of physical wasting and as a metaphor for a lustful life.

The remainder of Ps. 102 is made into David's sermon on grace as he summarizes and comments on his past experience of 'waker care/ that with this wo bygane' (line 564). He acknowledges that the wrath of God, 'provokt by ryght had off my pride disdayne' (line 574), and Wyatt's David remembers how God broke his pride:

> for thou didst lyfft me up to throw me downe
> to tech me how to know my sellff agayne.
> Wherby I knew that helples/ I shold drowne[39]
>   (lines 575–7)

A distinctive feature of Wyatt's interpretation of verse 10 ('A facie ire indignationis tue: quia elevans allisisti me') is the motive attributed to God: 'to tech me how to know my sellff agayne'. Wyatt's imitation also gives prominence to the biblical theme of writing for the spiritual benefit of future generations:

> to our discent thys to be wrytten semith
> Off all confortes as consolation best
> and thei that then shalbe regenerate
> shall praise the lord therfore both most & lest
>
> (lines 597–600)

(scribantur hec in generatione altera: et populus qui creabitur laudabit dominum) (Ps. 101[102]:18)

Wyatt's David, like Aretino's (but unlike the biblical psalmist), also urges God that 'the tyme at hand' is the right time to redeem 'syon from sins Aw' and from original sin: 'this frailte that yokyth all manekynd' (line 581). In the middle of this fifth psalm David considers a future 'when thi grace this Syon thus redemith' (line 593), and

> When in one chirche the peple off the lond
> And remes bene gaderd to serve/ to lawd/ to pray/
> the lord above so just and mercyfull (lines 609–11)

David himself does not hope to live long enough 'to se that terme', but he repeats the substance of his prayer on human mortality and divine immortality: all things in heaven and earth shall perish, but God will endure to 'tourne and translate' them (line 624), or to change and transform them in recurrent cycles of redemption and renewal.

In the prologue to the sixth psalm the Narrator confirms David's perception that the exiled 'sprite off god' had returned, thereby making him the prophet and poet, or a medium for the expression of 'grete thinges

> as shalme or pype letes owt the sownd inprest
> by musikes art forgid to fore and fyld (lines 636–7)

Wyatt's David is now God's instrument. However, David overreaches himself yet again, when he attributes the revival of the 'sprite of confort in hym' as a sign of complete reconciliation 'unto the lordes grace'. Wyatt's Narrator adopts a familiar tone in his reference to 'our david',

> but our david jugith in his intent
> hym sellff by penance clene owt off this cace
> wherby he hath remission off offence   (lines 644–6)

In the company of the Narrator, 'we' are wiser than David who (Wyatt's Narrator states firmly) had mistaken the 'owtward dede' which is only a symptom of penitence ('the sygne of fruyt alone') for 'ryghtfull penitence'

> wich is alone the hert retornd agayne
> and sore contryt   (lines 653–4)

In the context of the Narrator's statement, and of David's realization voiced in his psalm, the constituents of 'ryghtfull penitence' are made clear to Wyatt's readers.

The root of David's problem remains his pride. He has learnt many lessons from his spiritual experience, but he is still described as having to fight off

> the slye assault
> off vayne alowance off his voyde desert   (lines 656–7)

This David proceeds to do in his sixth psalm, where he acknowledges that God's mercy, rather than man's merits, redeems a sinner. Wyatt's David at last throws himself on the mercy of God who, instead of making the punishment fit the crime, is understood to seek

> rather love
> For in thi hand/ is mercys resedence
> By hope wheroff thou dost our hertes move
> (lines 680–2)

David's heart is moved by his hope of God's mercy which will be bestowed far in excess of his obvious demerits. He argues, if mercy were 'putt . . . in restraint', and

> if just exaction demaund recompense
> Who may endure o lord? who shall not faynt
> At such acompt?[40]   (lines 677–9)

Paradoxically David's cry *de profundis* is uttered from a superior position. He has called on God to be his 'borow' to bail him out

> From depth off sinn & from a diepe dispaire
> from depth off deth/ from depth off hertes sorow
> from this diepe Cave off darknes diepe repayre
>
> (lines 664–6)

(Out of the depe call I unto the (o Lorde))

(1535 Bible, Ps. 129[130]:1)

He has set his 'confydence' in God, in that he has confided his 'hert . . . hope . . . plaint . . . overthrow' and his 'will to ryse'[41] to God's ear, and has been sustained by the 'piller' and 'stay' of 'mercys promesse that is alway just' (line 686). David's reaffirmation of faith in God's 'propertie' of 'grace and favour' culminates in his prophecy that

> plenteus rannzome shall com with hym I say:
> And shall redeme all our iniquitie   (lines 693–4)

A measure of David's spiritual recovery is seen again in his return to human society and his consideration of 'all *our* iniquitie'. In this conclusion to the penultimate psalm Wyatt's David articulates Christian teaching, and regains his standing as a representative type of humanity. The theme of redemption recurs throughout this psalm and Wyatt's Narrator takes it up in his final prologue:

> This word redeme that in his mowght did sownd
> did put david it semyth unto me
> as in a traunce to starre apon the grownd
> and with his thowght the heyght of hevin to se
> where he beholdes the word that shold confownd
> the sword off deth   (lines 695–700)

David's contemplation of the Word is a divine gift, bringing inner peace and confidence (based on contempt of self), which is promoted by the highest states of prayer. David's contemplation connotes the superior aspect of compunction (described by Gregory and by Fisher in terms of love as well as fear) which influenced devotional, pastoral and mystical literature well into the sixteenth century.[42] He stares 'apon the grownd' in an attitude of humility, but he perceives the 'heyght of hevin'. The mystical nature of this

vision is suggested by the repeated image of mortality as a
veil, and by David's trance-like posture and appearance.
As in Aretino the Narrator reports that David's vision was
of the Word, or Christ, given 'mortall habitt', or human
life, by the Virgin Mary, the 'mortall mayd' who clothed
the Word in flesh. The incarnation gives rise to the paradoxical 'eternall lyff in mortall vaile', or the life of Christ,
which is subsequently sacrificed so that according to
Christian teaching death shall die. As David in his trance
contemplates the crucifixion,

> He seith that word/ when full rype tyme shold come
> do way that vayle/ by fervent affectione
> torne off with deth/ for deth shold have her dome
>
> (lines 703–5)

The tearing of the veil signifies both mortality and the life
of Christ, hence (paradoxically), 'that mortall vaile hath
immortalite' whereby 'david [hath] assurance off his iniquitie' (lines 709–710), or the certainty of forgiveness for
his sin.

In the second half of the prologue to the last penitential
psalm, the Narrator sees into David's heart, and presents
his thought processes in direct speech. The substance of
David's reasoning is a confession of Christian faith, that
the God who did not

> forbere his sonne
> from deth for me and can therby convert
> my deth to lyff/ my synn to salvation
> both can & woll a smaller grace depert
> to hym that suyth by humble supplication
>
> (lines 712–16)

Finally, in the seventh psalm David prays for grace

> not by desert/ but for thyn own byhest
> In whose ferme trowgh thou promest myn empyre
> to stond stable   (lines 729–31)

David's complete humility and subjection to God is an
outward sign of his inner salvation or soul's health which
has been achieved in the course of the poem by his genuine

contrition or repentance, sincere confession or self-knowledge, and a vision of Christian satisfaction yet to come:[43]

> Shew me by tyms thyn Ayde
> For on thy grace I holly/ do depend.
> and in thi hand sins all my helth is stayde
> do me to know/ what way thou wolt I bend
> For unto the I have reysd up my mynd.
>
> Tech me thy will/ that I by the may fynd
> the way to work the same in affection
>
> (lines 757–61, 765–6)

The final prologue and psalm echo the first prologue and psalm by returning to the historical setting for the whole poem in the life of King David; Wyatt took little from Aretino. In the first prologue the Narrator had described David as attacked and conquered by profane Love to whom he yielded as he 'stode and trauncyd', thereby forgetting God and himself. In the first psalm David's peremptory tone to God had been coupled with an acute self-pity and his misplaced confidence that merely because God had heard 'the voyce off my complaint' (line 170), therefore,

> He shall do mak my sensis by constraint
> Obbey the rule that reson shall expres   (lines 174–5)

Finally, the contrite, humble David, having confessed his sins and his need for divine grace, amends his life, and experiences a vision of divine love. The double aspect of compunction – dread and desire – secures David's contrition, confession and satisfaction. He sets about restoring peace in both Israel and the 'inward syon', by ending the civil war, 'sufferd by god my sinne for to correct' (line 722), within the kingdom and within the king. David turns to face his temporal enemies assured that God will revive his spirit

> within the ryght that I receyve by the
> wherby my lyff off danger shalbe quyte   (lines 770–71)

He concludes the process of his repentance by acknowledging his integrity in terms of the discipline and consolation of obedient service to God:

> For thyn ame I thy servant ay most bownd
>
> (line 775)

In the recurrent pattern of alternating prologue and psalm the reader comes to the prologues for emotional respite and moral and theological stocktaking. The rôle of the Narrator throughout Wyatt's poem has been to control the reader's response to David's prayers and meditations. He preserves a distance between the reader and David – at one point by introducing an anonymous observer to corroborate his comments, and at another point by encouraging the reader to judge 'our david' according to his criteria. The Narrator even takes over the rôle of Nathan, the admonitory prophet, to counsel the reader. The narrator's assurance that God's 'mesureles marcys' are an 'infinite tresure | tresure termeles that never shall defawte' (lines 526–8), and freely available to 'prodigall sinners', such as David, is intended to comfort the reader. There is never any indication in the poem that David is aware of the Narrator who is thus preaching to an audience beyond the poem – its readers. The 'homily' on the psalm texts continues as the Narrator describes how David recovered his spiritual equilibrium after meditating on God's promise of grace, 'that gratis ... to men doth depert', and of mercy

> gaine whome shall no assaute
> off hell prevaile/ by whome ...
> off hevin gattes Remission is the kay   (lines 530–2)

John Fisher had expressed a traditional view of David as the author of the seven penitential psalms, when he said that 'he was a synner as we be/ but he dyde holsome penaunce makynge this holy psalme wherby he gate forgyvenes & was restored to his soules helth'.[44] The descriptions and commentaries of Wyatt's Narrator present the seven penitential psalms as evidence for the spiritual biography of David as a true penitent. Wyatt's representation of the course of David's repentance would have had a strong appeal to the interests and sympathies of contemporary readers familiar with the seven penitential psalms which were always included in the laity's Books of Hours and Primers as a devotional sequence. The spirituality of the late fifteenth and early sixteenth centuries was characterized by its focus on the personal relationship of an individual with God in private prayer rather than on traditional forms of communal worship.[45] The treatments of these seven psalms by Fisher, Aretino and Wyatt in their different versions reflect this contemporary spirituality. In each version the sinner's analysis of his self is expounded by the voice of the preacher or narrator so that the reader is encouraged to take an objective view of the redemption of a 'grievous' sinner. David's spiritual recovery was exemplary. For Fisher, the object in retelling David's story was that we simpler sinners

by the example of hym warned/ instructe/ and monysshed/ despayre not in ony condycyon/ but with true penaunce ... aske of our blessyd lord god mercy and forgyveness[46]

Such a view of the utility of the story was shared by both Catholics and Protestants alike. In his *The obedience of a Christen man* published in 1528, William Tyndale had observed that

The adultery of David with Barsabe is an ensample/ not to move us to evell: but yf (whyle we folow the waye of ryghteousnes) any chaunce dryve us asyde/ that we despere not. For yf we saw not soch infyrmytes in Gods electe/ we which are so weke and fall so ofte shulde utterly despeare and thinke that God had cleane forsaken us[47]

Wyatt's treatment of the penitential sequence offers an exemplum for the instruction of his readers, not a model for their devotions. He would have sympathized with the views of Christian humanists who regarded good literature

– and particularly a good poem – as a moral incentive to a virtuous life.[48] There is no evidence to suggest that Wyatt sought to identify himself with the persona of David. The poem is not presented by Wyatt as a vehicle for a personal statement of his own, nor has it been preserved as such.

By contrast Wyatt's three satires, and his epigram 'Syghes ar my foode, drynke are my teares' are presented as direct addresses to named individuals, which would have encouraged the first readers of these poems to associate the speakers in them with their author. The epigram, which echoes Wyatt's 'Defence' written in the Tower of London in May 1541, is addressed, in line 7, to Sir Francis Brian who was clearly supposed to regard this epigram as an expression of Wyatt's personal reaction to imprisonment.[49] Surrey associated Wyatt with the speaker in this epigram since he alluded to its last lines in his own epigram 'My Ratclif, when thy rechlesse youth offendes':

> Yet Salomon sayd, the wronged shall recure
> But Wiat said true, the skarre doth aye endure

recalling Wyatt's

> Sure I am Brian this wounde shall heale agayne
> But yet alas the scarre shall styll remayne[50]

The heading in the Blage manuscript to Wyatt's poem 'Who lyst his welthe and eas Retayne' also testifies to a contemporary tradition among Wyatt's friends, which associated him with the speaker in this poem:[51]

> *V. Innocentia*
> *Veritas Viat Fides*
> *Circumdederunt me inimici mei*

This heading names Wyatt and proclaims his innocence, surrounding his name with truth and faith as if to protect his person or his reputation from the enemies which have surrounded the speaker. Circumstantial evidence has been used to link this poem with Wyatt's imprisonment in the Bell Tower in May 1536, when Anne Boleyn was executed. The last lines of the poem support the association of the speaker with the author named in the heading:

> Wyt helpythe not deffence to yerne
> Of innocence to pled or prate
> Ber low, therffor, geve god the sterne
> For sure circa Regna tonat

The last line of the heading is a taken from Ps. 16[17]:9, and identifies the speaker in the poem with the psalmist.

The only other instance where Wyatt may be associated with the persona of a biblical psalmist is to be found in his close paraphrase of Ps. 37 which is not one of the penitential psalms. The themes of Ps. 37 suggest that Wyatt may have selected it (like the Senecan models for other poems including 'Who lyst his welthe and eas Retayne') as an appropriate expression for a moral truism and a personal lament on what he called elsewhere the 'Slipper toppe of courtes estates'.[52] This psalm, and Wyatt's imitation of it, takes the form of an instruction in a series of injunctions to a second person.

> Altho thow se th'owtragious clime aloft
> Envie not thowe his blinde prosperitye
> The welth of wretches tho it semith soft
> Move not thy hert by theyre felicitye.
> They shalbe found like grasse turnd into hay
> And as the herbes that wither sodenlye.
> Stablisshe thy trust in god seke right alway
> And on the yerth thowe shalte inhabite longe[53]

(Ps. 37, lines 1–8)

Like the biblical Ps. 37, Wyatt's paraphrase may have consoled or encouraged its readers, but it may also have served to confirm the faith of that Tudor moralist who resolved at the end of 'Who lyst his welthe and eas Retayne' to 'Ber low' and 'geve god the sterne'.

Wyatt probably wrote at least one other psalm version, which is now lost. The text of his Ps. 37 in the Arundel manuscript is followed by a poem entitled 'Th'argument', beginning 'Somtyme the pryde of mye assured trothe'. This would appear to be the introduction to another psalm version.[54] Immediately after the concluding lines of the 'argument' –

> Myne Earle this doute my hart did humble than
> For errour so might murder Innocentes
> Then sang I thus in god my Confydence[55]

– the Arundel manuscript (which is the only witness to the text) lacks eight leaves (folios 120–7). The last line implies that a psalm of personal devotion articulating positive themes followed. If Wyatt did write a psalm to express his own thoughts and feelings in a devotional mode, then it would appear to have been lost with the missing folios. As in the epigram 'Syghs ar my foode . . .' the direct address to an individual – here, probably Surrey – would have encouraged contemporary readers of Wyatt's 'lost psalm' to identify the psalmist or speaker with the author.

The comments by Wyatt's contemporaries transmitted with the text of his penitential psalms associate Wyatt as author with the persona of the Narrator rather than with that of the psalmist David. In John Harington's printed edition of the text (1549) the heading 'Th'Auctor' has been supplied to each of the prologues, not the psalms.[56] Surrey's sonnet 'The great Macedon . . .' which was added (probably after Wyatt's death) to Wyatt's holograph manuscript as a heading or prologue to the seven penitential psalms assumes that contemporary readers would see a connexion between the poem and Nathan's admonition to David: Wyatt's poem is described as 'a myrrour clere',

> Where Rewlers may se . . .
> The bitter frewte of false concupiscence

and be awakened 'out of their synfull slepe'.[57] Surrey's sonnet suggests that Wyatt may have seen King David – the royal lover guilty of manslaughter, if not murder, in

the pursuit of illicit passion – as representing Henry VIII
rather than himself. According to Thomas Sackville
Wyatt's poem

> singes the fall
> Of David dolling for the guilt he wrought
> and Uries deth which he so dereli bought[58]

Such views would place Wyatt's poem in the *de casibus*
tradition later epitomized in the popular Elizabethan
anthology *A Myrrour for Magistrates* (1563),[59] but, as both
Fisher and Tyndale testify, contemporary attitudes to the
way the David and Bathsheba story functioned as an
exemplum were not so restricted. Elsewhere Surrey com-
memorated Wyatt's 'rare wit . . . employde to our avayle
Where Christe is tought'.[60] The wording on the title page
of the first printed edition of Wyatt's penitential psalms
recommends the poem as 'very pleasaunt & profettable to
the godly reader'.[61]

In October 1549 Sir Thomas Smith, one of Edward VI's
two secretaries of state, was imprisoned in the Tower of
London with the Duke of Somerset and several members
of Somerset's household.[62] During his imprisonment
Smith wrote eleven metrical psalm paraphrases and eight
prose collects or prayers for his companions' devotions.
He also composed three stanzaic lyrics or 'songues . . . to
pas the tyme there', which he called 'other psalmes', since,
although they contain echoes of various biblical psalms,
they are not based on any particular psalm texts.[63] Wyatt's
imitation of the seven penitential psalms – combining the
Narrator's hortatory, descriptive commentary and David's
ruminative, lyrical devotions – may be compared with
Smith's 'other psalme' beginning 'Whie shall we still in this
prison abid?'.[64] Like Wyatt's sequence, Smith's 'other
psalme' projects the voices of two speakers in the representation of an individual's spiritual crisis. In Smith's poem,
however, the unnamed psalmist is represented not only in
colloquy with himself but also with the authoritative voice

of God. The psalmist's crisis of faith is enacted and resolved through these exchanges without the separate commentary of a narrator.

The poem begins with a series of direct questions reminiscent of the form and content of several biblical psalms:

> Whie shall we still in this prison abid?
> Shall we still in these Cabons remayn?
> Wilt thou yet from us thi face away hid?
> And keepe us continually in this disdayn?[65]
>
> (MS Royal 17 A xvii, fol. 24^v)

In the second and third stanzas Smith's 'psalmist' righteously proclaims the innocence of himself and his companions:

> If we have offended, as thei do to us laye
> And as the brute doth go about
> Let them us kill, let our lives decaye
> Let us never herafter alive com out[66]   (fol. 25^r)

But he then reverts to questions which begin to sound impudent and challenging. Three short, parallel sentences lead up to a sustained climax which marks the end of the first section of the poem, and introduce the theme which is developed in the next six stanzas:

> What meane thes tales? what meane thes talkes?
> Whi do thei thus upon us lye?
> Is there no god that now on earth walkes?
> Suche false sclaunderours for to espie?   (fol. 25^r)

The injustice of the prisoners' situation has shaken the speaker's faith, and made him echo the 'fool' (from Ps. 14 and others), who 'said in his heart, there is no God'.[67] Smith's 'psalmist' is poised on the brink of despair. In the second section of the poem it is immediately apparent that by using the singular pronoun, this psalmist distinguishes himself from his companions. The main verbs are in past tenses, and the form of the 'psalme' suggests the speaker's sense of an audience besides God (addressed as 'thou' in line 3): either his companions (signified by 'we' in the first section), or a reader to whom he relates his spiritual history in a dramatic, personal style.

Since the 'psalmist' has found no satisfactory answers to his initial questions, he becomes dejected and reports to his audience

> I had thus conceived, in my mynd
> The wicked flaterer, speedith best
> Thei save themself most, that be unkind
> The just man hath, I see, no rest[68]

> Whan troble cometh, than most is his part
> Whan welth retorneth, he is most suspect
> He is lest pleasaunt, that hath a true hart
> Still flaterie is preferrid, and truthe is reject   (fol. 25ʳ)

His self-conscious 'I see' restores the ruminative style of the meditation, merging a personal form with aphoristic generalizations on the just man's fate in an immoral world. The 'psalmist' comes to the same conclusion as his biblical counterpart who saw the wicked flourish and take power for themselves: his own virtue and innocence are in vain.[69] The application of this conclusion to himself is emphasized in the next line with a return to direct speech and the triple repetition of 'I':

> I will, I said, if I do escape

However, the past tense of 'I said' indicates that the 'psalmist' is no longer addressing God, or himself. The 'psalme' becomes a reported meditation:

> I will, I said, if I do escape this
> Turne my lief, an other waye
> Be pleasaunt, and a flaterer, as some other is
> What need I tell truth, and my self cast away

> The wicked I see doth gaine, most riches
> The wethercock scapeth best, every wind
> What neede I needles, cast me in distres?
> To perills of death, or grief of mynd[70]   (fol. 25ᵛ)

He assesses his chances of survival in a world abandoned by God:

> I can, I think, scape, as well as the best
> I knowe all the waies, to the wood
> I can hold my peace, or I can say lest
> And I can if I will, be most mild of mood
>
> God doth not regarde, god doth not see
> God lettith the world, goo on wheeles   (fol. 25ᵛ)

and concludes with an ironic recommendation of hypocrisy to 'all true harted men' who 'seyng such daungiers, following their heeles', 'maie learne of me'; as in Wyatt's third satire the 'true harted' were really intended to learn something different.

In the third and fourth sections the style of the poem changes again as a dialogue between the dispirited 'psalmist' and God is presented in direct speech:[71]

> Thus in my folie, I semed to speak
> But god me than, did reprehend
> Thow doest not regarde, the later wreak
> Thow doest not consider, what is the end
>
> If with patience I suffer them for to call
> And mak myn examples, variable
> Wilt thou from my grace, streightway fall
> With a mynde so doubtfull, and so unstable?   (fol. 26ʳ)

God berates the 'psalmist' for his impatience and lack of faith, and then reminds him sternly of divine omnipotence in a series of rhetorical questions deploying antithetical parallelisms (in imitation of biblical poetic forms):

> Whose is riches? whose is need?
> Whose is to mak sad? whose to make fain?
> Whose to give comfort? whose to make the hart bleed?
> Whose to poure on honour? and whose to give disdain?
>
> Is there any thou doest trust, better than me?
> Or whom thou doest tak, to be more wise?
> Is there any, thinkes thou, more carefull of thee?
> That can let thee fall easelier, and soner arise?[72]   (fol. 26ʳ)

The fourth section, in which the rebellious 'psalmist' is brought to his knees in prayer, follows immediately.

There is no comment on God's words, but the psalmist states that he was moved by them to repentance:

> I was ashamed of myself, and I moorned in myn hart
> (fol. 26ᵛ)

In the last seven lines the 'psalme' reverts to the present tense, and an immediate, personal invocation: the 'psalmist' is contrite and humble

> I crie thee o Lorde most humbly mercie
> Pardon me o god, heale my soules smart
> To thi goodnes I submitte, my cause hoolye   (fol. 26ᵛ)

The doubt and despair with which he began are dispelled, and the 'psalmist' ends with a confession of faith:

> I have no god, but thee alone
> I have no father, Cousyn, nor freend
> I have no Master, to whom I shuld moone
> Therfore thou o Lorde, shalt make myn eend[73] (fol. 26ᵛ)

These final lines confirm the speaker's repentance.

Like Wyatt's penitential psalms, Smith's poem offers its readers an affective exemplum of repentance. The blatant blasphemy of Smith's 'psalmist' would have discouraged any pious reader from identifying with this speaker, but it might have enabled and encouraged that reader to learn from the experience represented. The 'psalmist's' ironic recommendation of hypocrisy is reminiscent of satire, and Smith exaggerates this feature. Like Wyatt's satires, the 'other psalme' dramatizes the Tudor courtier's moral dilemma: how to survive and succeed in 'the press of courts' without sacrificing peace of mind and an 'honest name' by 'feeding' on 'innocent blood'.[74] Although Smith composed his 'other psalme' in prison and in peril of his life, it does not function as a vehicle for the expression of personal devotion. 'Whie shall we still in this prison abid?' reveals a devout man articulating personal reactions to his situation by imitating a generic concept of the biblical psalms as divine poems or 'songs'. The speaker in this 'other psalme' may represent any individual, including Smith, but, like Chaucer's Dan Geoffrey or Wyatt's speaker in his third satire, this other 'psalmist' is a literary persona who cannot be identified simply with the individual who wrote the poem.

Smith created his 'other psalme' by analogy with the biblical texts as examples of a poetic 'kind' with the proven capacity to teach and delight as a source of spiritual comfort and guidance. Wyatt's poem offers a more psychologically complex examination of his psalmist's dilemma, exploiting subtle but recognizable stages in the development of a traditional pattern of contrition, confession and satisfaction or amendment of life.[75] Alongside Smith's 'other psalme' the structure of Wyatt's poem as a single, unified sequence of prayer, meditation and homiletic comment becomes more apparent.

The issues raised by these poems anticipate some of the problems raised by later meditative, lyric verse which represents the personal experience and inner life of a well-projected and eloquent speaker or poetic persona, such as Sidney's Astrophil, Shakespeare's sonneteer, or the speaker in Herbert's *Temple*. The better the poem, the greater the temptation to assume that the feelings expressed by the speaker within it represent the 'particular greefes eyther of body or soule' of the poet.

3

'PARTICULER PRAYERS OF PARTICULAR PERSONS, IN PARTICULAR GREEFES EYTHER OF BODY OR SOULE'

OCCASIONAL VERSES BY THE EARL OF SURREY, AND OTHERS (1535–1554)

In 1581, Anthony Gilby defined the unique significance of the Psalms:

whereas al other scriptures do teach us what God saith unto us, these praiers ... teach us, what we shal saie unto god[1]

Sixteenth-century commentators encouraged individuals to recognize representations of their own experiences and emotions in psalms, and to use them as models for personal prayer and meditation:

here shall you see paynted as in a most lively Table, in the person of king David, such things as you have felt and shall continuallye feele in your selfe[2]

This evidence that 'David and the other saintes of God' had 'felt the same infirmities that we doe, both corporall and spiritual' was a matter of history, and a source of reassurance which 'for most singular comfort may be marked in the meditation of the Psalmes'.[3] Meditation on the Psalms was an act of 'imitation' to be practised as a devotional exercise in the course of an individual's spiritual life. The Genevan translators recommended that the Psalms should be 'well weyghed and practysed':[4] that is, that the reader should first ponder the meaning of the words and evaluate the significance of the experience represented, and that he should subsequently use the texts as vehicles for his own devotions and meditations.

Before the reader could apply the content of the relevant psalm to his own condition he had first to understand the text and to identify with its author. Calvin had found that to identify his personal experience with David's 'was no small help . . . too the understanding of the Psalmes', and in expounding 'the inward meanings' of David and the other psalmists he believed he was dealing with 'things wherwith I am well acquaynted'.[5] In 1559 the English Genevan translators encouraged Queen Elizabeth (who had recently succeeded to the throne) to identify her experiences with King David's 'perils and persecutions that he susteyned before he came to the royall dignitie'.[6] Elizabeth was urged to imitate David in her life, and to depend upon God's help as David had done 'in hys greatest afflictions'.

The which considerations may move you . . . to the same or lyke meditacions and prayers, as David used in his distres, that you may also finde like comfort whensoever affliction shall assayle you[7]

The Psalms must have had a special appeal for prisoners. John Hooper, the Protestant martyr, wrote expositions of certain psalms as spiritual exercises 'in the time of his trouble, when (no doubt) he was talking in spirit with God', 'ex carcere & vinculis'.[8] He had also written to his wife advising her which psalms 'be for the purpose when the minde can take no understandyng, nor the hart any joye of gods promises' and from which she would 'learne both patience & consolation' in her 'anguish of mind'.[9]

During the recurrent upheavals in the official religion and politics of England between 1534 and 1559, prisoners in the Tower of London and elsewhere wrote their own occasional prayers and meditations in imitation of psalms. In such circumstances prisoners approached the Psalms in the expectation of finding vehicles for their own supplications to God, sources of comfort in their affliction, guides to their spiritual self-scrutiny, and patterns for remaking their spiritual identities. Such expectations are evident in their selection and 'weighing' of particular psalms, and contributed to the prisoners' treatments of those texts in their devotional 'practice' and 'lyke meditacions, as David used in his distres'.[10]

While Thomas More was a prisoner in the Tower of London (1534–5) he wrote five 'devout and vertuouse instruccions, meditacions and prayers'.[11] One of these 'devout prayers' was in Latin, 'collected oute of the psalmes of David', and consists of verses selected from different psalms. This prayer is in the tradition of such devotional texts as the so-called 'Psalter of St Jerome' found in Books of Hours, and the new compilations *Psalmi seu precationes* attributed to John Fisher.[12] More also composed an English prayer (later entitled 'A godly meditacion') which he wrote in the margins of his Book of Hours.[13] The substance of the Latin and the English prayers is related to annotations in More's hand found in the margins of his Latin Psalter.[14] These annotations represent More's 'weighing' of the Psalms, the 'devoute prayer' in Latin and the 'godly meditacion' in English represent his 'practice' in following that live devotional tradition which had placed the Psalms at the core of the literature of Christian spirituality. Both prayers are inventive imitations in that no attempt has been made to follow the sense of any single psalm. The 'godly meditacion' in English is in More's handwriting, and may have been composed four days before his execution.[15] There is not the same direct connexion between the Psalter annotations and the English prayer as that which exists between the annotations and the Latin prayer,[16] but all have been attributed to the period of his imprisonment, and reflect the same concerns.

In his Psalter annotations More noted particularly the applications of psalm themes to those 'in tentatione' and 'in tribulatione'.[17] He selected only those psalms containing references to personal suffering or national calamity, and passed over psalms of praise and thanksgiving. There are, for example, six comments on Ps. 30 [31]: the second, alongside the sixth verse ('In manus tuas commendo spiritum meum') is 'periclitantis aut morientis oratio', the prayer of someone in great danger or at the point of death; the fourth, at verse 14 ('Super omnes inimicos meos factus sum opprobrium et vicinis meis valde, et timor notis meis'), is 'infamia et periculo'; the sixth, at verse 23 ('Quam magna multitudo dulcedinis tuae domine'), is 'consolatio spiritus in tribulatione'.[18] At Ps. 87 [88]:4 ('Estimatus sum cum descendentibus in lacum: factus sum sicut homo sine adjutorio') More wrote 'in tribulatione vehementi et in carcere', and there are three other specific references to imprisonment in his Psalter annotations.[19]

The text of More's English prayer or 'godly meditacion' consists of fifty-four lines added in the upper and lower margins of his Book of Hours on the pages containing the offices for prime, terce and sext. The position of these lines is important, and must have had some significance for More. The first line is placed adjacent to an illustration of the Nativity, and the last is added on a page facing an illustration of the Crucifixion, alongside the prayers for the hour at which Christ was reputed to have been nailed to the Cross. The location of the prayer on these particular pages of the book, and their association with these devotional pictures, probably reflect More's desire to imitate the life of Christ; his desire to 'bere the crosse with christ' is brought out clearly in the other works composed during his imprisonment – the *Treatise upon the Passion* and the *De Tristitia Christi*.[20]

More's prayer has been called a 'psalm' because it is related to the themes of the psalms in the offices for prime, terce and sext which it accompanies, and because it imitates the parallel forms of the Psalms.[21] The first psalm for prime, Ps. 53 [54], has the printed rubric 'in quo docetur vir justus in adversis laudare deum' ('in which the just man is taught to praise God in adversities').[22]

More's prayer begins with a request for God's grace

To sett the world at nought.
To sett my mynd faste uppon the
And not to hange uppon the blaste of mennys mowthis
To be content to be solitary
Not to long for worldely company[23]

The parallelisms emphasize the theme of renunciation of worldly affairs:

Lytle & litle uttrely to caste of the world
And ridde my mynd of all the bysynes therof

and the desire

to lene un to the cumfort of god
Bysyly to labor to love hym

More prays for grace

gladly to bere my purgatory here
To be joyfull of tribulations

and

To walke the narow way that ledeth to life
To bere the crosse with christ.

To have continually in mynd the passion that christe suffred
    for me[24]

He resolves to give thanks for Christ's 'benefitys', and

To thynke my mooste enemyes my best frendys
For the brethern of Joseph could never have done hym so mych good with theire love & favor as they did hym with theire malice & hatered

The last lines are a summary and evaluation of the spiritual ideals the suppliant has prayed for, and the 'worldely sub-stauns' he has renounced:

These mynds are more to be desired of every man than all the trea-sore of all the princis & kyngis christen & hethen were it gathered & layed to gether all uppon one hepe

The psalms in the offices for these hours also emphasize the suppliant's isolation and tribulation:

Quoniam alieni insurrexerunt adversum me, et fortes quaesierunt animam meam (Ps. 53[54]:3)

Omnes gentes circuierunt me (Ps. 117[118]:10)

They include reference to the suppliant's decisive leaning towards God and away from man

Bonum est confidere in domino: quam confidere in homine
(Ps. 117[118]:8]

to his faith in tribulation

Ad dominum cum tribularer clamavi (Ps. 119[120]:1)

and to his belief that God watches over the righteous and will not let his foot slip from the narrow way

Non det in commotionem pedem tuum . . .
Dominus custodiat introitum tuum & exitum tuum
(Ps. 120[121]:3 & 8)

More imitated the Psalms not only in his marginalia and 'devout prayers' but also in his conduct during the period of his trial. At the beginning of Ps. 38[39]

Dixi custodiam vias meas: ut non delinquam in lingua mea.
Posui ori meo custodiam: cum consisteret peccator adversum me

More wrote in his Psalter margin 'maledictis abstinendum' ('evil words are not to be employed').[25] We may infer from such weighing and practising of psalms that his intention was to re-make his spiritual identity in preparation for a martyr's death, and to become in (Coverdale's words), 'a new David: a man accordynge unto the wyll of God'.[26]

In March 1543 Thomas Sternhold and Philip Hoby were committed to the Fleet prison in London, charged with supporting the Protestant opinions of Anthony Parson who was 'burnt for heresies against the sacrament of the Altar'.[27] Sternhold, who was not charged with heresy, was released in the following September. He was the author of thirty-seven metrical psalm paraphrases, but his treatment of one in particular stands out from the others.[28]

Sternhold's Ps. 120 is the personal prayer of one who supplicates God to save his soul from hypocrisy, and laments his association with liars and slanderers:

> In trouble and in thrall,
> Unto the lorde I call,
> And he doeth me comforte:
>   Deliver me I saye.
> From lyars lyppes alwaye,
> And tongue of false reporte[29]   (lines 1–6)

The threats to Sternhold's psalmist are external, but in Coverdale's translations the biblical psalmist laments the deceit of his own 'false tonge':

Delyver my soule, O Lorde, from lyenge lippes, and from a disceatfull tonge.
What rewarde shall be geven or done unto the, thou false tonge?
                              (Great Bible, Ps. 120:2–3)

Coverdale's psalmist goes on to prescribe 'myghtie & sharpe arowes, with hote burnynge coales', as suitable punishments to inflict on himself, whereas in Sternhold's psalm the arrows and fire are indicative of the pain endured by others subject to slander:

> Howe hurtfull is the thyng,
> Or els howe doeth it styng,
> The tongue of suche a lyer?
>   It hurteth no lesse I wene,
> Then arowes sharpe and kene
> Of whote consumyng fier   (lines 7–12)

Here the psalmist's conjecture ('I wene') suggests that he does not actually share the situation of those who suffer the sting of a liar's tongue, but he identifies with them, and it is clear from the first lines of the psalm that he also has his own troubles, 'in thrall'.

In the second half of Sternhold's imitation the psalmist's imaginative sympathy with the victims of slander leads to his active involvement on their behalf. He regrets dwelling with the Ishmaelites who openly persecute 'the folke elect' or chosen people of Israel:

> Alas to long I dwell,
> With the sonne of Ismaell,
> That Chedar is to name.
>   By whom the folke elect
> And all of Isaacks sect,
> Are put to open shame   (lines 13–18)

(Wo is me, that I am constrayned to dwell with Mesech, and to have myne habitacion among the tentes of Cedar)
        (Great Bible, Ps. 120:5)

Sternhold's references to the 'shame' of 'the folke elect' are his own inventive responses to the biblical verse and may imply reference to the detention of several notable London Protestants in the Fleet prison at the same time as himself.[30] Sternhold's imitation of Ps. 120 concludes:

> With them that peace did hate,
> I came a peace to make,
> And set a quiet lyfe.
>   But whan my worde was tolde,
> Causeles I was controlde,
> By them that would have stryfe   (lines 19–24)

(My soule hath longe dwelt amonge them, that be enemies unto peace. I laboured for peace, but when I spake therof, they made them to batayll)   (1535 Bible, Ps. 120:6–7)

Sternhold's penultimate line

> Causeles I was controlde

does not originate from the biblical psalm. (Cf. however 'impugnabant me *gratis*' Ps. 119[120]:7). Sternhold's line explains the psalmist's current predicament 'in trouble and in thrall'. The key word is 'causeles': either the psalmist was restrained unreasonably – controlled without cause – or he was restrained even though he had no active cause to plead; perhaps also, he was causeless – without a cause – once the 'worde' of his peace mission 'was tolde'.

Although there is no external evidence to connect this psalm with events in 1543, there are also apparently no literary sources to account for Sternhold's departures from the sense of the biblical model. It is possible therefore that these lines could refer to his outspoken defence of Parson's rights, and to his own subsequent imprisonment. In such a situation Sternhold would probably have been drawn to speak alongside the psalmist in Ps. 120 (and to adapt the meaning) because he regarded the psalmist's situation as parallel to his own. During his imprisonment Sternhold would have been made aware of the 'open shame' of those Protestants who considered themselves 'the folke elect', and would have had good cause to pray for protection 'from lyars lyppes . . . And tongue of false report'. Just as More lamented the influence of the 'Turks' or Protestant heretics in his Psalter annotations, so Sternhold may have regarded the actions of the Privy Council against Protestant policies in 1543 as parallel to those of the 'Ishmaelites'.[31] In the context of national events in 1543 Sternhold's Ps. 120 reflects his weighing of the Psalms as containing 'Prayers agaynst the enemies of the Church', and the 'histories' of God's 'folke elect'.[32] The interaction of his interpretative and inventive methods of imitation in this paraphrase draws the attention of a reader already familiar with the text of Ps. 120 to the action and motives of the persecuting Ishmaelites. If Sternhold's psalm does belong to this period then his imitation has political as well as personal significance.

It is characteristic of the Earl of Surrey as a poet that the crises of his life were occasions for writing poetry. Periods of imprisonment gave rise to poems such as 'When Winde-

sor walles sustained my wearied arme', 'So crewell prison
...' and 'London, hast thow accused me'.[33] The occasional
nature of these poems is apparent even from their opening
lines, and it seems likely that Surrey intended the poetic
personae in them to represent himself. Throughout his
short life Surrey's rash temperament and 'heady will'
prompted him to extreme actions, and he was imprisoned
five times between 1537 and 1547 in London and at
Windsor Castle.[34]

Surrey's metrical versions of Pss. 55, 73, and 88 are
usually attributed to the period of his final imprisonment
in the Tower of London in December 1546;[35] he was executed in January 1547. The choice of these psalms, with
themes of despair and acute misery, a trial of faith, and the
denunciation of treachery by former friends, seems peculiarly appropriate to these last weeks.

Surrey's imitation of Ps. 55 is unfinished, and lacks the
external corroboration necessary to relate it to his personal
situation. On the other hand, in both the contemporary
manuscript sources of Surrey's psalms, the texts of his Pss.
73 and 88 are prefaced by verse epistles (to Sir George
Blage and to Sir Anthony Denny, respectively);[36] these
testify to the author's troubled circumstances, and indicate
that the composition of these two psalms at least, was
related to Surrey's personal situation. Surrey's treatment of
Ps. 88 especially presents the kind of internal evidence
which, when combined with the external evidence
afforded by the letter to Denny, can sustain an interpretation of this text as the 'particuler prayer' of a 'particular
person' in a 'particular greefe'. His version of Ps. 73 is too
close to the original, and too dependent upon the interpretative paraphrase by Campensis, for his treatment of
these sources to reveal more than his sympathy with the
thoughts and feelings of the biblical psalmist.[37] However,
Surrey's selection, evaluation and imitation of each of these
three psalms suggest that they have the same provenance;

and so the argument for Surrey's application of Ps. 88 as his 'particuler prayer' may be extended to stand, by analogy, for these three psalms.

In March 1546, Surrey was recalled from his command of the English forces at Boulogne and replaced by his rival, Edward Seymour.[38] The following July he was imprisoned at Windsor for voicing his bitterness against Seymour. Although Surrey was soon released, he was not reinstated in his office, and he remained in England at court. Enforced leisure about this time may have provided the opportunity for him to begin his meditations on the vanity of human wishes contained in the paraphrase of five chapters from Ecclesiastes.[39] Similarities between the ideas and diction of Surrey's version of Ecclesiastes and those of his Ps. 88 suggest that both were written at about the same period, but that the version of Ecclesiastes is unlikely to be later than his version of the psalm.[40]

Surrey's epistle to Denny serves as a prologue to his version of Ps. 88, and must refer to his situation after August 1546. Surrey described how his 'errour, depe imprest, Began to worke dispaire of libertye'[41]

> When recheles youthe in an unquiet brest,
> Set on by wrath, revenge and crueltye,
> After long warr pacyens had opprest,
> And justice wrought by pryncelye equitie

The 'wrath, revenge and crueltye' could be interpreted as referring to Seymour's actions, the 'long warr' may refer to Surrey's experiences in France, and the 'pryncelye' judgement to his imprisonment at Windsor in July 1546 on the orders of Henry VIII. If 'libertye' is to be interpreted literally, then the psalm probably belongs to the Windsor imprisonment, if it is to be interpreted figuratively or spiritually, then it may well belong to the period of his final imprisonment. The final couplet indicates that 'David, the perfyt warriour' taught him how to seek 'pardon' for his 'fault' in the psalm which follows. Surrey focussed on those 'perfyt' aspects of David's identity most like his own: the 'warriour' and the persecuted poet.

Surrey's choice of Ps. 88 as a model indicates that he was studying the Psalms for personal guidance. More had noted its usefulness 'in tribulatione vehementi et in carcere', and Campensis and Coverdale had also related the situation of the psalmist to imprisonment.[42] John Hooper wrote in 1553 that Ps. 88 contains 'the prayer of a man that was brought into extreme anguish and misery, and, beyng vexed with adversaries and persecutions, saw nothyng but death and hell'.[43] Hooper stressed the theme of a trial of faith and its resolution since, although the psalmist 'felt in himselfe, that he had not onely man, but also god, angrye towardes hym',

yet he by praier humbly resorted unto god, as the onely porte of consolation, and in the middes of his desperate state of trouble, put the hope of his salvation in him whom he felt his enemye

The Catholic and the Protestant martyrs' expectations of this psalm were similar, and were probably shared by Surrey. Hooper also regarded Ps. 88 as a model for spiritual self-examination. He recommended it to his wife in her 'anguish of mind', promising

after that god hath made you to know what you be of your self, he wil doutles shew you comfort, & declare unto you what you be in Christ hys only sonne

Surrey's treatment of Ps. 88 suggests that his imitation may be divided into three sections.[44] In the first and last sections (lines 1–18 and 35–44), Surrey speaks alongside the sense of verses 1–9 and 13–18, whereas the middle section of his psalm (lines 19–34) reflects a more inventive manner of imitation.

As an example of his more straightforward interpretative method Surrey's lines 11–12,

The burden of thy wrath it doth me sore oppresse,
And sundrye stormes thow hast me sent of terrour and
distresse

may be compared with verse 7 of the original (here in Coverdale's translation):

Thyne indignacyon lyeth harde upon me, and thou hast vexed me with all thy stormes   (Great Bible, Ps. 88:7)

Surrey has added indications of personal sorrow in specifying 'stormes . . . of terrour and distresse', and, in his paraphrase of verse 18, by emphasizing the violence of his separation from 'they whome no myschaunce could from my love devyde' (line 43). The biblical psalmist had indicated that he was separated from his friends by God:

My lovers and frendes hast thou put awaye fro me, and hyd myne acquayntaunce out of my syght   (Great Bible, Ps. 88:18)

However, Surrey attributed the separation not to God but to the malice of an unnamed power seeking his 'greater greif':

> For they whome no myschaunce could from my love devyde
> Ar forced, for my greater greif, from me their face to hyde
> (lines 43–4)

Such departures from the sense of the biblical model are significant but relatively minor by comparison with the extended and subtle adaptation of the biblical verses 10–13, which represents the core of Surrey's personal meditation or 'practice' on Ps. 88:

15]   My duraunce doth perswade of fredom such dispaire
       That, by the teares that bayne my brest, myne eye sight doth
            appaire.
       Yet did I never cease thyne ayde for to desyre,
       With humble hart and stretched hands for to appease thy yre.
       Wherfore dost thow forbeare, in the defence of thyne,
20]   To shewe such tokens of thy power, in sight of Adams lyne,
       Wherby eche feble hart with fayth might so be fedd
       That in the mouthe of thy elect thy mercyes might be
            spredd?
       The fleshe that fedeth wormes can not thy love declare,
       Nor suche sett forth thy faith as dwell in the land of dispaire.
25]   In blind endured herts light of thy lively name
       Can not appeare, as can not judge the brightnes of the same.

Nor blasted may thy name be by the mouth of those
Whome death hath shutt in sylence, so as they may not
    disclose.
The livelye voyce of them that in thy word delight
30] Must be the trumppe that must resound the glorye of thy
    might.
Wherfore I shall not cease, in chief of my distresse,
To call on the till that sleape my weryd lymes oppresse.
And in the morning eke, when that the slepe is fledd,
With floods of salt repentaunt teres to washe my restles
    bedd.[45]

As in Sternhold's psalm, the interaction between the inventive and interpretative qualities of Surrey's imitation focusses the reader's attention on these verses where Surrey's invention is at its strongest and the meaning of his meditation overlaps least with that of the psalmist. Given the nature of Surrey's circumstances indicated by the epistle to Denny, the inference is here that the Christian poet is 'figuring forth' his own spiritual anxiety: he is the maker of the psalm imitation and the persona within it.

The biblical psalmist had asked God, in a series of parallel questions, to relieve his sufferings before death, because after death it would have been too late for him to receive God's loving kindness:

Shall thy lovyng kyndnes be shewed in the grave, or thy faythfulnesse in destruccion? Shall thy wonderous workes be knowen in the darcke, and thy ryghtyousnes in the lande where all thinges are forgoten?   (Great Bible, Ps. 88:11–12)

The implied answer to these questions is 'no'. In Surrey's version the psalmist declares

The livelye voyce of them that in thy word delight
Must be the trumppe that must resound the glorye of thy
    might   (lines 29–30)

because,

The fleshe that fedeth wormes can not thy love declare
    (line 23)

Neither can 'suche . . . as dwell in the land of dispaire', 'sett forth thy faith' (line 24). Extrapolating from the first ques-

93

tion in the biblical verse 12 ('Shall thy wonderous workes be knowen in the darcke?'), Surrey states that the light of God's name cannot appear in blind, hardened hearts unable to appreciate the brightness of that light (lines 25–6). The biblical darkness metaphor for the afterworld in verse 12, and the Hebraic parallel form in verses 11 and 12, probably suggested to Surrey the antithesis of blindness and light (or sight). He imitated this development of the biblical metaphor with an inventive parallel reference to sound and silence in the following couplet:

> Nor blasted may thy name be by the mouth of those
> Whome death hath shutt in sylence, so as they may not
> disclose   (lines 27–8)

The prominent repetition of 'can not' at the beginning of line 26, echoes line 23:

> The fleshe that fedeth wormes can not thy love declare

which summarizes the idea of the biblical verses. (The imagery, however, is not from these biblical verses.)

The delayed main verb 'declare' in line 23 (also given prominence as the last word in the line) seems to have provided the foundation for Surrey's inventive imitation of the biblical idea. Surrey's version of Ps. 88:10–12 (his lines 19–30) imitates the biblical parallelisms in a series of imaginative variations on the biblical theme, which depend on the multiple senses of 'declare' – to 'explain', or 'elucidate', to 'show', to 'prove' and also to 'proclaim' or 'announce formally' – all of which were current in Surrey's lifetime.[46] Almost all the verbs in the middle section of Surrey's psalm – 'shewe', 'spredd', 'sett forth', 'appeare', 'judge', 'blasted' (or the variant reading 'blazed'), 'disclose', 'resound' – may be read as synonyms for 'declare'.

Surrey not only responded to the conceptual parallelisms at the centre of Ps. 88 but he also adapted the grammatical and rhetorical parallelisms which are especially evident in the Vulgate (Ps. 87[88]:11–13)

Nunquid mortuis facies mirabilia ... Nunquid narrabit aliquis in sepulchro misericordiam tuam ... Nunquid cognoscentur in tenebris mirabilia tua

Instead of repeated interrogative forms requiring a negative response to signify that the dead cannot praise God, Surrey made repeated use of negative forms coupled with synonymous verbs: 'can not ... declare ... can not appeare ... can not judge ... nor blasted ... not disclose'. When these verbs are interpreted as synonyms for the multiple senses of 'declare', they convey the meaning of the biblical verse which is about praise (or rather no praise). However, when they are read without the underlying senses of 'declare', the different verbs may evoke many different associations for a Christian. 'Blasted' and 'resound', in combination with death and silence on the one hand, and 'livelye voyce' with 'trumppe' and 'glorye' on the other hand, suggest the Last Judgement.[47] (In this Christian allegorical context, the 'light of thy lively name' signifies Christ.) The metaphorical richness of association in this inventive passage has been carefully designed to accommodate Surrey's expression of his own concerns and purpose as a Christian with sixteenth-century religious and literary sensibilities.

Surrey also strengthened the emotional resonance of the antithesis between life and death in this section of his psalm by relating the Christian spiritual status of 'dispaire' and 'delight' (lines 23–4 and 29–30) to eternity in hell or in heaven respectively. The affective quality of this antithesis is reinforced by Surrey's juxtaposition of macabre literal images of death with figurative images redolent of the same physicality. (The mouths of the dead must be inert and silent, but the mouths of the elect should be active and praising. The mouths of worms feed on dead flesh, but the mouths of feeble-hearted humanity should feed on faith.) As a result of these tactics of affective writing, faith and the active praise of God are recognized as constituents of life and of eternal 'delight' hereafter.

Surrey's radical treatment of this central section of Ps. 88 can thus be seen as above all a Christian poet's meditation on life, death and judgement. The poet is dying, 'My restles bodye doth consume and death approcheth fast' (line 6). His 'soule is fraughted full with greif of follies past' (line 5), nevertheless, he sees his hardship and misery as a result of the wrath of God:

> The burden of thy wrath it doth me sore oppresse
> (line 11)

> The scourgis of thyne angrye hand hath made deth seme
> full sweet   line 40)

Because he recognizes that his position is dependent upon the will of God, he attempts to emphasize his repentance by praying day and night. His purpose is to move God 'To shewe such tokens of thy power' that feeble hearts may be fed with faith, and

> in the mouthe of thy elect thy mercyes might be spredd
> (lines 20–2)

The poet hopes to be among 'thy elect', and his psalm is part of his effort to show himself that he is.

Although the climax of Ps. 88 is unusual in that it brings no relief or new insight to the biblical psalmist, in Surrey's version the poet resolves

> To call on [God] till that the sleape my weryd lymes oppresse.
>   And in the morning . . .
> With floods of salt repentaunt teres to washe my restles bedd
> (lines 32–4)

The poet's decision is based on his understanding that

> The livelye voyce of them that in thy word delight
> Must be the trumppe that must resound the glorye of thy
>   might.
>   *Wherfore* I shall not cease, in chief of my distresse,
> To call on the   (lines 29–32; my italics)

Lines 29–31 are not derived from the biblical text of Ps. 88.

Surrey's inventive imitation shows him to have been less concerned than the biblical psalmist to move God to mercy, but much more concerned to persuade himself in what he called his 'wretched state', that God's mercy was still available.[48] Surrey acknowledged that his temptation was to despair, thus his wretched state was above all spiritual desolation. By imitating such a psalm in this way, Surrey 'declares' himself. Whereas More's 'godly meditacion' may be regarded as his attempt to remake his spiritual identity in preparation for a martyr's death, Surrey weighed the meaning of Ps. 88 in search of the 'secrets of his owne hart', and a comforting assurance of his salvation.[49]

This application of psalms became associated with Protestant spirituality. Expectations of the Psalms as prayers 'containing the alterations of every mans hart and conscience' and 'moste present remedies against all tentations and troubles of minde and conscience' drew Surrey 'to the peculiar examination of himself' through his meditation on Ps. 88.[50] He described prayer as the 'frute of faith whereby/god doth with synne dispence'.[51] He must, therefore, have regarded the completion of his meditation as a sign of grace. In the prologue to his Ps. 73 Surrey confessed to George Blage

> The soudden stormes that heve me to and froo
> Had welneare perced faith, my guyding saile[52]

In his version of Ps. 55, Surrey recognized God's purpose in striking 'The conscyence unquiet' to be a test or proof of 'their force in fayth whome he sware to defend', and found 'ease' in 'th'other Psalme of David': 'Iacta curam tuam super dominum et ipse te enutriet'.[53] It may be that Surrey's meditations on these psalms gave him the spiritual comfort, 'pacience graft in a determed brest' and 'mirth and rest', which he described in the last poem he wrote as planted 'in the hart where heapes of griefes were grown'.[54]

Surrey had earlier sought to fashion literary memorials to Wyatt by regarding Wyatt's psalms as monuments to his reputation as a poet.[55] It may be, therefore, that, when creating a poetic persona for himself in his prison poems, Surrey also intended his psalms to stand as literary memorials to himself: by sending them to friends accompanied by explanatory epistles Surrey, in effect, set up these psalms as monuments to his own reputation as a poet.

In October 1549 it was the turn of Surrey's rival, Edward Seymour, Duke of Somerset to find himself a prisoner in the Tower. Among those imprisoned with him were William Cecil (later Lord Burghley), and Sir Thomas Smith; they were released by February 1550.[56] Smith's eleven metrical psalm paraphrases, and eight prose 'collectes or prayers', were written about the same time as his 'other psalmes' 'in the Tower of London ... to pas the tyme there'.[57] Some of these works provide detailed insights into the prisoners' situation, political interests and religious beliefs.

Like More and Surrey, Smith 'weighed' the Psalms and selected texts for his paraphrases, collects and 'other psalmes', which were relevant to his own situation. With two exceptions (Pss. 145[146] and 146[147]) he chose personal prayers of the afflicted, including requests for justice, comfort and deliverance:

> Give me comfort and lief again for the honour of thi name
> And for thi justice sake bring me out of trouble and blame
>
> (MS Royal 17A xvii, fol. 4ᵛ)

(Quycken me (o Lorde), for thy names sake, and for thy rightuousnesse sake brynge my soule out of trouble)

> (1535 Bible, Ps. 142[143]:11)

Like Sternhold he responded to contemporary expectations of the Psalms as 'Songues' of David and so adopted appropriate, short-line stanzaic forms for his imitations.

Smith's eleven psalm paraphrases are versifications of Coverdale's English Psalms in the 1535 Bible. His version

of Ps. 54[55], however, shows some inventive adaptation.
The first two stanzas of Smith's Ps. 54[55] are close, interpretative imitations of Coverdale's 1535 text:

> Do thou o Lorde
> My prayer heare
> Thine help I do abid
> To my peticion
> Encline thin eare
> Do not thee from me hid
>
> Tak heed to me
> My god, I say
> And heare me in my pain
> How piteously
> I moorn and pray
> and lamentably complain   (fol. 12ʳ)

(Heare my prayer (O God) and hyde not thy self fro my peticion.
Take hede unto me and heare me, how piteously I mourne & com-
playne   (1535 Bible, Ps. 54[55]:1–2)

Throughout Smith's paraphrase of this psalm each six-line
stanza corresponds to a single verse in Coverdale's prose
model; the exceptions are verses 19 and 23 which occupy
two stanzas each, and verse 15 which was omitted (probably because the imprecation 'Let death come hastely upon
them, and let them go downe quick in to hell, for wickednes is amonge them in their dwellinges' (1535 Bible) was
either inappropriate for a man in Smith's situation or dis-
tasteful to him).

All Smith's other adaptations of Coverdale's Ps. 54[55]
appear to have been made to express his personal response
to his situation as a political prisoner. The sixteenth-
century psalmist identified himself with the biblical psalmist whose enemies 'lay many snares'

> And such as be at peace
> With god, thei cast
> streight into bandes   (fol. 13ᵛ)

(Yee they laye hondes upon soch as be at peace with him)
                         (1535 Bible, Ps. 54[55]:20)

He remained confident, however, that God would hear his prayer, and at the end of his psalm Smith assured himself that God would 'cast down' the malicious enemies

> That thus do stand
> Against thi crown   (fol. 14ʳ)

There is no crown in Coverdale's translation of Ps. 54[55], neither here at the end, nor in verse 19 where Smith introduced a heavenly crown as the property or attribute of 'god that sittes on high' (fol. 13ᵛ). In Smith's version the crown may be seen as a symbol of temporal authority, divinely invested in God's anointed, and Seymour's nephew, Edward VI. (Smith's oppressors, who would 'not bow' to God's 'great justice ... Nor his comaundementes heare', must have been the Privy Council led by John Dudley, Earl of Warwick subsequently Duke of Northumberland.)[58] Smith also used the simile of 'a ship that hath lost her helme' with reference to the fears for England which overwhelmed him and the 'horrible dread' which made his 'hart ak' (fol. 12ᵛ). Smith's introduction of the ship and crown imagery reflects their significance for him as a Protestant Secretary of State. Like Sternhold, he was responding to contemporary expectations of a psalm as a vehicle for lamenting the national catastrophes which had befallen God's elect. The seventh collect or prayer identifies the group of prisoners as Protestant statesmen unable to separate their own 'perill and danger' from the 'wofull estate of this Realme':

We can not forget o Lord in all our cares and thoughtes at this present tyme the wofull estate of this Realme ... to which thou haest vouchsaved to give the true knowledge of thi veritie & gospell
                                                      (fol. 22ʳ)

The influence of Smith's weighing of the Psalms is also evident in his collects. Smith and his colleagues, lamenting the 'cyvil dissencon' in England,[59] prayed:

Let not the heathen & papistes laughe us to skorn and ask where is our god   (fol. 22ʳ)

(The ungodly layeth wayte for the just . . . But the Lorde laugheth
him to scorne)   (1535 Bible, Ps. 36[37]:12–13)

(Wherfore shall the Heithen saye: where is now their God?)
                                                       (Ps. 78[79]:10)

To a reader familiar with the Psalms, Smith's imitation of
Ps. 78[79] in particular evokes the context of a national
lament. (This context was later exploited by the Protestant
martyr John Bradford in his inventive meditation on Ps. 79
(1554–5) in which the restoration of Catholicism in
England under Mary Tudor is likened to the destruction of
the Temple in Jerusalem.)[60]

The last psalms selected by Smith (Pss. 145[146] and
146[147]) the 'psalmes of thanksgiving' reflect an improvement in the prisoners' situation.[61] Speaking closely
alongside the psalmist, Smith wrote 'Never in Princes, put
yow yowr trust', and 'The Lord looseth men out of prison
stroung' (fols. 17^v, 18^v). These themes are also imitated in
Smith's last collect, where he wrote

Somwhat o our Lord God we have comfort . . . Some libertie and
token is graunted us   (fol. 22^v)

and offered 'humble thankes' for this improvement in their
circumstances. But, also in accordance with the warning in
Ps. 145[146], his attitude in this collect remained wary and
sceptical:

Mannes promises, and semblaunces, profers and enlargementes be
doubtefull, and as all men be, so thei be variable, uncertaigne,
unstable, chaungeable, and not to be trusted to   (fol. 23^r)

The collects are the occasional prayers of 'particular
persons in particular greefes', who considered themselves
'falsely accused, and wrongfully sclaunderid, and
oppressed by false witnesses' (fol. 20^v). Believing that their
lives were threatened, they prayed

that neither our bloodes may hereafter be required . . . nor we in
the meane space suffer undeservid persecution, and crueltie
                                                           (fol. 20^r)

Their particular fears are made evident in the themes of their prayers in which they ask the Holy Spirit to

> so fill our mynds ... that when so ever we shalbe called to answer, no subtyletie interrogatorie, nor malytious question may over-throw us (fol. 21ʳ)

In the last of his three 'other psalmes' Smith lamented the inconstancy of his world in which

> This day made new Duke, Marques, Earle, or Baron
> Yet maie the ax, stand next the dore (fol. 27ʳ)

He also invoked God's 'mercie' for England:

> look upon this poore Isle
> Let not truthe be oppressed, nor innocentes slayn
> ... comfort our most loving King (fol. 27)

Despite the title 'other psalmes', the last three items in Smith's manuscript are not imitations of specific psalms, but they too represent his meditative weighing and practising of psalms. With the exception of the second 'other psalme' which has been discussed in another context,[62] these inventive imitations, like the collects and the interpretative psalm paraphrases, preserve the form and function of personal prayers and meditations: the suppliant addresses himself directly either to God or to his own soul.

In the first of his 'other psalmes' (which follows the last collect, without a title), Smith shows how thoroughly he has assimilated and transformed *publica materies* into his private property by meditative 'weighing' and 'practising' of the Psalms. His 'psalme' begins with phrases and parallel questions suggestive of Ps. 2:1:

> What meane thei thus to fret and fume?
> What meane thei thus to fare? (fol. 24ʳ)

(Why do the Heithen grudge? Why do the people ymagyn vayne thinges?) (1535 Bible, Ps. 2:1)

Smith's 'thei' and 'thus' become explicit in the context of this biblical psalm (i.e. 'the Heithen grudge ... ymagyn vayne thinges') and of his own imitations of other psalms.

102

In the second stanza he addresses God in imitation of themes and phrases from Ps. 26:

> Thou knowest, o Lorde, how I have walked
> Thow knowest what I have doon   (fol. 24ʳ)

(Be thou my judge (O Lorde) for I walke innocently)
                                (1535 Bible, Ps. 25[26]:1)

In the following stanza he assimilated the form and content of Ps. 7:4–5:

> If I have gone about to hurt any man
> Or for to sowe discorde
> Than let them hurt me as thei can
> And help me not o Lorde   (fol. 24ʳ)

(Yff I have rewarded evell unto them that dealt frendly with me or hurte them that without eny cause are myne enemies: Then let myne enemie persecute my soule, & take me)
                                (1535 Bible, Ps. 7:4–5)

Smith's fourth and fifth stanzas draw on Ps. 120:8 and 2[63]

> But if I have alwais sought for peace
> And labored discord to remove   (fol. 24ʳ)

> From lyeing lippes, and sclaunderous tongues
> Now Lorde thou me defend   (fol. 24ᵛ)

and the 'psalme' ends with echoes of Ps. 9:2 among others as poetry of praise and prayer

> Than shall I be glad, and in the rejoyce
> Than shall I praise thi name   (fol. 24ᵛ)

A further example of inventive weighing and practising of the Psalms may be seen in the four-line meditation written by Somerset, 'Frome the toware the day before my dethe 1551', which is preserved in a different manuscript:

> Fere of the lord is the beginneng of wisdume
> Put thi trust in the lord with all thine hart
> be not wise in thyne owne conseyte
> but fere the lord and fle frome evele[64]

Somerset's quotations from Pss. 111:10; 4:5; 37:27 must have been intended as an admonition to himself and his heirs, and also perhaps as a memorial for posterity of his state of mind as he prepared to die.

The exclusive choice of biblical models for personal devotion was typical of Protestant sensibilities, but was not confined to Protestants as the examples of meditative weighing of psalms in the *Psalms or prayers* attributed to John Fisher or in More's annotations and 'devout prayers' demonstrate. The prisoners' own immediate circumstances stimulated the interpretative and inventive imitations which they composed in response to contemporary expectations of the Psalms.

However, by the end of Edward VI's reign, if not earlier, an element of convention had become attached to the making of metrical psalms. The publication of Sternhold's thirty-seven metrical psalms in 1549 had stimulated production of numerous other versions.[65] This element of convention dominates the psalms produced by the next generation of 'Tower psalmists', which included members of the Duke of Northumberland's family imprisoned after the Duke's failure to secure the crown for his daughter-in-law, Jane Grey, at the death of Edward VI in July 1553.[66] Two of the Duke's sons, John, Earl of Warwick, and Robert Dudley (later Earl of Leicester) shared a cell in the Beauchamp Tower from February 1554 until their release in October. The metrical versions of Ps. 55 by Warwick, and of Ps. 94 by Robert Dudley, were probably written during their imprisonment.[67] (The brothers also left other more permanent records of themselves by scratching their names and arms on the walls of the Beauchamp Tower.)

There are close correspondences between the diction and themes of the two brothers' psalms which were also written in the same metre.[68] By their choice and treatment of their biblical models, the brothers emphasized their bitterness at the treachery of former friends, and prayed for vengeance.[69] Nevertheless certain features of style distinguish the work of the two writers.

In Warwick's imitation nouns are rarely unqualified, and yet most of his adjectives add little or nothing to the sense of his psalm. The 'wicked swarminge flockes' of his bestial enemies have 'cruell ravening myndes', and their hypocrisy, which operates 'under face of frendlye faithe', leaves him a 'helples wretche' with a 'trobled quyv'ring hart' singing God's 'thanckfull prayse' 'bothe night and day and every houre'.[70] He appears to revel in bombastic language and simple alliterative sound effects: he prayed for

> the swiftfull pigeons guyftes
> that scape I might by farr floen flight/ from all their devillishe
> driftes   (lines 5–6)

(O that I had winges like a dove, for then wold I flye awaye, and be at rest)   (Great Bible, Ps. 55:6)

Warwick's treatment of Ps. 55 is freer and more artfully self-conscious than Smith's paraphrase, but his version does not carry the political significance which Smith introduced with the images of crown and ship symbolizing authority and stability in church and state. The battle image in Warwick's version,

> my god and kinge
> That hast me garded aye/ withe thye tryumphant shylde
> From fearfull force of furious foes/ and graunted me the
> fielde   (lines 18–20)

seems to have been suggested by Coverdale's 1539 translation (Ps. 55:18); but the opportunity afforded by the military metaphor for alliteration in line 20 also seems to have stimulated Warwick's imagination. Like Smith, he responded to the hunting metaphor implicit in Coverdale's 1535 translation of verse 18, 'them that laye waite for me', in his

> When they had lead their frawdful snares to snarle me fast
> in tripps   (line 26)

Warwick's bitterness is emphasized throughout his psalm. At the beginning, he introduced an imprecatory tone which is not found in Coverdale's, Surrey's or Smith's versions of Ps. 55[71]

> Geve eare to me my god / and heare my mourning voyce
> breake down the wicked swarminge flockes / that at mye fall rejoyce
> whose cruell ravening myndes / to worke my bane are bent
> (lines 1–3)

Warwick's 'mourning voyce' was consistently and heartily energetic in planning violence and vengeance. He enlarged on the imprecations in verse 15 (which Smith had omitted from his paraphrase), and prayed for the continual torment of his oppressors rather than their immediate death:

> devour them Lorde / consume them every echone
> And throw them in the dredfull pit / wheare they shall stintles mone
> (lines 13–14)

Finally, he cursed those

> Whoe with faire Clokes of truce / and fawninge lowlye bowes
> Have trait'rouslye conspyred my death
> (lines 23–4)

and appealed to God to

> send consuming plages / for their desertes moste due
> That thrust so sore mye giltles blood / their tryaunts handes t'embrue
> (lines 29–30)

(Coverdale's translation of verse 15 begins

> Let death come hastely upon them, and let them go downe quick into hell
> (1535 and 1539)

Surrey had written:

> Such soden surprys quicke may them hell devoure)

Robert Dudley's use of language, and, in particular, the use of alliteration in his paraphrase of Ps. 94, resembles his older brother's, but is less exuberant. In general, Robert's style is plainer than Warwick's, and his paraphrase is also closer than Warwick's to the sense of his biblical model

O mightie Lorde to whome / all vengeaunce doth belonge
and just revendge for their desertes / whiche do oppresse by
   wronge
Thye praid fore presence shew / thow judge and rightuouse
   guyde
And pay them with a due rewarde / that swell in hatefull pryde
(lines 1–4)

(O Lord God, to whom vengeaunce belongeth: thou God to whom vengeaunce belongeth, shew thy self. Aryse thou judge of the world, & rewarde the proude after theyr deservynge)
(Great Bible, Ps, 94:1–2)

The many superficial exaggerations in the Dudley's psalms, coupled with their overall conservative treatment of the sense of their biblical models, suggest that the brothers may have had a more perfunctory attitude to their meditations than some of the other Tower psalmists. Perhaps they turned to literary activity because other more energetic outlets for expression of their frustrations were denied them: writing psalms and marking walls (in these instances at least) could be seen as comparable ways of making memorials to one's self and of passing the time. Both activities are forms of self expression yet both are conventional. By the mid 1550s Warwick's expectations of the Psalms must have been influenced by an awareness of psalms as fashionable models for contemporary verse as well as 'perfect patterns' for personal prayers 'against the enemies of the Church' and the Dudley family.[72]

The different imitations of the Psalms by More, Sternhold, Surrey, Smith and the Dudleys were new works created within a live devotional tradition. They derive their affective and poetical qualities primarily from those of the original models, but these qualities also depend upon the literary sensibilities of the individual 'psalmists'.

Surrey's success and Warwick's relative failure, in literary terms, may be assessed from their processes of imitation; poems differ, as Scaliger said, 'quae imitamur, quibus imitamur, & quomodo imitamur'.[73] Warwick appears to have found in his chosen psalm an image of his own state of mind in a particular situation, but there is no evidence that he weighed the model attentively, as Vives had said, 'ut simili artificio & ipse quod animo destinarit, perficiat'.[74] Warwick's artistic failure represents, for the most part, his failure to digest and assimilate the model before turning it into the embodiment of his own will as an occasional personal meditation. Surrey was drawn 'to the peculiar examination of himself' by the coincidence of his situation, 'in tribulatione vehementi et in carcere', with what he understood to be that of the psalmist. His weighing of the psalm was assimilated in practice to his own 'lyke meditacion' in so far as the psalm taught him how to speak to God independently, as well as alongside the psalmist by exploiting traditional formulae of expression.

The common generic expectations of psalms as models for personal prayer and self-examination provided each of the individual prisoners with opportunities to find spiritual consolation, and to strengthen the faith on which he relied in adversity. The same psalms stimulated the expressions of different persons experiencing similar situations. Surrey, Smith and Warwick all wrote imitations of Ps. 55 in prison and within a period of about eight years. We can compare their versions of verses 12–14 with that by Coverdale:

Yf it were myne enemie that reuyled me, I coude beare it: or yf one that ought me euell will dyd threaten me, I wolde hyde myself from him.
But it is thou my companyon, my gyde and myne owne familier frende.
We had swete and secrete communicacion together, and louyngly walked we together in the house of God.

(1535 Bible, Ps. 54[55]:12–14)

> Ne my declared foo wrought me all this reproche;
> By harme so loked for, yt wayeth halfe the lesse.
> For though myne ennemyes happ had byn for to prevaile,
> I cold have hidd my face from venym of his eye.

It was a frendly foo, by shadow of good will,
Myne old fere and dere frende, my guyde, that trapped me;
Where I was wont to fetche the cure of all my care,
And in his bosome hyde my secreat zeale to God

(Surrey, Ps. 55, lines 18–25)

Surrey's imitation of verse 12 emphasizes the sense of vulnerability caused by the fact that his enemy was not 'my declared foo', explaining how different the effect would have been had he expected 'harme', and how he could have hidden from the 'venym of his [foe's] eye' even if his 'ennemyes happ had byn for to prevaile'. His imitation of verses 13 and 14 parallels the hypothetical situation in facing a 'declared foo' with the actual situation of a 'frendly foo' who 'trapped' him 'by shadow of good will'. Surrey preserved the triple parallelism of the biblical model, 'myne old fere and dere frende, my guyde', and enhanced the poignancy of the betrayal by explaining his dependence on a relationship which provided 'the cure of all my care'. He does not, however, follow the biblical form of a direct address to a familiar second person. In the last line quoted, the words 'secreat' and 'God' are all that remains of the biblical model: Surrey specifies that the intimacy betrayed was 'my secreat zeale to God'. Surrey's introduction of the basilisk metaphor into verse 12 is subtly appropriate to the sense of a foe who causes 'all this reproche'. There is no waste of words in Surrey's carefully structured imitation of these three verses.

> If it were myn enimie
> I wolde it beare
> Or one that I did knowe
> To have born me ill will
> I wolde not feare
> Tavoide this overthrowe.
>
> But now it is
> Even thou I see
> My compaignion, guide, and freend
> Myn olde familiar

That hurtes me,
That makes me doubt theend.

Sweet communicacions
Have we had togither
And secretely have we talked
In the howse of the Lord
Hither and thither
Full lovingly have we walked

(Smith, Ps. 54[55], fol. 13ʳ)

Smith's version follows the sense, words and form of the biblical model very closely. He retained the reproach to the false friend 'thou' in verse 13, and extended the triple parallelism by making 'familiar' a noun. The effects of the betrayal are specified: 'this overthrowe' and a hurt 'that makes me doubt theend'. His additions to verse 14, 'hither and thither', were obviously useful in making the rhyme and filling out the stanza, but they are also appropriately descriptive of the action.

For yf they had bene foes/ that wold display their yre
Then warn'd thearby I might have bene/ as by the flambe
    from fyre
but even my mates they weare/ that seem'de to holde me
    deere
Whan under face of frendlye faithe/ they bredd this doulefull
    cheere   (Warwick, Ps. 55, lines 9–12)

Warwick's version undermines the sense and the tonal subtlety of the biblical model. He abandoned the parallelisms, substituting 'my mates' for the emotionally resonant triple parallelism in verse 13. He reduced the image of intimate friends' confiding to one of the banal appearance, or 'face', of 'frendlye faithe'. In verse 12 he introduced the irrelevant and inappropriate simile of 'the flambe from fyre'. The effect of his false friends' treachery is 'yre' and 'this doulefull cheere'.

Smith's version is the most interpretative paraphrase whereas the others are both inventive. There are however striking differences between the two inventive versions.

Since Surrey and Warwick were imitating the same model in much the same situation, these differences can only be explained in personal terms. The differences between their psalms register their different abilities to comprehend and to emulate the model: first, the nature of their critical responses to the original, considering the art or procedure by which it was accomplished, and recognizing its potential for imaginative exploitation (*quae imitantur*); secondly, their artistic ability to exploit their own resources of language and senses of decorum in representing with a similar artifice their purposes, and their perceptions of the model (*quibus imitantur et quomodo imitantur*). Vives observed that the power to imitate was affected by the sort of thing which is natural to mankind.[75] Each imitation must reflect that which is proper or natural to that particular imitator: it is the product of his reading, literary tastes and sensitivity, as well as of his personal situation and intentions.

The content of Surrey's psalms is no more 'original' because they were written at a time of personal distress than any of his other mature literary works (including his imitations of Virgil or of Petrarch), and they are no more peculiarly his own than, for example, Wyatt's or Sternhold's. In all these writers it is the expression of their imitations, which reveals that unique impression or image which is proper to each individual mind: *oratio speculum mentis*. The development of a literary personality – the mind reflected in the discourse – is a slow growth. It is not the ephemeral circumstances in which the various authors wrote their psalms, which differentiated either their work or the personalities reflected in their work. Erasmus wrote

The individual natural talents of men (*singula mortalium ingenia*) have a certain native property of their own, which has such force that, when fitly disposed by nature to this or that kind of speaking it strives after another to no effect

(Habent singula mortalium ingenia suum quiddam ac genuinum, quae res tantam habet vim, ut ad hoc aut illud dicendi genus natura compositus, frustra nitatur ad diversum)[76]

4

'HOLYE SONGES OF VERITIE'

THOMAS STERNHOLD AND PSALMS 'FOR THE RECREATION OF ALL SUCH AS DELIGHT IN MUSICKE' AND 'FOR THE COMFORTYNG OF SUCHE ... IN THE COMMON PRAYERS IN THE CHURCH'

Whereas the selection and treatment of psalms by the writers in prison reflect their pursuit of consolation and spiritual guidance in response to 'particular greefes eyther of body or soule', the selection and treatment of psalms by writers of 'holye songes' reflect a more altruistic concern for the spiritual needs of a wider audience.

These authors wrote and published psalm versions suitable both for reading aloud and for musical settings, and their imitations of the model texts reflect another sixteenth-century generic expectation of psalms. They sought to emulate the meaning and expression of a 'celestial Orpheus' whose songs had 'strength and force' to make men 'spiritual and heavenly', and to provide 'for the comforte and consolacyon of soch as love to rejoyse in God and his worde'.[1] They employed appropriate English metrical forms 'in such sort that [the Psalms] maye the more decently and wyth more delyte of the mynde be reade and songe of al men'.[2]

Although the earliest surviving example of metrical psalms in the form of holy songs to be printed in England is Coverdale's *Goostly psalmes and spirituall songes* (c. 1535), this work appears to have had little influence on the subsequent development and tradition of such holy songs in England.[3] The book was banned and burned in the later years of Henry VIII's reign.[4]

In England the sixteenth-century vogue for such metrical versions of the Psalms originated in the courts of Henry VIII and Edward VI where poetry and song were established forms of recreation.[5] After 1543 the influence of Catherine Parr promoted a taste for Protestant devotional literature among members of the royal household. Catherine's own devotional works – her *Prayers or Medytacions . . . collected out of holy woorkes* (1545) and *The Lamentacion of a synner* (1547) – indicate the religious atmosphere which influenced Henry VIII's younger children, Elizabeth and Edward, during the last five years of Henry's reign.[6] The vogue for holy songs was established by the publication of the work of a member of the royal household, Thomas Sternhold, who served both Henry VIII and Edward VI as a groom of the King's Robes during the 1540s.[7]

There is no evidence that Sternhold knew Coverdale's *Goostly psalmes*. Whereas Coverdale's songs are heavily dependent on Lutheran songs for both form and content, there is no trace of this influence in those of Sternhold. Moreover, there is no reason to assume that he shared Coverdale's apprehensive and puritanical reaction to secular songs and verses. Whereas Coverdale's epistle 'unto the christen reader' indicates that he, like Becon later, regarded his psalms and canticles as sacred, moral antidotes to profane 'balettes of fylthynes',[8] Sternhold's attitudes and intentions, stated in his dedication to Edward VI, were entirely positive. Sternhold praised the piety and zeal of the young king who took '*more* delyghte' in 'holye songes of veritie than in anye fayned rimes of vanitie'.[9] In his statement songs of 'veritie' and those of 'vanitie' are both credited with a capacity to 'delight', the more obvious moral contrast is between 'veritie' and 'fayned', although 'fayned rimes' are neither derided nor excluded.

Sternhold's holy songs were written to instruct and delight a specific audience. The dedication implies that they were royal command performances:

I am encouraged to travayle furdre in the sayed boke of psalmes, trustyng that as your grace taketh pleasure to heare them song somtimes of me, so ye wyll also delyghte not onlye to see and reade them your selfe, but also to commaunde them to be song to you of others: that as ye have the psalme it selfe in youre mynde, so ye maye judge myne endevoure by your eare[10]

Sternhold envisaged three ways of taking pleasure from his psalms: private reading, singing and making mental comparisons between his interpretative imitations and the normative liturgical translations (either in Latin or in English). Private reading needs no further comment. Sternhold specifically stated that his psalms had been and were to be sung.[11] However, English music publishing was then in its infancy and there is no music in any of the early editions printed by 1553, nor are there any directions for named, existing tunes to be applied to them. Sternhold's paraphrases were written in rhyming fourteener lines which were printed in octavo format as two shorter lines of eight and six syllables, or alternating four- and three-stress lines; each couplet was laid out on the page as a stanza by indenting the first letter. The rhythms of a wide range of popular tunes could have been easily adapted to accompany psalm paraphrases written in this metrical form.[12] Alternatively, Sternhold's psalms could have been sung to brief repeated melodies improvised on existing tunes associated with either secular songs or even plain-song. Such 'dittying' and improvisation would have been consistent with the musical activities and capabilities of non-professional musicians and song-writers at court.[13]

Sternhold also expected that the king and his household would be able to recognize and appreciate the novel features in his imitations by comparing them with the normative texts. In the dedication he wrote, 'as ye have the psalme it selfe in your mynde,' not if, 'so ye may judge myne endevoure by your eare'.[14] Daily repetition of literal translations of psalms in devotional exercises and the liturgy would have impressed the psalm texts on the minds of his audience. Sternhold expected them to observe the similarity, and to value the 'continuity-in-change' between his paraphrases and the text of 'the psalme it selfe'.[15]

The psalms selected by Sternhold afford considerable variety of themes and forms. Among the nineteen psalms in the first edition, for example, Ps. 1 and Ps. 29 contain impersonal statements on moral and religious themes; in Pss. 2, 34, 49 and 78 the psalmist speaks as a preacher or teacher (in the Great Bible Ps. 78 is headed 'An instruccyon of Asaph'); Ps. 25 and Ps. 32 are the prayers of a penitent; Ps. 120 and Ps. 123 contain pleas for divine help; Ps. 103 and Ps. 128 are songs of praise and blessings, and the remaining psalms selected contain personal affirmations of faith.

In his dedication, Sternhold offered extravagant

thankes to almyghtye God, that hath appoynted us suche a Kynge and governour, that forbyddeth not laye men to gather and leaze in the lordes harvest, but rather commaundeth the reapers to cast out of their handfulles among us, that we maye boldly gather wythout rebuke[16]

The 'reapers' were biblical scholars and translators such as Tyndale, Joye and Coverdale. Sternhold did not claim to be a scholar or an exegete who could 'searche out the secret misteries hydden in the booke of Psalmes',[17] but his dedication indicates that by offering psalm versions to Edward he thought he was offering him a source of guidance in both temporal and spiritual affairs. Sternhold commended Edward's knowledge of 'the fountaines of the scriptures' which he regarded as

the verye meane to attayne to the perfyte governement of this your realme, to goddes glory, the prosperitie of the publique wealthe, & to the comforte of all youre majesties subjectes[18]

Sternhold emphasized the doctrinal value of the Psalms which, he acknowledged, 'by the opinion of many learned menne, comprehendeth theffecte of the whole Byble'.[19]

Sternhold acquired a reputation as a writer solely as a

maker of 'holye songes';[20] he is not known to have written anything else. When imitating his literary models, he responded to the poetry of the Psalms with varying degrees of success. Sternhold's paraphrase of Ps. 1 is characteristic of his usual treatment of psalms as holy songs:

The man is blest that hath not gon
by wycked rede astraye,
Ne sate in chayre of pestilence,
nor walkt in sinners waye.
But in the lawe of God the Lorde,   5
doeth set his whole delyght,
And in that lawe doeth exercyse,
hym selfe both day and nyght.
And as the tree that planted is
fast by the ryver syde: 10
Even so shall he bryng forth his frute
in his due tyme and tyde.
His leafe shall never fall a waye
but floryshe styll and stande,
Eche thyng shal prosper wonderou[s] wel[l]   15
that he doeth take in hande.
So shall [not] the ungodly doe,
they shalbe nothyng so,
But as the dust whiche from the earth,
the windes dryve to and fro.   20
Therfore shall not the wicked men,
in judgement stande upright,
Ne yet in counsel of the just,
but shalbe voyde of myght.
For why the waye of godly men,   25
unto the lorde is knowen,
And eke the waye of wicked men,
shall quite be overthrowen[21]

In this instance Sternhold chose to speak alongside the Vulgate text: 'Beatus vir, qui non abiit in consilio impiorum, et in via peccatorum non stetit, et *in cathedra pestilentiae* non sedit.'[22] However, some of the impact of the poetic movement at the beginning of the original, which is preserved in the liturgical Latin and English translations, has been lost in Sternhold's paraphrase. In Coverdale's

Great Bible translation the description of the sinner's progress is preserved in three verbs of action: 'walked ...
stonde ... sytt'. By contrast, Sternhold's first three main
verbs, 'gon astraye ... sate ... walkt', evince his failure to
respond to the poetic progression embodied in this
sequence of verbs.

Besides the literal conservatism and occasional stylistic
ineptitudes of Sternhold's paraphrases their most insistent
and persistent characteristics are metrical regularity and
simple rhyme schemes. Although metrical regularity can
reflect the constraint imposed upon a poet by the need
either to fit his words to pre-existing tunes, or to make his
verses suitable for musical improvisation, nevertheless
such metrical regularity would also have assisted a moder-
ately literate singer to read and remember these holy
songs, and to sing them to brief melodies repeated stanza
by stanza. The stress patterns and metre of Sternhold's
holy song resemble the stress patterns and metre of ballads
such as 'The Nutbrown Maid'.[23] Comparisons may also be
made with contemporary verses written by a professional
court musician and poet such as John Heywood whose
praise of the Princess Mary (written in 1534) was later
published in Tottel's *Songes and Sonettes* (1557):[24]

> Geve place you Ladies and be gon,
> Boast not your selves at all:
> For here at hande approcheth one,
> Whose face will staine you all.
>   The vertue of her lively lokes,
> Excels the precious stone:
> I wishe to have none other bokes
> To read or loke upon   (lines 1–8)

All these verses were written to be sung, probably to an
instrumental accompaniment; they were thus intended for
performance in some kind of social activity.

Sternhold's verse often suggests the rhythm of an iambic
line with alternate weak and strong stresses, but his choice
of language (like that of many of his contemporaries) con-

tains a preponderance of monosyllables.[25] Sternhold's songs show his preference for pairs of alliterative synonyms, some of which like 'tyme and tyde' (line 12) were popular and proverbial phrases.[26] But the pairing of 'styll and stande' (line 14) is more artful, since it involves a pun on 'styll' having the senses of 'constantly' and 'motionless'. He also used a sprinkling of obsolescent words like those found in contemporary court song-books and verse anthologies: examples from his paraphrases of Psalms 1 and 120 are 'eke', 'rede', and 'wene'. There are also redundant phrases used to fill out the line of verse.[27] However, the repetition of phrase and rhyme, such as that which occurs at the end of Sternhold's Ps. 1, is not always redundant:

> ... the waye of godly men
> ... is knowen
> ... the way of wicked men
> ... overthrowen

Here the repetition gives appropriate emphasis to the moral statement, and a sense of finality to the conclusion of this didactic psalm. Elsewhere, repetition of sound, word and idea emerges as a positive and characteristic feature of Sternhold's style. The sound play at the beginning of his Ps. 6 is expressively contrived:

> Lord in thy wrath reprove me not
> though I deserve thyne Ire:
> Ne yet correcte me in thy rage,
> O lorde I thee desyre[28]

The parallel half lines emphasize the pathos of the contrast in sense, and the similarity in sound, of 'deserve' and 'desyre'. The next lines echo with the four-fold repetition of 'for':

> For I am weake, therfore O Lorde,
> of mercy me forbeare   (My italics)

The rhyme 'quake for feare' also provides an internal half-rhyme 'weak ... quake'. The repetition of an idea in doublet forms like 'reprove ... ire' and 'correct ... rage' (as in the examples from his Ps. 1) not only reflects the literary tastes of Sternhold and his contemporaries[29] but also represents the Hebraic parallelisms in the original psalms and hence is found in many other versions. He did not use these doublets at least simply to fill out the line.

Besides the Vulgate, Sternhold made extensive use of Coverdale's Great Bible translation (1539); he also adopted the interpretations of different translators and paraphrasts. Sternhold's use of the Great Bible Psalms is particularly evident in his paraphrase of Ps. 6:7 where, at this date, use of the word 'beauty' in translations of this verse is confined to Sternhold and to Coverdale's 1539 Bible.[30] For his paraphrase of Ps. 19:12 & 13, Sternhold took over Coverdale's wording

Who can tell, how oft he offendeth? Oh clense thou me fro my secrete fautes. Kepe thy servaunt also from presumptuous synnes, lest they get the dominion over me

and added his own taste for alliteration:

> But lorde what earthly man doeth know
> *how oft he doth offend*?
> Than *clense* my soule from *secret* sinne
> my lyfe that I may mende.
> And *kepe* me that *presumpteous sinnes*
> prevayle not over me[31]   (My italics)

(Similarly, 'oft offende' and 'presumpteous' here are readings peculiar to Coverdale and Sternhold at this date.) By contrast, Sternhold's phrase 'the mightie & the riche'[32] in his version of Ps. 34:10 echoes the Vulgate's 'Divites', or Coverdale's 1535 Bible translation 'the rich'. (The paraphrase by Campensis, and Coverdale's Great Bible translation denote the Hebrew metaphor 'lyons'.)

Sternhold's rendering of Ps. 73:6

> Wherby they be full gloriouslye
> in pride so high extolde,
> And in their wrong and violence,
> be wrapt so many folde[33]

seems to be indebted to Campensis who introduced the idea of being enfolded as in a garment, which is not found in the Vulgate nor in either of Coverdale's Bibles.[34] However, there can be little doubt that Sternhold has assimilated Coverdale's English translation of the Campensis paraphrase into his own metrical paraphrase of Ps. 103:5:

> Lyke as the *egle casteth her byll,*
> whereby her age renueth   (Sternhold)

lyke as the *aegle casteth* awaye *hyr byl* when it waxeth all croked for oldenesse and receaveth a new one, so thou ... shalt receave the floure of youth agayne[35]   (Campensis)

Only Campensis and Sternhold use the image of the discarded eagle's bill at this date.

Later sixteenth-century imitations of the Psalms, which followed Sternhold's example, have restricted our appreciation of his achievement and originality. Sternhold created his metrical paraphrases by interpreting the biblical models which were available to him in a variety of source texts, and by assessing these sources in relation to his own values and intentions.

The inventive qualities of Sternhold's literary expression may be demonstrated from his response to a celebrated simile in Ps. 103:14–16:

> The Lord that made us knoweth our shape
> our moulde and fashion just,
> Howe weake and frayle our nature is
> and howe we be but dust.
>   And howe the tyme of mortall men
> is lyke the widdering hay,
> Or lyke the floure right fayre in felde
> that fadeth full soone away.
>   Whose glosse and beautie stormy wyndes,
> doe utterly disgrace,
> And make that after their assautes,
> suche blossomes have no place[36]

Sternhold's 'the floure ... fayre in felde that fadeth full soone' extends the alliteration prominent in the Vulgate and in Coverdale's translation of this verse, which obviously appealed to his literary tastes.[37] His image of 'widdering hay' makes the conventional biblical simile for man's brief span of life more elaborate and pointed than Coverdale's simple translation: 'the dayes of man are but as grasse' (Great Bible). Similarly, in imitating the antithetical parallel theme of flourishing life, Sternhold emphasized the physical beauty of the flower ('right fayre' with 'glosse and beautie'), which is ravished by time and the elements. Sternhold's image of 'blossomes' gives fragile substance to the object of beauty, and contrasts with the unspecific reference to 'it' in the Vulgate's 'pertransibit in illo'. Finally, Sternhold added a poignant tone in depicting the effects of 'stormy wyndes' which by the violence of their action 'utterly disgrace', assault and displace the transient and fragile beauty of the blossoms. (Sternhold's elaboration, 'stormy wyndes', in verse 16 may have been suggested by the English translation of the paraphrase by Campensis: 'touched with any sharpe wynde'.[38]) In such small-scale inventive details Sternhold's imitations reflect his attempt to revitalize the public lyrical expression of *publica materies* in mid sixteenth-century English verse.

Sternhold appears to have been the first Englishman to write metrical psalms as 'holye songes' for the recreation of the court. The question arises therefore as to where and how Sternhold found precedents for his songs. Unlike Luther and Coverdale, Sternhold restricted himself to psalm texts, and his style, his attitudes and, to some extent, his purpose in paraphrasing selected psalms were different from those of Coverdale.

The closest analogues to Sternhold's paraphrases are the French metrical versions by Clément Marot (*c.* 1496–1544).[39] Marot began to write metrical psalm paraphrases around 1532, most probably at the behest of Marguerite of Navarre, the pious and learned sister of Francis I.[40] Marot's psalms, like Sternhold's, were dedicated to his king, sung

at court and printed and reprinted during the poet's lifetime for circulation among a wider audience. Marot had
also used contemporary vernacular and scholarly sources
for his psalms, including the Latin paraphrases by Campensis.[41] (Apart from the first fifteen psalms, Marot and
Sternhold selected only six psalms in common.)[42]

However, Marot's paraphrases are much freer with the
literal sense of the Psalms than Sternhold's; this indicates a
different attitude or approach to the biblical texts. A telling
example of Marot's radical reorganization of a biblical
psalm text may be seen in his inversion of the celebrated
opening of the Psalms: 'Beatus vir qui . . . '

> Qui au conseil des malins n'esté
> qui n'est au trac des pecheurs arresté,
> qui des mocquers au banc place n'a prise,
> Mais nuict et jour la loy contemple et prise
> De l'eternel, et en est desireux:
> Certainement *cestuy-là est heureux*[43]

Marot was characteristically an inventive imitator. He also
used a wide variety of different verse forms and rhyme
schemes for his psalms, whereas, with two exceptions
Sternhold only used the divided fourteener couplet.

There is no evidence that Sternhold had any direct
knowledge of Marot's paraphrases. However, Marot's
poetry was known by English contemporaries, and his
influence on English poetry has been detected in some of
Wyatt's secular poetry.[44] Wyatt's penitential psalms
(printed in 1549) have been cited as Sternhold's exemplars,
but since Wyatt based his imitations on Aretino's Italian
prose model which bears no resemblance to Marot's or
Sternhold's psalms, there seems little point in looking to
Wyatt for a connexion.[45] During the late 1540s there were
first-hand literary connexions between the French and
English royal households through the presence of French-
men at the English court. Edward VI had a Calvinist
French tutor, Jean Bellemain, but a much more likely
source for the transmission of French influence on the

literary sensibilities of Sternhold and some of his contemporaries at court may be identified with the person of
Nicolas Denisot (1515–59).[46]

Denisot was a poet, painter, courtier (and French
government spy) who had been connected with the
humanist circle at Nogent-le-Rotrou as one of the founders
of the *Pléiade*. He came to England in 1547, temporarily
rusticated from the French court where he had served as a
'gentilhomme de la chambre' to Francis I. Denisot's
literary talents, evident in his *Noëls* of 1545 and *Cantiques
du nouvel advènement de Jésus-Christ* of 1553, were devoted
to stimulating and fostering the religious sensibilities of the
readers and singers of his lyrics.[47] When Edward VI succeeded to the throne Denisot sought to ingratiate himself
with his new masters and to enhance his reputation as a
poet and scholar by dedicating Latin verses to the young
king.[48] He was appointed tutor to Edward Seymour's
three daughters and remained in England until 1549, the
year of Sternhold's death. Denisot was thus in the right
place at the right time to have stimulated the devotional
literary tastes of Sternhold's contemporaries in the English
royal households. There is ample proof that he succeeded
in interesting some of the younger generation in the pious
activities and works of Marguerite of Navarre (who died in
December 1549): Denisot compiled an anthology of elegiac
verses as a tribute to Marguerite which was published in
Paris in 1551; it contained Latin verses by Seymour's
daughters.[49]

Since Denisot's stay in England resulted in poetic tri-
butes to Marguerite, and since Denisot himself had written
and advocated the writing of holy songs, he may well have
influenced others in court circles (including Sternhold) by
extolling the psalm paraphrases of Clément Marot who
had once been Marguerite's secretary. Members of the
English court would have found Denisot's taste for devotional poetry congenial. The tastes of the royal household,
stimulated by the influence of Catherine Parr, may well

have provided Sternhold with a further incentive to follow the example of the French in making metrical psalms.

Unlike the majority of Wyatt's and others' lyrics for Tudor court circles, Sternhold's holy songs were not circulated only in manuscript copies among a small group of people, but rapidly found their way into print.[50] The first edition, containing nineteen paraphrases and entitled *Certayne Psalmes chosen out of the Psalter of David and drawen into Englishe metre* [1549?], was immediately reprinted. An enlarged edition in which a further eighteen metrical psalms by Sternhold had been added, was published in December 1549 about four months after his death.[51] By 1553 this edition had been reprinted at least nine times. The printer was Edward Whitchurch who had been imprisoned in the Fleet at the same time as Sternhold in 1543.[52]

The fact that Sternhold regarded 'holye songes' as comparable with 'fayned rimes' may have helped to account for the popularity of his psalm paraphrases which obviously appealed to the literary tastes of a wide English public who would have bought 'fayned rimes of vanitie' as well as these 'holye songes of veritie'. In spite of his position at court and the dedication to the king, Sternhold must also have considered the requirements of a wider public. He paraphrased Ps. 9:11:

> Sing psalmes therfore unto the lord,
> that dwelth in Syon hyll:
> Publishe among the people playne,
> hys counsels and hys wyll[53]

Sternhold's patron, Edward VI, would have encouraged his attempt to 'publishe' God's will among 'the people playne' by means of vernacular texts and easily remembered stanzaic verses.

The publication of Sternhold's *Certayne Psalmes* established a vogue for metrical psalm paraphrases, and Sternhold had many imitators. In 1549 John Hopkins, a young Oxford graduate, added seven of his own psalm paraphrases to the posthumous edition of Sternhold's thirty-seven psalms. In a short preface found after Sternhold's last psalm, Hopkins explained that his seven additional psalms were included 'that the booke may ryse to his just volume' (a phrase which could indicate a printer's commission), and as a tribute to the dead poet's 'exquisite dooinges'.[54] There was no actual partnership between Sternhold and Hopkins.

The success of Sternhold's *Certayne Psalmes chosen out of the Psalter* provoked a flurry of activity, and numerous volumes appeared with similar titles. Wyatt's version of the seven penitential psalms, published by John Harington of Stepney as *Certayne psalmes chosen out of the psalter* in December 1549, was dedicated to William Parr, Catherine's brother. In 1550 Harington published William Hunnis's *Certayne Psalmes chosen out of the Psalter*, and in 1553 Francis Seagar's *Certayne Psalmes select out of the Psalter* was printed and published by William Seres.[55] Such publications have led to the association of Sternhold's work and reputation with those of others who followed his example. Also in 1549–50, William Seres published *Certayne Chapters of the proverbes of Salomon drawen into metre by Thomas Sterneholde*; the printer was John Case. In the dedication to Sir Thomas Spek, Case explained that

The copye of thys boke was delivered me by a frende of myne beynge sometyme servaunte unto maister Thomas Sterneholde, *whereby it is to be conjectured*, that the same were putte in metre by hym, yet not so parfectly perused, by reason of sodaine deathe, as perchaunce he would have done, if he hadde longer lyved[56]

(My italics)

However, there is no evidence to attribute any of the contents of this book to Sternhold. It contains a metrical version of Proverbs (chapters 1–11), which was reprinted in the same year as the work of John Hall;[57] it also contains three chapters of Ecclesiastes in metre, variant texts of which are attributed reliably in manuscript sources to Surrey, and metrical paraphrases of Psalms 88, 31 and 51 which have also been attributed to Surrey;[58] the last poem in the book is an anonymous 'ballade: Againste nigardy, and riches'. It is clear that the printer's 'frende' and the publisher expected the book to sell because it carried Sternhold's name.[59]

The vogue for 'Certayne Psalmes' in metre established by Sternhold was not restricted to printed versions, although it was only in print that anyone could hope for commercial gain. In 1551 William Forrest, the king's 'humble orator', wrote fifty new paraphrases of 'Certaigne Psalmes ... added to maister Sterneholdis'; Forrest regarded Sternhold as the 'firste' and 'beste of all psalmysters', and saw himself as Sternhold's unworthy successor.[60] He therefore modestly dedicated his manuscript of 'Certaigne Psalmes' to Edward Seymour rather than the king:

> As Sternholde/ highest in framynge of psalmes,
> unto the higheste/ can destynate his doings;
> bicawse I cannot so highe reache the psalmes:
> unto meaner then dignyte of kings:
> (as unto your grace) I make my offerings[61]

The manuscript was a new year's gift; there is apparently no record of Seymour's reaction to this compliment.

Hall's 'Certayne Psalmes of David, drawen in metre' first appeared in the 1550 reprint of his Proverbs: 'Whych Proverbes of late were set forth, Imprinted and untruely entituled, to be thee doynges of Mayster Thomas Sternhold, late grome of the Kynges Majesties robes'. In spite of this statement on the title page it is likely that Hall intended his book to be compared with Sternhold's, since his dedication to 'John Bricket of Elton' bears a striking resemblance to part of Sternhold's dedication of his *Certayne Psalmes* to Edward VI:

I thought you had more delite and pleasure to reade or to heare, or sing the word of god in metre then anye other rymes of vanitie & songes of baudy[62]

Hall was proud of his work and his moral intentions. But in his 'Preface to the Reader' he affects modesty, asking the reader not to compare his 'simple and unlearned exercyse'

to the learned and exquisit doynges of other men, as though my desyre were to have the vayne glory & the prayse of men, but rather like as I have bestowed tymes herein that myghte have bene worsse occupyed[63]

He makes his intentions clear by railing against an earlier printed anthology of secular verse – the *Court of Venus* – and by proclaiming

let this be as now sufficiente to admonish the, to turne thyne exercyse from vyce to vertue, to turne thy talke from fylthenesse to godlynes and thy hole lyfe from evyll to good[64]

Sternhold's dedication suggests that his holy songs were intended to supplement the secular lyrics circulating in the court, but the psalms of John Hall were clearly intended to replace secular lyrics wherever they were circulating.

Revised versions of Hall's eight psalms from the reprint of his *Proverbes* were included in his *Courte of Vertue* (1565)[65] which, as its title implies, was intended to provide the moral antidote to the *Court of Venus*. In the prologue he described the earlier anthology as satisfying the indecent cravings of 'fylthy mynde[s]'.[66] In response to the injunction of 'Arete or lady vertue'

> To make a boke of songes holy,
> Godly and wyse, blamyng foly

Hall indicates that he undertook his work of compiling 'Ryght sober songes godly and sadde' in order to 'procure' men 'to goodnes'.[67]

The *Courte of Vertue* contains a variety of moralized secular themes metamorphosized into godly lyrics. Biblical paraphrases make up almost half the contents of the book, and amongst these, psalm paraphrases predominate. The other texts include moral 'parodies' of some of Wyatt's lyrics known to have been contained in the *Court of Venus*. (Wyatt's family lived in the vicinity of Hall's home town of Maidstone.) Hall's lyrics have titles such as 'A Song of the lute in the prayse of God and disprayse of Idolatorie'[68] which is based on Wyatt's 'My lute awake!' and follows the stanza form and refrain of Wyatt's lyric from the *Court of Venus*. Hall's 'ditie' of 'Blame not my lute' also follows the form, refrain and tone of a Wyatt lyric, but it does so in order to lament 'the wycked state and enormities of most people, in these present miserable dayes', including those who

> abuse the lute
> With sinfull songes of lechery[69]

Some of the lyrics have printed tunes.

The Prologue and the titles of Hall's non-biblical lyrics establish the moral and the literary contexts for his holy-song psalms. The literary context is clearly that of secular verse conventions. In the prologue the poet describes how he became the champion of Lady Vertue who appeared to him in a dream vision accompanied by feminine personifi-cations of 'hope' and 'love':

> Me thought they compaste me about,
> Standing as in a syrcle trayne,
>
> Forsothe it was a semely syghte,
> My harte therin dyd muche delyghte[70]

In his dream, the ladies 'so bryght' greet the poet courte-ously. In lines which parody the speaker's erotic vision in Wyatt's 'They fle from me that sometyme did me seke' the poet describes how

> She tooke me then in hyr armes twayne,
> And thus to me she sweetly sayde[71]

They 'embrace' him 'gently' and command his services in combating the 'synne and vyce' of those 'untrue' who regard 'their owne wyt and wyll, And wyll not harke gods worde'.[72]

In his metrical psalms Hall's method of imitation is interpretative: his texts remain close to Coverdale's prose translations in his English Bibles. The only notable exception occurs in the opening of his Ps. 130 where Hall perhaps imitates the metaphor of the cave from Wyatt's version of this penitential psalm:

> From care of harte that cave so depe,
> So hath my soule my sinnes abhorde:
> Repentantly I humbly crepe,
> And call to thee for helpe O lorde[73]

Hall was a physician and he identified himself with the example of 'Noble kyng David' whom he regarded as a 'good phisicien', 'wryting medcines for the soule' and bestowing 'godly love' to 'comfort all his race'.[74]

The provision of godly alternatives to popular songs was not solely a sixteenth-century phenomenon. The fourteenth-century bishop of Ossory, Richard de Ledrede, had had religious texts set to popular tunes in an effort to counter the appeal of secular vernacular lyrics.[75] It is not surprising, therefore, that a Catholic writer and publisher like Richard Verstegan (or Rowlands) – motivated by a quite different kind of piety from Hall's – should also write in a tradition which might otherwise appear to a modern reader to be essentially a Protestant, puritan one.

Verstegan's *Odes in Imitation of the seaven penitential psalmes* (1601) was dedicated to Catholic Englishwomen, 'the vertuous ladies and gentlewomen readers of these ditties', with the express hope that

sweete voyces or virginalles may voutsafe so to grace them, as that thereby they may be much bettered and the rather yf it shal please you to obtaine of some skilful Musitian, such requisite tunes, as may unto them be best fitting[76]

Verstegan concluded his dedication with the following verses indicating his devotional purpose:

> The vaine conceits of loves delight
> I leave to *Ovids* arte,
> Of warres and bloody broyles to wryte
> Is fit for *Virgils* parte.

Of tragedies in doleful tales
Let *Sophocles* entreat:
And how unstable fortune failes
Al poets do repeat.

But unto our eternal king
My verse and voyce I frame
And to his saintes I meane to sing
In them to praise his name[77]

Like Sternhold, Verstegan did not condemn secular themes, he simply expressed a preference for religious subjects. Verstegan's perceptions of psalms as a lyric genre is evident in his title *Odes*; despite the title there is no attempt to imitate any classical form, and no printed music. Each of the seven psalms is in a different metre including the common measure of Sternhold's psalms, divided poulter's measure, octosyllabics and one in pentameters; they are described in the head title as being seven psalms 'to so-many several tunes of Musick'. Besides the penitential psalms Verstegan's book includes verses on 'The Fifteen Mysteries of the Rosarie', 'Epithetes of our Blessed Lady', 'Our Blessed Ladies Lullaby', 'The Triumphe of feminyne Saintes' as well as several other devotional or hortatory works in metre, including a linked sequence of seven sonnets entitled 'Visions of the worlds instabillitie'. The last item in the book is entitled: 'Verses of the worldes vanitie, supposed to bee made by S. Bernard. And translated into English to bee sung to the tune they beare in Latin'.

Verstegan's penitential psalms are mainly interpretative imitations in which he is speaking alongside a literal prose translation, more or less verse by verse. The source is the Vulgate rather than any of the newer translations derived from the Hebrew:

But when o Lord thy heavy hand
No day or night I could withstand,
But that in anguish overworne
My conscience prickt as with a thorne[78]

(Verstegan, Ps. 31[32], lines 13–16)

130

(Quoniam die ac nocte gravata est super me manus tua: conversus sum in erumna mea, dum configitur spina)   (Vulgate, Ps. 31[32]:4)

(For thy hande is hevy upon me daye and nyght, and *my moysture is lyke, the drouth in Sommer*)

(Great Bible, Ps. 32:4, and similarly all English Protestant Bibles following the Hebrew)

In his paraphrases of Ps. 129[130] and Ps. 101[102] Verstegan used a more inventive method of imitation:

> Ev'n from the depth of woes
> Wherein my soule remaines,
> To thee in supreame blis
> O Lord that highest raignes,
>   I do both call and cry:
>   T'is deep hart-sorrowes force
> That moves me thus to waile,
> T'is pittie Lord in thee
> Must make it to availe,
>   Thyne eares therefore aply
>
> (Ps. 129[130], lines 1–10)

(De profundis clamavi ad te domine: domine exaudi vocem meam. Fiant aures tuae intendentes: in vocem deprecationis meae)

(Ps. 129[130]:1–2)

Verstegan has introduced a parallel situation into his imitation: the location of his psalmist's soul in the 'depth of woes' is contrasted with the extreme opposite, 'supreame blis'. The psalmist is placed at the opposite extreme from God. Verstegan's psalmist also specifies his own and God's motives in this stark relationship: his 'deep hart-sorrowes force' is contrasted with God's 'pittie'.

In Verstegan's imitation Israel or Zion acquires a contemporary religious and political significance:

> His people he affects
> He wil not leave destrest,
> The thralled he wil free
>
> (Ps. 129[130], lines 36–8)

(Et ipse redimet Israel)   (Ps. 129[130]:8)

In the sixth penitential psalm there are oblique references
to persecuted English Catholics as God's 'afflicted flock'

> Let thy afflicted flock
> Comfort in thee retaine,
> From dauning day to night,
> From night to day againe,
> Let stil their hope endure
>
> (Ps. 129[130], lines 26–30)

(A custodia matutina usque ad noctem: speret Israel in domino)
(Ps. 129[130]:6)

Verstegan interprets the 'orationem humilium' as 'the
plaint, Of faithful folk, thrall'd in untruths restraint'.[79]

Like Sternhold, Verstegan could rely on his readers'
ability to recognize and appreciate the significance of 'his
best endevours'[80] in adapting or enlarging on the sense of
the biblical model. These seven psalms were a familiar
feature of the Primer in daily use by the Catholic laity.[81]
Verstegan's invention amplifies the original to provide
comfort for contemporary Catholic readers in their
oppression.

The earlier metrical psalmists, like Sternhold, had
exploited the literary resources of the more popular contemporary 'fayned rimes' in the making of their 'holye
songes'. However, by 1580, the popularity of psalms in
England gave concern to some lest they should be under-
valued. In his translation of Beza's paraphrases (dedicated
to the Dudley brothers' sister, Catherine Hastings, Countess of Huntingdon) Gilby lamented 'that the Psalmes in
English are in manie places read rather for taske as it were,
and for fashion sake, than for good devotion and with
understanding'.[82] By the 1580s, therefore, it was possible
to reverse the process previously adopted by Sternhold and
others – to exploit this 'fashion', as well as the contemporary popular vogue for metrical psalms as vehicles for
devotional praise – in order to glorify the image of the
Queen:

As prayer in sadnes is mete:
In myrthe so godly songes to synge
For Christen men lo this is fytte[83]

The combination of religious and political themes which
is delicately balanced in Verstegan's *Odes*, as in Sternhold's
Ps. 120 and Smith's 'other psalme' is found in a cruder
form, and applied in a different context, in two psalm imitations by William Patten. Patten's metrical imitations of
Ps. 72 and Ps. 21 are occasional poems published in 1583
and 1598 respectively to commemorate Queen Elizabeth's
twenty-fifth and fortieth accession-day anniversaries.[84]
Psalms with appropriate themes have been carefully selected. Ps. 72 celebrates the 'soothsay & wish of many blessings' by David for the reign of Solomon his son whom
Patten identifies with Elizabeth. Ps. 21 'blessed David did
make for himself & hiz peple too rejoys at Gods allmighty
poour & mercy against hiz enimyez',[85] and in Patten's imitation reference is made to the defeat of the Armada:

11 Against Thee & Her in damnable dezire,
   One prank (amoong the rest) most execrabl
   Assayd they in mallis, mischeef, swoord & fire,   1588
   Which yet too acheeve (alas) they wear unabl:
   What gat they by that practis detestabl?
   But slaughter & flight and most infamoous shame,
   With a freating corzey perpetuall too their name.

12 Tiz thoow that makest them run awey apace,
   Thy bowstring iz it, that in a full despight,
   Terribly shall flyrt them at their very face:
13 Avauns thy self O Lord God in thy might,
   So shall we sing all cheerfull in delight,
   Thy praiz, thy glory, and celebrate with all,
   Thy puissant poour that Reinz & ever shall[86]

Patten's Ps. 72 was printed with a simple tune as a
broadside ballad for mass circulation. Yet, like Sternhold,
Patten wrote with two audiences in mind; the presentation
manuscript copy of his Ps. 21 (without music) survives
among the Royal manuscripts now in the British

Library.[87] A Latin paraphrase (attributed to Campensis) was printed parallel with each of his English imitations. Patten's scholarly aspirations are also evident in the heading to his Ps. 72 in which he explains his choice of English metre:

Like az the ditti thearof waz in Ebru vers, so apted heer in English meeter into Seaven Septenariez, the rather for honoour of oour Souereinz name, that is in Ebru ELIZABETH, in oour toong, The Seaventh of my God[88]

Patten's compliment to the Queen is based on an analogy with the personal devotion which is implied by the psalm form:

> Justis triumphs within her Landz we see,
> In coours full az the Moon, dooth Peas aboound:
> By Seaz & fluds extends her sooveraintee,
> Her enmiez croouch & lik dust from the groound,
> Her freendship sought by kings aboout her roound,
> The Dutch, the Dane, the Moscovite & Sweathen,
> With theez the very Infidellz & Heathen[89]

Metrical psalms had also been used as a medium for occasional, devout and patriotic praises by Thomas Bownell in the reign of Mary. Bownell celebrated Mary's accession with metrical paraphrases of selected verses from three psalms of thanksgiving which were published with Richard Beeard's *Godly Psalme, of Marye Queene* (1553).[90] Thomas Bentley included a prose version of Ps. 118 written to celebrate Elizabeth's accession in his *Monument of Matrones*.[91]

Besides the selected psalms for recreation, instruction and praise, there were also complete metrical psalters for public worship in church or for private devotion at home. In 1549 the printer Robert Crowley published his own metrical paraphrases of all the psalms with a single four-part setting based on traditional 'playn songe' chant.[92] However in the same year Cranmer issued the first Book of Common

Prayer which adopted Coverdale's 1539 prose translation
of the Psalms, and Crowley's psalter was not used in the
liturgy.

Matthew Parker also produced English metrical versions of all the Psalms, which could have been used in the
liturgy as a public and ordered expression of a community's corporate response to God's presence, and a declaration of Christian doctrine.[93] In selecting the contents of his
book Parker made lavish provision for the application of
his psalms in public worship: he paraphrased all the Psalms
in sequence and used the title *Psalter*; he included metrical
versions of hymns and canticles with directions for antiphonal singing by 'the quiere' and 'rectors' (men's voices)
in some texts.[94] Moreover, each of his psalms is prefaced
by an interpretative 'argument' or summary in verse
(usually of two or three lines) and each psalm is followed
by a brief prose collect containing a petition related to the
psalm theme.

Parker probably wrote his metrical psalms about 1556
while in retirement during the reign of Queen Mary.
During this period there would have been no opportunity
to use an English psalter in the liturgy, and some of the
liturgical features of *The whole Psalter translated into English
Metre* as finally printed about 1567 may have been later
accretions. Meanwhile, however, during Mary's reign,
Parker's psalms, like Sternhold's and others', could have
provided holy songs for the recreation and private devotions of Parker's household. In a long verse prologue 'Of
the vertue of Psalmes' Parker explained the dual purpose of
his paraphrases: to please God, to instruct and delight all
honest men who should, according to the Apostle Paul

> make melodye,
> To God geve thankes in song.

> Judge Reader well: my good entent,
> so thinke that God be pleasde[95]

Parker also pointed out that

135

In other bookes: where man doth looke,
　　but other wordes seeth he:
As proper hath: this onely booke,
　　most wordes his owne to be.

It is a glass: a myrrour bright,
　　for soule to see his state[96]

This verse prologue, like Coverdale's and Hall's, attacks and banishes secular love songs which 'worke mens myndes: but bitter gall, by phansies pevishe playes'.[97]

Depart ye songes: lascivious
　　from lute, from harpe depart:
Geve place to Psalmes: most vertuous,
　　and solace there your harte.

Ye songes so nice: ye sonnets all,
　　of lothly lovers layes:
Ye worke mens myndes: but bitter gall,
　　by phansies pevish playes.

Herein because: all mens delight,
　　bene diverse founde in mynde:
I tournd the Psalmes: all whole in sight,
　　in rythmes of divers kynde.

Us song should move . . .

God graunt these Psalmes: might edifie,
　　that is the chiefest thing

Parker's psalter also reveals his humanist moral, scholarly and literary concerns in ways which can be seen as representative of many other sixteenth-century psalmists' attitudes. In his prologue, Parker provided a list of his scholarly sources indicating a humanist preference for patristic authorities and contemporary Christian Hebraists:

So Vatablus: and Pellicane,
　　in truth were not rejecte:
Nor Munster yet, or Pagnyne playne
　　in tonges were fled for secte.

Who more will searche: how here it goes,
　　let him the Hebrew trye:
Where wordes were skant: with texts or glose
　　that want I did supplye[98]

It has been said that Parker 'shews rather the ability of the Scholar than the feeling of the Poet'.[99]

Parker's text of Ps. 1, unlike Sternhold's, shows his awareness of the triple parallelisms in the first verse

> Man blest no doubt: who walkth not out,
>   in wicked mens affayres:
> And stondth no daie: in sinners waie,
>   nor sitth in scorners chayres[100]

Printed in the margin alongside the English text are references to these 'triades': the words *ambulare*, *stare* and *sedere* are bracketed together, similarly *impii*, *peccatores* and *derisores*; *consilia*, *viae*, *cathedrae*. Parker's work demonstrates his literary interests. He employed a variety of stanzaic verse forms in the continental humanist tradition established by Buchanan's Latin paraphrases.[101] This variety was emphasized by the way the psalm texts were laid out on the page, although this layout sometimes gives the impression that a wider variety of forms has been used than is actually the case: those indicated by each of the eight psalm tunes printed to accompany the *Psalter* are simple combinations of eight and six syllables. The rhyme words in many psalms were indicated in the printed text by red and black brackets which tend to make the verses look intricate.[102] Parker's dedication 'To the Reader' includes a defence of metrical composition, and invokes the names of 'Ambrose sage and worthy Bede' amongst others.[103] Parker took particular care to point his psalms and other verses metrically. He issued the following instructions to the reader on the eloquent delivery of his verse:

> But reade it round: and hacke it not,
>   as jumblyng short and long:
> Expresse them sound: and racke them not,
>   as learners use among.
>
> Accent in place: your voyce as needth,
>   note number, poynte, and time:
> Both lyfe and grace: good reading breedth,
>   flat verse it reysth sublime[104]

Parker's verse was 'raised sublime' by the eight settings for his *Psalter* composed by Thomas Tallis. Tallis, the most outstanding English composer of his time, provided moving melodies with four-part harmonies.[105] An introduction to Tallis's tunes printed at the end of the *Psalter* describes what was considered their relative emotional significance.[106] An index of psalms with marks to identify each tune suggests which tune is appropriate for each psalm. The eight tunes provided a link with the older liturgical tradition whereby the psalms were intoned in accordance with a series of eight tones.[107] Tallis's music has syllabic underlay with bar lines to point the phrasing as the punctuation points the text. The tunes consist for the most part of two note values with some simple provisions for making the melody represent the sense of the words: the first syllable of 'majestie' is lengthened for emphasis in the second tune; 'kynges', in the third tune, is treated similarly and the last word of the phrase 'the kynges aryse' is set to a rising interval of a tone. There is also some provision for adapting the texts to the tunes. There are two different versions of Ps. 32 for example, each in a different metre to be sung to different tunes. In other instances a singer's choice of phrase – and hence metre and tune – within a single psalm is indicated typographically: Ps. 42 is printed with some two-syllable phrases in parentheses so that these phrases may be omitted to make the psalm fit Tallis's fifth tune; (they are not included in the text of Ps. 42 which is printed as a syllabic underlay to the fifth tune). Similarly, in Ps. 95 metrical alternatives to the second half of each line are printed together and linked by brackets:

> O come in one: { let us sing to the Lord: / to prayse the Lord:
>
> And hym recounte: { for the stay of our wealth: / our stay and wealth

The textual underlay of this psalm printed to the fourth tune is in octosyllabics.[108]

The importance of the music was such that the text of the holy song was rearranged to fit the tune. Among the preliminary matter of this psalter, Parker quoted Basil the Great's view that in the Psalms the holy ghost had mixed 'in his forme of doctrine the delectation of musike, to thintent that the commoditie of the doctrine might secretlye steale into us, while our eares bee touched with the pleasauntnes of the melodie'.[109]

In the last years of his life, Parker, by then archbishop of Canterbury, commissioned a new setting of his own version of Ps. 107 from the composer Thomas Whythorne, master of the music in the archbishop's chapel.[110] Although the music is not known to survive the commission encouraged Whythorne to make his own metrical paraphrase of the same psalm; one holy song begat another.

Parker wrote his psalms some ten years before they were printed. Yet even though he emerged from his rural retirement to become Elizabeth's first archbishop of Canterbury, it was Sternhold's psalms, not Parker's, which provided the basis of the metrical psalter which was adapted for liturgical use in the Elizabethan Church.

Sternhold's thirty-seven psalms were adapted for liturgical use by English Calvinists living in Geneva during the reign of Mary. These Marian exiles adopted the practice of using metrical psalms as liturgical songs, which was a feature of Genevan spirituality. Calvin had used Marot's psalms supplemented by new versions by Theodore Beza for this purpose.[111]

When the English Protestants arrived in Geneva, they may well have recognized in Sternhold's holy songs (and in Hopkins's supplement to them) English counterparts to Marot's psalms, and sought to adapt Sternhold's texts for similar liturgical purposes. In 1556 Jean Crespin published an edition of fifty-one English metrical psalms for the use of the resident English community.[112] Each psalm was printed with a monodic, unharmonized tune; those for Pss. 128 and 130 for example are adaptations of the French tunes for these psalms. William Whittingham was one of the chief editors responsible for this Genevan liturgical book.[113]

The indebtedness to Sternhold is clearly acknowledged on the title-page of the metrical psalms, which also states that corrections were made to Sternhold's original thirty-seven psalms in order to achieve a more faithful rendering of the Hebrew texts:

One and Fiftie Psalmes of David in Englishe metre, wherof .37. were made by Thomas Sterneholde: and the rest by others. Conferred with the hebrewe, and in certeyn places corrected as the text, and sens of the Prophete required

The general preface, addressed to 'our bretherne in England', bears witness to the editors' high regard for Sternhold, 'hym whome for the gyftes that God had gevyn him we estemed and reverenced', but does not mention his name. The preface explains why corrections were considered necessary, on what principle they were made, and also hints that the incentive came from contact with Hebrew scholars in Geneva:

Nowe to make you privie . . . why we altered the ryme in certeyne places, of hym whome for the gyftes that God had gevyn him we estemed and reverenced, thys may suffice: that in this our entreprise, we did onely set God before our eyes and therfore wayed the wordes and sense of the Prophete: rather consideringe the meanyng therof, then what any man had wrytt, and chiefly beinge in this place where as moste perfite and godly judgement dyd assure us, and exhortations to the same encorage us, we thoght it better to frame the ryme to the Hebrewe sense, then to bynde that sense to the Englishe meter and so either altered for the better in suche places as he had not attayned unto, or els where he had escaped parte of the verse, or some tymes the whole, we added the same[114]

The final appeal of the editors was to the judgement of 'the learned' – the Christian Hebraists.

The Genevan editors' emendations removed many, but

not all, of the individual interpretative details and literary features in Sternhold's (and in Hopkins's) work. Sternhold's paraphrase of Ps. 103:6, for example,

> The Lord with justice doth *revenge*
> all such as be opprest:
> *The pacience of the perfit man*
> is turned to the best[115]

was changed to

> The lorde with justice doth *repaye*
> all suche as be oppreste:
> *So that their suffrings and their wrongs*
> are turned to the best[116]   (My italics)

In spite of the Anglo-Genevan's claim to have 'Conferred with the hebrewe, and in certeyn places corrected as the text, and sens of the Prophete required'[117] there is no more basis in the Hebrew text for the Genevans' 'repaye' than Sternhold's 'revenge'; and there is no scriptural justification for the sense of the second half of the verse in either paraphrase.[118] However, Sternhold's 'The pacience of the perfit man' is a memorable resonant phrase, and his interpretation of this verse successfully conveys the psalmist's positive confident mood. It was nevertheless dropped by the editors and replaced with a more explicit line. At the end of Ps. 103 Sternhold's latinate diction was also lost in the Genevan revisions:[119]

> Ye angels and ye *vertuous* men
> *laude* ye the lord   (Sternhold; my italics)

> Ye Angels which are great in power
> praise ye   (Geneva, 1556)

The Genevans omitted Sternhold's artful diction and replaced it with plainer language better suited to a popular Calvinist audience. Alliteration was added as another device likely to make the metrical psalms easier to remember. In the 1556 edition of Ps. 1:4 Sternhold's 'His leafe shall never fall a way' (Ps. 1, line 13) became 'Whose leaf shall never fade nor fall'.[120]

The Genevan editors' liturgical requirements also led to important changes in their presentation and layout of the metrical psalms in print. Sternhold's dedication to Edward VI, which was obsolete by 1556, was removed. Hopkins's supplementary preface to his seven psalms was also dropped, because the Genevan psalms were printed as a uniform collection in a single numerical sequence rather than as an anthology of the works of different individual authors. Sternhold's verse prefaces or 'arguments' before each psalm, which had been retained in the London editions published until 1553, were omitted and replaced by longer explanatory prose prefaces, and scholarly notes were occasionally added in the margins.[121] The Genevan editors also added verse numbers and musical notation. All these editorial changes produced a more uniform and anonymous style, thus facilitating the communal use of a slightly closer paraphrase of the Hebrew Psalms as liturgical songs in accordance with Calvinist practice.

Sternhold's name remained a feature of the self-advertising title-page of the original Genevan, and then the Elizabethan or Anglo-Genevan editions of English metrical psalms.[122] But, after John Day's 1561 London edition of *Four score and seven Psalmes*, all reference to the changes made to Sternhold's psalms 'as the sens of the Prophete required' was omitted.[123] Sternhold's connexion with the metrical psalter may have had some tactical advantage for puritan elements in the Elizabethan Church, since his name and holy-song book were associated with the piety and musical recreations in court circles during Queen Elizabeth's childhood. Sternhold's name and possible 'authority' may have helped to make the Anglo-Genevan psalter acceptable and 'alowed according to thordre appointed in the Quenes majesties Injunctions' of 1559 which related to singing in Church.[124]

The metrical psalter was apparently 'sung in all parochial

churches' until the end of the seventeenth century.[125] For almost 150 years therefore, this Anglo-Genevan (the so-called 'Sternhold and Hopkins') psalter was probably the most familiar English verse known to the majority of Englishmen. Harmonized vocal and instrumental settings of the 'church tunes' for the Anglo-Genevan psalter were first published by John Day in about 1563. Thomas East (Est) later commissioned some of the best composers of the day (including John Dowland and Giles Farnaby) to harmonize the psalm tunes for his edition of

The. Whole. Booke. of Psalmes; With their Wonted Tunes, as they are song in Churches, composed into foure parts ... Wherein the Church tunes are carefully corrected, and thereunto added other short tunes usually song in London, and other places of this Realme ... 1592[126]

Some of the tunes associated with these psalms remained in continuous use for more than four centuries and thus represent one of the most enduring English musical traditions.[127]

The popularity and predominance of this liturgical version has affected Sternhold's reputation which has been founded not on his own texts but on the Genevan and later Anglo-Genevan adaptations of his texts. The effect of Anthony Wood's late-seventeenth-century garbled but influential account of Sternhold was to align Sternhold's motives with those of Coverdale in his *Goostly psalmes*, or with those of Hall in his *Courte of Vertue*. Wood, elaborating on John Bale's brief notice of Sternhold[128] in his catalogue of British writers, stated that Sternhold was 'a most zealous reformer, and a very strict liver' who became

so scandaliz'd at the amorous and obscene songs used in court, that he forthsooth turn'd into English metre 51 of David's Psalms, and caused musical notes to be set to them, thinking thereby that the courtiers would sing them instead of their sonnets, but [they] did not, only some few excepted[129]

Wood's statement contains three crucial errors. First, the mention of fifty-one psalms with music indicates that he was describing the 1556 Genevan psalms and not Sternhold's own texts from any of the pre-1553 London editions which include Sternhold's dedication to Edward VI.[130] Secondly, Wood has confused the attitudes of his source, John Bale, with those of Sternhold, and thus attributed motives to Sternhold which could have been more appropriately attributed to Bale. Thirdly, Wood has implied that Sternhold's psalms were not well received by his contemporaries, but the existence of twelve editions surviving from Edward's short reign is a powerful argument to the contrary.

Sternhold often interpreted the biblical texts according to his own readings of various sources. It is important to recognize that his interpretative imitations were not for worship but, in the first instance, for godly recreation in Edward's Protestant court, and secondly, for popular edification and enjoyment.[131] If Sternhold was too successful in popularizing holy-song psalms for the good of his own reputation, and if the subsequent imitations of his holy songs have masked our appreciation of Sternhold's originality, at least the vogue he helped to establish may be seen to have been a formative influence on public taste in general. Whereas prayers and meditations had by their nature a restricted audience, the form and content of holy songs reached a wider public through the mass circulation of printed copies. Sternhold may have lost a personal reputation, but he gained a popular image.[132]

The qualities peculiar to a holy song, which distinguish it from a personal meditation are brought into sharper focus by the fate of Surrey's Ps. 88, first in the version printed by Case in 1549–50, and subsequently in the adaptation by Seagar published in 1553. Neither Case (who attributed all 'the copye of thys boke' to Sternhold), nor Seagar, seems to have been aware that the poem was by Surrey.[133]

There are several discrepancies between the printed text of 1549–50 and the received text from London, British Library, Additional MS 36529. For example, Case's text has 'wery bones' for 'weryd lymes' (line 32), and 'follow' for 'swallow' (line 42).[134] However, the sense of three lines of the psalm is completely different: Surrey's line

> Why dost thou not appeare, O Lord   (line 36)

was printed as

> Why dost thou lorde appaese

In lines 29–30 the climax of Surrey's personal meditation on this psalm

> The livelye voyce of them that in *thy word* delight
> *Must* be the trumppe

appears as

> The lyvely voice of them,
>   that in *thys worlde* delyght:
> *Nor* be the trumpe   (My italics)

Surrey's strong personal conviction has been reduced to a negative platitude about worldly delights. The turning point of Surrey's meditation has been discarded.

Case printed Surrey's long lines of poulter's measure (alternate rhyming lines of twelve and fourteen syllables) as half lines in order to accommodate them to the octavo format which was commonly used in such books. (Puttenham accused 'common rimers, or their Printer for sparing of paper', of cutting long lines 'in the middest, wherein they make in two verses but halfe rime'.)[135]

The process of depersonalizing the sense and style of Surrey's meditation on Ps. 88, begun in the 1549–50 version, was later taken much further by Francis Seagar in his *Certayne Psalmes* (1553). Seagar, basing his work on a copy of Case's version, turned Surrey's psalm into a holy song with a four-part musical setting.

The layout of Case's edition formed the basis for Seagar's adaptation of the original poulter's measure into the common measure stanza associated with the psalms of Sternhold and his followers (lines of 8.6.8.6 syllables rhyming in the shorter lines). In the 1549–50 text of Surrey's psalm each measure is presented as a sentence indicated aurally by rhyme and marked graphically by a full stop. The strong pauses which fall at the ends of the twelve-syllable lines are indicated by colons; weaker medial pauses after the sixth and eighth syllables in the twelve- and fourteen-syllable lines respectively are marked by commas. Thus Ps. 88 begins

> O lorde upon whose wyll,
>   dependeth my welfare:
> To call upon thy holy name,
>   since day nor night I spare.   (1549–50 edn)

Seagar adapted the 1549–50 text to make it fit his printed tune more easily:

O Lord up on whose ho ly wyll

De pen deth my wel fare:

To call up on thy ble ssed name

Since daye nor nyght   I   spare[136]

The stanza form accords with the length of the tune, and the metrical punctuation of the lyric corresponds with the rhythm of the tune (rests ▬ are used to indicate strong pauses at the end of each line, just as each new line begins with an upper-case letter). At the end of the stanza, the melodic decoration on the penultimate syllable slows the pace and emphasizes the sense of closure evident in the completion of the rhyme.

In order to accommodate this tune Seagar has had to supply two syllables to that part of Surrey's poulter's measure which forms the first line of each new stanza. Seagar consistently made up these lines with synonymous phrases, intensifiers and some additional explanatory phrases:

juste requeste   (Surrey, 1549–50 edn, line 3)

juste, & ryght request   (Seagar, 1553)

The dreade   (Surrey, 1549–50, line 39)

The feare so greate   (Seagar, 1553)

fleshe that fedeth wormes   (Surrey, 1549–50, line 23)

fleshe in earth, that feadeth wormes   (Seagar, 1553)

Occasionally one such change has led to another, as in lines 1 and 2 where the additional adjective in 'holy wyll' led Seagar to change Surrey's 'holy name' into 'blessed name' to avoid repetition. These changes add nothing to the meaning of Surrey's lines; they were required solely to provide a metrical form which could be easily associated with such psalm tunes.

A pattern of revision emerges showing that, besides changing the metre of the whole psalm, Seagar paid special attention to the most inventive parts of Surrey's personal meditation. For example, Seagar's psalmist, unlike Surrey's, was not cast headlong into a bottomless pit so that his enemies would be pleased:

> Oh lorde thou haste me caste,
>   headlonge to please my foo:
> Into a pytte all bottomeles,
>   wher as I playne my woo
>   (Surrey, 1949–50 edn, lines 9–10)

> Lorde *in thy wrath*, thou hast me cast
>   Into *the* pyt *of payne*:
> Wherin I *mourne, and* playne my wo
>   *That I byde and sustayne*   (Seagar, 1553: my italics)

Seagar's revision removed the personal implications of Surrey's imitation and reverted to a more literal paraphrase of the biblical verse 6, but Seagar is still closer to Surrey than to the Bible:

(Thou hast layed me in the lowest pytt, in a place of darcknesse and in the depe)   (Great Bible, Ps. 88:6)

He has reworked the substance of Surrey's lines and weakened their impression of pathos and bitterness. Both the emotive apostrophe 'Oh' and the specific reason given for the action of God have been omitted. Instead, Seagar has anticipated the sense of the next biblical verse by substituting a cause dependent on God's 'wrath', and elaborating on the description of the psalmist's situation. The last line of Seagar's stanza is redundant according to the sense of both models, but it is a metrical necessity for the sake of the tune. Seagar appears to have looked back at the biblical model and interpreted the sense of Coverdale's '*the* lowest pytt' as hell rather than imprisonment as Surrey had done in the context of verse 8: '. . . I am so fast in preson'.[137]

By contrast, Seagar's 'payne my harte' is no closer to the biblical psalm verse than Surrey's 'bayne my brest' (line 16). The change seems gratuitous except in so far as it helps to depersonalize the style of Surrey's psalm imitation which was linked to his paraphrase of Ecclesiastes 4 by the use of the same image: 'teares that bayned all ther brest'.[138]

This process of depersonalizing Surrey's meditation is best illustrated by the fate of lines 25–7 which form part of the central climax of his Ps. 88. Lines 25–6 were simply omitted by Seagar presumably because they were not derived from the biblical model. (Seagar's version is thus four lines shorter than might be expected from his usual method of treating Surrey's psalm.) In line 27 Seagar appears to have deliberately deflated the vigour of Surrey's expression in the course of expanding the line to fit the music:

> Nor blasted may thy name,
>   be by   (Surrey, 1549–50 edn)

> Thy name no prayse, can have at all
>   Even by   (Seagar, 1553)

The even quality of Seagar's line would have made it easier to sing than Surrey's. The form, sense and style of Surrey's psalm were revised consistently to make the model psalm public property, and to revise Surrey's imitation of the model in accordance with Seagar's and his contemporaries' expectations of psalms as holy songs.

Seagar's book also contains adaptations of two of Surrey's other psalms which had been printed by Case in 1549–50 as the work of Sternhold. However, Seagar evidently regarded them all as his own work since he began his verse dedication

> When I had these psalms finished
> And into Metre brought[139]

We would now call them plagiarized texts, but Seagar's claim could also indicate that he and his publisher, William Seres, regarded such metrical psalms, like their biblical models, as public property. Just as composers in their harmonized settings adapted the church tunes associated with Anglo-Genevan psalms – the musical *publica materies* – so Seagar in his holy songs adapted Surrey's private meditations on selected psalms.

All the metrical versions of psalms in the form of holy songs were intended to be sung. They were written in similar patterns of regular stanzaic verses – mainly in short, end-stopped lines of eight or six syllables. Such patterns were suitable for simple, repeated musical settings, and allowed different texts to be sung to the same tunes. Regularity and uniformity are important characteristics of these psalm paraphrases for singing. The aesthetic properties of many sixteenth-century holy-song psalms depend on their musical settings.

Musicke is as the more delicate meates, and as the finer apparell: not in deede necessary simply, but profitablie necessary for the cominesse of life[140]

Even simple melodies can transform the most ordinary of texts into stirring, affective songs: 'flat verse it reysth sublime'.

The immediate as well as the enduring popular success of many holy-song psalms depended to a considerable

degree on the suitability of their respective musical settings. Thomas Whythorne cited Augustine on the Psalms
which are said

> to bee framed bi meaziurz good, þe eazier to repeat
> so þat meaziurz being but meeterz, and meeterz rithms to bee
> it argiuz þat þe hol salter with miuzik doth agree[141]

In 1571 Whythorne published new harmonized settings to
some of his own metrical psalms and to prose texts by
Coverdale.[142] The music enhanced the appeal of the doctrine conveyed by the text. The two principal functions of
holy songs – recreation and instruction – were thus interdependent.

Luther and Coverdale had written their holy songs to
infuse the practices of contemporary church music with
popular-song traits, so that the people could sing them.
Calvin had recommended French metrical psalms to
'chacun qui désire se resjouir honnestement selon Dieu'.[143]
Later the holy-song vogue helped to stimulate the taste for
lyric more generally, and to a higher degree of musical
sophistication. In 1588 William Byrd, probably the most
outstanding English musician of his generation, published
*Psalmes, Sonets, & songs of sadnes and pietie made into Musicke
of five parts . . . for the recreation of all such as delight in Musicke*.[144] The lyrics of the first ten songs are psalm verses in
metre; the majority are new paraphrases to suit the new
music, but two are from the Anglo-Genevan psalter. Byrd
included 'Reasons briefely set downe by th'auctor to perswade every one to learne to sing'. Besides being beneficial
to health, Byrd notes that no instrumental music is 'comparable to that which is made of the voyces of Men' and
that 'The better the voyce is the meeter it is to honour and
serve God therewith'.[145] Such views help to explain why
guides to reading music and to singing were printed
among the preliminary matter to some editions of Anglo-
Genevan metrical psalms.[146]

The period contribution to generic expectations of
psalms was thus to emphasize traditional perceptions of the

inherent mode of procedure in the biblical Psalms. This had long been recognized as a certain kind of teaching in its most affective form, and was defined by thirteenth-century scholars as the lyric mode of praise and prayer (*modus laudis et orationis*).[147] Sixteenth-century commentators on the Psalms, such as Calvin, cited Augustine and their own experience in support of their view that 'le chant a grand force & vigueur d'esmouvoir & enflamber le coeur des hommes, pour invoquer & louer Dieu d'un zèle plus vehement & ardent'.[148] There could be no better nor more appropriate 'chansons' than psalms which acted like 'aiguillons pour nous inciter à *prier* & *louer* Dieu'.[149] This perception of their *modus laudis et orationis* was given form and substance in English in the 'holye songes of veritie'. After the impact of Sternhold and his followers the psalm was regarded primarily as a vernacular lyric.

5

'A HEAVENLY POESIE ... OF THAT LYRICALL KIND'

SIR PHILIP SIDNEY AND THE COUNTESS OF PEMBROKE 'SINGING THE PRAISES ... OF THAT GOD, WHO GIVETH US HANDS TO WRITE, AND WITS TO CONCEIVE'. PART ONE – SIR PHILIP SIDNEY

The achievement of the later sixteenth-century English psalmists was to regenerate their contemporaries' expectations of psalms as poetry, and to make English metrical psalms a suitable vehicle for contemporary devotional poetry. This was largely the work of one man, Sir Philip Sidney, aided by his sister Mary Herbert, Countess of Pembroke. Like earlier English psalmists, the Sidneys read and interpreted the Psalms with the help of several scholarly translations and commentaries; they also drew on the conventions established by the vernacular metrical psalmists of the previous generation in France as well as England. Sternhold had transposed the Psalms into popular lyrics which could be sung to common-measure tunes; Sidney's art reconstituted the inherent capacity of the Psalms as devotional poetry 'of that Lyricall kind', to move, teach and delight a sophisticated contemporary readership.[1] He was the first poet in English to seek to provide each psalm with a different verse form. Moreover, only two of the stanza forms of the forty-three psalms paraphrased by Sidney can be found in any of his other poetry. Sidney did not select psalms according to personal needs on any specific occasions in his life (as the prison psalmists, including Surrey, had done), nor according to any particular convention of personal devotion (as Wyatt had done in his version of the penitential psalms). Sidney, like Wyatt, exploited the biblical models disinterestedly.

The process of Sidney's poetic imitation was itself a mode of praise and prayer: 'a heavenly poesie'.[2] Sidney's imitation of the Psalms was a literary act of devotion. Both the devotional and literary elements of this act are represented in his version of Ps. 34:3

> Come then and join with me,
> Somewhat to speake of his due praise,
> Strive we that in some worthy phrase
> His Name may honourd be[3]

(O prayse the Lorde with me, and let us magnifie his name together) (Great Bible)

During the 1580s Sidney embarked on a complete psalter of extraordinary metrical virtuosity, but at his death in 1586 he had paraphrased only Psalms 1–43. The Countess of Pembroke completed her brother's project about 1594, working to principles of interpretation and by methods of imitation employed by Sidney and implicit in his forty-three psalms.[4]

Modern critical opinion has tended to disparage Sidney's literary activity as an imitator and therefore to regard his psalm paraphrases as early, experimental works.[5] According to Theodore Spencer, the 'intrinsic merit' of Sidney's psalms 'is small, for they almost never rise from the ground of ordinariness ... They are experiments in metrics and, in a smaller degree experiments in vocabulary'; Spencer argued that Sidney's 'creative energy' was indicated 'in a mechanical way' by his use of a wide range of different metres.[6] This view has been accepted by other critics. It was modified slightly by Hallett Smith who suggested that 'Sidney compiled what might be regarded as a School of English Versification', and in this form it seems to have dominated subsequent assessments of Sidney's psalms.[7]

Sidney's contemporaries had a different view; they

understood that paraphrase was a highly skilled process, and one best reserved for a well-learned man.[8] The duty of the humanist poet as a moral teacher, and the end to which he applied his art, was the exploitation of those works which he considered appropriate for the promotion of sound judgement. As biblical poetry, the Psalms had the capacity to promote spiritual values, wisdom and eloquence simultaneously. The art of the psalm imitator, like any other imitator, lay in transposing the poetic biblical models into decorous forms and language. It was, as Ascham had said, a matter of making 'a good choice, & right placing of wordes':

For all soch Authors, as be fullest of good matter and right judgement in doctrine, be likewise alwayes, most proper in wordes, most apte in sentence, most plaine and pure in uttering the same.[9]

Sidney's *Defence of Poesie* is probably the best guide to his intentions and his methods as an English metrical psalmist. The *Defence* implies that in striving to honour God's name 'in some worthy phrase' he was offering both praise, and thanks as a poet for 'the immortall goodnes of that God, who giveth us hands to write, and wits to conceive'. The 'worthy phrase' figuring forth 'that unspeakable and everlasting bewtie, to be seene by the eyes of the mind, onely cleared by faith' could be 'employed' with 'heavenly fruites, both private and publike, in singing the praises of ... God'.

For what else is the awaking his musical Instruments, the often and free chaunging of persons, his notable *Prosopopeias*, when he maketh you as it were see God comming in his majestie, his telling of the beasts joyfulnesse, and hils leaping, but a heavenly poesie ...? the holy *Davids* Psalms are a divine *Poeme*[10]

The *Defence* also testifies to Sidney's evaluation of David as a particular kind of poet. Of the three kinds of poet described

The chiefe both in antiquitie and excellencie, were they that did imitate the unconceiveable excellencies of God[11]

Sidney's view of David as a *vates* or prophet made him consider it his duty to respect and elucidate the original author's meaning, and to do so as an interpretative imitator. Sidney was imitating David, but David had imitated the 'unconceiveable excellencies of God'.[12]

Sidney had argued in the *Defence* that the function of poetry is 'the winning of the minde from wickednes to vertue'.[13] Like Scaliger he believed that 'the final end' of poetry, as of 'learning' or

This purifying of wit, this enriching of memorie, enabling of judgement, and enlarging of conceit, which commonly we cal learning . . . is, to lead and draw us to as high a perfection, as our degenerate soules made worse by their clay-lodgings, can be capable of[14]

The poet was regarded as a better teacher than the philosopher, because poetry has a peculiar power to mitigate the effects of man's 'infected wil' which keeps him from reaching to that perfection apprehended by his 'erected wit': the 'sweete delights of Poetrie' which have 'softened and sharpened' 'hard dull wittes' can move 'men to take that goodnesse in hand, which without delight they would flie as from a stranger'.[15] It was part of Sidney's purpose in his psalms to exploit this power:

as vertue is the most excellent resting place for al worldly learning to make his end of, so *Poetry* being the most familiar to teach it, and most Princely to move towards it, in the most excellent worke is the most excellent workeman[16]

An understanding and appreciation of Sidney's creative process in speaking alongside the psalmist, in particular his attention to detail and sifting of scholarly sources, indicates a more ambitious purpose than the creation of a mere 'School of English Versification'. Sidney's close and learned paraphrases of 'heavenly poesie' would have enhanced the effectiveness for him of the traditional dual functions of psalms as vehicles for devotion and for religious instruction. Sidney's imitations could have been employed whenever such vehicles were required; it was the Countess's view that the substance of the divine poem remained unchanged:

> That heaven's King may daigne his owne transform'd
> in substance no, but superficiall tire
> by thee put on[17]

Sidney's search for 'some worthy phrase' to further these ends, may be demonstrated by a close analysis of his process of imitation. He meditated on the texts of the Psalms 'weighing' them before he 'practised' them, as the Genevan translators of 1559[18] had urged, in order to ensure that he understood them. He studied attentively the meaning and the style of the texts, and for this purpose consulted and collated several translations, paraphrases and learned commentaries.[19] The search for 'some worthy phrase' required the exercise of the 'learned discretion' of a 'right poet'.[20]

Sidney's two main sources were Coverdale's Great Bible translation of the Psalms (as used with the Book of Common Prayer from 1549), and the Geneva Bible Psalms first published in 1559. The following example from Ps. 22 shows how closely Sidney spoke alongside these biblical models:

> Our Fathers still in thee their trust did beare,
> They trusted and by Thee deliverd were.
> They were set free when they upon Thee called,
> They hop'd on Thee, and they were not appalled.
> But I a worm, not I of mankind am,
> Nay shame of men, the people's scorning game.
> The lookers now at me poore wretch be mocking
> With mowes and nodds they stand about me flocking
> Let God help him (say they) whom he did trust;
> Let God save him, in whom was all his lust.
> And yet ev'en from the womb thy self did'st take me;
> At mother's breastes, thou didst good hope betake me
>
> (Ps. 22, lines 11–22)

> Our fathers trusted in thee:
> they trusted, and thou didest deliver them.
> They called upon thee, and were delivered:
> they trusted in thee, and were not confounded.

But I am a worme, & not a man:
a shame of men, and the contempt of the people.
All they that se me, have me in derision:
they make a mowe and nod the head, saying,
he trusted in the Lord, let him deliver him:
let him save him, seing he loveth him.
But thou didest drawe me out of the wombe:
thou gavest me hope, even at my mothers breasts
(Geneva Bible, Ps. 22:4–9)

But Sidney was not a slavish imitator of any single source. As he wrote, he selected images and phrases from among his different sources, exercising that sense of decorum, which he regarded as proper to a poet: that is, observing and respecting in an appropriate manner 'the dignitie of the subject'.[21] When interpreting divine prophecies Sidney exercised his 'learned discretion' as a poet even more carefully, perhaps, than when he ranged only 'within the Zodiack of his owne wit'[22] as a maker of secular fictions.

The detail of Sidney's discretion in selecting phrases from among his Calvinist sources may be seen in his imitation of Ps. 34:

> His Angels Armys round
> About them pitch who him do feare,
> And watch and ward for such do beare
> To keep them safe and sound.
>   I say but tast and see
>   How sweet how gracious is his grace
(Ps. 34, lines 25–30)

(The Angel of the Lord pitcheth rounde about them, that feare him, and delivereth them. Taste ye & se, how gracious the Lord is)
(Geneva Bible, Ps. 34:7–8)

The image of 'armies' and the specified taste of 'sweetness' in Sidney's imitation emphasizes the protective function of the angel's presence and so enhances the impact of the biblical image. Such additions are interpretative. The army image and the genitive plural in 'Angels Armys' were borrowed from either the Latin paraphrase 'angelorum copiis' by Beza or the English translation of this paraphrase by Anthony Gilby:

the Lord ... doth campe about them with the invincible armies of his Angels[23]

Sidney's phrase 'How sweet' was also influenced by Beza, and probably through Gilby's English translation: 'taste his most comfortable sweetnes'. However, the details of the function of the angels in Ps. 34:7 were most probably suggested by the marginal gloss to this verse in the Geneva Bible:

though gods power be sufficient to governe us, yet for mans infirmitie he appoynteth his angels to watch over us[24]

Sidney's phrase 'watch and ward' may have been taken from Golding's translation of Calvin's commentary: 'the Angelles keepe watch and ward about us'.[25] (This phrase and Sidney's own 'safe and sound' emphasize the meaning of the biblical verse, and preserve the style of the parallelism in traditional English two-stress alliterative phrases.) Sidney's use of the Genevan glosses may be seen more clearly in his imitation of Ps. 27:

> Though Father's Care, and Mother's love
> Abandond me   (lines 49–50)

The Geneva text is

Thogh my father and my mother shulde forsake me
(Ps. 27:10)

but the gloss in the margin reads

He magnifieth Gods love towards his, which farre passeth the most tender love of parents towards their children[26]

Sidney's paraphrase regenerates the meaning of the biblical verse by reference to the gloss which specifies those attributes of parenthood – care and love – which are to be compared with the love of God.

Sidney's choices from his different sources seem to have

been made in order 'that the truth may be the more palpable', and to have been guided by the principle recognized
in his *Defence*, that subtle arguments require familiar illustrations or they 'will by few be understood, and by fewer
graunted'.[27] Sidney often made the truth 'more palpable'
by extending images or themes in the biblical psalm
model. In his imitation of Ps. 18:5, for example, he introduced a striking simile:

> Like in a winding sheet, wretch I already lay
> All ready, ready to my snaring grave to go

(The sorowes of the grave have compassed me about: the snares of
death overtoke me)   (Geneva Bible)

This use of the winding sheet simile must have been suggested by Beza's paraphrase

Iacebam quodammodo fasciis sepulchralibus obligatus

and in particular by Gilby's translation:

I did lie as it were wrapped in my winding sheete, even snarled with
the snares of death[28]

The sense of the immediacy of an actual funeral, its
attendant emotion and finality were the result of Sidney's
imaginative regeneration of such sources. The pun on
'already' ('thus early' and 'all prepared') and the triple repetition of 'ready' are Sidney's contribution to the impact of
this verse. Sidney was thus not merely an editor of other
texts; he was seeking to create palpable effects on the
readers of his poetry.

The affective impact of his interpretative imitations was
also strengthened by the introduction into one psalm of
imagery borrowed from another, in order to re-reveal the
meaning of the psalmist. In his imitation of Ps. 26:9 for
example, Sidney adapted an image from the Genevan
translation of Ps. 40:7 ('in the rolle of the boke it is writen
of me'), adding a devotional apostrophe and alliteration for
emphasis. His

> Sweet lord, write not my soul
> Within the sinners' roll (Ps. 26, lines 28–9)

gives a greater sense of an urgent personal plea than the Genevan translation of this verse:

Gather not my soule with the sinners (Ps. 26:9)

Such details would seem to have been selected and deployed in this way for their capacity to 'strike, pearce [and] possesse, the sight of the soule' in order to communicate doctrine affectively according to the recognized *modus agendi* of the Psalms.[29] Moreover, the fact that readers familiar with the Psalms would have recognized the sources of such borrowed images, and thus been able to respond to Sidney's originality in adapting them to new contexts, would have further enhanced their impact.

Sidney's paraphrase of Ps. 6 provides a more extended opportunity to study his methods of imitating heavenly poesie of that lyrical kind. His main source text appears to have been Coverdale's translation from the Great Bible or the Prayer Book. Sidney's choice of 'displeasure' and 'beauty' are particularly reminiscent of this translation:

> Lord, let not me a worme by thee be shent,
>   While Thou art in the heat of thy displeasure:
> Ne let thy rage, of my due punishment
>   Become the measure (Sidney, Ps. 6, lines 1–4)

(O Lorde rebuke me not in thy indignacyon: neyther chasten me in thy dyspleasure) (Great Bible, Ps. 6:1)

> Woe, lyke a moth, my face's beauty eates
>   And age pull'd on with paines all freshness fretteth:
> The while a swarm of foes with vexing feates
>   My life besetteth (Sidney, Ps. 6, lines 21–4)

(My bewtie is gone for very trouble, & worne awaye because of all myne enemyes) (Great Bible, Ps. 6:7)

However, the images of the worm and the moth in lines 1 and 21 of Sidney's imitation appear to have been borrowed from other psalms. Once again the starting point for Sidney's imaginative interpretation may be seen in the Geneva Bible marginal gloss:

myne eye is eaten as it were with wormes[30]

The term moth comes from Ps. 39:11 which echoes the theme and diction of Ps. 6

when thou with rebukes doest chastise man for iniquitie, thou as a moth makest his beautie to consume[31]   (Geneva Bible, Ps. 39:11)

Beza's prose paraphrase of Ps. 6 was a likely source for Sidney's

> Woe ... my face's beauty eates
>   And age pull'd on with paines all freshness fretteth
>   (Ps. 6, lines 21–2)

and the English translation by Gilby,

Sorowe doth consume my face, I waxe wrinkled and old[32]
                                            (Beza, Ps. 6:7)

could have suggested not only the idea of aging (with the effect of wrinkles understood in Sidney's image of the fretted freshness of youth) but also Sidney's choice of language. 'Woe' was probably derived from Gilby's 'sorowe'. Sidney's 'my face's beauty' combined Gilby's 'my face' with Coverdale's 'my bewtie'. The moth simile is fully integrated into Sidney's imitation of Ps. 6, and seems germane to the context of a night scene established in his previous stanza:

> Lo, I am tir'd, while still I sigh and groane:
>   My moystned bed proofes of my sorrow showeth:
>   My bed, while I with black night mourn alone
>   With my tears floweth   (lines 17–20)

The subsequent image of 'a swarm of foes' in Sidney's line 23 also supports the simile borrowed from Ps. 39 because it is an apt metaphorical echo of the two ideas of the insect and destruction. The realistic and horrifying image of the eaten face would have had a special affective power for an

Elizabethan reader. But, because the poet's imagination has imposed itself on the available material by introducing images borrowed from other psalms, the total substance of the 'divine Poeme' remains unaltered.

The affective qualities of Sidney's imitation are not confined to his exploitation of metaphor. The level of emotional intensity is raised and sustained in various subtle ways. The first half of Sidney's Ps. 6 emphasizes the penitent psalmist's personal supplications by the use of repeated apostrophes and imperatives:

> But mercy, lord, let Mercy thyne descend
> For I am weake, and in my weakness languish;
> Lord help, for ev'en my bones their marrow spend
>   With cruel anguish.
>
> Nay ev'n my soul fell troubles do appall;
>   Alas, how long, my God, wilt Thou delay me?
> Turne Thee, sweet lord, and from this Ougly fall
>   My Deare God stay me.
>
> Mercy, O Mercy lord, for Mercy's sake,
>   For death doth kill the Witness of thy glory;
> Can of thy prayse the tongues entombed make
>   A heavnly story?   (lines 5–16)

Line 13 echoes line 5 with its repetitions of 'mercy' as a plea for pity, and for the protection of 'mercy' as an attribute of God. The insistent cries for mercy and help become more pathetic and emotional in the almost flattering, personal appeals 'sweet lord' and 'My Deare God'. The affective quality of these desperate pleas ('for Mercy's sake') is quite different from Coverdale's translation 'for thy mercyes sake' (Ps. 6:4). It is even different from the tone of Sidney's line 1

> Lord, let not me a worme by thee be shent

where the reader is distanced from the psalmist by the unattractive image of the worm, and perhaps also by the literary archaism 'shent'.[33] When these details are compared with the impersonal formality of 'thy displeasure', 'the measure' 'of my due punishment' (in lines 1 to 4), the poetic movement within Sidney's poem may be seen to be towards a greater emotional intensity in the depiction of the psalmist's predicament, and thus a stronger appeal to the reader's will.

Sidney's treatment of verse 5,

> For death doth kill the Witness of thy glory;
> Can of thy prayse the tongues entombed make
>   A heavnly story?   (lines 14–16)

preserves the structure of the biblical verse: the assertion of an argument for mercy, followed by a rhetorical question. But in this verse Sidney's 'learned discretion' in assimilating and transforming his sources was also matched by his 'undeceiving skill'[34] in regenerating the biblical model by a more inventive process of imitation. Death is personified, and the image of 'tongues' is used by Sidney to represent man by his unique capacity for speech, which enables him to praise God.[35] The image of 'tongues entombed' is vivid, complex and emotionally resonant; it is therefore more striking and more memorable than the simple statement in Coverdale's translation for example:

For in death no man remembreth the: and who wyll geve the thankes in the pyt?   (Great Bible, Ps. 6:5)

Sidney also introduced the emotive word 'kill' (in spite of the effect of tautology), and increased its impact by placing it after dulling, alliterative repetition in 'death doth'. (His use of the phrase 'witness of thy glory' echoes Cranmer's use of 'witness' as a martyr (or, one who testifies for Christ by death) in the Prayer Book collects.) By contrast, the tone of the last verse is softened, and the reader's attention is drawn to God's gentleness in response to the psalmist's pleas:

> The lord my suite did heare, and gently heare,
>   They shall be sham'd and vext, that breed my crying,
>   And turn their backs, and strait on backs appeare
>   Their shamefull flying   (lines 29–32)

Nevertheless, Sidney's imitation maintains the sense of Coverdale's translation which was also adopted by the translators of the Geneva Bible,

All myne enemyes shalbe confounded and soore vext: they shalbe turned backe and put to shame, sodenly   (Ps. 6:10)

In Sidney's paraphrase, however, the psalmist's enemies 'turn their backs' (instead of being turned back as in the literal translation), which simultaneously signifies their shame and their intention to retreat.

Such deft details and the small-scale adaptations and borrowings in this psalm may be seen to have evolved from Sidney's imaginative meditation on the psalm in his study of several sources, and from a sensitive appraisal of the psalmist's art or 'poesie'. In this and many of his other psalms Sidney's process of imitation exploited the similarity and continuity-in-change between normative devotional models and well-established literary traditions of imitating these model texts.

The range of different metres and verse forms in Sidney's psalms, and the display of an occasionally inventive verbal wit, could be regarded as an exception to his preference for interpretative methods. But these features are also part of his process of imitating source texts, and characteristic of his usual methods as a poet-interpreter, or 'vates'.

Although no one had been able to discover in which metres the Psalms might have been written, the 'knowledge' that they were somehow metrical seems to have allowed a free choice of metres and verse forms.[36] It would seem that Sidney had welcomed this licence to introduce variety of form as a way of making a personal, but also responsible, contribution to his imitation of 'heavenly poesie'. There were few poets who could match Sidney's dexterity and poise in handling English verse, or meet his requirement of

peasing each sillable of eache word by just proportion, according to the dignitie of the subject[37]

The exceptional range of different metrical forms in Sidney's psalms may have been a reaction to the simpler, old-fashioned ballad metres typical of holy songs in general and of the Anglo-Genevan psalter in particular.[38] Although Sidney's psalms are mainly in accentual iambics, he did not use the common measure of holy songs.[39] However, precedents for metrical variety in psalm paraphrases were to be found in some of his sources. Beza's *Psalmorum Davidis ... latina paraphrasi illustrati, ac etiam vario carminum genere latine expressi* (1580) was modelled on Buchanan's Latin verse paraphrases.[40] Moreover, Marot had used a wide range of French verse forms and some of these were adopted by Sidney and the Countess.[41]

Another explanation of Sidney's metrical ingenuity is that, encouraged by such precedents, he exercised his own skill and sense of literary decorum to provide an expressive complement 'according to the dignitie of the subject': a variety of forms to match the range of themes and styles recognized in the Psalms. French neo-Latin poets connected with Sidney's circle realized that one type of verse did not suit all kinds of psalm.

And so since I should judge that not all shoes were appropriate for all feet, I would also reckon that so great a number of diverse themes of psalms could not be treated appropriately in one kind of metre (*carminis*): and that it would be much more appropriate if they were represented in various kinds of metrical odes

(itaque cum iudicarem non omni pedi omnem calceum aptum esse, existimabam quoque non uno carminis genere tot tamque diversa psalmorum argumenta commode tractari posse: multoque fore commodius, si variis odarum generibus describerentur)[42]

Sixteenth-century English commentators on the Psalms, such as Sidney's associate Arthur Golding, had also shown themselves well aware of the relationship in the Psalms between their expressive styles, form and content. Golding wrote in his dedication of Calvin's commentaries on the Psalms:

And forasmuche as it consisteth cheefly of prayer and thanksgiving, or . . . of invocation . . . and requireth rather an earnest and devout lifting up of the minde, than a loud or curious utterance of the voice: there be many unperfect sentences, many broken speeches, and many displaced words: according as the voice of the partie that prayed, was eyther prevented with the swiftnesse of his thoughtes, or interrupted with vehemency of joy or greef, or forced to surcease through infirmitie[43]

Sidney's tactical application of formal ingenuity can be seen in the following examples from his paraphrase of Ps. 13. His choice of verse form was influenced partly by this psalm's theme of an individual's affliction expressed in 'broken speeches', and partly by Coverdale's phrasing of the first verse in the Great Bible translation. The length and rhythm of Sidney's first stanza, for example,

> How long, O Lord, shall I forgotten be?
> What? ever?
> How long wilt Thou Thy hidden face from me
> Dissever?   (Ps. 13, lines 1–4)

was suggested by Coverdale's prose:

Howe longe wylt thou forget me O Lord? for ever?
How longe wilt thou hyde thy face fro me?

There are several small but crucial changes to the biblical model in Sidney's paraphrase. First, he dissected the opening question by advancing the position of the first important apostrophe. Thus the exclamations or 'broken speeches' of lines 1 and 2 suggest the psalmist's 'vehemency of . . . greef'. Secondly, the rhyming pronouns 'I' and 'Thy' draw attention to the theme of the psalmist's personal relationship with God. Thirdly, Sidney changed the mood of the verb in the first question, thereby making the psalmist's situation central, and implying that the psalmist is passive and must wait for God to bestow mercy on him. The second half of Sidney's synonymous parallelism stresses the active power of God, which is an important theme of the biblical psalm. The repeated second person pronouns of line 3 both have strong stresses, since the iambic metre causes stress to fall on 'Thou', and the internal rhyme with 'I' (in line 1) emphasizes 'Thy'. The sense of this line is thus dominated by the references to God. Sidney's verb 'Dissever', which has considerably more emotive force than the passive implications of 'hyde' in Coverdale's translation, lends the psalmist's alienation from God a physical dimension which complements the biblical anthropomorphism. 'Dissever' not only implies violent action it also looks and sounds emphatic: it comprises a line of verse in itself, and its delayed final position in the sentence implies that it has been anticipated by the reader's syntactical expectations.

Throughout his Ps. 13, Sidney's five two-part stanzas imitate the 'substance' of the five biblical verses. In the second stanza,

> How long shall I consult with carefull sprite
>   In anguish?
> How long shall I with foes' triumphant might
>   Thus languish?   (lines 5–8)

(Howe longe shall I seke councell in my soule? & be so vexed in myne hert? how longe shall myne enemye triumphe over me?)
(Great Bible, Ps. 13:2)

the emphasis is on the psalmist's affliction rather than his enemy's active triumph, and the length of the first part of the biblical verse has been cut in order to maintain a 'biblical' parallel structure in grammatical form, rhythm and rhyme. The short-line rhymes are virtually self-rhymes, and Sidney used them to reiterate the idea of the psalmist's passive suffering; this idea is developed at the climax of the psalm where Sidney's paraphrase follows the form of the biblical verses with three imperatives:

> Behold me, lord, let to Thy hearing creep
>   My crying:
> Nay give me eyes, and light, least that I sleep
>   In dying   (lines 9–12)

(Beholde, & heare me, O Lord my God: lighten myne eyes, that I slepe not in death)
(Geneva Bible, Ps. 13:3)

The imperative 'heare me' in verse 3 is expanded to take on the character of a suppliant's humble plea: let my crying creep to thy hearing. The biblical parallels, between sight and sound and between God and the psalmist, have also been extended, but in a different direction from the biblical text. Having appealed to God to see and hear him, Sidney's psalmist changes his mind (as if 'prevented with the swift-nesse of his thoughtes') and asks instead for 'eyes, and light' or the means to perceive, and perception, so that he might not sleep in dying, but, by implication perhaps, so that he might wake to glory.[44] The verbs denoting the psalmist's action (and passivity), 'creep' and 'sleep', are also emphasized by their final positions and by rhyme. In stanza 4 Sidney preserved the dominance of the psalmist's voice by changing the direct speech of the 'Foe' to an in-direct form:

> Least my Foe bragg, that in my ruin hee
>   Prevailed,
> And at my fall they joy that, troublous, me
>   Assailed   (lines 13–16)

(Lest myne enemye saye: I have prevayled agaynst him: for yf I be cast downe, they that trouble me will rejoyse at it)
                                            (Great Bible, Ps. 13:4)

Sidney's verb 'bragg' offsets the consequent loss of energy in the foe's reported speech. The conclusion of Sidney's divine poem is a sudden anti-climax or reversal:

> No, No I trust on thee, and joy in Thy
>   Great Pity.
> Still therfore of Thy Graces shall be my
>   Song's Ditty   (lines 17–20)

(But I trust in thy mercie: mine heart shal rejoyce in thy salvacion: I wil sing to the Lord, because he hathe delt lovingly with me)
                                            (Geneva Bible, Ps. 13:5)

None of Sidney's known sources concludes this psalm with such a dramatic emotional outburst. But the style of this sudden shift of position is reminiscent of some of Sidney's final lines from secular love sonnets.[45] The last line of Sidney's psalm identifies the psalmist as a poet of that lyrical kind, and, as Louis Martz has suggested, there is 'perhaps a touch of the art of sacred parody in the use of a favorite lover's rime'.[46]

The other inventive quality of expression used by Sidney is verbal wit. Sidney's humanist literary training and Protestant principles would have led him to respect the meaning and the style of the primary biblical sources more than those of the other sources. Even where Sidney appears to have been 'faining notable images'[47] he was often responding to a word or suggestion implicit in these biblical sources. In Sidney's imitation of Ps. 22 the psalmist is brought by God's 'power'

> Unto the dust of my death's running hower
> (Ps. 22, line 38)

Coverdale's Great Bible and the Genevan translation supplied 'the dust of death' (Ps. 22:15), but the image of the hour glass here is Sidney's invention. It is a traditional concept, and also a powerful metaphorical 'translation'[48] of the theme of man's mortality. The effect of the visual image is to conflate the dust of man's death with the sands of time slipping through the glass; but even this action may have been suggested to Sidney by the parallelism in the previous psalm verse:

I am *powred out* lyke water, & all my bones are out of joynt, my hert also in the middest of my body is even lyke *meltynge* waxe
(Great Bible, Ps. 22:14; my italics)

In Ps. 25 Sidney paraphrased the Genevan translation of verse 7

Remember not the sinnes of my youth, nor my rebellions

as

> But Lord remember not
>   Sins brew'd in youthfull glass,
> Nor my Rebellious blott,
>   Since my youth and they do passe
> (Ps. 25, lines 25–8)

Sidney's psalmist implies, perhaps, that such sins are only a weak brew, more innocuous when in a youthful glass (which has still the sands of time to run into it) than the heinous offences of a seasoned sinner. The association of sins with stains or 'blotts' is also traditional. The psalmist's excuse, 'Since youth and [sins] do passe', is logical, but perhaps irrelevant, thus the poet's pun on 'Sins' and 'Since' may be an ironic qualification of the psalmist's excuse. The parallels of sound match the parallels in verse structure. Later in this psalm Sidney contrasted the psalmist's 'Rebellious blott' with God's 'spotless verity' (Ps. 25, line 39).

Sidney's imitation of Ps. 28:3 contains further examples of his inventive, imaginative responses to words and ideas in the source texts:

> Link not me in self same chain
>   With the wicked working folk
>   Who, their spotted thoughts to cloak,
>   Neighbors friendly entertain
>   When in hearts they malice meane   (lines 11–15)

(Drawe me not awaie with the wicked, and with the workers of iniquitie: which speake friendly to their neighbours, when malice is in their hearts)   (Geneva Bible, Ps. 28:3)

The chain image may have developed from an association with the verb 'drawe ... awaie' in the Geneva Bible, and from the idea of being joined to the wicked who will be punished. The 'spotted thoughts' of deceit are to be understood in the context of Sidney's interpretations, as the antithesis of 'spotless verity', in Ps. 25, line 39, for example. The terseness of Sidney's style in phrases like 'wicked working folk' and 'Neighbors friendly entertain' is an imitation of the biblical poetic style comparable with his use of parallelisms.[49]

Elsewhere in his psalms Sidney demonstrates his ability to suggest the language of direct speech, and, where appropriate, to translate biblical idioms into contemporary English. Sidney's line

> Aha! Sir, now we see you where we should
>   (Ps. 35, line 54)

conveys the pride and scorn of the psalmist's enemies more dramatically than either Coverdale's 'Fye on thee' or the Genevan translators'

Aha, aha, our eye hathe sene   (Ps. 35:21)

Further examples of his ability to construct vivid English interpretations of Hebraic idioms occur in his versions of Ps. 41:9 and Ps. 10:4 and 11:

> O yea, my Friend to whom I did impart
>   The secrets of my heart,
> My Friend I say, who at my table sate,
>   Did kick against my state   (Ps. 41, lines 29–32)

(Yea, my familiar friend, whome I trusted, which did eat of my bread, hathe lifted up the hele against me) (Geneva Bible, Ps. 41:9)

Sidney's repetition of 'my friend' in line 31 emphasizes the pathos and irony implicit in its use in line 29. His exact parallelism intensifies the bitterness of the psalmist whose trust and hospitality have been betrayed, and whose judgement has thereby been proved faulty. Sidney's style successfully blends the Hebraic and the English: he not only emphasized the parallel structure of the verse but also translated the Hebraic idiom 'eat of my bread' into an appropriate modern idiom: 'sat at my table'. The Geneva Bible depicts the action of the false friend, somewhat euphemistically, as lifting up the heel; in Sidney's imitation the verb 'kick' is direct, forceful and therefore appropriate for the violent, physical action it denotes. Sidney draws out the meaning of the psalmist, and manages to communicate his sense of hurt at this disloyalty.

In Sidney's Ps. 10 the crafty, wicked man who 'plagues the poore the most he can' and thrives, saying defiantly 'in his bragging heart, This gotten bliss shall never part', also

> rather much . . . fancys this
> That Name of God a fable is   (lines 15–16)

He assumes that God's sight

> now hoodwinkt is,
> He leasure wants to mark all this   (lines 47–8)

(God . . . hideth awaie his face & wil never se)

(Geneva Bible, Ps. 10:11)

Sidney's choice of the word 'hoodwinkt' brings an irreverent, colloquial tone to the speech of the blasphemer who derides fables (and, by implication, poetry) in the same breath as he proclaims his atheism.

Sidney's use of the French metrical psalter by Marot and Beza enables us to compare their different treatments of the same psalms, and hence to identify the differences between the literary personalities reflected in their work. In his version of Ps. 38 Sidney imitated Marot's verse form, and a detailed comparison of the two versions indicates that Sidney must have had the French text in front of him as he wrote. Moreover, the textual interpretations and stylistic features of Marot's psalm, which Sidney rejected in the course of preparing his own version, help us to identify the personal qualities of Sidney's expression, his sensibilities and *mentis character*.

In spite of the general influence of the French version on the form of his imitation, Sidney's psalm follows the sense of the English Bibles closely. The Genevan translation of verse 1,

O Lord, rebuke me not in thine angre, nether chastise me in thy wrath

and Coverdale's translation of verse 2,

For thyne arowes styck fast in me, and thy hande presseth me sore

provided the matter of Sidney's opening:

> Lord while that thy rage doth bide,
>   Do not chide
> Nor in anger chastise me;
> For thy shafts have pierc't me sore,
>   And yet more,
> Still Thy hands upon me be   (Ps. 38, lines 1–6)

Perhaps 'shafts' seemed a more 'poetical' word than arrows, but Sidney's phrase 'pierc't me sore' was probably suggested by a combination of Coverdale's phrase 'press-eth me sore' and the parallel situation, 'styck fast'. Each symmetrical half of the stanza corresponds to one biblical verse, and in this stanza Sidney has even managed to imitate and 'figure forth' the comparable binary structure of the parallelism in each of the biblical verses. Sidney has thus made a genuine attempt to correlate form and style in his psalm, and to imitate the style of the biblical models, which is evident in his usual English source translations.

By contrast Marot had allowed a complete stanza for each biblical verse; his version of Ps. 38 is thus twice the length of Sidney's:

> Las! en ta fureur aigue
>   Ne m'argue
> De mon faict, Dieu tout-puissant:
> Ton ardeur un peu retire,
>   N'en ton ire
> Ne me puni languissant.
>
> Car tes fleches descochées
>   Sont fichées
> Bien fort en moy, sans mentir:
> Et as voulu, dont j'endure,
>   Ta main dure
> Dessus moy appesantir[50] (Marot, Ps. 38, lines 1–12)

Although 'sans mentir', for example, is mere padding, most of the details added by Marot (like 'aigue', 'mon faict', 'tout-puissant', 'ardeur un peu retire', 'languissant' in stanza 1), are relevant amplifications of the sense of the two biblical verses. Marot's additions obscure the poetic form of the original: line 4 is redundant; and the triple parallelism 'fureur', 'ardeur', 'ire' (in stanza 1) distorts the formal balance between the two verses. The effect of Marot's inflated style is to exaggerate the psalmist's distress ('languissant') by indecorously aggravating and personalizing God's reaction ('tout-puissant', 'as voulu, dont j'endure').

Sidney's sensibilities did not allow him to respond to this elaborate and inventive method (which had led Marot to imply a criticism of God in line 10), nor to Marot's comparatively indulgent style. In verse 5 Marot had lingered with gory detail on the psalmist's suffering:

> Mes cicatrices puantes
>   Sont fluantes
> De sang de corruption.
> Las, par ma folle sottie
>   M'est sortie
> Toute ceste infection[51]   (lines 25–30)

Sidney's interpretation of the same verse,

> My wounds putrify and stink,
>   In the sinck
> Of my filthy folly lai'd   (lines 13–15)

preserves the terse style and substance of the literal biblical translation. Sidney followed his usual practice of selecting words from the English Bibles and combining them with his own ideas for the sake of more affective expression. In Coverdale's translation the psalmist's 'woundes styncke', in the Geneva Bible they are 'putrified', and in both translations this condition is attributed to the psalmist's 'folyshnesse'. Sidney incorporated this idea of foolishness into a new metaphor: a sink of filth. In his interpretation the psalmist's wounds thus putrify and stink because they have been physically 'lai'd' in 'the sinck of ... filthy folly'. Sidney's idea coheres logically and poetically, with reinforcement from the sound play in 'putrify', 'stinck', 'in', 'sinck', 'filthy', thus impressing the reader's mind and ear simultaneously.

However, Sidney must still have had Marot's psalm before him, and in his interpretation of verse 6 Sidney did not disdain the French paraphrase:

> Tant me fait mon mal la guerre,
>   Que vers terre
> Suis courbé totalement:
> Avec triste & noire mine
>   Je chemine
> Tout en pleurs journellement   (lines 31–6)

> Earthly I do bow and crooke,
>   With a look
> Still in mourning chear arayd   (lines 16–18)

Under the influence of the French, Sidney displayed his own inventive verbal wit and English, Protestant sensibilities. (The Geneva Bible translation of Ps. 38:6 is 'I am bowed, and croked very sore: I go mourning all the daye.') Marot had enlarged on the pathos of the psalmist's situation 'courbé vers terre avec triste et noire mine'. Sidney combined the essential diction of the literal English translation: 'bowed and croked ... mourning' with two ideas borrowed from Marot's extended paraphrase, which gave him the opportunity for significant witty effects. Sidney's 'Earthly' in line 16 must have evolved from Marot's 'vers terre' (line 32), and so means 'towards the ground'. However, 'earthly' is also proper for mankind or Adam's 'clayey race'.[52] The psalmist is depressed because he is mortal and frail: under the influence of his 'degenerate soules clay-lodgings'[53] he has been drawn into 'filthy folly'. (Calvin, who was described as 'well practized and tryed in the affaires and troubles of this world', mentions 'lustes' of the flesh in his commentary on this and the previous verse.)[54] Sidney's oxymoron 'mourning *chear*' combines the literal sense of the biblical verse with Marot's image 'triste et noire *mine*'. Verbal wit is also evident in Sidney's paraphrase of verse 7

> In my reines hot torment raignes,
>   There remains
> Nothing in my body sound   (lines 19–21)

The Geneva Bible supplied the source of Sidney's punning figure in 'reines' and the sense of heat in 'burning':

For my reines are ful of burning, & there is nothing sounde in my flesh

Marot's psalm provided 'tourmenté' (in line 39). But it was Sidney's sixteenth-century English sense of verbal wit which led him to combine these component details, and to exploit the sound play, in 'reines . . . raignes . . . remains'.

The inventive qualities of Sidney's expression are more evident in the second half of his Ps. 38 where he allowed himself more freedom to adapt the language of the English prose translations. With one exception, he also apparently stopped looking at Marot's psalm; Sidney probably wrote 'I attend' in imitation of the French 'j'attends'.[55] In his interpretation of verses 13 and 14 Sidney has imitated the style of the biblical parallelism, but not the actual words or phrasing of the English Bibles:

> But I like a man become,
>   Deaf and dumb,
> Little hearing, speaking lesse;
> I ev'en as such kind of wight,
>   Senseles quite,
> Word with word do not represse   (lines 37–42)

(But I as a deafe man heard not, and am as a dumme man, which openeth not his mouth. Thus am I as a man, that heareth not, & in whose mouth are no reprofes)   (Geneva Bible, Ps. 38:13–14)

Sidney's interpretation compresses the biblical model by deleting the repetition of 'man', 'mouth' and the forms of 'hear', but the consequent need (in line 40) to refer back to the previous verse results in the clumsy phrase 'such kind of wight'. Nevertheless Sidney has imitated the emphatic parallelism between the physical senses in verse 13 ('deaf . . . hearing', 'dumb . . . speaking') (lines 38–9) and the conceptual parallelism ('Deaf and dumb', 'senseless quite') in the two interdependent verses. Thus the psalmist does not argue or 'represse' in the sense of oppose 'Word with word' because he remains insensible to his enemies, described in Sidney's paraphrase of verse 12 as,

> Speaking ev'ill, thinking deceit   (line 36)

In his paraphrase of verse 17 Sidney followed the sense of the Genevan translation, but borrowed and transformed the image of a repressive neighbour from Coverdale's translation of verse 11:

> Sure I do but halting go,
> And my woe
> Still my orethwart neighbour is
>
> (Sidney, Ps. 38, lines 49–51)

(My lovers and my neyghbours dyd stande lokynge upon my trouble) (Great Bible, Ps. 38:11)

(Surely I am ready to halte, and my sorow is ever before me) (Geneva Bible, Ps. 38:17)

Instead of being deserted by friends and neighbours who ought to have been supportive, Sidney's psalmist is accompanied by his sorrow imagined as a repressive neighbour. Sidney's metaphor makes the continued presence of the abstraction more poignant and vivid. It is yet another instance of the poet's 'undeceiving skill' in 'heavenly poesie': imitating or figuring forth 'the generall notion with the particuler example' for the sake of more affective expression.[56]

An examination of Sidney's methods provides evidence of his careful study of a range of scholarly and literary sources, and of his personal integrity as an interpreter, critic and poet in combining them in his own imitations. The inventive qualities of his imitations were deployed with tact and discrimination. For example, without compromising the integrity of what he believed to be the psalmist's meaning and style, he extended the imagery of the model and borrowed images from other psalms always in search of the 'worthy phrase'.

The style of his psalms shows his respect for the biblical models. He was not only diligent in expressing his notion of the author's meaning but also in 'a certaine resembling and shadowing out of the forme of his style and the maner of his speaking'.[57] Yet the manner of speaking is also distinctively Sidney's own: he deployed his talent as a poet in English with evocative imagery, serious, witty word play and a unique command of metrical forms. By comparison the uniformity and simplicity characteristic of holy-song lyrics make their expressions of *publica materies* essentially anonymous.

The variety of forms in Sidney's psalms would not have inhibited their musical performance. The fundamental beat, the 'tactus' or 'pulse' of a piece of music provided a constant pattern, analogous to the formal framework of metre in a verse text, but the number of notes placed against this pulse in a song varied according to the rhythm of the text.[58] Since the metres and stanza forms of about a third of Sidney's psalms derive from those in the French metrical psalter, the tunes associated with these French psalms could easily have been adapted to Sidney's corresponding English texts.[59] By contrast with airs and consort songs set to harmonized instrumental settings, or with the contrapuntal vocal settings of madrigals, the convention in writing tunes (or melodic rhythms) for metrical psalms was to set one note to each syllable. In general, contemporary practice allowed considerable flexibility of accent or stress: the basic pulse of the music and metrical pattern of the lyric may be 'punctuated' by a variety of rhythmic features; these include the stress and intonation patterns of the language, its pauses, or control of speed and emphasis.[60] Metrical form is ultimately founded on such features; however metrical form is constituted and recognized, the constancy of a pulse ensures that there is, for example, no inherent difficulty in singing an English lyric, such as Sidney's Ps. 38 written in accentual trochaics, to music for Marot's French version of Ps. 38 written in quantitative trochaics.

Although Sidney is not known to have been a practical musician, he is known to have enjoyed music, and to have recommended that his 'songs' should be sung.[61] This is important because for Sidney and his contemporaries the terms 'poem' and 'song' could be synonymous in certain circumstances. According to Sidney's argument in the *Defence* the Book of Psalms is a divine poem because, as he believed, 'even the name of Psalmes ... being interpreted, is nothing but Songs'.[62] The same words: songs, *carmina*, *numeri*, were applied to music and to verse since they were both metrical. If a song is sung however then a tune is provided to accompany the lyric. Virtually any text may be sung. Nevertheless, in Sidney's collection of miscellaneous poems, 'Certaine Sonnets', there is ample evidence that he was capable of contrafaction: writing new lyrics (with complex verse forms) according to the pulse of existing tunes.[63] Sidney's 'The fire to see my wrongs for anger burneth' and 'The Nightingale, as soone as Aprill bringeth' (sonnets 3 and 4) were both written 'To the tune of *Non credo gia che piu infelice amante*' which Frank Fabry associated with a text and musical setting in a Winchester manuscript collection of Italian villanelles and early madrigals (*c.* 1566).[64] However, in each of the cases where Sidney has written new lyrics to fit either these Italian *poesia per musica* models, or the French psalm tunes (of about the same date), the exercise would not have required specialist musical skill: as John Stevens has indicated, it required syllable counting, metrical organization and rhythmic shaping; Sidney was highly adept at such exercises.

The French tune for Beza's trochaic metre in Ps. 42 is regarded as one of the best; it was composed later than the text (although the text was subsequently revised in part).[65] Sidney used the same formal scheme for his version of Ps. 42; this psalm thus provides an excellent opportunity to study the effects of an appropriate setting for Sidney's text.

Ps. 42, Beza (Geneva, 1551) & Sidney

179

3   Ainsi mon âme altérée
     ...   coeur qui souspire [1562]
     So my soul in panting playeth,

4   Seigneur Dieu de tes ruisseaux
     ...   a-près [1562]
     Thirsting on my God to look.

5   Va toujours criant, suyvant
     My soul thirsts indeed in me

6   Le grand, le grand Dieu vivant.
     After   ever   living thee;

7   Helas   donques   quand sera - ce
     Ah, when comes my blessed being,

8   Que verray de Dieu la face
     Of Thy face to have a seing?

[*] 1565: ♩ ♩ for ♩ ♩ (1551 etc.)

As in the majority of holy songs only two note values are used throughout this sixty-note tune which would have to be repeated six times in order to sing the seven stanzas of both the French and English psalms. Even in this first stanza there is no sustained attempt at a mimetic relation-ship between the words and music, although several opportunities might have suggested themselves. In line 2 the printed rhythm for 'Poūrchăssānt' (♩ ♩ ♩) takes no account of the lively potential in the sense of the verb of motion, and the same musical phrase is repeated in line 4 with the textual underlay 'Sēignēur Diēu' where the syl-labic weight is at least better distributed (cf. Sidney's

'Seēkiňg sōme ♩♩♩). In line 7 the exclamation 'Hélas' (♩♩) (cf. Sidney's 'āh, whěn') is represented melodically by an upward interval of a third. The final melodic interval of the tune is printed as a rising semi-tone which in the first stanza at least, reflects the intonation pattern for a question. The best indication of the matching of musical and textual form in this stanza is the use of the repeat to represent the parallel between the panting hart (in lines 1–2) and the thirsting psalmist (in lines 3–4).

Without the exercise of considerable flexibility in performance the regular twelve-beat melodic line of this psalm cannot match the subtlety of Sidney's variety of expressive speech rhythms. The addition of these dignified but plain, slow-tempo tunes and their constant repetition stanza by stanza, tends to obscure the sense, and to depress the lively variety of Sidney's verbal expression.

It is unlikely that Sidney used the music of the French psalter except in so far as it followed the formal framework of line length and stanza structure in the French verse texts.[66]

Moreover, since only about a third of his psalms use the metres and stanza forms of the French psalter, if Sidney's psalms were intended to be sung, the French tunes would only be appropriate for a third of his texts. By contrast with his imitations of Italian and other literary lyrics in 'Certaine Sonnets', Sidney's imitation of the verse forms of the French psalter does not suggest a serious attempt at contrafaction.

In the case of most songs for which settings survive, however, musical settings were composed for existing lyrics. (William Byrd's *Songs of sundrie natures ... lately made and composed* (1589) for example, contains a lyric first published without music in *The Paradyse of daynty devises* (1576)[67] as well as Sidney's tenth song from *Astrophil and Stella*.) It is more likely, therefore, that if Sidney's psalms were written to be sung the musical settings would have been supplied by specialists at a later date. Such settings could be based on any melody including those associated with French or English psalms, and secular songs.

However, there is no music, nor any reference to tunes, in a presentation manuscript of Sidney's complete psalter prepared on behalf of the Countess of Pembroke for the Queen.[68] If the Countess had considered music an essential part of Sidney's project, it seems inconceivable that she would not have commissioned settings; there would surely have been no shortage of willing composers.[69] Nevertheless, it seems that only two settings (for treble voice and lute) exist; settings of penitential psalms (51 and 130) by the Countess were included in a manuscript song book dating from about 1616.[70] Sidney's psalms, like any other lyrical poetry, were and are amenable to musical setting.

However, the aesthetic properties of Sidney's psalms, unlike those of most holy songs, are essentially literary: the product of his capacity as a particular kind of poet to move and delight readers solely by the power of language. The affective qualities of his psalms – their capacity to 'strike, pearce [and] possesse, the sight of the soule' – is not dependent on actual music.[71] They are words set in such 'delightfull proportion' that they did not need to be 'either accompanied with, or prepared for the well enchanting skill of Musicke': they were already music of a sort.[72] It was in the nature of lyrical poesie by its 'measures and concordes of sundry proportions' to seem to 'counterfait the harmonicall tunes of the vocall and instrumentall Musickes'.[73]

Puttenham described numerous stanza forms which 'may best serve the eare for delight, and also . . . shew the Poets art and variety of Musicke';[74] but he also warned that the more complex and extended rhyme schemes, which serve 'to declare high and passionate or grave matter, and also . . . art', are not satisfying to 'the rude and popular eare'

and therefore the Poet must know to whose eare he maketh his rime, and accommodate himselfe thereto, and not give such musicke to the rude and barbarous, as he would to the learned and delicate eare[75]

Sidney wrote his 'musicke', or verse of that lyrical kind, for the 'learned and delicate eare'; he was also as Puttenham would have said 'his crafts maister'.[76]

Horace had written in his *Ars poetica* that 'the man who combines pleasure with usefulness wins every suffrage, delighting the reader and also giving him advice':

> omne tulit punctum qui miscuit utile dulci,
> lectorem delectando pariterque monendo[77]

The reader's delight came from admiration of the poet's skill in giving new life to old or traditional subjects and persuasive authority to new subjects: from the surface detail of exquisite craftsmanship, as well as from the deeper moral satisfaction and insights gleaned from well-tempered poetic *sententiae*. According to Jacques Peletier

L'ofic¢ d'un Poet¢, ¢t d¢ donner nouueaute aus chos¢s vielh¢s, auto-rite aus nouu¢l¢s, beaute aus rud¢s, lumier¢ aus obscur¢s, fo¢ aus douteus¢s, e a tout¢s leur natur¢l e a leur natur¢l tout¢s[78]

The Countess of Pembroke lamented that her brother's psalms were left unfinished: 'Had Heav'n so spar'd the life of life to frame the rest', but of all his literary work, she nevertheless chose them to embody his 'fame' as a poet.[79] Just as Surrey had epitomized Wyatt's reputation as a good poet and a good man in his praise of Wyatt's psalms, so the Countess proposed Sidney's psalms as 'Immortall Monuments of [his] faire fame'.

Several English writers cited biblical poetry in their defences of poesie, but none gave such prominence and appreciation to the Psalms as Sidney in his *Defence*.[80] I believe that Sidney would have regarded his psalms as a fulfilment of his 'vocation' as both a poet and an apologist for poetry.

In 1554, the year Sidney was born, his uncles, the Dudley brothers, had written their impassioned but conventional psalm paraphrases in the Tower, and the last of the pre-Anglo-Genevan editions of Sternhold's psalms had been published. Some thirty years later Sidney's psalms reversed that convention established by Sternhold of realizing the psalms' lyric mode of praise and prayer in holy songs for the 'popular eare'. Through the influence of his reputation as a poet and his literary achievement in these psalms Sidney restored the art of 'poesie' to English imitations of the Psalms.

6

'A HEAVENLY POESIE ... OF THAT LYRICALL KIND'

PART TWO – THE COUNTESS OF PEMBROKE

More than two thirds of the Sidney–Pembroke psalter is the work of the Countess of Pembroke. A. B. Grosart regarded her psalm versions as 'infinitely in advance of her brother's in thought, epithet and melody', and later modern assessments of the two psalmists have tended to favour the Countess's literary achievement.[1] However, since the sample of her work is about twice as large as his, it inevitably provides more examples of stylistic and interpretative felicities. Not enough attention has been paid to the similarities in their processes of imitating the Psalms.

In her dedicatory poem, addressed to the 'Angell spirit' of her dead brother, the Countess proclaimed her 'zealous love' which was unfolded in the 'world of words', for no 'other purpose but to honor thee'. To Sidney's psalms

> (Immortall Monuments of thy faire fame,
>   though not compleat ...
> Yet there will live thy ever praised name)

she added her own, describing them as

>   theise dearest offrings of my hart
> dissolv'd to Inke ...
>   sadd Characters indeed of simple love[2]

The Countess mingled Christian and familial pieties, since her completion of his psalter was an act of devotion not only to God but also to her brother: 'the wonder of men',

>   sole borne perfection's kinde,
> Phoenix thou wert, so rare thy fairest minde

Heav'nly adorn'd, Earth justlye might adore,
  where truthfull praise in highest glorie shin'de[3]

(She signed herself 'the Sister of that Incomparable Sidney'.) She may also have had another, more personal interest in his project. In 1586 the Countess lost not only her brother but also her parents: her father died on 5 May, her mother on 11 August, and Philip on 17 October. The Sidneys had been a close family, they wrote affectionate letters to each other and enjoyed each other's company. In these circumstances the Countess may also have turned to the Psalms for her own spiritual guidance and solace. There is no evidence that she was actively involved with Sidney's psalms before his death, but she had completed drafts of all her psalms by 1594.

Sixteen manuscripts of the Sidney–Pembroke psalms survive.[4] The best witness to the texts of Sidney's forty-three psalms is Samuel Woodford's incomplete but careful transcript (now Oxford, Bodleian Library, Rawlinson poet. 25)[5] of one of the Countess's working copies. This working copy had contained thirty-seven psalms (by Sidney or his sister) which she had crossed out or marked for revision. Since all the deletions and annotations have been reproduced by Woodford, it is possible to trace the processes of the Countess's many revisions and emendations of her own psalms as well as those of her brother's. She made substantial and repeated revisions to her own psalms, and is aptly described in Ringler's often-quoted phrase as 'an inveterate tinkerer'.[6] Comparison of the texts in Woodford's transcript with those in the Penshurst manuscript copied by John Davies of Hereford for presentation to the Queen, shows that the Countess's revisions of Sidney's work were relatively limited and tentative.[7] Her respect for Sidney's achievement is evident not only in the pattern of her revisions of her work but also in the way she adopted his methods for her own imitations of psalms.

The Countess was not an innovator: she did not try to

change her brother's conception of the work, and she used the same biblical and scholarly sources. Like Sidney, she also adapted the metres, stanza forms and rhyme schemes of the French metrical psalter.[8] She recognized that her contribution to their psalter was 'inspird' by him and she referred to it as

> this coupled worke, by double int'rest thine:
> First rais'de by thy blest hand, and what is mine
> inspird by thee, thy secrett power imprest[9]

The Countess's own versions do not represent any further significant development in the English metrical psalm as a literary kind. She accepted and adopted her brother's view of the Psalms as 'holy Davids . . . divine Poeme' in which the psalmist's 'heavenly poesie' could best find expression in the best contemporary English verse: 'that Lyricall kind of Songs and Sonets'.[10] She also adopted certain features of Sidney's poetic practice in an attempt to make their psalter into a single work bearing the impression of Sidney's eloquence.

However, because of the sort of thing which Vives said was natural to mankind (*quod genus sunt homini naturalia*),[11] like every other psalmist the Countess has her own personal eloquence and literary personality. Samuel Daniel assured her that the psalms had given 'Eternitie' 'Unto thy voyce':

> And this is that which thou maist call thine owne[12]

Her perceptions and imitations of Psalms 44–150 are often remarkably individual and forceful. A characteristic strength of her poetry arises from the ways in which she ruminated on literal translations, with the help of glosses and commentaries on the Psalms, in order to build (usually extensively) on implicit themes. J. C. A. Rathmell has commented on the vitality of her interpretations, which derives from her sense of personal involvement with the procedures in the models of her imitations:

it is her capacity to appreciate the underlying meaning that vivifies her lines ... By recreating the Psalms as Elizabethan poems, the Countess compels us to read them afresh[13]

Nevertheless, the quality of her work is uneven, and it often appears that her understanding of and sympathy with the psalmist's divine poem exceeded her own proficiency as a writer. While Sidney's psalms may be seen as a fulfilment of his 'unelected vocation' as a Christian poet, her psalms exemplify the self-education of a novice poet. G. F. Waller has suggested that those most heavily revised and abandoned versions among Psalms 44–80 were practice pieces in which the Countess discovered and developed her own skills as a metrical psalmist.[14]

The Countess's personal eloquence as a poet is characterized by her response to and handling of suggestive metaphors in her models. Like Sidney, she turned to Calvin's commentaries on the Psalms and to Beza's paraphrases for guidance on the meaning and significance of the biblical models.

Calvin's commentaries, which draw attention to the metaphorical qualities of the Hebrew poetry, provided a stimulus to her own imagination and wit. Ps. 44 marks the beginning of the Countess's section of the psalter, and illustrates some of her characteristic methods. Her treatment of verse 2 (in lines 5–8) is particularly interesting:

> Lorde, our fathers true relation
> Often made, hath made us knowe
>
> How thy hand the Pagan foe
> Rooting hence, thie folke implanting,
> Leavelesse made that braunch to grow,
> This to spring, noe verdure wanting[15]
>
> (Ps. 44, lines 1–2, 5–8)

The biblical psalmist had contrasted the position of the heathen, who (according to the Geneva Bible) were 'driven out' and 'destroyed', with that of his own fore-fathers who were 'planted in' and 'caused to growe'. The Countess's imitation extends this biblical metaphor of planting and growth under the influence of Calvin's explanation that the psalmist

compareth the old inhabiters of the land of Canaan to trees, bicause they had taken root there by long continued possession. Therfore the sodein alteracion that happened, was like as if a man should pluck up trees by the rootes, and plant other in their steedes[16]

Calvin's tree metaphor is subsumed in the Countess's image of the two branches (in lines 7 and 8) which correspond to the progeny of the 'Pagan foe' and 'thie folke'. Her meaning is made clearer by reference to Calvin once again:

there is added another Metaphor, wherby the faithfull shew how it came to passe through the blissing of the Lord, that the chozen people multiplyed: like as in processe of time a tree is the more strengthened in the place that hee hath gotten, by spredding forth farre, aswell his boughes, as his rootes

The Countess's earlier draft of this psalm made the parallel between the image of physical destruction and that of fertility more obvious:

> Our fathers Lord by hearing
> Have made us understand
>
> How rooting nations, them thy hand
> Did plant and planted nourish
> The stock prophane did leafelesse grow
> The faithfull branch did flourish[17]

Her revised version is denser, with more varied rhythms, but lines 7 and 8 are consequently more obscure. She was over-ingenious in changing the point of contrast from the simple antithetical parallelism: 'stock prophane ... faithfull branch' to 'that braunch' and 'this'. However, the revision makes a more complex rhetorical figure, and demonstrates that the dislocated syntax in the later version was deliberate.

Some of the Countess's most striking figurative language is derived from Beza's prose paraphrases in the English translation by Gilby, which had been dedicated to her aunt. Several notable passages in her version of Ps. 139 provide insights into her processes of imitation, and her literary tastes. The Geneva Bible translation of verses 7 and 8:

Whether shal I go from thy Spirit? or whether shal I flee from thy presence?
If I ascend into heaven, thou art there: If I lie downe in hel, thou art there

provided the substance and structure of the Countess's imitation.

> To shunn thy notice, leave thine ey,
> O whither might I take my way?
> To starry spheare?
> Thy throne is there.
> To dead mens undelightsome stay?
> There is thy walk, and there to ly
> Unknown, in vain I should assay
>
> (Ps. 139, lines 22–8)

The Countess found scholarly precedents for her exploitation of the antithetical parallelism in lines 24 and 26, and for her figurative periphrasis (line 26), in Gilby's translation of Beza's paraphrase:

If I shal even go up and flie up into *the verie heavens*, verelie there shal I find thee: contrariwise, if I lie downe in *the close places of the grave*, behold againe there shal I perceive thee[18]

Like Beza, and unlike all the translators of the English Bibles, she restricted the range of her psalmist's reference to the physical universe. In the same vein she contributed the metaphors which connote God's 'presence' in anthropomorphic terms: 'Thy throne ... thy walk'. As Coburn Freer has said (in a different context), she is careful of observed detail and rigorously logical.[19] Although the binary structure of each of the two biblical verses is represented in her double parallelism, 'To ...? To ...? There ... and there ...', the Countess made the complete stanza her sense unit, combining the two verses into a single entity. The form and varied rhythms of her stanza are well matched with the sense; for example, 'Unknown' (line 28) completes the sense of the previous line, but receives an appropriate emphasis from its position at the beginning of the last line of the stanza.

The influence of Beza's paraphrase is particularly evident in the Countess's version of the next verse:

Let me take the wings of the morning, & dwell in the uttermost partes of the sea   (Geneva Bible, Ps. 139:9)

since it supplied her with the figure of the rising and setting sun and the verbs 'lend' and 'flee'

the sunne it selfe arising up, should lend me his most swift wings, whereby I might flee even into the farthest part of the west[20]

Her own literary taste encouraged her to develop the witty play on 'light' and 'flight' in lines 29 and 30:

> O Sun, whome light nor flight can match,
>   Suppose thy lightfull flightfull wings
>   Thou lend to me
>   And I could flee
>   As farr as thee the ev'ning brings:
>   Ev'n ledd to West he would me catch,
>   Nor should I lurk with western things
> (Ps. 139, lines 29–35)

In verse 15, the biblical psalmist 'expresse[s] metaphorically' what Calvin referred to as 'the inestimable woorkmanshippe whyche appeareth in the shape of mannes bodye':[21]

My bones are not hid from thee, thogh I was made in a secret place, & facioned beneth in the earth   (Geneva Bible, Ps. 139:15)

Characteristically the Countess developed Calvin's emphasis on craftsmanship with well-visualized images of building and embroidery in her imitation.

> Thou, how my back was beam-wise laid,
>   And raftring of my ribbs, dost know:
>   Know'st ev'ry point

> Of bone and joynt
> How to this whole these partes did grow,
> In brave embrod'ry faire araid,
> Though wrought in shopp both dark and low
>
> (Ps. 139, lines 50–6)

Gilby's translation of Beza's 'compāges', 'the joining of my bones', provided the basis of the Countess's 'raftring of my ribbs', but not for the house-building metaphor which her imitation implies. Beza's simile 'as it were with needle worke' was also the basis for her embroidery metaphor depicting the physical beauty of the human body.[22] The final detail in line 56 of the dark workshop was probably derived from Golding's translation of Calvin's commentary on this verse, which refers to a 'craftesman . . . with a peece of worke in some darke denne'.[23]

In Ps. 141:7 the Countess developed a metaphor from Beza's paraphrase to represent the contrary sense of the worthlessness rather than the beauty, of the psalmist's frame or bones which are broken and disperst by death.

> Mean while my bones the grave, the grave expects my bones,
> Soe broken, hewn, disperst, as least respected stones,
> By careless Mason drawn from caves of worthless quarry
>
> (Ps. 141, lines 19–21)

(Our bones lie scattered at the graves mouth, as he that heweth wood or diggeth in the earth) (Geneva Bible, Ps. 141:7)

Here too the Countess responded to the biblical simile by emphasizing the physical action which dominates the sense of Beza's paraphrase:

In the meane season, we do lie not onlie as dead men: but also even as the hewers of stone do cut here and there the peeces of stones, so are we scattered, and our bones cast to and fro, at the mouth of the grave[24]

The carelessness of the mason was suggested by 'here and there' and 'to and fro' in Gilby's translation of Beza. But she has personalized and dramatized the situation on her own initiative both by using a singular pronoun and by personifying the grave through the effect of zeugma in line 19

> ... my bones the grave, the grave expects my bones

The additional figures of chiasmus and epizeuxis (or 'the coocko spel')[25] in this line also demonstrate her taste for those rhetorical ornaments which were considered poetical.

The Countess, like her brother, always restricted the most inventive features of her imitations to the detail of her interpretative paraphrase, and used the resources for imagery which she found in her scholarly sources in order to make the truth 'more palpable'.[26] She then developed these resources according to her own capacities to comprehend, evaluate and regenerate David's 'heavenly poesie' as late Elizabethan poetry. She was most successful when she was able to develop images which were already explicit or implicit in the biblical verses and the commentaries.

In this respect her imitation of Ps. 73:6–7 may be contrasted with Surrey's more inventive methods. The Countess's practice was to extend rather than expound the biblical similes

> Therefore with pride, as with a gorgious chaine
> Their swelling necks encompassed they beare;
> All cloth'd in wrong, as if a robe it were:
> So fatt become, that fattness doth constraine
> Their eies to swell
>
> (Ps. 73, lines 16–20)

(Therefore pride is a chaine unto them & crueltie covereth them as a garment. Their eyes stand out for fatnes)
(Geneva Bible, Ps. 73:6–7)

The Countess's inventive detail in line 17 of the 'swelling necks encompassed' elaborates on Beza's interpretation:

they . . . testifie with how great pride and fiercenes their heart swelleth, by the verie apparel of their bodie adorned with chaines, with gold, and pretious stones[27]

Her imitation generates a vivid impression of bloated self-importance and self-indulgence; the laboured rhythm of line 17 enhances the associations of the visual image, all the essential features of which were inherent in her usual sources: Calvin had commented

fatnes maketh folkes eyes to swell outward ... David ... Metaphorically expresseth the pryde, wherwith the ungodly be puffed up by reason of too much fulnes[28]

By contrast, Surrey's imitation of verse 7 had expounded the biblical simile and transformed it into a vehicle for his sharp criticism of the misuse of power by those

> Whose glutten cheks slouth feads so fatt as scant their eyes
> be sene.
>   Unto whose crewell power most men for dred ar fayne
> To bend and bow with loftye looks, whiles they vawnt in their
> rayne
>   And in their bloody hands, whose crueltye doth frame
> The wailfull works that skourge the poore with out regard of
> blame[29]   (Ps. 73, lines 14–18)

As with Surrey's sonnet 'Th' Assyryans king ...' it 'is tempting, but not necessary, to see in this poem a covert allusion to Henry VIII'.[30] However just as the interpretations of Calvin and Beza informed the Countess's imitation so the paraphrase by Campensis had provided the stimulus to Surrey's imagination:

Every man that meteth them, is afrayde of them by reason of theyr power, whych is waxen so greate, that they gyve no force whether theyr wyckednesse and vyolence (wherby they oppresse the poore) be knowne or no[31]

Thus the differences between the versions by the Countess and by Surrey reflect not merely differences of intention and personal eloquence but also the nature of the different scholarly sources which informed their understanding and interpretation of the biblical models.

The weaknesses of the Countess's psalms like her strengths often arise from her characteristic literary tastes

and powers of expression. She has a tendency to overdo
the surface detail of rhetorical ornamentation, and to lose
control of the larger imaginative infrastructure of her own
psalm imitations. The application of her usually good
attention to detail is occasionally too localized. Coverdale
had translated Ps. 73:16,

Then thought I to understande this, but it was to harde for me

Surrey's psalmist explains his dilemma in terms of intellectual failure to penetrate divine mysteries:

And as I sought wherof thy sufferaunce, Lord, shold groo,
I found no witt cold perce so farr, thy holly domes to knoo,
And that no mysteryes nor dought could be distrust

(Ps. 73, lines 35–7)

The Countess independently generated images with visual
qualities and implying physical action:

So then I turn'd my thoughtes another way:
Sounding, if I, this secrets depth might find;
But combrous cloudes my inward sight did blynd

(Ps. 73, lines 46–8)

The visual image is apt, given the traditional reference to
intellectual perception as 'inward sight', but in the larger
context of the psalm verse, the associations of her mixed
metaphors lead to incongruity: while sounding the depths
(sea, understood) the psalmist was blinded by 'combrous
cloudes' (sky, understood). (Gilby had translated Beza's
paraphrase '. . . howbeit, I could not rid my selfe of these
most troublesome cogitations'.)[32] In Ps. 88:1, the biblical
psalmist had cried day and night before God; the Countess
dissipated this sense of intense continuous action by periphrasis,

Both when the sunn the day
The treasures doth display
And night locks up his golden wealth

(Ps. 88, lines 4–6)

Such a poetical device of ornamentation is contrary to the
mood of the poem. The 'treasures' and 'golden wealth'

represent the sunlit universe of the God of creation, and are out of place. They import irrelevant associations thereby changing the tone of the psalmist's voice from lament to praise at the point where the tone of penitential lament needs to be firmly established.

The Countess often reveals her inexperience as a writer by improvising her own metaphorical details, rather than developing those she found in her usual sources. She was more dependent on Calvin and Beza than Sidney appears to have been, and she was more elaborate and copious in her treatment of borrowings from these commentators. Sidney had used these same sources but had also observed more carefully the terse quality of the biblical psalmists' styles. The differences between his uses of the sources and hers arise from differences in taste and from the disparity between their practical experience as writers.

Coburn Freer has commented that the Countess's rhythms are not as subtle and varied as her brother's, and that the variety of metrical forms in her psalms appears to have been chosen more arbitrarily.[33] The brief example from Ps. 139 demonstrates that she could vary her rhythms with interest and subtlety. In her imitation of Ps. 100 (*Jubilate deo*) the Countess matched form and content very deliberately: she represented this psalm's lyric mode of praise and prayer by exploiting a form more traditionally associated with a secular convention for praise and devotion: the sonnet.

> 1 O all you landes, the treasures of your joy
>   In mery shout upon the Lord bestow:
>   Your service cheerfully on him imploy,
>   With triumph song into his presence goe.
> 2 Know first that he is God; and after know
>   This God did us, not we our selves create:
>   We are his flock, for us his feedings grow:
>   We are his folk, and he upholds our state.
> 3 With thankfullnesse O enter then his gate:
>   Make through each porch of his your praises ring,
>   All good, all grace, of his high name relate,

4   He of all grace and goodnesse is the spring.
     Tyme in noe termes his mercy comprehends,
     From age to age his truth it self extends   (Ps. 100)

There is a close correspondence between the structure of
the biblical psalm (which in the Bishops' Bible is divided
into four verses) and the argument of the Countess's
sonnet. She rejected the opportunity to make the opening
phrases of her first two quatrains parallel each other in the
manner of several of Sidney's secular sonnets, or of some
of the biblical translations of this psalm.[34] Her final couplet
lends an apt weightiness to the concluding *sententia*, and
the last word – 'extends' – is a triumphant summary of the
psalmist's teaching: mercy and truth stretch into eternity.

There is often a wistful quality to the Countess's imitations of those psalm verses which depict the emotional
states of the speaker – a quality which distinguishes her
work from both Surrey's and Sidney's. In Ps. 73 the biblical psalmist is troubled because the wicked prosper, and
God, who is truly 'lovynge unto Israel', apparently allows
the wicked to oppress the righteous.

Lo, these are the ungodly, these prospere in the worlde, and these
have ryches in possession   (Great Bible, Ps. 73:12)

Surrey had paraphrased this verse

     In terrour of the just thus raignes iniquitye,
   Armed with power, laden with gold, and dred for crueltye
                              (Ps. 73, lines 27–8)

While Surrey's psalmist sees prosperity and riches as
adjuncts of a power maintained by fear, the Countess's
psalmist relates this prosperity to a state of personal
happiness:

     See here the godlesse Crue, while godly wee
        Unhappy pine, all happiness possesse:
        Their riches more, our wealth still growing lesse
                              (Ps. 73, lines 34–6)

Her rhetorical manipulation of syntax has introduced an
implied relationship between the godly and the godless,

like that between the two pans of a balance for weighing gold: so as the riches of the 'godlesse Crue' increase, the 'wealth' of the godly grows less. Whereas Surrey had realized the physical properties of weight and colour in his image of iniquity 'laden with gold', the Countess made 'riches' into a metaphor for a psychological state, and thereby offered a new reading of the psalm verse.

All the English Bibles translate the final clause of Ps. 88 as a statement that, either God hid the psalmist's friends from him, or else the friends hid themselves. The Countess's imitation of this verse softens the resentful tone of the biblical psalmist by emphasizing the distance, rather than the cause of the separation:

> Who erst to me were neare and deare
> > Far now, O farr
> > Disjoyned ar:
> > And when I would them see,
> > Who my acquaintance be,
> As darknesse they to me appeare   (Ps. 88, lines 73–8)

(Thou hast removed al my friends and companions farre from me, that I see nothing anie-where, but meere darknes)[35]

(Beza, tr. Gilby)

Beza supplied the two distinctive elements of her imitation: the references to distance and darkness. However, whereas Beza had focussed on the situation of the psalmist, the main subject of the Countess's stanza is the psalmist's lost nearest and dearest. This emphasis gives her imitation a wistful quality as the psalmist reflects on the friends, 'Far now, O farr', and on the nature of their relationship; the final impression is of personal loss and fading memories. The mood she has successfully evoked is a reflexion of her personal eloquence.

As she developed the potential of the figurative language in the Psalms, the Countess did not scruple to borrow imagery associated with a pagan, classical tradition. This had not been Sidney's practice in his psalms. In her imitation of Ps. 73:10 the Countess conspicuously substituted

the classical metaphor of the cornucopia for the biblical
metaphor of a cup running over:

> Their horne of plenty freshly flowing still
>> (Ps. 73, line 29)

(waters of a ful cup are wrung out to them)
>> (Geneva Bible, Ps. 73:10)

Similarly, at the end of her version of Ps. 55 she introduced
a metaphor of death (but not specifically of the Fates),
shearing the half-spun thread of man's life:

> their life-holding threed so weakly twin'd
> That it, half-spunne, death may in sunder sheare
>> (Ps. 55, lines 71–2)

The usual biblical figure of speech for a man's life is the
number of his days, thus all the contemporary English
Bibles translate this verse '. . . shall not lyve out halfe their
dayes' (Great Bible, Ps. 55:23).[36] Although Sidney's
psalms do not employ such classical imagery, these two
topoi are so commonplace in literature that there was no
breach of decorum in the Countess's application of them
here; their general 'literary' quality is matched by such
phrases as 'Zephyrs nest' (Ps. 67, line 30) and 'sweete
Auroras raine' (Ps. 110, line 16). By utilizing such figures
the Countess helped to revitalize biblical poetics according
to a tradition by which Orpheus was seen as a figure for
David and Urania had become a Christian muse.[37]

The Countess imitated her brother's secular poetry as
well as his imitations of David's 'heavenly poesie'. She
began her version of Ps. 73 by incorporating an allusion to
the fifth *Astrophil and Stella* sonnet.

> It is most true that God to Israell
>> I meane to men of undefiled hartes
>> Is only good, and nought but good impartes.
> Most true, I see, allbe allmost I fell
>> From right conceit into a crooked mynd;
>> And from this truth with straying stepps declin'd
>>> (Ps. 73, lines 1–6)

> It is most true, that eyes are form'd to serve
> The inward light ...
>
> It is most true ...
>
> True, and yet true[38]
>
> (*Astrophil and Stella* 5, lines 1–2, 5, 14)

This is sacred parody. The biblical psalmist's assertion of truth and the qualification 'Neverthelesse', must have helped to put Sidney's sonnet into the Countess's mind:

(Truly God is lovynge unto Israel: even unto soch as are of a cleane hert? Neverthelesse my fete were almost gone, my treadynges had well nye slypte) (Great Bible, Ps. 73:1–2)

There are implicit thematic links here between Astrophil's notion of 'inward light' (reason or understanding) and the emphasis of the Countess's psalmist on 'undefiled hartes' which think 'right conceit[s]'.[39] Similarly, there are links between on the one hand, the psalmist's praise of God's goodness and his fear of error or physical slipping, and on the other hand, Astrophil's rational, moral argument and his own failure to sustain it ('True, and yet true that I must Stella love', line 14).

In her imitation of Ps. 51:6,

> My trewand soule in thy hid schoole hath learned
>
> (Ps. 51, line 21)

(therefore hast thou taught me wisdome in the secret of mine heart)
(Geneva Bible, Ps. 51:6)

the Countess has developed Calvin's reference to 'a froward scholer' from Golding's translation.[40] But in doing so she seems to have recollected the penultimate line of *Astrophil and Stella* 1, in which Astrophil – the novice poet – having studied 'inventions fine', bites

> My trewand pen

and is told by his muse 'looke in thy heart and write'. The Countess too was a novice poet when she began her psalm imitations. In her version of Ps. 73:25 the psalmist asks,

O what is he will teach me clyme the skyes?

(Ps. 73, line 73)

For the reader who recognizes her allusion to the opening line of *Astrophil and Stella* 31,

With how sad steps, ô Moone, thou climb'st the skies

the implication must be that Sidney was her teacher in the art of poesie of 'that Lyricall kind'. Such allusion was probably deliberate; it is partly an indication of the Countess's regard for her brother as a poet. It is also, more importantly, part of her effort to give their 'coupled worke' – the whole psalter – the character or 'marke' of Sidney's 'sweet sprite':

So dar'd my Muse with thine it selfe combine,
as mortall stuffe with that which is divine[41]

The Countess saw her brother as having established the canons of a poetic suited to the most cultivated Protestant sensibilities in late Elizabethan England. Sidney had defended poetry against the abuse of hostile critics: by arguing in *The Defence* that 'the end & working of [poetry] ... being rightly applied, deserveth not to be scourged out of the Church of God';[42] and by setting a standard for the 'right' application of poetry in his forty-three psalms. John Donne, who lamented that the Psalms were 'So well attyr'd abroad, so ill at home' in those holy songs used in Church, celebrated the 'Sydnean Psalmes' by 'this Moses and this Miriam' for the way in which they 're-reveal[d]', 'In formes of joy and art', those songs 'which heavens high holy Muse' had 'Whisper'd to David'.[43] When she addressed her brother's 'Angell spirit', the Countess expressed her belief that

all of tongues with soule and voice admire
Theise sacred Hymnes ...
thy works so worthilie embrac't
By all of worth[44]

The example of Sidney's 'divine' Muse provided, she thought, 'lightning beames' which gave 'lustre' to her own psalms.[45] She completed his psalter by combining her own 'mortall stuffe with that which is divine', and by producing a full repertoire of psalms in a heavenly poesie for the most cultivated of Christian souls in devotion. Her 'mortall stuffe' – her concentration on poetic detail in the elaboration of metaphor, and the introduction of images based on *topoi* familiar to the cultivated reader – is part of her higher purpose in developing Sidney's poetic ideal. The nature of her achievement cannot be appreciated in isolation from the literary ambitions and achievements of her brother, and from the whole tradition of English psalm versions. In combining her Muse with Sidney's and completing the psalter as his memorial, she helped to set the seal on her contemporaries' expectations of psalms as the best kind of lyrical poetry. Thereafter, the English archetype of devotional poetry was the Sidneys' idea of a psalm.

7
EPILOGUE

The choice of biblical psalms as models to imitate was promoted by a renaissance view of man placed by God at the
centre of the world with the power and responsibility to
shape his own nature. In the oration by Pico della Mirandola 'on the dignity of man' Adam is told by God

We have set thee at the world's center that thou mayest from
thence more easily observe whatever is in the world. We have made
thee neither of heaven nor of earth, neither mortal nor immortal, so
that with freedom of choice and with honor, as though the maker
and molder of thyself, thou mayest fashion thyself in whatever
shape thou shalt prefer. Thou shalt have the power to degenerate
into the lower forms of life, which are brutish. Thou shalt have the
power, out of thy soul's judgment, to be reborn into the higher
forms, which are divine[1]

The dignity of man is his God-given capacity for judgement. This capacity enables him to kindle the divine spark
within himself, and to nurture that better part of his nature
which will allow him to fashion a better self. The human
potential for honour or degeneracy is great, and in order to
exercise this freedom to choose, the individual needs to
discover the attributes of his own nature.

In these circumstances, and in an age in which emphasis
on a personal religion was renewed, the individual
required models for self-examination and standards for
self-assessment before he exercised his judgement. The
biblical psalmists had faced this problem directly: 'What is
man, that thou art myndfull of him?' (Ps. 8:4); the biblical
psalm, therefore, was seen as the most appropriate model.
Meditation on the Psalms helped the individual to define
the responsibilities of his position, to articulate his spiritual
problems and to realize his relationship with God. The

psalm model's peculiar importance derived from its representation of an individual's self revelation in direct and
artful colloquy with God.

Renaissance scholars rediscovered the literary qualities
of these devotional models in the original language by
making new Latin translations and commentaries. Translations into the vernacular also allowed many laymen to
appreciate the literary qualities of these poetic texts which
they had repeated in Latin for centuries. It was not possible
to adopt sincerely the psalmist's words as one's own unless
they had been understood. Hence, many of the sixteenth-
century psalmists, including Wyatt, Surrey, Sternhold and
Sidney, made efforts to understand and interpret the
meaning of the biblical psalmists by consulting the latest
scholarly paraphrases and commentaries. They took seri-
ously the opportunity offered by the example of the psalmist for spiritual rebirth and self-making.

Imitation of the Psalms in life as well as literature promoted a consciousness of self, which was expressed in lyric
and dramatic forms emphasizing the emotional intensity of
personal experience. This consciousness and expression of
self provided an obvious paradigm for different literary
kinds of introspection and devotion. Renaissance poets
learnt to apply a Judaeo-Christian concept of the unique
integrity of an individual's sentient self in their writing by
imitating inherited themes and forms of biblical poetry.
The eloquent and sentient 'I', whose voice emerges from
their lyrical poetry, is a direct descendant of the psalmist:
Petrarch had written both psalms and sonnets. The English
renaissance sonneteer pretended to voice his personal
meditation and devotion to a secular idol in a contemporary social context. By convention the poetic personae of
Elizabethan sonneteers tease their audiences with names
and details which seem both to hint at simple connexions
between life and literature, and at the same time to deny
such connexions as simplistic. This sonneteer wears a
mask: 'I am not I', says Astrophil, and then pleads play-

fully 'pitie the tale of me'.[2] By contrast the psalmist is conventionally bare-faced before heaven. Nevertheless, because metrical psalms were poetic expressions of devotion to God's truth, they lent credence to other personal expressions of emotional intensity in different forms of English secular poetry. The reader could feel more comfortable with expressions of emotional intensity in such poetry, since he knew that in the Psalms they had been sanctioned by religious experience mediated through a divinely inspired model.

By the later sixteenth century, the vogue for metrical psalms had helped to establish a new decorum for Protestant poetics. The contrast between the elaborate ironies and self-contradictions of the sonneteer on the one hand, and the psalmist's expression of truth in a direct yet artful colloquy with God on the other, became an issue in Sidney's poetry: what constitutes a stylistic decorum for Truth? Astrophil had repented that his 'best wits still their owne disgrace invent' (sonnet 19, line 5). In the seventeenth century the same issue recurs in Herbert's poetry.[3]

> Must all be vail'd, while he that reades, divines,
> Catching the sense at two removes?
>
> ('Jordan I', lines 9–10)

The answer given to Herbert's speaker at the end of 'Jordan II' is

> There is in love a sweetnesse readie penn'd:
> Copie out only that, and save expense

This 'sweetnesse' is in the Bible:

> Oh Book! infinite sweetnesse! let my heart
> Suck ev'ry letter, and a hony gain,
> Precious for any grief in any part;
> To cleare the breast, to mollifie all pain
>
> ('The H. Scriptures I', lines 1–4)

The poem 'Antiphon I' makes explicit the speaker's recourse to the biblical poetry of the Psalms in 'The Church'. Herbert's speaker has rediscovered the biblical poetic that Wyatt, Surrey and Sidney had practised in their imitations of psalms.

When Barbara Lewalski called the Sidney–Pembroke psalter 'a secure bridge to the magnificent original seventeenth-century religious lyric in the biblical and psalmic mode' she implied limitations to the intrinsic value and originality of the Sidneys' paraphrases and those of their earlier sixteenth-century predecessors.[4] Before we cross that 'bridge' it would be as well to pause, and perhaps with hindsight as readers of *The Temple* and *Paradise Lost*, to consider what were the most significant and valuable achievements of the sixteenth-century psalmists.

There are four outstanding figures whose psalm versions contributed most to the development of an English biblical poetic. Wyatt's psalm paraphrases, drawing on a devotional tradition of penitential exercises, and on an Italian literary model, brought the divine poetry of the Psalms firmly into the English poetic repertoire. In his seven penitential psalms Wyatt set up the figure of David as an exemplum to help the reader to understand his own nature, and to realize his own capacity to be reborn into a higher form of existence – a reformed spiritual nature, or as Coverdale said 'a new David: a man accordynge unto the wyll of God'.[5] Wyatt was a pioneer of the poetry of meditative introspection, and his initiative established the co-existence of psalms and sonnets as English literary kinds.

Surrey placed himself in the situation of the psalmist, and attempted to discover through his imitations of select psalms his own spiritual character as 'a new David'. He wrote relatively few psalms, but they were important and meaningful to him personally, reflecting as they did his imaginative life of the spirit. With hindsight Surrey's psalms appear to represent the epitome of the new literary kind: he wrote with a sure touch, and managed to convey the literal sense of the biblical models by combining the detail of scholarly interpretation with studied personal relevance. His psalms are impressive and moving both as poetry and as responsible biblical paraphrase.

Sternhold's psalms are both public declarations and private manifestations of religious feeling in England during the second half of the sixteenth century. When his holy songs were adopted as adjuncts to the English liturgy between 1559 and 1696, their simple ballad metres imprinted the elements of Protestant spirituality on the hearts and minds of English people; they helped to establish the character of English hymnody which prevails to this day.

The Sidney–Pembroke psalter placed the English metrical psalm on a par with the best psalm paraphrases in French and Latin. The 'delicate eare' for 'poesie' of such readers as Donne, Fulke Greville, Sir John Harington, Samuel Daniel and Jonson was satisfied, as the Sidneys confirmed what Wyatt and Surrey had demonstrated on a smaller scale fifty years earlier, that there was poetry in paraphrase. During a period from 1535 (or thereabouts) to 1585 English poets had rediscovered the poetry of praise and prayer in the Psalms, and had responded with copious eloquence and imagination to all the traditional perceptions and expectations of the Psalms as personal prayers, meditations, various modes of divine poetry and song, instructions and thanksgivings.

Sidney's psalms practically exhausted the formal possibilities for new developments in the metrical psalm as a literary kind. Nevertheless metrical psalms by priests, poets, scholars and other laymen continued to proliferate throughout the seventeenth century.[6] Herbert's 'The 23d Psalme' is a holy song in which he has adapted the form and style of the Anglo-Genevan psalter, and followed the sense of the literal translations by Coverdale and others. Herbert gave this psalm paraphrase many characteristic details of his own, including an emphasis on the mutual relationship between the 'God of love' and the psalmist, and in the last lines evidence of the psalmist's concern to find fit 'praise' to match God's eternal 'sweet and wondrous love'. However, neither Herbert nor Milton, for example, could find any new directions for the fixed kind of metrical psalm, although Milton in particular proved to be eminently capable of transforming the English poetic repertoire in other kinds.

Sidney's achievement encouraged later poets to a heightened appreciation of the imaginative and formal possibilities of the Psalms as affective models of devotional poetry and meditation. His influence on *The Temple* (1633) is well known.[7] The variety and expressiveness of Herbert's verse forms in 'The Church' serve – like Sidney's in his psalms – to multiply the personal praises of an eloquent Christian poet.

Paradoxically poems such as 'Sighs and Grones', 'Longing' and 'Complaining' have a closer affinity to Sidney's psalms than 'The 23d Psalme', but they are not actually psalm paraphrases. As a result it is sometimes difficult to tell the difference between Sidney's psalms and Herbert's 'sacred poems and private ejaculations' in *The Temple*.

> Do not beguile my heart,
>   Because thou art
> My power and wisdome. Put me not to shame,
>   Because I am
> Thy clay that weeps, thy dust that calls
> (Herbert, 'Complaining', lines 1–5)

> Do not, Lord, then me forsake,
>   Do not take
> Thy deare presence farr from me;
> Hast O Lord, that I be stayd
>   By thy aid:
> My salvation is in thee
> (Sidney, Ps. 38, lines 61–6)

Herbert shared Sidney's facility in handling flexible lyric verse forms; it is their poise and control of rhythm which suggests their speakers' dignified but impassioned colloquy with God.

With hindsight it appears that the tactics of Sir Thomas Smith in his 'other psalmes' anticipate some of those in *The*

Temple. The significance of such an observation is that the patterns of religious experience and feeling in the Psalms, in particular the quality of the relationship between God and the psalmists, as well as the literary repertoire in which these patterns were repeatedly embodied, provided not only model resources but also a challenge for very different writers.

Although Milton's psalms have more significance for the study of Milton than of the metrical psalm tradition, they should also be seen in terms of that tradition: in particular, the public contexts of Sternhold's popular holy songs and Smith's political commentary, and the personal applications of psalms as vehicles for the 'particuler prayers of particular persons in particular greefes eyther of body or soule'.[8] Milton's 'Let us with a gladsome mind' (Ps. 136) is a holy song written in hymn-metre septenaries by a pious youth of fifteen. His selection of Psalms 80–88 for paraphrases written twenty-four years later in April 1648 seems to be related to his fears for the Church and to his controversial pamphlets of that period. In this public context he used Sternhold's common measure as reminiscent of the holy songs sung in Church and chamber by Anglicans and Puritans alike. When these psalms were published in 1673 Milton included notes on his own translations from the Hebrew texts, and was careful to distinguish his strict paraphrase from his local elaborations of the biblical models: for example, the image of the death bed added in his Ps. 88:10

> Wilt thou do wonders on the dead,
>   Shall the deceased arise
> And praise thee *from their loathsome bed*
>   *With pale and hollow eyes?*[9]

The sequence of Psalms 1–8, each in a different metre, which Milton wrote during the second week of August 1653 is different. These psalms, like Surrey's, probably had a more personal significance and reflect Milton's reactions to his recent blindness

> mine eye
> Through grief consumes, is waxen old and dark
> I'the midst of all mine enemies that mark
>
> (Ps. 6, lines 13–15)

The sequence may be seen to represent an attempt to come to terms with his affliction as a trial of faith by God: the final psalm, Ps. 8, is a hymn of praise to the Creator who has 'crowned' man 'With honour and with state', and placed all the creatures in a providential order 'under his lordly feet'. In testifying to the continuation of the metrical psalm tradition according to the criteria of the sixteenth-century psalmists, Milton's psalms also suggest that the permissible options for the development of the established kind had indeed been exhausted.

Seventeenth-century poets not only wrote new psalm paraphrases in the various forms of devotional lyric poetry but also wrote new religious lyrics influenced by that concept of the psalm as the most excellent form of poetry expressed by Sidney in *The Defence of Poesie*. Drayton's *Harmonie of the Church*, Herbert's *Temple* and Traherne's *Thanksgivings*, for example, may thus be described as 'other psalmes'. In this sense it may be true that the 'greatest paraphrases of the Psalms of David ever written . . . are embodied in the texture of *Paradise Lost*'.[10]

APPENDIX: A GUIDE TO ENGLISH PSALM VERSIONS PRINTED 1530–1601 (EXCLUDING BIBLES AND PRIMERS)

This finding-list is provisional. I have recorded every work so far known to me which contains a new English psalm version (in prose or metre) and was printed during the period 1530–1601 (e.g. from Joy's first prose psalter to Verstegan's metrical paraphrase of the seven penitential psalms).

I have included some new compilations drawn from existing psalm versions (e.g. no. 80, John Mundy's musical settings of Coverdale's prose texts from the Book of Common Prayer, and of Anglo-Genevan metrical texts in *Songs and Psalmes* (1594)). However, I have neither attempted to record systematically those works, such as devotional compilations, sermons and rhetorical guides, which include quotations from psalms subsumed into new works, nor have I listed works entitled 'psalm' or 'psalter', which are not versions of the biblical psalms (e.g. see further A. C. Southern, *Elizabethan Recusant Prose 1559–1582* (London & Glasgow, [1950]), pp. 219–23 on the 'Jesus Psalter'). Nevertheless, where such works were printed in books which are listed here for other reasons then these works are also noted (e.g. no. 12, Fisher's *Psalmes or prayers* (1544)).

Since this list is intended as a guide to different versions of psalms I have not included reprints of the Bible, the Psalms (from Coverdale's Great Bible of 1539) reprinted with the Book of Common Prayer, nor have I included the various devotional primers from the 1530s and 1540s many of which reprint psalms from Joye's translations of either 1530 or 1534. (See further A. S. Herbert, rev. T. H. Darlow & H. F. Moule, *Historical Catalogue of Printed Editions of the English Bible 1525–1961* (London & New York, 1968); C. C. Butterworth, *The English Primers (1529–1545) Their Publication and Connection with the English Bible and the Reformation in England* (Philadelphia, 1953).) For the convenience of the reader the four English Bibles containing new translations of the Psalms from this period are listed separately at the end of this note.

Items 1–85 are listed chronologically under the date of the earliest surviving edition recorded in the revised *Short Title Catalogue* (*STC²*). Each entry is in three parts:

(i)   date, name of person responsible for English text, title, place of publication and printer;
(ii) brief description of psalm version(s) comprising (or incorporated in) the contents of the book;
(iii) *STC²* number, shelfmark of copy consulted, and a brief note of any subsequent editions, including variant titles.

Wherever possible I have tried to verify the contents of each work by inspecting a copy of it myself. In the few cases where this has not been possible, I have recorded the work as 'unseen', citing the authority for the title and attribution if not *STC²* (e.g. No. 41, *The Comentarye of Musculus* (1565–6?)). Where I have not been able to examine a copy of the earliest edition, or where the title page of the copy is lacking, the title from a subsequent edition is given within square brackets (e.g. no. 45, *Ane compendius Buik* [1567], *STC²* 2996.5, with title from the edition of 1600, *STC²* 2997).

Items 86–90 (numbered in square brackets) list psalm versions recorded in the sixteenth century but which appear not to have survived.

The names of editors, translators or authors of English

versions and the titles of anonymous books are included in the General Index.

English Bibles Containing New Translations of the Psalms.

(1) Coverdale Bible: *Biblia The Bible/ that is, the holy Scripture of the Olde and New Testament, faithfully and truly translated out of Douche and Latyn in to Englishe* ([Cologne or Marburg?], 1535).
STC² 2063; D & M 18.

(2) Great Bible: *The Byble in Englyshe, that is to saye the content of all the holy scrypture, bothe of the olde and newe testament, truly translated after the veryte of the Hebrue and Greke textes, by the dylygent studye of dyverse excellent learned men, expert in theforsayde tonges* (London, 1539).
STC² 2068; D & M 46.

(3) Geneva Bible: *The Bible and Holy Scriptures Conteyned in the Olde and Newe Testament. Translated according to the Ebrue and Greke, and conferred With the best translations in divers langages. With moste profitable annotations upon all the hard places, and other things of great importance as may appeare in the Epistle to the Reader* (Geneva, 1560).
STC² 2093; D & M 107.

(4) Bishops' Bible: *The . holie . Bible . conteyning the olde Testament and the newe* (London, 1568).
STC² 2099; D & M 125.

I   1530   [GEORGE JOYE (1495–1553)]

The Psalter of David in Englishe purely and faithfully translated aftir the texte of Feline: every Psalme havynge his argument before/ declarynge brefly thentente & substance of the wholl Psalme.
[Antwerp, Martin de Keyser]

Pss. 1–150 in English prose translated from Martin Bucer's Latin (1529). Pseudonymous ded. signed 'Johan Aleph' on sig. A1ᵛ; contemporary attribution to Joye, see C. C. Butterworth & A. G. Chester, *George Joye* (1962), pp. 54–60 and G. E. Duffield's introduction to facsimile edn (1971).

STC² 2370; B. Lib., C.17.a.2.
Other edns [1532?] *STC²* 2371, and [1542?] 2374 (with collects).
D & M 3.

2   1534   GEORGE JOYE

> Davids Psalter/ diligently and faithfully trans-
> lated by George Joye/ with breif Arguments
> before every Psalme/ declaringe the effecte
> therof.
>   ([Antwerp], 'Martyne Emperowr')

Pss. 1–150 in English prose translation from Ulrich Zwingli's Latin (1532) with brief explanatory 'arguments' heading each psalm. See C. C. Butterworth & A. G. Chester, *George Joye* (1962), pp. 128–34.

STC² 2372; C.U.L., Syn. 8.53.89.
D & M 9.

3   [1534]
          [WILLIAM MARSHALL (fl. 1533–7)]

> An exposition after the maner of a contempla-
> cyon upon the .li. psalme/ called Miserere mei
> Deus.
>   (London, John Bydell for Wyllyam Marshall)

English prose translation of Savonarola's exposition of Ps. 51. Many later editions: *STC²* 21789.6 (Rouen, 1536) includes Savonarola's exposition of Ps. 31 in a similar English prose translation. *STC²* 21790 (Paris, 1538) includes the Latin text of Ps. 51 printed parallel with the English exposition and a new English translation of the psalm incorporated into the exposition; (initial letters of the Latin and English psalm verses are printed in red); the head-title indicates that the exposition was 'made at the latter ende of hys dayes' by 'Hierom of Ferrarye' [i.e. Savonarola]. See also Abraham Fleming's edn (1578) *STC²* 21797, no. 57 below.

STC² 21789.3, formerly 21795; C.U.L., Syn. 8. 53.41.
STC² 21790; B.Lib., C.36.c.2.
Variant titles (as *STC²*): *An exposytion upon* ... [1535?] *STC²* 21789.4; *A goodly exposycyon...* (*c.* 1540) *STC²* 21793; *A meditacyon...* [1536] *STC²* 21799; *An other meditation* [1555?] *STC²* 21799.2.

4   1535   [MILES COVERDALE (1488–1568)]

> A Paraphrasis/ upon all the Psalmes of David/ made by Johannes Campensis/ reader of the Hebrue lecture/ in the universite of Lovane/ and translated oute of Latyne into Englyshe.
> [Antwerp, widow of Christopher von Ruremond]

Paraphrases of Pss. 1–150 in English prose translated from J. Campensis, *Psalmorum omnium* (1534), *STC²* 2354 (printed in Paris for Thomas Berthelet of London). English version attributed to Coverdale by J. Bale (*Scriptorum illustrium ... Catalogus* (1557), p. 721); see also J. F. Mozley, *Coverdale and his Bibles* (1953), pp. 60–4, 324.

STC² 2372.4; Lincoln Cathedral Lib. (on Bodl. film 51). Anr edn *STC²* 2372.6, formerly 14620 (London, 1539); B. Lib., 3090.a.8.

5   [1535?]   MILES COVERDALE

> Goostly psalmes and spirituall songes drawen out of the holy Scripture, for the comforte and con-

solacyon of soch as love to rejoyse in God and his worde.

([Southwark], Johan Gough)

Contains metrical versions (beginning fol. 32^r) of Pss. 11 [12], 2, 45 [46], 123 [124], 136 [137], 127 [128] (x 2), 50 [51] (x 2), 129 [130], 24 [25], 67 [68], 13 [14], 147, 133 [134] with tunes for each; see M. Frost, *English & Scottish Psalm & Hymn Tunes* (1953), pp. 293–339. Also contains metrical versions of ten commandments, creed and canticles all in English. (There is a table of contents on the last leaf.) For Lutheran sources, see J. Bale, *Scriptorum illustrium ... Catalogus* (1557), p. 721 'Cantiones Witenbergensium'.

STC^2 5892; Oxford, Queen's College, Sel.d.81 and Bodl. facsimile, Facs.c.21.

6   1536

> Storys and prophesis out of the holy scriptur/ garnyschede wiih [sic] faire ymages/ and with devoute praeirs/ and thanckgevings unto God.
>   (Antwerp, Symon Cowke [Simon de Cock])

Extracts from biblical texts and new devotional compilations translated from Dutch, with many illustrations. Contains new English version of Ps. 51 (sig. I1^r–I2^r); not Joye's translation.

STC^2 3014; Bodl., Douce B. 205.

7   1537   MILES COVERDALE

> A very excellent and s[we]te exposition upon the [two and] twentye Psalm[e] o[f] David, called in latyn Dominus regit me, & nihil. Translated out of hye Almayne into Englyshe by Myles Coverd[ale].
>   (Southwark, James Nycolson for Jhon Gough)

Prose exposition of Ps. 23 translated from a paraphrase by Luther with variant text of 1535 Bible translation interspersed in exposition. See Coverdale, *Remains*, ed. G. Pearson (Parker Soc., 1846), pp. 282ff.

STC² 16999; Bodl., Tanner 33.
Anr edn with additions [1538], *STC²* 17000.

8   1537

> An exposicyon of the .xv. psalme made by mayster Erasmus of Rotherdame in whiche is full purely declared the pure and clene behavoure that ought to be in the pure churche of Chryst which is the multytude of all trewe chrysten people.
> (London, John Waylande)

Contains: 'the texte' of Ps. 15 (with numbered verses i-vi); 'A Paraphrase' of the same; and exposition, all in English prose translated from Erasmus's *De puritate ecclesiae* (1536).

STC² 10495; Bodl., Antiq. f.E.$\frac{1537}{1}$.

9   1539   RICHARD TAVERNER (1505?–75)

> An Epitome of the Psalmes, or briefe meditacions upon the same, with diverse other moste christian prayers, translated by Richard Taverner.
> (London, [R. Bankes? for A. Clerke?])

Contains Christian prayers on themes loosely inspired by each psalm e.g. Ps. 1 'A prayer for true Godlynes'; Ps. 2 'For the true knowledge of Christe'; Ps. 60 'For strength of mynde to beare the crosse', with Lord's Prayer, 'Ave Maria' (censored in B. Lib. copy), Creed & Ten Commandments. Also 'The Principal Prayers of the Byble' gathered by Taverner (new register) with other prayers and graces. Translated from Wolfgang Fabricius Capito, *Precationes Christianae ad imitationem psalmorum compositae* (1536). Ded. to Henry VIII.

*STC*² 2748 formerly also 23710; B. Lib., C.53.i.25.
Anr edn of *The summe, or pith of the .150. psalmes of David reduced in to a forme of meditations* (1539), *STC*² 2747.5.

10   1540   [MILES COVERDALE]

The Psalter or boke of Psalmes both in Latyn and Englyshe, wyth a Kalender, & a Table the more eassyer and lyghtlyer to fynde the psalmes contayned therin.
                (London, Richard Grafton)

Pss. 1–150 in English prose printed in parallel columns with 'the comon texte in Latyne, which customably is redde in the churche'. English translation attributed to Coverdale by J. F. Mozley, *Coverdale and his Bibles* (1953), pp. 195–200.

*STC*² 2368; Bodl., Douce BB.71.
D & M 56.

11   1542   [THOMAS BECON (1512–67)]

Davids Harpe ful of moost delectable armony, newely strynged and set in tune by Theodore Basille.
                (London, John Mayler for John Gough)

Head title: 'Davids Harpe, The hundred & fyftene Psalme, called in Latin, Credidi propter, wyth a fruytfull exposicion and godly declaracion of the same' [i.e. Ps. 116: 10–19]. Also contains at end 'The Cxlv Psalme' (sig. M7ʳ-M8ʳ). Ded. to George Brooke, Lord Cobham. See Becon, *Early Works*, ed. J. Ayre (Parker Soc., 1843), pp. 262ff.; *H & L*³ D14.

*STC*² 1717; C.U.L., Syn. 8.54.59³.

12   1544   [JOHN FISHER (1469–1535)]

Psalmes or prayers taken out of holye scripture.
(London, Thomas Barthelet, 25 April)

Contains English prose translation of Ps. 21 [22] 'The complaynt of Christ on the Crosse' (sig. L1^r-L5^r) and Ps. 100 'A psalme of thankes gyvyng' (sig. L5^{r-v}), also fifteen original prayers composed mainly of unmarked psalm verses: each prayer is called a 'psalme' (sig. A2^r-K8^v). Printed on vellum with coloured title page and royal arms painted on title leaf verso. (Only one other such royal presentation copy from Henry VIII known, see *Haus der Bücher*, and *L'art ancien* auction sale 54 (Basle, 27 Sept. 1978), lot 14.) Translated from *Psalmi seu precationes D.Jo.Episcopi Roffensis* (Cologne [1525?]) repr. London, 18 April 1544 (*STC*^{2} 2994); 23 Aug. 1544 (*STC*^{2} 2995); 1568 (*STC*^{2} 2995^a) etc. See *H & L*^{3} P282 and K17.

STC^2 3001.7; Oxford, Exeter College, 9M.3001+.
See *STC*^{2} 3002ff. for eighteen subsequent edns up to 1601.
STC^2 3009 Anr edn (with additions) *The psalmes or praiers ... commonly called the Kynges psalmes* (London, H. Wykes, 1568).

13   1546   ANNE ASKEWE (1521–46)
              ed. JOHN BALE (1495–1563)

The first examinacyon of Anne Askewe, latelye martyred in Smythfelde, by the Romysh popes upholders, with the Elucydacyon of Johan Bale.
[Wesel, D. van der Straten]

Contains 'The voyce of Anne Askewe out of the 54. Psalme of David, called + Deus in nomine tuo + ' on sig. f. 7^r (i.e. after the colophon); English metrical paraphrase.

STC^2 848; Bodl., 8°C.46 Th. Seld.
Anr edn [1585?] *STC*^{2} 849.

14   1547   SIR ANTHONY COPE (d. 1551)

A godly meditacion upon .xx. select and chosen
Psalmes of the prophet David, as wel necessary to
al them that are desirsus to have the darke wordes
of the Prophet declared and made playn: as also
fruitfull to suche as delyte in the contemplation of
the spiritual meanyng of them. Compiled and
setfurth by Sir Anthony Cope Knight.
                    (London, Jhon Daye)

Contains prose expositions of themes from Pss. 1, 6, 12,
13, 23, 32, 49, 51, 73, 84, 90, 102, 103, 104, 116, 121, 130,
138, 139, 146, ded. to 'Katherine [Parr] Quene of
Englande' as a new year's gift.

STC² 5717; B. Lib., 697 g.11.

15   1547   MILES COVERDALE

Devout psalmes and colletes, gathered and set in
suche order, as may be used for dayly meditacions.
                (London, Edwarde Whitchurche)

Psalms from Coverdale's Great Bible (1539) version:
Monday: Pss. 1, 5, 6, 8; Tuesday: Pss. 12, 14, 15, 22; Wed-
nesday: Pss. 25, 27, 31, 32; Thursday: Pss. 34, 37, 39, 41;
Friday: Pss. 51, 52, 54, 55; Saturday: Pss. 59, 61, 62, 67;
Saturday afternoon: Pss. 77, 79, 80, 86; Sunday: Pss. 90,
95, 100, 103.

STC² 2999 formerly also 20478; C.U.L., Syn.8.54.100².
Anr edn (1550) STC² 3000.
Also [1550?] STC² 2999.5 formerly 20479.

16   1548   JOHN BALE

A Godly Medytacyon of the christen sowle, con-
cerninge a love towardes God and hys Christe,

compyled in frenche by lady Margarete quene of
Naverre, and aptely translated into Englysh by
the ryght vertuouse lady Elyzabeth doughter to
our late soverayne Kynge Henri the .viii.

([Wesel], D. van der Straten)

Contains English metrical paraphrase of Ps. 14 (fols.47^v-
48^r) formerly attributed to Elizabeth, but repr. as Ps. 23
(sic) in Bale's *An Expostulation or complaynte agaynste the
blasphemyes of a franticke papyst of Hamshyre* (London
[1551]), sig. C6^v (*STC*^{2} 1294); see D. S. Kastan, *Notes &
Queries*, n.s., xxi (1974), 404–5. Elizabeth's translation of
Le Miroir de l'âme pecheresse (1531) by Marguerite of
Navarre was edited by Bale with ded. to Elizabeth and
conclusion by him.

STC^2 17320; Bodl., Malone 502.
Other edns *STC*^{2} 17320.5ff.

17   1548   MILES COVERDALE

The Psalter or Boke of the Psalmes, where unto is
added the Letany and certayne other devout
prayers. Set forth wyth the Kynges moste
gracious lycence.

(London, Roger Car, for Anthoni Smyth)

Contains Pss. 1–150 from 1535 Coverdale Bible texts.

STC^2 2375; B. Lib., C.25.b.2
Cf. *STC*^{2} 2379, and 2379.5 'out of the Byble First Prynted
in southwarke by James Nicolson' (*D & M* 55).

18   1548   MILES COVERDALE

The Psalter or psalmes of David after the transla-
cion of the great Bible, poincted as it shalbe song
in Churches.

(London, R. Grafton)

*STC*² 2375.5; New York Public Lib. (unseen; title from *STC*²).

For anr edn (1549), see below no. 21.

19 1548

> [Devo]ut meditacions, [psal]mes and praiers [to]
> bee used aswell in the morning as eaventyde,
> gathered out of the holy scriptures and other
> godly writers.
>
>   (London, Edwarde Whitchurche)

Contains English prose version (slightly adapted from Coverdale's 1539 translation) of Ps. 103 (sig. A3ᵛ-5ʳ); a text headed 'Psalme', beginning 'Blessed be the lorde God of Israel' (sig. B1ʳ-2ʳ); 'The voyce of the devout Christian man to God', compiled from psalm verses (sig. B3ʳ⁻ᵛ) with 'The voyce of God unto man' (cf. Ps. 32) (sig. B3ᵛ-4ʳ), see also sig. B4ʳ–C1ᵛ; Ps. 24 [25] (sig. D5ᵛ-7ᵛ); Ps. 12 [13] (sig. D7ᵛ-8ʳ); Ps. 30 [31] (sig. D8ʳ-E1ʳ); Ps. 133 [134] (sig. E2ᵛ); see also prayer for 'Whan we laye us down to rest' compiled from psalm verses (sig. F1ʳ).

*STC*² 2998.5; Cambridge, Mass., Harvard University, *STC* film 1745.
Cf. *STC*² 2999, formerly 20478 (a different compilation); see above no. 15.

20 1549   JOHN BALE

> A dialogue or Communycacyon to be had at a
> table betwene two chyldren, gathered out of the
> holy scriptures, by Johan Bale, for his .ii. younge
> sonnes Johan and Paule.
>
>   (London, Richarde Foster)

Contains English metrical paraphrase of Ps. 130 'called De profundis' signed 'Johan Bale. Anno M.D.XLIII' on verso of title leaf.

*STC*² 1290; Bodl., Douce B. 55.
Repr. in his *An Expostulation or complaynte agaynste the blasphemyes of a franticke papyst of Hamshyre* [1551], sig. C7ʳ (*STC*² 1294).

21   1549   MILES COVERDALE

> The psalter or psalmes of David after the translacion of the great Byble, poynted as it shall be sayed or song in Churches.
> (London, Humfrey Powell for Edwarde Whitechurche)

Contains Psalms 1–150 in Coverdale's English prose translation first published in the Great Bible of 1539. Other editions include liturgical texts: e.g. *STC*² 2376.5 (1549) printed with an adaptation of the BCP for lay clerks; *STC*² 2377 includes the order for matins and evensong during the year, litany and suffrages, and other prayers.

*STC*² 2376; Cambridge, Emmanuel College, S1.4.29.
Anr edn of *STC*² 2375.5 (1548).
Other edns e.g. *STC*² 2377 (Aug. 1549); 2378 (Sept. 1549).

22   1549   ROBERT CROWLEY (1518?–88)

> The Psalter of David newely translated into Englysh metre in such sort that it maye the more decently, and wyth more delyte of the mynde, be reade and songe of al men. Wherunto is added a note of four partes, wyth other thynges, as shall appeare in the Epistle to the Readar. Translated and Imprinted by Robert Crowley.
> (London, Robert Crowley)

Pss. 1–150 in English metre translated from Latin of Leo Juda (d. 1542) to whom, Crowley says in his epistle, 'God hath reveyled ... those thynges that were unknowne to them that before hym translated the Psalter out of the Ebrue' (sig. ++2ʳ). See *Grove's Dictionary* (1954), vi,

957–8; P. Le Huray, *Music & the Reformation* (1978), pp. 371–2; A. B. Emden, *Biographical Register* ... *1501–40* (1974), pp. 153–4.

STC² 2725; B. Lib., C.36.e.25.

23   [1549?]
THOMAS STERNHOLD (d. AUG. 1549)

Certayne Psalmes chosen out of the Psalter of David, and drawen into Englishe Metre by Thomas Sternhold grome of the kynges Majesties Roobes.
(London, Edouardus Whitchurche)

English metrical paraphrases of Pss. 1–5, 20, 25, 27 [28], 29 (misnumbered 19), 32, 33 [34], 41, 49, 73, 78, 103, 120, 122 [123], 128 (misnumbered 138) ded. to Edward VI. Each psalm headed by metrical 'argument'.

STC² 2419; B. Lib., G.12147.
Anr edn (1549) *STC²* 2419.5. Cf. *STC²* 2420, no. 24 below. See Chart of Editions in *STC²*, i, 99–103.

24   1549   THOMAS STERNHOLD
JOHN HOPKINS (d. 1570)

Al such Psalmes of David as Thomas Sternehold late grome of the kinges Majesties Robes, didde in his life time draw into English Metre.
(London, Edwarde Whitchurche)

Contains Sternhold's nineteen metrical psalms from his *Certayne Psalmes* (*STC²* 2419) with the addition of Pss. 6–17, 19, 21, 43, 44, 63, 68 also by Sternhold. John Hopkins's seven psalms: Pss. 30, 33, 42, 52, 79, 82, 146 begin after his preface signed J. H. on sig. G2ᵛ. Each psalm headed by metrical 'argument'.

STC² 2420; C.U.L., Syn.8.54.157.

Other edns (1551) *STC²* 2422, 2423, 2424 *Psalmes of David drawn into English Metre by Tomas Sterneholde*; (1553) *STC²* 2424.2; [1553?] *STC²* 2424.4, 2424.6 (formerly 2421), 2424.8 (formerly also 2421); (1553) *STC²* 2425, 2426; [(1554) *STC²* 2426.5 (lost)].

25   1549   SIR THOMAS WYATT (1503–42)

> Certayne psalmes chosen out of the psalter of David/ commonlye called thee .vii. penytentiall psalmes, drawen into englyshe meter by Sir Thomas Wyat Knyght, wherunto is added a prologe of the auctore before every psalme, very pleasaunt & profettable to the godly reader.
> (London, Thomas Raynald and John Harryngton)

Contains lengthy metrical paraphrases of Pss. 6, 32, 38, 51, 102, 130, 143. Linking narrative prologues in metre are derived from Pietro Aretino's Italian prose version of the penitential psalms (1534). Ded. to William Parr (brother of Catherine Parr) by John Harryngton (of Stepney); see H. V. Baron, 'Sir Thomas Wyatt's Seven Penitential Psalms' (1977), pp. 171–9.

STC² 2726; C.U.L., Syn.8.54.156.

26   [1549–50]
     [HENRY HOWARD, EARL OF SURREY (1517–47)]

> Certayne Chapters of the proverbes of Salomon drawen into metre by Thomas Sterneholde, late grome of the kynges Magesties robes.
> (London, John Case for Willyam Seres)

Contains metrical versions of Pss. 88, 31 and 51 (sig. F1ʳ-F7ᵛ) now attributed to Surrey. Ded. to Sir Thomas Spek by Case states: 'The copye of thys boke was delivered me by a . . . servaunte unto maister Thomas Sterneholde, whereby it is to be conjectured, that the same were putte in metre by hym' (sig. A2ᵛ). Text of Ps. 88 differs from those in B. Lib., Additional MS 36529 and Arundel Castle, Harington MS; see *Surrey Poems*, ed. E. Jones (1964), pp. 98–9, and *Arundel Harington MS*, ed. R. Hughey (1960), i, 127–8. Surrey's Pss. 31 and 51 are not known from other sources. Cf. Seagar's revised and plagiarized versions of these three psalms in his *Certayne Psalmes* (1553), *STC²* 2728, no. 31 below; see C. A. Huttar, *English Miscellany*, xvi (1965), 9–18, and M. Rudick, *Notes & Queries*, n.s., xxii (1975), 291–4. Also contains metrical versions of Proverbs 1–11 and Ecclesiastes 1–3, neither of which are by Sternhold. For Hall's Proverbs see *STC²* 12631, no. 27 below; for Surrey's Ecclesiastes see manuscripts cited above.

*STC²*2760; B. Lib., C.25.a.29.

27   1550   JOHN HALL (1529?–66?)

> Certayn chapters taken out of the Proverbes of Salomon, wyth other chapters of the holy Scripture, & certayne Psalmes of David, translated into English metre, by John Hall. Whych Proverbes of late were set forth, Imprinted and untruely entituled, to be thee doynges of Mayster Thomas Sternhold, late grome of the Kynges Majesties robes, as by thys Copye it may be perceaved.
> (London, Thomas Raynalde)

Contains 'Certayne Psalmes of David, drawen in metre' beginning on F7ʳ: Pss. 25 [misnumbered xxi], 33 [34], 53 [54], 64 [65], 111 [112], 112 [113], 113 [114], 145. No music. Ded. to John Bricket of Eltham. Cf. *Certayne Chapters of the proverbes of Salomon drawen into metre by Thomas Sterneholde* [1549–50] *STC²* 2760, no. 26 above; cf. also Hall's variants on these psalms in his *Courte of Vertue* (1565) *STC²* 12632, no. 40 below.

STC² 12631; C.U.L., Syn.8.55.129.
Also two other edns [1550?] and one [c. 1553].

28   1550   WILLIAM HUNNIS (d. 1597)

Certayne Psalmes chosen out of the Psalter of
David, and drawen furth into Englysh meter by
William Hunnis servant to the ryght honorable
syr Wyllyam Harberde Knight Newly collected
& imprinted.
(London, the wydowe of Jhon Herforde, for Jhon
Harrington)

Contains six metrical psalms in contrasting moods: Pss.
51, 56, 57 (Latin incipits all 'Miserere'), Pss. 113, 117, 147
('Laudate'), with four canticles or hymns. No music.

STC² 2727; C.U.L., Syn.8.55.130.

29   1550   THOMAS PAYNELL (fl. 1528–68)

The Piththy and moost notable sayinges of al
Scripture, gathered by Thomas Paynell: after the
manner of common places, very necessary for al
those that delite in the consolacions of the
Scriptures.
(London, T. Gaultier, at the costes of R. Toye)

Contains very brief English prose extracts from seventy-
four psalms beginning sig. G4ʳ, published for 'mans consolation, & learning' (A1ᵛ). Ded. to Mary Tudor.

STC² 19494; B. Lib., C.25.a.15.
Other edns [1552?] *STC²* 19495, and (1560) *STC²* 19496.

30   1553   THOMAS BOWNELL (fl. 1553)

A Godly Psalme, of Marye Queene, which
brought us comfort al, Through God, whom
wee of dewtye prayse, that gives her foes a fal. By
Rychard Beeard.
(London, Wyllyam Griffith)

Contains metrical paraphrases of Pss. 145 [146]: 1–2, 7–9; 146 [147]: 6, 10; 148: 11–12 by Thomas Bownell beginning A7ʳ. (Beard's *Godly Psalme* is a song of praise for Catholics' release from persecution at the accession of Queen Mary and is not based on a biblical text.) Musical setting for four parts to Beard's 'Godly Psalme' could also be used for Bownell's texts.

STC² 1655; Cambridge, Trinity College, C.20.1¹ (on *STC* film 486).

31   1553   FRANCIS SEAGAR (fl. 1549–63)
          [HENRY HOWARD, EARL OF SURREY]

Certayne Psalmes select out of the Psalter of David, and drawen into Englyshe Metre, wyth Notes to every Psalme in iiii parts to Synge, by F.S.
          (London, Wyllyam Seres)

Metrical paraphrases of Pss. 88, 31, 51, 112, 130, 138, 140–47, 149, 43, 64, 120, 70 each set to one of two tunes. Seagar signs ded. to Lord Russell. For music see M. Frost, *English & Scottish Psalm & Hymn Tunes* (1953), pp. 339–42. Pss. 88, 31 and 51 are plagiarized, revised versions of Surrey's psalms printed as Sternhold's in *Certayne Chapters of the proverbes* [1549–50], *STC²* 2760, no. 26 above. See further C. A. Huttar, *English Miscellany*, xvi (1965), 9–18; M. Rudick, *Notes & Queries*, n.s. xxii (1975), 291–4.

STC² 2728, formerly also 22134; C.U.L., Syn.8.55.69.

32   1554   THOMAS BECON

A confortable Epistle/ too Goddes faythfyll people in Englande/ wherein is declared the cause of takynge awaye the true Christen religion from them/ & howe it maye be recovered and obtayned agayne/ newly made by Thomas Becon.

(Strasburgh) [i.e. really Wesel? J. Lambrecht?]

Contains at end on sig. D5ᵛ a metrical version of Ps. 103 'for a thankesgeving unto God/ immediatly after hys deliveraunce out of pryson' (16 Aug. 1553 – 22 Mar. 1554). Also, on sig. D7ᵛ, a metrical version of Ps. 112.

*STC*² 1716; Bodl., 8° E.26 Art BS.

33 [1554]   JOHN KNOX (1514?–72)

[a percel of the .vi. Psalme expounded.]
[London? John Day?]

Contains the opening of Knox's English prose exposition of Ps. 6 dedicated and addressed within the text to his mother (dated May 1554). Completed by 1556? and printed as *An Exposition uppon the syxt Psalme of David, wherein is declared hys crosse, complayntes and prayers* (*STC*² 15074.6) which incorporates verses from Ps. 6 in a new translation. Anr edn (revised) *A Fort for the afflicted. Wherin are ministred many notable & excellent remedies against the stormes of tribulation*, ed. Abraham Fleming (London, 1580), *STC*² 15074.8.

*STC*² 15074.4; Bodl., Arch. A.f.107 (imperfect, title from running head title).
Other edns *STC*² 15074.6; Bodl. film 323. *STC*² 15074.8, formerly 15072; Bodl., Arch. A.f.2.

34 1556
[ed. WILLIAM WHITTINGHAM (1524?–1579)]

One and Fiftie Psalmes of David in Englishe metre, wherof .37. were made by Thomas Sterneholde: and the rest by others. Conferred

with the hebrewe, and in certeyn places corrected
as the text, and sens of the Prophete required.
(Geneva, John Crespin)

First Genevan edition of metrical psalms based on but
different from London editions of Sternhold's thirty-seven
psalms and Hopkins's seven psalms: texts revised, see nos.
23–4 above. Includes anon. versions of Pss. 23, 51, 114,
115, 130, 133, 137 attributed to W. W. [i.e. Whittingham]
in later editions. All with printed tunes, short prose prefaces (or 'arguments'), also some interpretative marginalia.
See M. Frost, *English & Scottish Psalm & Hymn Tunes*
(1953), p. 3. See further *The Whole Booke* (1562), *STC*[2]
2430, no. 38 below; Table of Liturgies in *STC*[2], ii, 87–90.

STC[2] 16561, formerly also 11723; Bodl., Tanner 9.
See also *STC*[2] 2426.8 (52 pss. [Wesel, 1556?]); 16561a (62
pss., Geneva, 1558); 2427 (65 pss., London, 1560); 16562
(80 pss., pr. abroad, 1561); 16563 (87 pss., Geneva, 1561);
2428 (87 pss., [London] 1561); 2429 (82 pss., London,
1561); 2429.5 (*The Residue*, 77 pss., London, 1562).

35   1557

The Psalmes of David translated accordyng to the
veritie and truth of th' Ebrue, wyth annotacions
moste [profitable].
([Geneva, M. Blanchier])

English prose translation incorporating variants (some of
which were later incorporated in the Geneva Bible Psalms)
on Coverdale's 1539 Bible or BCP texts. The Preface
divides Psalms into five classes: 'prophetie, doctrine, consolation, prayer, and thankesgeving' (p. 4). Each psalm
prefaced by brief prose 'argument' reprinted from Whittingham's Calvinist sources (see his 1556 edn of metrical
psalms, no. 34 above). Brief comments including biblical
cross references and glosses on Hebrew words (cf.
Whittingham's edn & Geneva Bible (1560)).

*STC*² 2383.6; Bodl., Arch.A.g.12.
D & M 2331 (p. 491).

36   1559

> The Boke of Psalmes, where in are conteined
> praiers, meditations, praises & thankesgiving to
> God for his benefites toward his Church: trans-
> lated faithfully according to the Ebrewe, With
> brief and apt annotations in the margent, as wel
> for the declaracion of the mynde of the Prophet,
> as for the joyning together & continuance of the
> sentence.
>
>   (Geneva, Rouland Hall)

The first edition of the English prose translation for the
Geneva Bible Book of Psalms published separately before
the Bible (1560). Ded. to Queen Elizabeth dated from
Geneva, 10 Feb. 1559.

*STC*² 2384; Cambridge, Trinity College, C.7.50.

37   1562   JOHN HOOPER (d. 1555)

> A Exposition upon the .23. psalme of David full
> of frutefull and comfortable doctrin, written to
> the Citye of London by John Hooper, bushop of
> Gloceter and Worceter, and holye Martyr of God
> for the testimonye of hys truth. Wherunto is
> annexed an Apology of his, agaynst such as
> reported that he cursed Quene Mary, wyth cer-
> taine Godlye and comfortable letters in the ende.
>
>   (London, John Tisdale & Thomas Hacket)

Prose exposition of Ps. 23 beginning: 'The Lorde feedeth
me and I shall want nothinge'. See also Henry Bull's edn of
1580 (*STC*² 13743), no. 62 below. See Hooper, *Later
Writings*, ed. C. Nevinson (Parker Soc., 1852), pp. 184ff.

*STC*² 13752; Bodl., Tanner 30.

38   1562   [ed. WILLIAM WHITTINGHAM?]

The Whole Booke of Psalmes, collected into Englysh metre by T. Starnhold, J. Hopkins & others: conferred with the Ebrue, with apt Notes to synge them with al, Faithfully perused and alowed according to thordre appointed in the Quenes majesties Injunctions. Very mete to be used of all sortes of people privately for their solace & comfort: laying apart all ungodly Songes and Ballades, which tende only to the norishing of vyce, and corrupting of youth.

(London, John Day)

First edition of complete Anglo-Genevan metrical psalter with contributors' initials included in psalm headings i.e. Pss. 1–23, 25, 29, 32, 34, 41, 43–4, 49, 63, 66, 68, 73, 78, 103, 120, 123 attributed to T. S. [Thomas Sternhold] also Ps. 128 attributed to T. T. [Sternhold]; Pss. 24, 26–8, 30–1, 33, 35–6, 38–40, 42, 45–8, 50, 52, 54–62, 64–5, 67, 69–72, 74, 76–7, 79–99, 102 and 145 attributed to I. H. [John Hopkins]; Pss. 37, 51, 114, 119, 121, 129–130, 133, 137 attributed to W. W., also Pss. 124 and 127 attributed to W. [William Whittingham]; Pss. 51 (2nd version) and 53 attributed to T. N., also Pss. 75, 101, 105–6, 108–11, 115–17, 136, 138–45, 147, 149, 150 attributed to N. [Thomas Norton]; Pss. 104, 107, 112–13, 122, 125–6, 134 attributed to W. K. [William Kethe]; Pss. 118, 131–2, 135 attributed to M. [John Mardley?]; Ps. 148 attributed to I. P. [John Pullain]; Ps. 100 is anonymous in this edition. (N.B. Different attributions are made in some different editions.) Each psalm printed with music or directions for the application of a tune printed with another psalm; see M. Frost, *English & Scottish Psalm & Hymn Tunes* (1953), pp. 13–15. Also includes 'A shorte Introduction into the Science of Musicke, made for such as are desirous to have the knowledge therof, for the singing of these Psalmes' (sig. $+2^r- 7^r$); other canticles and hymns in English metre.

*STC*² 2430; B. Lib., C.25.g.3.
Many other edns see *STC*² 2430.5ff. (1563–1640 in *STC*²
period).

39   1564

> The Forme of Prayers and Ministration of the
> Sacraments &c. used in the English Church at
> Geneva, approved and received by the Churche
> of Scotland . whereunto besydes that was in the
> former bokes, are also added sondrie other
> prayers, with the whole Psalmes of David in
> English meter.
>
> (Edinburgh, Robert Lekprevik)

Contains metrical psalms with tunes from the Genevan
edn of *Four score and seven Psalmes* (1561) *STC*² 16563 and
the London edn of *The Whole Booke of Psalmes* (1562) *STC*²
2430, with the following new versions replacing those of
1562: Pss. 59, 76, 80, 81, 83 by Robert Pont; Pss. 102, 108,
110, 117, 118, 132, 136, 140, 141, 143, 145 by John Craig;
all with tunes. Versions of Pss. 24, 56, 75 and 105 by Craig
and of Ps. 57 by Pont are printed without tunes. See M.
Frost, *English & Scottish Psalm & Hymn Tunes* (1953), pp.
17–18. See further J. W. MacMeeken, *History of the Scottish
Metrical Psalters* (1872) and W. Cowan, 'A Bibliography of
the Book of Common Order and Psalm Book of the
Church of Scotland: 1556–1644', *Papers of the Edinburgh
Bibliographical Society*, x (1913), 71–98.

*STC*² 16577 (unseen, details from Frost of the copy in
Oxford, Corpus Christi College).
Many subsequent editions e.g. *STC*² 16578 (1566); also
*The Haill hundreth and fyftie Psalmes of David, in Ingl[ish]
meter, With utheris diveris Poyetis, quhilk completis the haill
Psalmes. As efter followis of the best Interpretouris* (Edinburgh,
Johue Scot, 1567), *STC*² 16578.5; and *The Cl . Psalmes of*

David in English metre . With the forme of Prayers (Edinburgh, Thomas Bassandine, 1575), *STC*² 16580.

40   1565   JOHN HALL

[The couurte of vertue contaynynge many holy or spretuall songes Sonettes psalmes ballettes shorte sentences as well of holy scriptures as others &c]
                  (London, Thomas Marshe)

Title supplied from the Stationers' Register for 1564–5. Contains metrical paraphrases of Pss. 25, 34, 54, 65, 112–15, 130, 137, 140, 145 each with a lengthy verse prologue. Hall is named in acrostic verses on sig. P1ʳ and at the end of the book. See *The Court of Virtue*, ed. R. A. Fraser (1961); cf. no. 27 above.

*STC*² 12632; Bodl., Douce W.26 (imperfect).

41   1565–6?
          [JOHN COXE (COCKIS) (fl. 1546–83)]

The Comentarye or exposition of Wolfegang Musculus uppon the li. psalme. Newlye translated out of Latine into Englishe the xii. of December.
                  (London, R. Serle for W. Lobley)

*STC*² 18307.5 (unseen, title from *H & L*³ C202).

42   1566   JOHN PITS (fl. 1566?)

A poore mannes benevolence to the afflicted Church.
                  (London, Alexander Lacy)

Contains metrical paraphrases of Pss. 67 and 100 each prefaced by a descriptive verse prologue on sig. B3ʳ-4ʳ.

*STC*² 19969; Bodl., 8° H.38Th.BS.

43 [*c.* 1567]   THOMAS BECON

> The Pomaunder of Prayer, by T. Becon.
> (London, John Daye)

Contains 'The vii Psalmes of the prophet David, with
Prayers made upon them', i.e. Pss. 6, 32, 38, 51, 102, 130,
143 in Coverdale's translation as 1539 Bible or BCP, pre-
ceded by a descriptive summary of each and followed by
the prayer 'taken out' of the psalm (fols. 35^r–54^r); also five
new prayers, entitled 'Meditations for the Soule', compiled
from different numbered psalm verses (fols. 29^v-32^r) (cf.
Fisher's *Psalmes or prayers* (1544 etc.), no. 12 above).
Includes portrait of Becon aged forty-one in 1553 on verso
of title leaf.

STC^2 1747.5 formerly 1745; Bodl., Douce B. 547.
Anr edn of *STC*^{2} 1744 (1558) which does not contain the
seven psalms or five prayers (cf. *STC*^{2} 1746 (1561) and
1746.5 (1563)).

44 [1567]   MATTHEW PARKER (1504–75)

> The whole Psalter translated into English Metre,
> which contayneth an hundreth and fifty Psalmes.
> (London, John Daye)

Contains lengthy verse prologue on virtue of the Psalms
with references to patristic commentators and humanist
biblical scholars; metrical paraphrases of Pss. 1–150 begin
on G3^r. Each psalm is prefaced by a short verse 'argument'
and followed by a prose collect related to the psalm's
themes. Attributed to Parker from acrostic verses prefixed
to Ps. 119; see V. J. K. Brook, *Life of Archbishop Parker*
(1965), p. 52. Eight musical settings (in four parts) by
Thomas Tallis beginning VV2^v; see M. Frost, *English &*
Scottish Psalm & Hymn Tunes (1953), pp. 374–93; P. Le
Huray, *Music and the Reformation* (1978), pp. 384–5, 218
and pl. 14. See further *H & L*^{3} W40.

STC^2 2729, formerly also 2439; Bodl., Douce BB. 233.

45 [1567]

> JAMES (d. 1553), JOHN (d. 1556) & ROBERT
> (d. 1557?) WEDDERBURN

[Ane compendius Buik . of Godly and Spirituall Sangis. Colletit out of sundrye partes of the Scripture, with sundrye uther Ballatis changeit out of prophaine sangis in godly sangis, for avoyding of sin and harlatry]
[Edinburgh, J. Scot]

Contains metrical psalms adapted from Lutheran sources, see A. F. Mitchell's edn (Scottish Text Soc., 1897), pp. 85–131, 136–7, 161–2. The enlarged 1600 edn (STC^2 2997) reprints Pss. 2, 12, 13, 15, 23, 33, 37, 64, 73, 83, 91, 114, 124, 130, 137, 145, 79, 51, 128 (many misnumbered) on sig. F2^v–H8^v); also Ps. 67 (sig. I3) and Ps. 31 (sig. K7). Cf. Coverdale's *Goostly psalmes* [1535?], no. 5 above. See further *H & L³* C299.

STC^2 2996.5 (unseen).
Title from anr edn (1600) STC^2 2997; B. Lib. C.39.d.63.
Anr edn [1578] STC^2 2996.7.

46 1568   HENRY BULL (d. 1575?)

[Christian Praiers and holie Meditations, as wel for Private as Publique exercise: Gathered out of the most godly learned in our time, by Henrie Bull. Whereunto are added the praiers, commonly called Lidleys praiers.]
(London, Thomas East for Henry Middleton)

Contains 'A Psalme to be sayd in the time of any common plague' (pp. 279–83) composed of psalm verses and other biblical texts; 'A Psalme of thankesgivinge for deliveraunce from the Plague' (pp. 283–5) composed entirely of selected psalm verses; also three prayers based on Ps. 1 (pp. 341–5) and two prayers based on Ps. 2 (pp. 345–7) attributed to

'Peter Martir' (cf. STC^2 24671, a different translation, see no. 48 below). See Parker Society reprint (1842) from STC^2 4029 (1570).

STC^2 4028; Bodl., Vet. A1 f.37 (imperfect, title from STC^2 4030 [1578?] (London, Henri Middleton) in C.U.L., SSS.34.20).
Other edns STC^2 4029ff.

47 [1568?] JAMES CANCELLAR (fl. 1564)

[A Godly Meditation of the Soule, concerning a Love towardes Christ ... Wherunto is added godlye Meditations, set forth after the Alphabet of the Queenes Majesties name.]
(London, H. Denham)

James Cancellar's edition of Elizabeth's *Godly Meditation of the Soule* translated from Marguerite of Navarre's *Miroir* (see STC^2 17320 (1548), no. 16 above), includes his own acrostic meditation (sig. H1^r-K6^v) on *Elizabeth Regina*, compiled principally from individual psalm verses in English prose adapted from Coverdale's translations. Reprinted in T. Bentley's *Monument of Matrones* (1582) STC^2 1892 (see no. 63 below).

STC^2 17320.5 (unseen, lacks title page); title from anr edn STC^2 17321 (London, H. Denham, 1580); Bodl., Mason CC.3.

48 1569 CHARLES GLEMHAN (fl. 1569)

Most Godly prayers compiled out of Davids Psalmes by D. Peter Martyr. Translated out of Latin into English by Charles Glemhan. G.
(London, William Seres)

A collection of brief prayers in English prose based closely on each of Pss. 1–150, some with two prayers from each.

Translated from Jonas Simler's edn of the Latin prayers by Pietro Martire Vermigli (1500–62); Simler's ded. dated 20 June 1564 from Zurich. (Cf. Henry Bull's *Christian Praiers* (1568) see no. 46 above for prayers from Pss. 1 and 2; also John Day's edn *Christian Prayers and Meditations* (London, 1569), *STC²* 6428 for prayers from Pss. 6, 32, 38, 51, 102, 130, 143 (the seven penitential psalms) on sig. A1ʳ-F8ᵛ.)

STC² 24671; C.U.L., SSS.47.39.
cf. *STC²* 6428; San Marino, Huntington Lib. (on *STC* film 214).

49   1569   WILLIAM SAMUEL (fl. 1551–69)

An abridgement of all the Canonical books of the olde Testament, written in Sternholds meter by W. Samuel Minister.
(London, William Seres)

For the Book of Psalms, each psalm reduced to a four-line adaptation in ballad metre, see sig. N3ᵛ-P6ʳ.

STC² 21690 formerly also 3044; B. Lib., C.12.d.19.

50   1571   ARTHUR GOLDING (1536?–1605?)

The Psalmes of David and others. With M. John Calvins Commentaries.
(London, Thomas East and Henry Middleton for Lucas Harison and Gorge Byshop)

Contains English prose translations of Pss. 1–150 each prefaced by a brief summary of contents and each followed by the translation of Calvin's Latin commentary, with Calvin's ded. to the reader (dated Geneva 23 July 1557). Golding's ded. to Edward de Vere, Earl of Oxford is dated London 20 October 1571. Includes a 'Table declaring the principal matters' of the commentaries at the end of the book.

STC² 4395, formerly also 2389; Bodl., LL.44 Th.

51   1571   THOMAS WHYTHORNE (1528–96)

Triplex, Of Songes, for three, fower, and five voyces, composed and made by Thomas Whythorne, gent the which Songes be of sundry sortes.

(London, John Day)

Contains metrical versions of Pss. 138 and 103 (four lines only); with Pss. 95, 100, 134 and 130 in Coverdale's prose as 1539 Bible or BCP, also a musical setting for one line from Ps. 123, see fols. 8, 19^v, 22^v, 23^v, 26, 27^v and 24^v. The tenor part-book contains Whythorne's preface describing the contents of the books. See *The Autobiography of Thomas Whythorne*, ed., J. M. Osborn (1961), pp. 178–92, Appendix VI and plate facing p. xlii.

STC^2 25584; B. Lib., L.R.39.a.6 (lacks tenor part). Bodl., Douce WW.62 (tenor part only).

52   157[2?]   ROBERT FYLLES (fl. 1562)

Godly prayers and Meditations, paraphrasticallye made upon all the Psalmes very necessary for al the godly, translated out of Frenche into Englishe.

(London, W. Seres)

Contains 150 English prayers 'taken out of the Psalmes, declaring briefly the substance and interpretation of the same, whiche booke is likewise printed in the Latin and Frenche tonges' (from ded. to Viscount Ferie of Hereford, sig. A4^r).

STC^2 10867; B. Lib., C.25.a.30(1).

53   1575   GEORGE GASCOIGNE (1542–77)

The Posies of George Gascoigne Esquire. Corrected, perfected, and augmented by the Authour.

(London, H. Bynneman for Richard Smith)

Gascoigne's metrical paraphrase of Ps. 130 composed 1563? included in 'flowers' section of *The Posies*, xxvi-xxviii. A preface to the psalm appears in Gascoigne's *A Hundreth sundrie Flowres* [1573], *STC²* 11635, pp. 372-3 wherein Gascoigne's 'De profundis' is said to 'have verie sweete notes adapted unto them'. An introductory sonnet describes the 'occasion of the wrighting hereof'. No music. See *Works*, ed. J. W. Cunliffe, ii (1910), 177.

STC² 11636; Bodl., Malone 791.
STC² 11635; Bodl., Wood 329.
Other edns (1575) *STC²* 11637 and *The Whoole woorkes* (1587) *STC²* 11638.

54   1577   HENRY BULL

A Commentarie upon the Fiftene Psalmes, called Psalmi Graduum, that is, Psalmes of Degrees: Faithfully copied out of the lectures of D. Martin Luther, very frutefull and comfortable for all Christian afflicted consciences to reade. Translated out of Latine into English by Henry Bull.
(London, Thomas Vautroullier)

English prose translations (as Geneva Bible) of Pss. 120–34; each psalm verse followed by lengthy commentary with summaries and biblical cross references in margins. Includes Luther's preface. (John Fox's Epistle to the reader indicates that Bull died shortly after completing his translation.)

STC² 16975; Bodl., 4° Rawlinson 524.
Other edns (1577 etc.) *STC²* 16975.5ff.

55   1577   THOMAS POTTER (fl. 1577?)

An Exposition upon the Cxxx. Psalme, Setting forth the comfortable doctrine of our justification and peace in Christ. Written by M. Luther: and

nowe newlye translated for the comfort of afflicted consciences, by Thomas Potter.
(London, Hugh Singleton)

Translated from Luther's text ('finished at Wittenberge, the first October 1533'); Potter's translation 'finished at Kingesdowne the 2. of March 1576'. Each psalm verse is followed by a lengthy commentary. Marginal corrections include quotations from the 'Geneva translation' (1560 Bible), see E5^r.

STC^2 16979.3, formerly 20137. Bodl., 8° S.322 Art.

56   [1577?]   G.C.

A Pitious platforme of an oppressed mynde, set downe by the extreme surmyzes of sundrye distressed meditations by, G.C.
(London, Thomas Gardiner and Thomas Dawson for R.B.)

Contains extended metrical meditations based on paraphrases of Pss. 1–5, 10, 15, 130.

STC^2 4269; San Marino, Huntington Lib. (on *STC* film 185).

57   1578   ABRAHAM FLEMING (1552?–1607)

A Pithie Exposition upon the .51. Psalme intituled, Miserere mei Deus, &c. Also a godly meditation, upon the .31. Psalme, intituled, In te Domine speravi. Written by Hierome of Ferrarie: And now newly augmented and amended, by Abraham Fleming.
(London, Thomas Dawson)

(Cf. [1534] tr. no. 3 above) English prose only. The psalm text is printed in full and followed by Savonarola's exposition which includes a verse by verse reprint of the psalm text. Texts from Geneva Bible of 1560. Ps. 31 begins on sig. I6ᵛ (treated as Ps. 51). Ded. to Gabriel Goodman, Dean of Westminster.

*STC*² 21797, formerly also 14504; B. Lib., C.25.a.30(2).

58   1578   [ed. RICHARD DAY (1552–1607?)]

A Booke of Christian Prayers, collected out of the auncient writers, and best learned in our tyme, worthy to be read with an earnest mynde of all Christians, in these daungerous and troublesome dayes, that God for Christes sake will yet still be mercyfull unto us.
(London, John Daye)

Contains devotional compilations entitled 'A comfort after craving of mercy gathered out of the psalmes' (fols. 71ʳ-72ʳ); and 'A Prayer to be sayd of such as be under the crosse' (fols. 122ʳ–123ʳ) composed from paraphrases of Pss. 13, 88 and others. Includes many illustrated page borders. R. D. signs ded. To the Christian Reader; see *H & L*³ B101.

*STC*² 6429; Bodl., Tanner 285.
See other edns *STC*² 6430ff.

59   1579   THOMAS ROGERS (d. 1616)

A Golden Chaine, taken out of the rich Treasure house the Psalmes of King David: also, the pretious Pearles of King Salomon; Published for the adorning of al true Christians which are the right Nobilitie, against the triumphant returne of our blessed Saviour, which is nigh at hande. By Thomas Rogers.
(London, Henrie Denham)

Prose compilations of occasional devotions (called links) from psalm verses arranged in three parts (instructions,

prayers and petitions, thanksgivings and praises), each
with psalm sources indicated in margins. Ded. to Queen
Elizabeth.

STC² 21235; Bodl., Vet.A1 f.128.
Anr edn (1587) *STC²* 21236.

60   1579   [ROBERT TRAVERS (fl. 1561–72)]

A Learned and a very profitable exposition made
upon the cxi Psalme.
            (London, Thomas Vautroullier)

English prose. Travers is named in Greek and described as
a fellow of Trinity College, Cambridge. The anon. ded. to
Trinity indicates that the 'worke was both made and
uttered in your Colledge, and for it alone: ... It cost him
the losse of his fellowship' (sig. ★2ᵛ); published as a memorial to the deceased Travers and as a means of admoni-
shing the College.

STC² 24180; Bodl., 8° S.322 Art.
Anr edn 'By R.T.' (1583) *STC²* 24180.3.

61   1580   ANTHONY GILBY (c. 1510–85)

The Psalmes of David, truely opened and
explaned by Paraphrasis, according to the right
sense of every Psalme. With large and ample
Arguments before every psalme, declaring the
true use therof. To the which is added a briefe
Table, shewing whereunto every Psalme is particularly to be applied, according to the direction
of M. Beza and Tremelius. Set foorth in Latine
by that excellent learned man Theodore Beza.
And faithfully translated into English, by Anthonie Gilbie.
      (London, John Harison and Henrie Middleton)

Pss. 1–150 in English prose paraphrases translated from Beza's Latin (Geneva, 1579 and London, 1580). Each psalm 'paraphrasis' prefaced by a short detailed 'argument' summarizing contents. Ded. by Gilby to Catherine Hastings (née Dudley), Countess of Huntingdon, dated from 'Ashby 7 March 1579'. (Latin edn ded. to her husband, 1580).

STC[2] 2033; San Marino, Huntington Lib. (on *STC* film 828).

Other edns (1581) *STC*[2] 2034, formerly also 2398; and (1590) enlarged, *STC*[2] 2035.

62   1580   JOHN HOOPER

Certeine comfortable Expositions of the constant Martyr of Christ, M. John Hooper, Bishop of Glocester and Worcester, written in the time of his tribulation and imprisonment, upon the XXIII. LXII. LXXIII. and LXXVII. Psalmes of the Prophet David. Newly recognized, and never before published.
                    (London, Henrie Middleton)

Lengthy prose expositions of Pss. 23 (repr. from 1562 edn *STC*[2] 13752 see no. 37 above), 62, 73 and 77 by Hooper, edited by Henry Bull (see A. F.'s Epistle to the Reader, sig. 4[r]). See Hooper, *Later Writings*, ed. C. Nevinson (Parker Soc., 1852).

STC[2] 13743; Bodl., 8° Z.599 Th.

63   1582
     THOMAS BENTLEY OF GRAY'S INN (fl. 1582)

The Monument of Matrones: conteining seven severall Lamps of Virginitie, or distinct treatises; whereof the first five concerne praier and meditation: the other two last, precepts and examples, as the woorthie works partlie of men, partlie of women; compiled for the necessarie use of both sexes out of the sacred Scriptures, and other approved authors, by Thomas Bentley of Graies Inne Student.

(London, H. Denham)

The first Lamp includes (p. 48), 'A praier of the Church' (i.e. Ps. 123 as 1539 Bible/BCP).

The second Lamp includes a prayer by Lady Jane Dudley 'a little before hir death' composed of psalm verses in prose paraphrase embedded in her new text (pp. 98–100); 'divers Psalmes, Hymnes and Meditations' by Lady Elizabeth Tyrwhit compiled from psalm verses in prose (begins p. 103); 'other godlie praiers taken out of the Psalmes, written by a godlie harted Gentlewoman' (pp. 215–20); a prayer 'out of the 143 Psalme', verses 8–10 (p. 226); a prayer 'out of the 119 Psalme, verses 9, 18, 34' (pp. 227–8).

The third Lamp includes: 'Right godlie Psalmes ... to be said of ... Queene Elizabeth' especially on 17 November, i.e. Ps. 18 (cf. Gilby's tr. of Beza's paraphrases, see no. 61 above) and Ps. 118 (pp. 253–7 and 258–60); 'Holie Praiers ... desciphering in Alphabeticall forme' *Elizabeth Regina* (pp. 280–96), reprinted from STC^2 17321 (1580) see no. 47 above; two prayers 'Collected out of the Psalmes' from Beza's paraphrases (begins p. 306).

The fourth Lamp contains a 'praier for the prosperous estate and flourishing reigne' of the Queen headed 'Psalme 72' (p. 712), cf. Patten's Ps. 72 (1583) STC^2 2368.3 see no. 69 below; 'The Dolefull Doove, Or Davids penitentiall Psalmes' as Coverdale's 1539 Bible and BCP (pp. 895–903); 'Other Psalmes or Praiers, compiled out of holie Scriptures, verie necessarie to be used of the afflicted soule, for obteining the remission of sinnes, and mitigation of miseries' (pp. 903–31); 'The Psalter, which S. Augustine composed out of everie Psalme of David a verse, for the use of his Mother' (pp. 937–43); cf. 'Shushanna hir Psalter, conteining verie devout praiers for remission of sinnes' (pp. 943–55); 'A forme of praier, conteining a paraphrasis of these words of David in his 119. Psalme: Order my steps in thy word, and so shall no wickednesse have dominion over me' (pp. 971–5); see also 'The Table' of contents (after p. 1000, i.e. at end of fourth Lamp) naming various occasional prayers as psalms.

The fift Lampe ... to bee used onlie of and for all sorts and degrees of women was published separately (1582) *STC²* 1893 and contains Ps. 22 'called The complaint of Christ on the Crosse' with a direction for women to say this psalm with or instead of the seven penitiential psalms 'in long and sore labour' (pp. 109–12); cf. directions to use Pss. 103, 30, 116 with text of Ps. 121 after childbirth (pp. 123–4), also Pss. 8, 127 and 128 (p. 154). All ded. to Queen Elizabeth.

STC² 1892; Bodl., 4° C.38 Jur. (Lamps 1–3).
STC² 1893; C.U.L., Syn.7.58.1. (complete).

64 1582
RICHARD ROBINSON, CITIZEN OF LONDON
(fl. 1576–1600)

Part of the Harmony of King Davids Harp. Conteining the first XXI. Psalmes of King David. Briefly & learnedly expounded by the Reverend D. Victorinus Strigelius Professor of Divinitie in the Universitie of Lypsia in Germanie. Newly translated into English by Rich. Robinson.
(London, John Wolfe)

Contains English prose argument, text and exposition translated from Strigelius's Latin (1562). Texts of Pss. 1–21 adapted from the Geneva translation (1560). Ded. to Ambrose Dudley, Earl of Warwick. Expositions include quotations and translations from classical literature, e.g. the exposition of Ps. 23 (1591 edn) cites Virgil, *Georgics*, 3;

that of Ps. 37 quotes from *Aeneid*, 2 and provides an English metrical paraphrase of the Latin.

*STC*² 23358; C.U.L., Syn.7.58.13¹.
See also *STC*² 23359ff. *A Proceeding in the harmonie* (Pss. 22–34) (1591); *A second proceeding* (Pss. 35–44) (1593); *A third . . .* (Pss. 45–61) (1595); *A fourth . . .* (Pss. 62–7) (1596); *A fift . . .* (Pss. 68–72) (1598).

65   1582
RICHARD STANYHURST (1547–1618)

Thee First Foure Bookes of Virgil his Aeneis Translated intoo English heroical verse by Richard Stanyhurst, wyth oother Poetical divises theretoo annexed.
(Leiden, John Pates)

Contains metrical paraphrases of Pss. 1–4 in English quantitative metres beginning on p. 86. Ps. 1 in 'Iambical verse'; Ps. 2 in 'Heroical and Elegiacal verse'; Ps. 3 in 'Asclepiad verse'; Ps. 4 in 'Saphick verse'; each psalm headed by a note on the selected metre. Ded. to 'my verie looving broother thee Lord Baron of Dunsanye' dated June 1582.

*STC*² 24806; Bodl., 90.b.36.
Anr edn (London, H. Bynneman, 1583) *STC*² 24807.

66   1582   [JOHN STUBBS 1543?–91]

Christian meditations upon eight Psalmes of the Prophet David. Made and newly set forth by Theodore Beza. Translated out of Frenche, for the common benefite, into the vulgare tongue by I.S.
(London, Christopher Barker)

English prayers based on Pss. 1, 6, 32, 38, 51, 102, 130, 143 with texts from Geneva translation (1560) in margin. Ded. to Lady Anne Bacon. For attribution to Stubbs, see *H & L*³

C148. Beza's *Chrestiennes Méditations* was first published Geneva, 1582.

*STC*² 2004; B. Lib., 3090.aaaa.7.
Anr edn [1583?] *STC*² 2005.

67   1583   [GEORGE FLINTON (d. 1585)]

> A Manual of Prayers Newly Gathered out of many and divers famous authours aswell auncient as of the tyme present.
>   [Rouen, George L'Oyselet]

Contains new prayers and psalm paraphrases of recusant provenance: Ps. 78 [79] (fol. 110ᵛ); Ps. 142 (fol. 52ᵛ); Ps. 139 [140] (fol. 56ᵛ); also More's Latin 'devoute prayer collected' out of the Psalms (fol. 59ᵛ) (Ps. 139 see *Complete Works*, xiii, ed. G. E. Haupt (1976), 215–25); and texts from Fisher's *Psalmes or prayers* (see no. 12 above): cf. 'A psalme' (fol. 97ʳ) and Fisher's 13th 'psalm' (1545 edn (*STC*² 3003.5), sig. L2ʳ-L6ᵛ), cf. 'A psalme' (fol. 100ᵛ) and Fisher's 14th 'psalm' (1545 edn, sig. L7ʳ-M1ᵛ), cf. 'A psalme' (fol. 103ʳ) and Fisher's 15th 'psalm' (1545 edn, sig. M2ᵛ-M6ᵛ), cf. 'A prayse' (fol. 108ᵛ) and Fisher's 15th 'psalm' this text only attributed to 'Io. Roffe' (i.e. John [bishop of] Rochester). See further *H & L*³ M27.

*STC*² 17263, formerly 14566; Bodl., 8° M.58 Th.
Many subsequent editions, mostly printed abroad or at English secret presses, see *STC*² 17264ff.

68   1583   WILLIAM HUNNIS

> Seven Sobs of a Sorrowfull Soule for Sinne. Comprehending those seven Psalmes of the Princelie Prophet David, commonlie called Poenitentiall: framed into a forme of familiar praiers, and reduced into meeter by William Hunnis, one of the Gentlemen of hir Majesties honourable Chapell, and maister to the children of the same.

Whereunto are also annexed his Handfull of
Honisuckles; the Poore Widowes Mite; a Dialog
betweene Christ and a sinner; divers godlie and
pithie ditties; with a Christian confession of and
to the Trinitie; newlie printed and augmented.
(London, Henrie Denham)

Contains extended adaptations of the seven penitential
psalms (6, 32, 38, 51, 102, 130, 143) in metre with a close
paraphrase of each psalm verse (printed in italics)
embedded in the new adaptations; also a Latin prose translation in the margins. Includes tunes for Pss. 6, 38 and 51
with directions for other psalms to be sung to one or other
of these, see M. Frost, *English & Scottish Psalm & Hymn
Tunes* (1953), pp. 459–67. Hunnis's fourth meditation in
his *Widowes Mite* (pp. 35–6) is 'gathered' from several
different psalms. Ded. to Frances Radcliffe (née Sidney),
Countess of Sussex. Entered *Stationers' Register*, 7 Nov.
1581 as *VII Steppes to heaven alias the vii Psalmes reduced into
meter*.

*STC*² 13975; Bodl., Arch. A.f.63.
Other edns (1585, 1587, 1589, 1592, 1597, 1600 etc.)
See *STC*² 13975.5ff.

69   1583
    [WILLIAM PATTEN (*c.* 1510–*c.* 1600)]

1583. Ann: foelicissimi regni Reginae Elizabeth:
XXVI. The Sallm by the olld Translation called
Deus Iudicium.
(London, Abel Jeffes)

English metrical adaptation of Ps. 72 published with a
simple tune and parallel Latin paraphrase from Johannes
Campensis, *Enchiridion Psalmorum* (1533). Head title of this
broadside indicates that this adaptation is an occasional
piece for Elizabeth's silver jubilee; 'Like az the ditti thearof
waz in Ebru vers, so apted heer in English meeter into

Seaven Septenariez ... for honoour of oour Sovereinz name, that is in Ebru Elizabeth.' For attribution to Patten see B. O'Kill, *Transactions of the Cambridge Bibliographical Society*, vii (1977), 32–3; and *H & L*[3] F47. See also no. 83 below.

STC[2] 2368.3; Colchester Public Lib., Harsnett Collection I.F.11.

70   1584
    [KING JAMES VI OF SCOTLAND (1566–1625)]

The Essayes of a Prentise, in the Divine Art of Poesie.
      (Edinburgh, Thomas Vautroullier)

Contains metrical version of 'The CIIII Psalme, translated out of Tremellius' in twelve eight-line stanzas (sig. N3[r]-N4[v]). (The new Latin translation by Tremellius of the Old Testament was first published 1579.)
See James's *Poems*, ed. J. Craigie, Scottish Text Soc., ser. 3, xxvi (1958).

STC[2] 14373; B. Lib., G.11237.
Anr variant edn (1585) *STC*[2] 14374.

71   1586   [THOMAS WILCOX (1549?–1608)]

A Right Godly and learned Exposition, upon the whole Booke of Psalmes: Wherein is set forth the true Division, Sence, and Doctrine contained in every Psalme: for the great furtheraunce and necessarie instruction of every Christian Reader. Newly and faithfully set forth by a Godly Minister and Preacher of the word of God.
(London, [T. Dawson] for T. Man & W. Brome)

Expositions of Pss. 1–150 based on the English translations of the Geneva Bible Psalms. For attribution to Wilcox see *Stationers' Register* 7 Feb., 1586.

*STC*² 25625; Bodl., Holkham e. 15.
Anr edn enlarged, *A very godly and learned exposition* (1591)
*STC*² 25626.

72   1587   RICHARD ROBINSON

>The Solace of Sion, and Joy of Jerusalem. Or
>Consolation of Gods Church in the latter age,
>redeemed by the preaching of the Gospell univer-
>sallye. Beeing a godly and learned exposition of
>the Lxxxvii. Psalme of the Princelye Prophet
>David: Written in Latine by the reverend Doctor
>Urbanus Regius Pastor of Christes Church at
>Zelle, in Saxonie. 1536. Translated into English
>by R. Robinson Citizen of London.
>   (London, [R. Jones])

Contains verse by verse prose translation of Ps. 87 with
lengthy exposition translated from the Latin of Urbanus
Regius (1489–1541). Ded. to Sir George Barne, Lord
Mayor of London by his 'humble Orator', Richard Robinson. Cf. *Harmony of King Davids Harp* (1582), no. 64
above.

*STC*² 20852; Bodl., 8° S.322 Art.
Other edns (1591 and 1594) *STC*² 20853 and 20854.

73   1588

>A Psalme and Collect of thankesgiving, not
>unmeet for this present time: to be said or sung in
>Churches.
>   (London, Deputies of Christopher Barker)

The 'Psalme of thankesgiving' (sig. A2ʳ–3ᵛ) is an occasional prayer in English prose compiled from adaptations
of different psalm verses in Coverdale's translation (as
BCP); psalm sources indicated in margins. Published to
give thanks for the defeat of the Spanish Armada: 'The

Angel of the Lord persecuted them, brought them into dangerous, darke, and slipperie places, where they wandering long to and fro, were consumed with hunger, thirst, colde, and sicknesse: the sea swalowed the greatest part of them' (sig. A3ʳ) (Cf. Pss. 48, 83, 35).

STC² 16520; Cambridge, Emmanuel College, S1.4.35.

74   1588   WILLIAM BYRD (1538?–1623)

> Psalmes, Sonets, & songs of sadnes and pietie, made into Musicke of five parts: whereof, some of them going abroad among divers, in untrue coppies, are heere truely corrected, and th' other being Songs very rare and newly composed, are heere published, for the recreation of all such as delight in Musicke: By William Byrd, one of the Gent. of the Queenes Majesties honorable Chappell.
>
>   (London, Thomas East)

Contains metrical versions of verses from Pss. 55, 123, 119 (pt 4 and 2 only), 13, 15, 12, 112, 6:1–2, 130:1–2 (sig. B1ʳ-C4ᵛ). Ded. to Sir Christopher Hatton prefaced by 'Reasons briefely set downe by th' auctor, to perswade every one to learne to sing'. Texts from Pss. 55 and 6 from Anglo-Genevan metrical psalms. Texts and music repr. in *The English Madrigalists*, ed. E. H. Fellowes, xiv (rev. P. Brett) (1965); see further P. Le Huray, *Music & the Reformation* (1978), pp. 223–4 and 386–7.

STC² 4253; Bodl., 85.d.8.
Other edns see STC² 4253.3ff.

75   1589   WILLIAM BYRD

> Songs of sundrie natures, some of gravitie, and others of myrth, fit for all companies and voyces. Lately made and composed into Musicke of

3.4.5. and 6. parts: and published for the delight of all such as take pleasure in the exercise of that Art. By William Byrd, one of the Gentlemen of the Queenes Majesties honorable Chappell.
(London, Thomas East)

Contains new metrical versions of the seven penitential psalms (i.e. 6, 32, 38, 51, 102, 130, 143) for three voices (sig. B1^r-B4^r); Ps. 133 for six voices begins sig. G3^r; Ps. 121 (six voices) begins sig. H2^r. Ded. to Sir Henry Carye (the Lord Chamberlain). Texts and music repr. in *The English Madrigalists*, ed. E. H. Fellowes, xv (rev. P. Brett) (1962).

*STC*² 4256; Bodl., [MS] Mus.Sch.E.453–8.
Other edns *STC*² 4256.5ff.

76 1589
RICHARD ROBINSON OF ALTON (fl. 1569–89)

A Golden Mirrour. Conteining certaine Pithie and figurative Visions prognosticating good fortune to England and all true English Subjectes, with an overthrowe to the enemies. Whereto be adjoyned certaine pretie Poemes written on the names of sundrie both noble and worshipfull.
(London, Roger Ward for John Proctor)

Contains 'A Psalme pend upon the Etimologie of the name of the right Worshipfull, Thomas Leigh of Adlington, in the Countie of Chester, Esquire: To the note or tune of, Domine ne in furore. Psalme .VI.': an adaptation of Ps. 6 (no music) in acrostic verses naming Thomas Leigh (begins sig. E4^r). Richard Robinson of Alton named in acrostic verses (sig. H3^v-H4^r). Proctor signs ded. to Gilbert Talbot.

*STC*² 21121.5, formerly 21119; B. Lib., C.21.c.13.

77   1590   THOMAS WHYTHORNE

Bassus. Of Duos, or Songs for two voices, composed and made by Thomas Whythorne Gent.
Of the which, some be playne and easie to be
sung, or played on Musicall Instruments, & be
made for yong beginners of both those sorts.
And the rest of these Duos be made and set foorth
for those that be more perfect in singing or
playing as aforesaid, all the which be devided into
three parts.
(London, Thomas Este)

Contains twelve songs with words from Ps. 119:1–45 in
Coverdale's prose as BCP (sig. A2^v-B4^v). Ded. to Francis
Hastings dated from London 19 Nov. 1590. Cf. Why-
thorne's *Songes* (1571), no. 51 above.

STC^2 25583; Bodl., Douce W.subt.30.

78   1591

ABRAHAM FRAUNCE (fl. 1587–1633)

The Countesse of Pembrokes Emanuel. Contein-
ing the Nativity, Passion, Buriall, and Resurrec-
tion of Christ: togeather with certaine Psalmes of
David. All in English Hexameters. By Abraham
Fraunce.
(London, Thomas Orwyn for William Ponsonby)

Extended metrical paraphrases of Pss. 1, 6, 8, 29, 38, 50,
73, 104 begin sig. D2^v. The ded. is to Mary Herbert (née
Sidney). Cf. Fraunce's secular companion volume *The
Countesse of Pembrokes Yvychurch* (1591).

STC^2 11339; Bodl., Wood 482.
(a variant of *STC*^{2} 11338.5 (1591)).

79 1593   JOHN UDALL (1560?–92)

מַפְתֵּחַ לְשׁוֹן הַקֹּדֶשׁ

That is the Key of the Holy Tongue: Wherein is
conteineid, first the Hebrue Grammar (in a
manner) woord for woord out of P. Martinius.
Secondly, A practize upon the first, the twentie
fift, and the syxtie eyght Psalmes, according to
the rules of the same Grammar ... Englished for
the benefit of those that (being ignoraunt in the
Latin) are desirous to learn the holy tongue; By
John . Udall.

(Leyden, Francis Raphelengius)

Contains Ps. 25 in English prose translation (in numbered
verses) heading word by word analysis of the Hebrew text
in the *Practize* section, pp. 5–78. This English text is very
similar to the various extant translations in English Bibles
but not identical with any one of these. Only Ps. 25 has
accompanying English translation. The work also contains
a brief Hebrew–English 'dictionary'.

STC[2] 17523; C.U.L., Syn.8.59.67.

80 1594   JOHN MUNDY (d. 1630)

Songs and Psalmes composed into 3. 4. and 5.
parts, for the use and delight of all such as either
love or learne Musicke: By John Mundy
Gentleman, bachiler of Musicke, and one of the
Organest of hir Majesties free Chappell of
Windsor.

(London, Thomas Est)

Contains in 'Psalmes' section settings of Pss. 146:1–2;
145:2; 143:1–2; 123:1 and 125:4 (Coverdale's prose texts as
BCP) and Pss. 69:1–2; 117; 128:1–3; 128:4–6; 47:1–2;
47:6–7; 95:1–2; 130:1–2; 149:1–2 and 25:1–2 (metrical texts

as Anglo-Genevan Psalters). Ded. to Robert Devereux, Earl of Essex. Texts and music repr. in *The English Madrigalists*, ed. E. H. Fellowes, xxxv^B (rev. P. Brett) (1961).

STC^2 18284; C.U.L., Syn.6.59.4. (Tenor part).

81   1596   EDMUND COOTE (fl. 1596)

The English Schoole-Maister, Teaching all his Scholers, of what age soever, the most easie, short, and perfect order of distinct reading, and true writing our English tongue that hath ever yet been knowne and published by any.
(London, the Widow Orwin for Ralph Jackson and Robert Dexter)

Contains Ps. 119:1–16 in Coverdale's translation as BCP in 'the practise to the English Schoole-maister', pp. 49–50; also Pss. 1, 4, 50:1–11, 51:1–10, 67, 104:1–9, 112, 113, 120, 126, 148:1–6 in metre from the Anglo-Genevan psalter (on pp. 52–63).

STC^2 5711; Dublin, Trinity College (in Scolar Press facsimile, Menston, 1968).

82   1597   HENRY LOK (1553?–1608?)

Ecclesiastes, otherwise called the Preacher. Containing Salomons Sermons or Commentaries (as it may probably be collected) upon the 49. Psalme of David his father. Compendiously abridged, and also paraphrastically dilated in English poesie, according to the analogie of Scripture, and consent of the most approved writer thereof. Composed by H. L. Gentleman. Whereunto are annexed sundrie sonets of Christian Passions heretofore printed, and now corrected and augmented, with other affectionate

Sonets of a feeling conscience of the same Authors.

(London, Richard Field)

Contains 'Sundry Psalmes of David [Pss. 27, 71, 119, 121, 130] translated into verse, as briefly and significantly as the scope of the text will suffer; by the same Author' on sig. I2^r–4^v (i.e. not part of the Christian Passions in 200 sonnets beginning after sub-title page on sig. I5^r). Ded. to Queen Elizabeth signed Henry Lok.

STC^2 16696, formerly also 2765; Bodl., 4° H.9Th.

83   1598   [WILLIAM PATTEN]

Anno foelicissimi Regni Augustae Reginae nostrae Elizabeth Quadragesimo primo, fauste iam incepto. Psal. terseptimus: Domine in virtute tua.

[London, Thomas Purfoot?]

English metrical adaptation of Ps. 21 (cf. Ps. 72 (1583)), from London, B. Lib., MS Royal 14B.l., printed with Latin paraphrase 'Ex versione Io. Campensis'. No music. (Cf. 1583 broadsheet, no. 69 above). Signed W. P. G. See B. O'Kill in *Transactions of the Cambridge Bibliographical Society*, vii (1977), 34. Ded. to Elizabeth for her fortieth anniversary as Queen. See further *H & L*^{3} A113.

STC^2 2368.5; Cambridge, Jesus College, B.3.29.

84   1600   [CHARLES LUMSDEN (d. 1630)]

An Exposition upon some select Psalmes of David, conteining great store of most excellent and comfortable doctrine and instruction for all those, that (under the burthen of sinne) thirst for Comfort in Christ Jesus. Written by that faithfull servant of God, M. Robert Rollok, sometime

Pastour in the Church of Edinburgh: And trans-
lated out of Latine into English, by C. L.
Minister of the Gospell of Christ at Dudingstoun.
(Edinburgh, Robert Waldegrave)

Prose argument, psalm text and commentary for each of
Pss. 3, 6, 16, 23, 32, 39, 42, 49, 51, 62, 65, 84, 116, 130 and
137 translated by Lumsden from Robert Rollock's Latin
(1599); see *H & L*[3] E178.

STC[2] 21276; B. Lib., 1011.aa.4.

85 1601
RICHARD VERSTEGAN (fl. 1565–1620)

Odes in Imitation of the seaven penitential
psalmes, with sundry other Poems and ditties
tending to devotion and pietie.
([Antwerp, A. Conincx])

Contains metrical paraphrases of Pss. 6, 32, 38, 51, 102,
130, 143 ded. to 'vertuous Ladies and Gentlewomen', with
twenty English metrical hymns of Catholic provenance.
The ded. is signed R. V., see *H & L*[3] O9. The seven psalms
were reprinted in reverse order as Elizabeth Grymeston's
in her *Miscelanea. Meditations. Memoratives* (London, 1604)
STC[2] 12407, sig. F1[r]-H1[r].

STC[2] 21359; Bodl., 8° C.98 Th.

[86]
Edmund Spenser, 'The seven Psalmes, &c.' (i.e. seven
penitential psalms] attributed to Spenser by his publisher
and printer William Ponsonby in 'The Printer to the
Gentle Reader' included in Ponsonby's edition of *Com-
plaints. Containing sundrie small Poemes of the Worlds Vanitie
... by Ed. Sp.* (London, 1591).

The following titles were included in Andrew Maunsell's *The First Part of the Catalogue of English printed Bookes* (London, 1595), and are not known to have survived. (See further F. B. Williams, 'Lost Books of Tudor England', *The Library*, 5th ser., xxxiii (1978), 1–14.)

[87] Lady Elizabeth Fane 'Her certaine psalmes of godly meditation in number 21. with a 102. proverbs. printed by Rob. Crowley: 1550 in 8'. (Maunsell, p. 85a).

[88] William Hunnis 'his abridgement, or brief meditation on certain of the Psalms in english meeter. Printed by Rob. Wier, in 8'. (Maunsell, p. 61a).

[89] Augustine Marlorat 'his praiers on the Psalmes, translated by Rodolph Warcup. printed by William How. 1571. in 16'. (Maunsell, p. 86a).

[90] Wolfgang Musculus, 'Exposition on the 51. Psalme, translated by John Stockwood. Printed for John Harrison the younger. 1586. in 16'. (Maunsell, p. 75a; cf. STC^2 18307.5)

NOTES

1 An Introduction

1 John Donne, 'Upon the Translation of the Psalmes by Sir Philip Sydney, and the Countesse of Pembroke his Sister', line 11, in John Donne, *The Divine Poems*, ed. H. Gardner (2nd edn, Oxford, 1978), pp. 33–5.

2 For the impact of the revival of Christian Hebrew studies on sixteenth-century biblical textual criticism and translation see: A. J. Baumgartner, *De l'enseignement de l'hébreu chez les protestants à partir de l'époque de la Réformation* (Lausanne, 1889); M. Brod, *Johannes Reuchlin und sein Kampf eine historische Monographie* (Stuttgart, 1965); H. de Vocht, *History of the Foundation and the Rise of the Collegium Trilingue Lovaniense 1517–1550* (Louvain, 1951); H. Hailperin, *Rashi and the Christian Scholars* (Pittsburg, 1963); B. Hall, 'Biblical Scholarship: Editions and Commentaries', in *The Cambridge History of the Bible*, vol. 3, *The West from the Reformation to the Present Day*, ed. S. L. Greenslade (Cambridge, 1963), pp. 38–93; G. Hammond, *The Making of the English Bible* (Manchester, 1982); G. L. Jones, *The Discovery of Hebrew in Tudor England: a Third Language* (Manchester, 1983); M. Krebs, ed., *Johannes Reuchlin 1455–1522 Festgabe seine Vaterstadt Pforzheim* (Pforzheim, 1955); L. Kukenheim, *Contributions à l'histoire de la grammaire Grecque, Latine et Hebraïque à l'époque de la Renaissance* (Leiden, 1951), pp. 88–129; F. Rosenthal, 'The Rise of Christian Hebraism in the Sixteenth Century', *Historia Judaica*, vii (1945), 167–91.

3 George Joye, *The Psalter of David in Englishe purely and faithfully translated aftir the texte of Feline* ([Antwerp], 1530), sig. A1ᵛ; see further Appendix, no. 1.

4 On Bucer, see C. Hopf, *Martin Bucer and the English Reformation* (Oxford, 1946), pp. 205–50.

5 Joye, *Psalter* (1530), sig. A1ᵛ.

6 For English psalm versions printed between 1530 and 1601 see above, Appendix pp. 211–59. Examples of contemporary manuscript copies of metrical psalm versions include the following: London, British Library, Additional MSS 12047–8 and 46372 (Sir Philip Sidney and the Countess of Pembroke), 30981 (John Croke, d. 1554), 36529 (Earl of Surrey); MS Egerton 2711 (Sir Thomas Wyatt (holograph), and Sir John Harington); MSS Harley 2252 (anon. of Ps. 130), 6930 (Davison brothers); Royal MSS 14 B l ([William Patten]), 17 A xvii (Sir Thomas Smith, possibly holograph), 17 A xxi (William Forrest), 18 B xvi (? James VI). Oxford, Bodleian Library, MSS Douce 361 (Sir John Harington),

Rawlinson Poet. 24 and 25 (Sir Philip Sidney and the Countess of Pembroke). For the contents of Arundel Castle, Harington MS see *The Arundel Harington Manuscript of Tudor Poetry*, ed. R. Hughey, 2 vols. (Columbus, Ohio, 1960).

7 For psalms as religious instruction see above pp. 30-4.

8 For psalms as private prayer see above pp. 27-30.

9 See H. Smith, 'English Metrical Psalms in the Sixteenth Century and their Literary Significance', *Huntington Library Quarterly*, ix (1946), 249-71; L. B. Campbell, *Divine Poetry and Drama in Sixteenth-Century England* (Cambridge, Berkeley & Los Angeles, 1959); B. K. Lewalski, *Protestant Poetics and the Seventeenth-Century Religious Lyric* (Princeton, New Jersey, 1979); for Wyatt's critics see above pp. 44-6, for Sidney's see p. 153.

10 Campbell, *Divine Poetry*, pp. 3-4.

11 For Hall and Verstegan see above pp. 126-32; see further above, Appendix, nos. 27, 40 and 85.

12 Thomas Becon, *Davids Harpe ful of moost delectable armony* (London, 1542), sig. A6ᵛ-A7ʳ; cf. H. Smith, *HLQ*, ix (1946), 259.

13 Becon, *Davids Harpe*, sig. B1ʳ.

14 For a note on Spenser's lost version of the seven penitential psalms see p. 258.

15 E. R. Curtius, *European Literature and the Latin Middle Ages*, tr., W. R. Trask (London, 1953, repr., 1979), p. 443.

16 For Johann Reuchlin's Hebrew and Greek studies see above n. 2, also L. Geiger, *Johann Reuchlin: sein Leben und seine Werke* (Leipzig, 1871, repr., 1964); R. Pfeiffer, *History of Classical Scholarship from 1300-1850* (Oxford, 1976), pp. 78-90; for Reuchlin's influence on English scholars including Colet, Fisher and More see G. L. Jones, *The Discovery of Hebrew*, pp. 86-97, 103, 168-74. For Erasmus's biblical scholarship see especially J. A. Froude, *Life and Letters of Erasmus* (London, 1894); C. A. L. Jarrott, 'Erasmus' Biblical Humanism', *Studies in the Renaissance*, xvii (1970), 119-52; M. O'Rourke Boyle, *Christening Pagan Mysteries: Erasmus in Pursuit of Wisdom* (Toronto, 1981); M. M. Phillips, *Erasmus and the Northern Renaissance* (London, 1949, repr., Woodbridge, 1981), esp. ch. 1 and 2; A. Rabil, *Erasmus and the New Testament: The Mind of a Christian Humanist* (San Antonio, 1972); W. Schwarz, *Principles and Problems of Biblical Translation: Some Reformation Controversies and their Background* (Cambridge, 1955), pp. 92-165. For Colet see K. K. Chatterjee, *In Praise of Learning: John Colet and Literary Humanism in Education* (New Delhi, 1974); J. H. Lupton, *A Life of John Colet, D. D.* (London, 1887); L. Miles, *John Colet and the Platonic Tradition* (London, 1962), pp. 1-30. For Vives see E. D'Ors, *et al.*, *Vivès humaniste espagnol* (Paris, 1941), esp. pp. 41-69; A.-J. Namèche, *Mémoire sur la vie et les écrits de Jean-Louis Vivès* (Brussels, 1841); F. Watson, *Luis Vives El Gran Valenciano 1492-1540* (Oxford, 1922).

17 *De tradendis disciplinis, seu de institutione christiana*, Bk i, in *Io. Lodovici*

Vivis Valentini Opera in duos distincta tomos (Basle, 1555), i, 442; cf. F. Watson, tr., *Vives on Education. A Translation of the 'De Tradendis Disciplinis' of Juan Luis Vives* (Cambridge, 1913), p. 30.

18 Vives, *Opera*, i, 444; cf. Watson, tr., *Vives on Education*, p. 33.

19 *The Fyrst Fower Bookes of P. Ovidius Nasos worke, intitled Metamorphosis, translated oute of Latin into Englishe meter by Arthur Golding Gent. A woorke very pleasaunt and delectable* (London, 1565). See further L. T. Golding, *An Elizabethan Puritan. Arthur Golding the Translator of Ovid's Metamorphoses and also of John Calvin's Sermons* (New York, 1937); J. Wortham, 'Arthur Golding and the Translation of Prose', *Huntington Library Quarterly*, xii (1949), 339–67.

20 Golding, tr., *The Psalmes of David and others. With M. John Calvins Commentaries* (London, 1571), sig. *5ʳ.

21 Ibid. For another example of this attitude, that 'of a good interpretour' expounding a difficult work for 'the ease of inferior readers', see *The seven first bookes of the Eneidos of Virgill, converted in Englishe meter by Thomas Phaer* (London, 1558), sig. X2ᵛ–3ʳ.

22 For the Psalms and the defence of poetry in England see Thomas Lodge, *Defence of Poetry, Music, and Stage Plays* (1579), P. Sidney, *The Defence of Poesie*, also called *An Apologie for Poetrie* (c. 1581–3), Puttenham, *The Arte of English Poesie* (1589), and John Harington, *A Preface or rather a Briefe Apologie of Poetrie* (1591), all reprinted in *Elizabethan Critical Essays*, ed. G. G. Smith, 2 vols. (Oxford, 1904, repr., 1971), see i, 71; 154 and 158; ii, 10 and 31; 207. See also Richard Stanyhurst's demonstration of quantitative metres in English employing Virgil's *Aeneid* i–iv and Psalms 1–4, in his *Thee First Foure Bookes of Virgil his Aeneis . . . wyth oother Poeticall divises* (Leiden, 1582), see Appendix, no. 65.

23 For Harington's comments see his *Preface or rather a Briefe Apologie of Poetrie* (1591) in *Elizabethan Critical Essays*, ed. Smith, ii, 198.

24 W. Wordsworth, Preface to *Lyrical Ballads* (1800) in *Wordsworth & Coleridge, Lyrical Ballads*, ed. R. L. Brett & A. R. Jones (London, 1968), p. 246; and, P. B. Shelley, *A Defence of Poetry* in *Political Tracts of Wordsworth, Coleridge and Shelley*, ed. R. J. White (Cambridge, 1953), pp. 195–206, esp. p. 201.

25 R. L. Montgomery, *Symmetry and Sense: The Poetry of Sir Philip Sidney* (Austin, 1961), p. 20.

26 *The Defence of Poesie. By Sir Phillip Sidney, Knight* (William Ponsonby, London, 1595), facsimile ed (Menston, 1973), sig. C1ᵛ; see further *Sir Philip Sidney An Apology for Poetry or the Defence of Poesy*, ed. G. Shepherd (Manchester, 1965, repr. 1967), pp. 159–60, n. lines 33ff.

27 *Defence of Poesie*, sig. C1ᵛ; see further *Apology for Poetry*, ed. Shepherd, p. 160. For a fuller discussion see above pp. 14–18.

28 *The Arte of English Poesie. Contrived into three Bookes: The first of Poets and Poesie, the second of Proportion, the third of Ornament* (London, 1589), repr. in *Elizabethan Critical Essays*, ed. Smith, ii, 1–193, see p. 3. For a fuller discussion see above pp. 18–23.

29 Ibid.

30 See A. Fowler, *Kinds of Literature: An Introduction to the Theory of Genres and Modes* (Oxford, 1982), p. 20; cf. R. L. Colie, *The Resources of Kind: Genre-Theory in the Renaissance*, ed. B. K. Lewalski (Berkeley, 1973), p. 29 for 'the connection of the literary kinds with *kinds* of knowledge and experience'.

31 H. Smith, *Elizabethan Poetry: A Study in Conventions, Meaning, and Expression* (Cambridge, Mass., 1952, repr., 1964), p. v.

32 *Iulii Caesaris Scaligeri, viri clarissimi, Poetices libri septem* (Lyon, 1561), p. 6, col. 1. Cf. Aristotle, *Poetics*, 1, 1447^a on 'varieties of mimēsis, differing from each other in three respects, the media, the objects, and the mode of mimēsis' tr. M. E. Hubbard in *Ancient Literary Criticism The Principal Texts in New Translations*, ed. D. A. Russell & M. Winterbottom (Oxford, 1972, repr., 1978), p. 90. I am particularly indebted to: G. P. Norton's two-part study of 'Translation Theory in Renaissance France', part 1 sub-titled 'Etienne Dolet and the Rhetorical Tradition', part 2 sub-titled 'The Poetic Controversy' in *Renaissance and Reformation*, x (1974), 1–13; xi (1975), 30–44; and Terence Cave's discussion of 'Imitation' in *The Cornucopian Text: Problems of Writing in the French Renaissance* (Oxford, 1979), pp. 35–77. Cf. T. M. Greene, *The Light in Troy: Imitation and Discovery in Renaissance Poetry* (New Haven & London, 1982). See further B. Weinberg, *A History of Literary Criticism in the Italian Renaissance*, 2 vols. (Chicago, 1961); E. J. Sweeting, *Early Tudor Criticism: Linguistic and Literary* (Oxford, 1940).

33 Vives, *Opera*, i, 492; tr., Watson, *Vives on Education*, p. 189.

34 Vives, *Opera*, i. 494

35 *The Institution of Christian Religion, written in Latine by M. John Calvine, and translated into English according to the authors last edition, by Thomas Norton* (London, 1578), sig. ★2^v.

36 *The Lives of the Noble Grecians and Romanes, Compared together by that grave learned Philosopher and Historiographer, Plutarke of Chaeronea: Translated out of Greeke into French by James Amyot ... and out of French into English, by Thomas North* (London, 1579), sig. ★8^r.

37 *Institution of Christian Religion*, sig. ★2^v.

38 Ibid.

39 Ibid.

40 Ibid.

41 Ibid., sig. ★3^v.

42 Ibid., sig. ★2^v.

43 *The newe testament both Latine and Englyshe ech correspondent to the other after the vulgare texte, communely called S. Jeroms. Faythfully translated by Myles Coverdale* (Southwark, 1538), sig. +3^v; for a bibliographical description see T. H. Darlow & H. F. Moule, revised A. S. Herbert, *Historical Catalogue of Printed Editions of the English Bible 1525–1961* (London & New York, 1968), no. 37; see further J. F. Mozley, *Coverdale and his Bibles* (London, 1953), pp. 180–95.

44 *The newe testament* (1538), sig. +3ᵛ, +4ʳ.

45 Ibid., sig. +4ʳ.

46 Ibid., sig. +2ᵛ, +3ʳ.

47 Ibid., sig. +3ʳ.

48 On sixteenth-century English Bibles and on biblical translation see *The Cambridge History of the Bible*, iii, 94–174; Schwarz, *Principles and Problems*; Darlow & Moule, *Historical Catalogue*; F. F. Bruce, *The English Bible: A History of Translations*, 2nd edn (London, 1970); C. C. Butterworth, *The Literary Lineage of the King James Bible* (Philadelphia, 1941); D. Daiches, *The King James Version of the English Bible: An Account of the Development and Sources of the English Bible of 1611 with Special Reference to the Hebrew Tradition* (Chicago, 1941); Hammond, *Making of the English Bible*; see further *Records of the English Bible*, ed. A. W. Pollard (Oxford, 1911) for a selection of primary source materials relating to the controversy surrounding early English translations of the Bible and the principles and practices of English translators from their various prefaces.

49 For useful general accounts of the theory and practice of sixteenth-century translators see F. R. Amos, *Early Theories of Translation* (New York, 1920), esp. pp. 48–70; C. H. Conley, *The First English Translators of the Classics* (New Haven, 1927); O. L. Hatcher, 'Aims and Methods of Elizabethan Translators', *Englische Studien*, xliv (1912), 174–92; L. G. Kelly, *The True Interpreter: A History of Translation Theory and Practice in the West* (Oxford, 1979); F. O. Matthiessen, *Translation An Elizabethan Art* (Cambridge, Mass., 1931, repr., New York, 1965); G. P. Norton, *The Ideology and Language of Translation in Renaissance France and their Humanist Antecedents* (Geneva, 1984); G. Steiner, *After Babel: Aspects of Language and Translation* (Oxford, 1975, repr., 1977); L. B. Wright, 'Translations for the Elizabethan Middle Class', *The Library*, 4th ser., xiii (1932), 312–31. Cf. also n. 32 above. See further Laurence Humfrey's *Interpretatio linguarum: seu de ratione convertendi & explicandi autores tam sacros quam prophanos* (Basle, 1559) for a monumental summary of ancient and humanist views of translation (Bk i) and imitation (Bk ii), drawn chiefly from the works of Cicero and those attributed to him; for a brief description in tabular form of the contents of Bk i see p. 201ff.

50 *Marcus Tullius Ciceroes thre bookes of duties, to Marcus his sonne, turned out of latine into english, by Nicolas Grimalde. Wherunto the latine is adjoyned* (London, 1558), sig. C 6ʳ (The preface to the reader).

51 Ibid., sig. C 3ʳ (The Epistles).

52 Ibid., sig. C 3ʳ⁻ᵛ.

53 Coverdale's remark appears in his address to the reader in his translation, *A Paraphrasis upon all the Psalmes of David, made by Johannes Campensis, reader of the Hebrue lecture in the universite of Lovane* (London, 1539), sig. A2ʳ; see further Appendix, no. 4.

54 *Dictionarium, seu Latinae linguae Thesaurus* (Paris, 1531), s.v. *paraphrasis*: 'non literam ex litera, sed sensum e sensu transfert, quasi iuxta loquens'

quoted in Norton, *Renaissance & Reformation*, x (1974), p. 12 n. 26; cf. Cave, *Cornucopian Text*, pp. 38–9 (Cave amends Norton's translation). I have not been able to consult the 1531 edition. This definition of *paraphrasis* does not appear in the 2nd edn (1543); cf. s. v. *paraphrasis*: 'Eiusdem sententiae per aliud sermonem expositio, & liberior interpretatio ...' (*Dictionarium*, 3 vols. (Paris, 1543), ii, fol. 1037ʳ). See also Norton, *Ideology & Language*, pp. 196–8.

55 Quintilian, *Institutio oratoria*, Bk X, v, 5, tr. H. E. Butler in Loeb Classical Library, 4 vols. (London & Cambridge, Mass., 1922, repr., 1961), iv. 114; cf. Cave, *Cornucopian Text*, p. 36.

56 *A Paraphrasis upon all the psalmes* (1539), sig. A2ʳ.

57 *The Psalmes of David, Truly Opened and explained by Paraphrasis, according to the right sense of everie Psalme ... set foorth in Latine by that excellent learned man Theodore Beza. And faithfully translated into English, by Anthonie Gilbie* (London, 1581), sig. A5ʳ; see further Appendix, no. 61.

58 For the reservation of *paraphrasis* to scholars by Johann Sturm and Roger Ascham see Ascham's *The Scholemaster Or plaine and perfite way of teachyng children ... the Latin tong* (London, 1570), Bk ii, s.v. *paraphrasis* in Roger Ascham, *English Works*, ed. W. A. Wright (Cambridge, 1904), repr., 1970), pp. 246–53 esp. 247: '*Paraphrasis* ... is onelie to be left to a perfite Master'.

59 Ibid., p. 248.

60 For renaissance views of *imitatio* cf. Ascham's (ibid., pp. 264ff.) and Humfrey's (*Interpretatio linguarum* (1559), pp. 209ff.) 'De imitatione, exercitatione et fine Interpretis'. For modern discussions see particularly Cave, *Cornucopian Text*, pp. 35–77, and Greene, *Light in Troy*, pp. 37–52.

61 On the range of *imitatio* cf. Greene, *Light in Troy*, pp. 37–52.

62 Ascham, *English Works*, ed. Wright, p. 264.

63 Ibid., pp. 266–7. Cf. 'quae imitamur, quibus imitamur, & quomodo imitamur' (Scaliger), see n. 32 above.

64 Ibid., p. 267; cf. Grimald, above p. 12; for a survey of Roman discussions of *imitatio*, especially the imitation of Greek authors, see Greene, *Light in Troy*, pp. 60–80.

65 Ascham, *English Works*, ed. Wright, p. 268.

66 Ibid., pp. 268–74; for a modern discussion of the sixteenth-century debate on *imitatio* see Greene, *Light in Troy*, pp. 171–96.

67 See Aristotle on the origins of poetry and differences between the objects of *mimesis* and on the source of tragic effect with respect to character, in *Poetics*, I, 1448ᵇ, 1448ᵃ, & III, 1454ᵃ tr. Hubbard, *Ancient Literary Criticism*, ed. Russell & Winterbottom, pp. 94, 92 & 110.

68 See Sidney's *Defence of Poesie*, sig. C1ʳ⁻ᵛ; also *Apology for Poetry*, ed. Shepherd, pp. 101 and 157–9.

69 Vives, see above n. 34.

70 Vives, *Opera* (1555), i, 495; cf. Quintilian, *Inst. orat.*, X, ii, 10 (Loeb ed., iv, 79); cf. Petrarch: 'Nec enim parvus aut index animi sermo est aut

sermonis moderator est animus. Alter pendet ex altero', *Epistolae Familiares* i, 9 in *Le Familiari Libri I–IV*, ed. U. Dotti (Urbino, 1970), p. 97.

71 *Ep. Fam.* xxiii, 19 in *Francisci Petrarchae Epistolae Selectae* ed. A. F. Johnson (Oxford, 1923), p. 132; tr., J. H. Robinson & H. W. Rolfe, *Petrarch The First Modern Scholar and Man of Letters: A Selection from his Correspondence* (New York & London, 1898), p. 290.

72 Seneca, *Ad Lucilium Epistulae Morales*, 84, 8, tr. R. M. Gummere in Loeb Classical Library, 3 vols. (London & Cambridge, Mass., 1920, repr., 1962), ii, 276–84 esp. 281; cf. R. S. Peterson's account of Ben Jonson's use of Seneca's moral epistles in *Imitation and Praise in the Poems of Ben Jonson* (New Haven & London, 1981), p. xv.

73 Vives, *Opera*, i, 493.

74 '. . . scribamus scilicet sicut apes mellificant, non servatis floribus, sed in favos versis, ut ex multis et variis unum fiat, idque aliud et melius', (blending many very different flavours into one, which shall be unlike them all and better). *Ep. Fam.* xxiii, 19 in *Petrarchae Epistolae*, ed. Johnson, p. 132, tr., Robinson & Rolfe, *Petrarch*, p. 291; cf. Seneca, *Ep. Mor.* 84, 3–5.

75 D. Erasmus, *Dialogus Ciceronianus* (1528), ed. P. Mesnard in *Opera omnia*, I, ii (Amsterdam, 1971), 652. Cf. the discussions of this passage by Terence Cave (*Cornucopian Text*, p. 45) and by Thomas Greene (*Light in Troy*, pp. 182–3). However, Erasmus's use of the word *meditatio* in this context indicates that he had in mind the process of the traditional monastic *lectio* and *meditatio*. For a discussion of this see J. Leclercq, *The Love of Learning and the Desire for God* (New York, 1961), pp. 18–21, 89–91.

76 On the *oratio speculum mentis* or *animi* topos see Cave, *Cornucopian Text*, pp. 43–4, and works cited.

77 For Puttenham's description of style see *Arte of English Poesie* (1589) in *Elizabethan Critical Essays*, ed. Smith, ii, 153–5, esp. 154.

78 Puttenham, *Arte of English Poesie* in *Elizabethan Critical Essays*, ed. Smith, ii, 148 and 154.

79 Ibid., pp. 147–8.

80 Erasmus, *Dialogus Ciceronianus*, in *Opera omnia*, I, ii, 703.

81 Horace, *On Poetry: The 'Ars Poetica'*, ed. C. O. Brink (Cambridge, 1971), p. 60 and pp. 208–12 (for commentary); trans., Ben Jonson, *Horace His Art of Poetrie Made English* (1640) in *Ben Jonson*, ed. C. H. Herford, P. & E. Simpson, 11 vols. (Oxford, 1925–52), viii (1947), 313. The 'Ars Poetica' was translated into English by Thomas Drant, *Horace his arte of poetrie, pistles, and satyrs Englished* (London, 1567), and by William Webbe in his *A Discourse of English Poetrie* (London, 1586). For discussion of the earlier French scholarly and critical debate on Horace's *fidus interpres* see Norton, *Ideology & Language*, pp. 57–110, esp. 90.

82 Scaliger, *Poetices*, p. 1, col. 2.

83 Ibid.; cf. Horace, *Ars Poetica*, lines 333–4 (Brink edn p. 67).

84 J. Du Bellay, *La Defense et illustration de la langue francoise* (Paris, 1561, fol. 8ʳ, (The *Defense* was first published in 1549.) See further Norton, *Renaissance & Reformation*, xi (1975), 35–7; Cave, *Cornucopian Text*, pp. 60–76; Greene, *Light in Troy*, pp. 189–96.

85 Du Bellay, *La Defense* (1561), fol. 9ᵛ.

86 Ibid., fol. 10ᵛ.

87 *Defence of Poesie*, sig. I 3ʳ⁻ᵛ (cf. *Apology for Poetry*, ed. Shepherd, pp. 138 and 228 n. lines 21 and 2).

88 Cf. Horace, *Ars Poetica*, line 131; for the legal sense of 'translation' in English see *OED*, translation, 5.

89 *Defence of Poesie*, sig. C2ᵛ (cf. *Apology for Poetry*, ed. Shepherd, p. 102). Cf. Scaliger, *Poetices* (1561), p. 1, col. 2 and tr., F. M. Padelford, *Select Translations from Scaliger's Poetics, Yale Studies in English*, xxvi (New York, 1905), p. 2.

90 *Defence of Poesie*, sig: B4ᵛ, C3ʳ, C1ʳ (cf. *Apology for Poetry*, ed. Shepherd, pp. 100, 103, 101).

91 *Defence of Poesie*, sig. C1ʳ (cf. *Apology for Poetry*, ed. Shepherd, p. 101). See further *Apology for Poetry*, ed. Shepherd, pp. 55–61; F. G. Robinson, *The Shape of Things Known: Sidney's Apology in its Philosophical Tradition* (Cambridge, Mass., 1972), pp. 108–22; L. S. Wolfley, 'Sidney's visual-didactic poetic: some complexities and limitations', *The Journal of Medieval and Renaissance Studies*, vi (1976), 217–41.

92 (My italics.) For a reprint of Gascoigne's anonymous edition (London [1573]) with an introduction by B. M. Ward, see *A Hundreth Sundrie Flowres From the Original Edition* (London, 1926).

93 T. Sebillet, *L'Art poetique françois. Pour l'instruction des jeunes studieux, & encor' peu avancez en la Poësie Françoise* (Paris, 1573), pp. 165, 166; see further Norton, *Renaissance & Reformation*, xi (1975), 34–5.

94 *L'Art poëtique de Jacques Peletier du Mans* (1555), ed. A. Boulanger (Paris, 1930), p. 105.

95 Ibid., p. 96; for Vives and Quintilian see above n. 70.

96 Du Bellay, *La Defense* (1561), fol. 13ʳ; cf. also Horace's distinction between the *fidus interpres* and the *doctus imitator*, lines 133–4 and 318 (Brink edn, pp. 60 and 66); the latter was translated as 'learned Maker' by Jonson, see *Ben Jonson*, ed. Herford & Simpson, viii, 325.

97 Du Bellay, *La Defense* (1561), fol. 9ʳ.

98 Puttenham, *Arte of English Poesie* in *Elizabethan Critical Essays*, ed. Smith, ii, 62; for a list of 'versifiers' noted for 'their learned translations' see Francis Meres, 'A Comparative Discourse of our English Poets with the Greeke, Latine, and Italian Poets', *Palladis Tamia* (1598) in *Elizabethan Critical Essays*, ed. Smith, ii, 322–3.

99 Puttenham, *Arte of English Poesie, Elizabethan Critical Essays*, ed. Smith, ii, 65.

100 Ibid., p. 64.

101 J. Harington, *A Preface, or rather a Briefe Apologie of Poetrie* in *Elizabethan Critical Essays*, ed. Smith, ii, 219; cf. Peletier (Boulanger edn p. 106) for

the views that a good translation was worth more than a poor 'invencion', and that well executed translations could enrich a language.

102 J. Harington, *A Preface* in *Elizabethan Critical Essays*, ed. Smith, ii, 204.

103 Ibid., p. 222; cf. Du Bellay's distinction between the learned 'translator' and treasonable 'traducteur' see above p. 22.

104 See R. Loewe, 'The Medieval History of the Latin Vulgate', in *The Cambridge History of the Bible*, vol. 2 *The West from the Fathers to the Reformation*, ed. G. W. H. Lampe (Cambridge, 1969), pp. 102–54.

105 Greene, *Light in Troy*, pp. 3, 4–27, esp. 3 and 20.

106 Ibid., p. 49.

107 For Greene's discussion of Petrarch's imitation of Virgil and Du Bellay's *Les Antiquitez de Rome* see *Light in Troy*, pp. 112–23 and 220–41.

108 For the influence of Jewish scholars, such as Rashi (Rabbi Solomon ben Isaac, 1040–1105), Abraham Ibn Ezra (1092–1167), Moses Kimchi (d. 1170?) and David Kimchi (1160–1235?), on Christian exegetes and Hebraists, notably Andrew of St Victor (d. 1175) and Nicholas of Lyra (*c.* 1270–1340) see B. Smalley, *The Study of the Bible in the Middle Ages*, 3rd edn (Oxford, 1984), pp. 149–72, 329–55; also G. L. Jones, 'The Influence of Medieval Jewish Exegetes on Biblical Scholarship in Sixteenth-Century England: with Special Reference to the Book of Daniel' (University of London, Ph.D., 1975) and Jones's introduction to his *Discovery of Hebrew*; see above n. 2.

109 Matthew Parker, *The whole Psalter translated into English Metre, which contayneth an hundreth and fifty Psalmes* (London [1567?]), sig. B3ᵛ. (I have amended the punctuation.)

110 'Athanasius in Psalmos', ibid., sig. B4ᵛ.

111 From 'The Argument' to the Psalms in the Geneva Bible: *The Bible and Holy Scriptures Conteyned in the Olde and Newe Testament. Translated according to the Ebrue and Greke, and conferred With the best translations in divers langages* (Geneva, 1560), fol. 235ʳ.

112 From Richard Hooker's *Of the Lawes of Ecclesiasticall Politie. The fift Booke* (London, 1597), ch. 37, p. 74.

113 From Calvin's epistle to 'the godly Readers', dated 23 July 1557 from Geneva, in Golding, tr., *The Psalmes of David* (1571), sig. *6ᵛ.

114 Ibid.

115 Thomas Wilcox, *A Right Godly and learned Exposition, upon the whole Booke of Psalmes* (London, 1586), sig. B1ʳ.

116 *The .holie. Bible. conteyning the olde Testament and the newe* (London, 1568), pt. 3, fol. 1ᵛ.

117 Gilby, tr., *The Psalmes of David* (1581), sig. a3ᵛ.

118 From John Jewel, Bishop of Salisbury's 'Controversy with M. Harding' in Jewel's *Works*, ed. J. Ayre, 4 vols., Parker Society (Cambridge, 1845–50), i, 333.

119 On *Psalmes or prayers taken out of holye scripture* see Appendix, no. 12.

120 On *A Golden Chaine, Taken out of . . . the Psalmes* (1579) see Appendix, no. 59.

121 *A Golden Chaine*, sig. a4^v–a5^r.

122 [*Christian Praieres and holie Meditations*] (London, 1568), pp. 283–5; see further Appendix, no. 46.

123 *A godly meditacion upon .xx. select . . . Psalmes* (London, 1547), sig. *3^r; see further Appendix, no. 14.

124 Cope, *A godly meditacion* (1547), sig. *2^v; see also *OED*, patron 9.

125 See Catherine Parr's *Prayers or Medytacions, wherein the mynd is stirred, paciently to suffre all afflictions here, to set at nought the vayne prosperitee of this worlde, and alwaie to longe for the everlastynge felicitee: Collected out of holy woorkes* (London, 1545); and her *The lamentacion of a sinner, made by the most vertuous Lady Quene Caterin* (London, 1547); see further J. K. McConica, *English Humanists and Reformation Politics under Henry VIII and Edward VI* (Oxford, 1965), pp. 7–8, 228–9, 251; and W. P. Haugaard, 'Katherine Parr: the Religious Convictions of a Renaissance Queen', *Renaissance Quarterly*, xxii (1969), 346–59.

126 *The Bible* (Geneva, 1560), fol. 235^r; cf. 'Proemial Annotations upon the Booke of Psalmes' in the Catholic English Old Testament: *The Second Tome of the Holie Bible Faithfully Translated into English, out of the Authentical Latin. Diligently conferred with the Hebrewe, Greeke, and other Editions in divers languages* (Douai, 1610), pp. 3–14 esp. 5–7.

127 *The Bible* (Geneva, 1560), fol. 235^r; cf. Lefèvre's preface to his *Quincuplex Psalterium. Gallicum. Romanum. Hebraicum. Vetus. Conciliatum* (Paris, 1508–9), in *The Prefatory Epistles of Jacques Lefèvre d'Etaples and Related Texts*, ed. E. F. Rice, Jr (New York & London, 1972), pp. 192–201.

128 Becon, *Davids Harpe*, sig. A8^r.

129 Ibid., sig. A7^v.

130 Cope, *A godly meditacion*, sig. *3^r.

131 Hooker, *Ecclesiasticall Politie*, p. 74.

132 Ibid., Hooker's remarks are based on Basil's Prologue to the Psalms; cf. Bishops' Bible prologue to Psalms see above n. 116.

133 See P. Riché, *Education et culture dans l'occident barbare VIe–VIIIe siècles, Patristica Sorbonensia*, iv (Paris, 1962), 515–6.

134 On the use of the primer and a short primer in the Middle Ages and sixteenth century as a first reading book see N. Orme, *English Schools in the Middle Ages* (London, 1973), pp. 62 and 258; T. W. Baldwin, *William Shakspere's Petty School* (Urbana, 1943), pp. 33–4, and pp. 191–215 for the early influence of the primer on Shakespeare's imagination. Cf. E. Pafort, 'A Group of Early Tudor School Books', *The Library*, 4th ser., xxvi (1946), 255–60 for the use of 'Expositio Hymnorum & Sequentiarum' in schools.

135 Bishop Hilsey's remarks are from his prologue to his *A Manual of prayers or the prymer in Englysh & Laten set out at length . . . by Jhon by*

Goddes grace, & the Kynges callyng, Bysshoppe of Rochester (London, 1539), sig. A4ᵛ.

136 *A Shorte Introduction of Grammar, generally to be used in the Kynges Majesties dominions* (London, 1549), sig. A3ᵛ; Lily (d. 1522) was Colet's choice as first master of St Paul's School.

137 Quoted from an edition of Buchanan's psalms (1582) in I. D. McFarlane, *Buchanan* (London, 1981), p. 267. For the pedagogic use of Buchanan's psalms by Johann Sturm, an associate of Ascham, and in Scotland (*c.* 1570), see ibid., pp. 257, 260–1. For editions published in London (1580) see McFarlane's Appendix A, ibid., pp. 500–6.

138 From Mulcaster's *The first part of the Elementarie* (London, 1582), p. 55.

139 From Colet's *Statuta Paulina Scholae* (1518) 'what shalbe taught', in Lupton, *Life of Colet*, Appendix A, esp. p. 280; cf. 'blotterature' and 'litterature' (ibid.).

140 From Wilson's *The arte of Rhetorique* (1560) ed. G. H. Mair (Oxford, 1909), p. 5.

141 Ibid.

142 Golding, tr., *The Psalmes of David* (1571), sig. ★4ᵛ.

143 Ibid.

144 Cope, *A godly meditacion*, sig. ★3ʳ.

145 Coverdale, tr., *A Paraphrasis upon all the Psalmes* (1539), sig. A2ʳ; see further, E. A. Gosselin, *The King's Progress to Jerusalem: some Interpretations of David during the Reformation Period* (Los Angeles, 1976).

146 Ascham, *English Works*, ed. Wright, p. 275 (cf. 2 Timothy 3:14–15). Cf. William Baldwin's assurance to readers of his anthology *A Treatise of Morall Phylosophye* (London, 1550 etc.): 'thinke not ... that I allow Philosophie to be Scriptures Interpretour: but rather woulde have it as an handemayden, to perswade suche thinges as Scrypture dothe commaunde' (sig. Ⱃ 5ᵛ).

147 For a copy of Sidney's letter to Edward Denny, dated Whitsunday 1580 from Wilton, see Oxford, Bodleian Library, MS Don.d.152, fols.3ʳ–4ᵛ, esp. 3ʳ; reprinted in J. M. Osborn, *Young Philip Sidney 1572–1577* (New Haven & London, 1972), pp. 535–40.

148 See above n. 110.

149 Cf. Pico della Mirandola's premise of man's 'mutability of character' and 'self-transforming nature' in his *On the Dignity of Man*, see *The Renaissance Philosophy of Man*, ed. E. Cassirer, P. O. Kristeller, J. H. Randall (Chicago, 1948, repr., 1971), pp. 223–54, esp. 224–5.

150 Cope, *A godly meditacion*, sig. ★2ᵛ.

151 Ibid.

152 Ibid., sig. ★3ᵛ (cf. 1 Samuel 16:14–23).

153 Becon, *Davids Harpe*, sig. A8ʳ.

154 Coverdale, 'Unto the Christen reader' in *Goostly psalmes and spirituall songes drawen out of the holy Scripture, for the comforte and consolacyon of soch as love to rejoyse in God and his worde* (London [1535?]) sig. +4ʳ⁻ᵛ.

155 Thomas Sternhold, *Certayne Psalmes chosen out of the Psalter of David, and drawen into Englishe Metre* (London [1549?]), sig. A3^r.

156 On the features of Hebrew poetry see J. L. Kugel, *The Idea of Biblical Poetry: Parallelism and its History* (New Haven & London, 1981); most of Kugel's examples of the 'parallelistic line' are from psalms see especially pp. 1–58 for Hebrew and English texts. See further R. ap Roberts, 'Old Testament Poetry: The Translatable Structure', *Publications of the Modern Language Association of America*, xcii (1977), 987–1004. For examples from Coverdale's Great Bible translation (1539) and Sebastian Münster's *Hebraica Biblia* (Basle, 1535) see also notes 157–61 below.

157 Cf. Ps. 8:5   מָה־אֱנוֹשׁ כִּי־תִזְכְּרֶנּוּ

    What [is] man that you-will-remember-him   (my translation)

    Quid est homo ut memoriam eius habeas   (Münster, fol. 574^r)

    Cf. Ps. 1:4   כִּי אִם־כַּמֹּץ אֲשֶׁר־תִּדְּפֶנּוּ רוּחַ:

    But as [the] chaff which [the] wind drives-away   (my translation)

    sicut palea, quam dispellit ventus   (Münster, fol. 571^v).

    (See also Ps. 129:4 and Ps. 90:10).

158 The Hebrew construct form is usually translated by noun + of +noun in English; see further Hammond, *Making of the English Bible*, pp. 49–51, esp. 51 for other examples of the construct in Coverdale's Psalms.

159 Cf. Ps. 124:7   נַפְשֵׁנוּ כְּצִפּוֹר נִמְלְטָה
                                   מִפַּח יוֹקְשִׁים
                 הַפַּח נִשְׁבָּר וַאֲנַחְנוּ נִמְלָטְנוּ

    Our-soul as-[a]-bird is-escaped
    from-the-snare [of the] fowlers
    the-snare is-broken and-we have escaped   (my translation)

    Anima nostra sicut avicula salvata est
    ex laqueo aucupum:
    laqueus diffractus est & nos liberati sumus   (Münster, fol. 626^v).

    Cf. Ps. 55:6   וָאֹמַר מִי־יִתֶּן־לִי אֵבֶר כַּיּוֹנָה
                               אָעוּפָה וְאֶשְׁכֹּנָה:

    And-I-said who will-give to-me wings as-[a]-dove
    I-will-fly-away and-will-dwell [i.e. in shelter]   (my translation)

    Et dixi: Quis dabit mihi pennam qualem habet columba
    avolarem enim & tuto quiescerem   (Münster, fol. 594^r)

160 Cf. Ps. 42:1   כְּאַיָּל תַּעֲרֹג עַל־אֲפִיקֵי־מָיִם
                     כֵּן נַפְשִׁי תַעֲרֹג אֵלֶיךָ אֱלֹהִים:

    As-[the]-hind pants for brooks [of] water
    so my-soul [i.e. feminine noun] pants towards-you O-God   (my translation)

    Sicut cerva inhiat rivis aquarum,
    sic anima mea desiderio fert ad te deus   (Münster, fol. 589^r)

161 Cf. Ps. 126:5 הַזֹּרְעִים בְּדִמְעָה

בְּרִנָּה יִקְצֹרוּ:

Those-who-sow in-tears (bedim'ah)

(berinnah) with-a-shout-of-joy shall-reap   (my translation and transliteration)

Qui seminant in lachrymis,

in exultatione metent   (Münster, fol. 627ʳ)

162 Sidney, Defence of Poesie, sig. B4ʳ (cf. Apology for Poetry, ed. Shepherd, p. 99). Cf. Peter Martyr Vermigli, Common Places (London, 1583), pt 3, ch. 12 '. . . divine Poems doo onlie sing of God, and celebrate him onlie' quoted in Campbell, Divine Poetry, p. 5. See further I. Baroway, 'The Bible as Poetry in the English Renaissance: An Introduction', Journal of English and Germanic Philology, xxxii (1933), 447–80; and the same author's 'Tremellius, Sidney and Biblical Verse', Modern Language Notes, xlix (1934), 145–9; see also Barbara Lewalski's discussion of the Psalms and biblical genre theory in Protestant Poetics, pp. 39–53.

163 For Coverdale's 1535 Bible see Darlow & Moule, Historical Catalogue, no. 18; for the Great Bible: The Byble in Englyshe . . . after the veryte of the Hebrue and Greke textes (London, 1539), pt 3, sig. AA2ʳ–DD3ᵛ, see Darlow & Moule, Historical Catalogue, no. 46; see further Mozley, Coverdale, pp. 261–305. Coverdale also produced the earliest surviving example of metrical psalms in the form of holy songs to be printed in England: Goostly psalmes and spirituall songes drawen out of the holy Scripture (London [1535]), on which see above pp. 112–13.

164 Cf. Luther's 'sein Zorn wahret einen Augenblick' in E. Clapton, Our Prayer Book Psalter (London, 1934), p. 62.

165 See Ps. 46:6 (cf. Vulgate & Jerome's 'iuxta Hebraeos', Clapton, Prayer Book Psalter. p. 107); Ps. 35:21; Ps. 40:15; Ps. 74:8; Ps.9:19 (cf. Luther 'dass Menschen nicht Ueber Hand krigen', Clapton, Prayer Book Psalter, p. 16).

166 See Pss. 18:22; 28:7; 118:6.

167 See Pss. 107:27; 37:40; 22:11; 16:4; 2:4 and 37:13.

168 Cf. Münster 'uni cor meum' (Clapton, Prayer Book Psalter, p. 207); cf. Vulgate 'declinavi' (Clapton, Prayer Book Psalter, p. 302).

169 Cf. Zurich Bible 'saugt es nit wenig nutzes' (ibid., p. 168).

170 Hunnis, Certayne Psalmes chosen out of the Psalter of David, and drawen furth into Englysh meter (London, 1550), sig. π1ᵛ: 'I have here picked oute . . . these psalmes folowing which no late wryter hath hytherto touched'; see further Appendix, no. 28. Forrest, Certaigne Psalmes of Davyd in meeatre/added to maister Sterneholdis/ and oothers 1551 in London, B.Lib., MS Royal 17A xxi; see further above pp. 125–6.

171 Crowley, The Psalter of David newely translated into Englysh metre (London, 1549), sig. ++2ʳ: 'I have made open and playne, that whiche in other translations is obscure & harde. Trustynge that some better learned, wyll hereat take occasion to adde more lyght.' Seagar, Certayne Psalmes select out of the Psalter of David and drawen into Englyshe Metre (London, 1553), sig. A3ʳ. See Appendix, no. 31.

172 'The Lover wounded with his Ladies beauty craveth mercy. To the Tune of where is the life that late I led' in *A Gorgeous Gallery of Gallant Inventions* (1578), ed. H. E. Rollins (Cambridge, Mass., 1926), pp. 39-42 esp. 40, lines 18-25; cf. Ps. 6 *The Piththy and moost notable sayinges of al Scripture, gathered by Thomas Paynell: after the manner of common places* (London, 1550), sig. H1ᵛ; see further Appendix, no. 29.

173 *The Complete Works in Verse and Prose of Samuel Daniel* ed. A. B. Grosart, 5 vols. (London, 1885-96), i, 81.

174 On Shakespeare's use of the Psalms see R. Noble, *Shakespeare's Biblical Knowledge and use of the Book of Common Prayer as Exemplified in the Plays of the First Folio* (London, 1935); R. E. Prothero, *The Psalms in Human Life* (London, [1903]), pp. 131-3. In the following examples Shakespeare's texts are quoted from *The Norton Facsimile The First Folio of Shakespeare*, ed. C. Hinman (London & New York, 1968) with the first line references (within scenes) as the relevant Arden Shakespeare editions.

175 Cf. further Ps. 18:1 (Bishops' Bible) for similar sense and quadruple parallelism; and Ps. 42:9 in the Anglo-Genevan metrical psalter: 'O Lord, thou art my guyde and stay, my rock and my defence'.

176 Cf. Ps. 8:4-5 (Great Bible and Geneva Bible).

177 Cf. *Romeo & Juliet*, II, ii, 28-32.

178 For Byrd's *Psalmes, Sonets, & songs* see Appendix, no. 74.

179 Drayton, *The Harmonie of the Church. Containing, The Spirituall Songes and holy Hymnes, of godly men, Patriarkes and Prophetes* (London, 1591), sig. A3ʳ.

180 On literary 'kinds' see above n.30.

2 Davids divine Poeme: Wyatt & Smith

1 John Fisher, *This treatyse concernynge the fruytfull saynges of Davyd the kynge & prophete in the seven penytencyall psalmes. Devyded in seven sermons* (London, 1509), sig. aa4ᵛ, *STC*² 10903. Fisher's sermons were preached before Margaret Beaufort, Countess of Richmond, and first published as the treatise in 1508.

2 On Wyatt's text and sources including Aretino's *I sette salmi de la Penitentia de David* (Venice, 1534, 1536 etc.) see H. V. Baron, 'Sir Thomas Wyatt's Seven Penitential Psalms: A Study of Textual and Source Materials' (University of Cambridge, Ph.D., 1977), esp. pp. 217ff. For an English translation of Aretino see John Hawkins, *Paraphrase upon the Seaven Penitentiall Psalmes of the Kingly Prophet* (Douai, 1635); extracts from Aretino's text (1536 edn) are quoted in *Collected Poems of Sir Thomas Wyatt*, ed. K. Muir & P. Thomson (Liverpool, 1969), pp. 358-90.

3 For the story of David and Bathsheba, see II Samuel [III Kings]:11-12. For renaissance views of David and their medieval antecedents see E. A. Gosselin, *The King's Progress to Jerusalem: Some Interpretations of David*

During the Reformation Period and their Patristic and Medieval Background (Los Angeles, 1976); also A. J. Minnis, *Medieval Theory of Authorship: Scholastic Literary Attitudes in the Later Middle Ages* (London, 1984), esp. ch. 3. Cf. I.-S. Ewbank, 'The House of David in Renaissance Drama', *Renaissance Drama* viii (1965), 3–40.

4 On the iconography of David and Bathsheba see L. Réau, *Iconographie de l'art chrétien* (Paris, 1955–59), ii (1956), 273ff.; E. Kunoth-Leifels, *Uber die Darstellungen der 'Bathseba im Bade': Studien zur Geschichte des Bildthemas 4. bis 17. Jahrhundert* (Essen, 1962); V. Leroquais, *Les Livres d'heures manuscrits de la Bibliothèque Nationale* (Paris, 1927–43); M. B. Parkes, *The Medieval Manuscripts of Keble College Oxford* (London, 1979), see pl. 88 of MS 39 for illustration by the Bedford Master of Bathsheba bathing.

5 For examples of English illustrations of Bathsheba bathing see Fisher, *Treatyse*, sig. aa2^r; *The Psalter or boke of Psalmes both in Latyn and Englyshe* (London, 1540), title leaf verso; see further E. Hodnett, *English Woodcuts, 1480–1535* (London, 1935).

6 See H. A. Mason, 'Wyatt and the Psalms', *The Times Literary Supplement*, 27 Feb. and 6 Mar., 1953, pp. 144 and 160 respectively; *Collected Poems*, ed. Muir & Thomson; R. G. Twombly, 'Thomas Wyatt's Paraphrase of the Penitential Psalms of David', *Texas Studies in Literature and Language*, xii (1970), 345–80; H. V. Baron, 'Wyatt's Seven Penitential Psalms'; *Sir Thomas Wyatt, The Complete Poems*, ed. R. A. Rebholz (Harmondsworth, 1978).

7 See H. A. Mason, *Humanism and Poetry in the Early Tudor Period* (London, 1959, repr., 1980), pp. 207–21; Twombly, *TSLL*, xii (1970), 352–80.

8 For Wyatt's use of Thomas de Vio Cajetan, *Psalmi Davidici ad Hebraicam veritatem castigati* (Venice, 1530) see Baron, 'Wyatt's Seven Penitential Psalms', pp. 243–8.

9 For Wyatt's revisions of his text in his own hand see London, British Library, MS Egerton 2711, fols. 86^r–98^v; see also *Collected Poems*, ed. Muir & Thomson, pp. 98–125; and Baron, 'Wyatt's Seven Penitential Psalms', pp. 255–321. For interpretations of Wyatt's handling of his Italian source see Baron, ibid., p. 221; and Twombly, *TSLL*, xii (1970), 355.

10 See H. Smith, 'English Metrical Psalms in the Sixteenth Century and their Literary Significance', *Huntington Library Quarterly*, ix (1946), 262–3. Cf. S. Greenblatt, *Renaissance Self-Fashioning: From More to Shakespeare* (Chicago & London, 1980), pp. 115–27 for the view that David's 'sexual aggression' is a metaphor for Henry VIII's 'abuse of power'.

11 Mason, *Humanism and Poetry*, pp. 180, 186, 198, see also pp. 217–20.

12 R. Southall, *The Courtly Maker, An Essay on the Poetry of Wyatt and his Contemporaries* (Oxford & New York, 1964); D. M. Friedman, 'The "Thing" in Wyatt's Mind', *Essays in Criticism*, xvi (1966), 375–81; Twombly, *TSLL*, xii (1970), 345–80; cf. also B. K. Lewalski, *Protestant*

Poetics and the Seventeenth-Century Religious Lyric (Princeton, 1979), pp. 237–8. See further C. W. Jentoft, *Sir Thomas Wyatt and Henry Howard, Earl of Surrey a Reference Guide* (Boston, 1980).

13 K. Muir, *Life and Letters of Sir Thomas Wyatt* (Liverpool, 1963), p. 256. For the debate with Mason on the dating of Wyatt's psalms (according to the dates of his imprisonments) see ibid., p. 256, n. 7 and Mason, *Humanism and Poetry*, p. 204.

14 See *Complete Poems*, ed. Rebholz, p. 454.

15 Twombly, *TSLL*, xii (1970), 356.

16 Greenblatt, *Renaissance Self-Fashioning*, p. 119.

17 See Twombly, *TSLL*, xii (1970), 347–8, 371–4; *Complete Poems*, ed. Rebholz, p. 454; Mason, *Humanism and Poetry*, pp. 215–19, esp. p. 219.

18 Twombly, *TSLL*, xii (1970), 355–7.

19 Mason, *Humanism and Poetry*, pp. 211–12; Lewalski, *Protestant Poetics*, p. 237.

20 Greenblatt, *Renaissance Self-Fashioning*, pp. 124–5.

21 In 1549 John Harington of Stepney published Wyatt's penitential psalms under the title *Certayne psalmes chosen out of the psalter of David ... whereunto is added a prologe of the auctore before every psalme*; each prologue is headed 'The Auctor'. (In his dedication to William Parr, Harington refers to Wyatt as the 'auctor' of the work.) See further Appendix, no. 25.

22 This and subsequent quotations from Wyatt's penitential psalms (except lines 100–153) are based on his holograph manuscript: London, British Library, Egerton 2711, fols. 86^r–98^v. (Cf. *Collected Poems*, ed. Muir & Thomson, pp. 98–125.) Quotations from lines 100–53 (wanting in Egerton) are from London, British Library, Royal 17A xxii, fols. 8^r–8^v; see further H. A. Mason, *Editing Wyatt An Examination of* Collected Poems of Sir Thomas Wyatt *together with suggestions for an improved edition* (Cambridge, 1972), pp. 140–54.

23 Wyatt added the phrase 'subject hertes' to the sense of Aretino's text. For Wyatt's treatment of the theme of Love as a cruel tyrant in his secular verse see esp. 'The lyvely sperkes that issue from those Iyes' (*Collected Poems*, ed. Muir & Thomson, p. 35); 'Love hathe agayne' (ibid., pp. 161–2); 'Off purpos Love chase first for to be blynd' (ibid., p. 83); 'Love and fortune and my mynde, remembre' (ibid., pp. 23–4); 'My galy charged with forgetfulnes' (ibid., pp. 21–2); 'I fynde no peace and all my warr is done' (ibid., pp. 20–21, esp. lines 5–8); 'Farewell, the rayn of crueltie' (ibid., pp. 11–12); 'Farewell, Love, and all thy lawes for ever (ibid., pp. 12–13).

24 Cf. Fisher, *Treatyse*, sig. aa 8^v: 'It is wryten in the gospell ... They that be hole nedeth no physycyen/ but a physycyen is nedefull unto them that be seke. The myserable synners whiche be thraste downe by the moost myserable sekenes of synne have grete nede of a medycyne to make theym hole ... and the more seke that a man is the better medycyne he hath nede of.'

25 Fisher associates 'compunccyon of the herte' with 'the inwarde sorowe
. . . whan we be sory for our synne' (ibid., sig. ii6ʳ), and explains, 'whan
the synner is prycked in his conscyence . . . remembrynge thabomyna-
cyon of his synnes/ anone yf he be very penytent teres shall trekell
downe from his eyen/ whiche is a grete token the holy ghoost is present
with that synner' (ibid., sig. ll6ʳ⁻ᵛ). Fisher is here drawing upon
traditional views of a psychology of the spiritual life, dominated by the
teaching of Gregory the Great. For a convenient summary of Gregory's
teaching on compunction and tears of penitence (*irriguum inferius*) see
J. Leclercq, *The Love of Learning and the Desire for God* (New York,
1961), pp. 37–9.

26 For this and subsequent quotations from Aretino's *I sette salmi* (1536)
see Wyatt's *Collected Poems*, ed. Muir & Thomson, pp. 358–90, esp.
366.

27 See *OED* disease 1 and 2, for senses of disquiet and of physical sickness
in Middle English and Early Modern English usage. Cf. Wyatt's line
200: 'esd not yet held he felith his disese'.

28 Cf. Fisher on 'that lyght of grace' (Ps. 31[32]:7), *Treatyse*, sig. dd1ʳ:
'From the eyen of almyghty god whiche may be called his grace shyneth
forth a mervayllous bryghtnes lyke as the beme that cometh from the
sonne.'

29 See Friedman, *Essays in Criticism*, xvi (1966), 375–81; for Campensis see
Baron, 'Wyatt's Seven Penitential Psalms', p. 281. (My italics.)

30 Fisher, *Treatyse*, sig. ff1ᵛ.

31 See T. N. Tentler, *Sin and Confession on the Eve of the Reformation*
(Princeton, 1977), esp. pp. 238–50.

32 On the contradictory impulses and effects of compunction see Leclercq,
Love of Learning, pp. 37–9.

33 On the 'tyranny' of sin, cf. Fisher, *Treatyse*, sig. ff4ʳ: 'who soever
serveth this malycyous and cursed lorde [synne] is in grete bondage and
servytude'; 'we be put downe . . . under the thraldome of synne' (ibid.,
sig. gg2ʳ).

34 On compunction and detachment see Leclercq, *Love of Learning*, p. 37.

35 Fisher, *Treatyse*, sig. ll3ʳ. On temptation as a cure for pride see
Leclercq, *Love of Learning*, p. 38.

36 See above notes 14 and 17.

37 Line 504 is Wyatt's addition; cf. Aretino and Campensis (*Collected
Poems*, ed. Muir & Thomson, p. 378) for emphasis on 'inward'. For
Wyatt's interpretation of Syon cf. also *OED* Zion: 'By Syon . . . is
understode sowles that are gyven to contemplacyon, where in oure
lorde . . . ys sewrely stabled', *Myrrour of our Ladye* (1450–1530).

38 For the image of the Bible as the food or bread of life cf. the poem
composed by Wyatt's friend Sir George Blage in prison (1546),
reprinted in Muir, *Life and Letters*, pp. 273–6, esp. 273; and pp. 258–9.

39 Wyatt may have borrowed the metaphor of drowning from Fisher's
exposition of Ps. 32:6 in which God's grace rescues the sinner from

drowning in floods of different sins and the 'transytory pleasures of thys worlde', *Treatyse*, sig. cc7ᵛ & dd1ᵛ.

40 Wyatt's doubling of the rhetorical question ('quis sustinebit') in the Vulgate Ps. 129[130]:3 emphasizes David's insistent tone.

41 Lines 669–70; Wyatt's addition to his sources, see *Collected Poems*, ed. Muir & Thomson, p. 386.

42 On the superior aspect of compunction and the influence of Gregory see Leclercq, *Love of Learning*, pp. 32–3.

43 For a description of 'Penaunce and the Partes of it' by a Protestant who had connexions with Wyatt's family see Thomas Becon's *A Potacion or drinkynge for this holi time of lent very comfortable for all penitent synners* (London, 1542), STC² 1749, sig. B6ᵛ and D1ᵛ ('Of contricion'), D6ʳ ('Of confession'), E7ʳ ('Of satisfaccion or amendment of lyfe').

44 Fisher, *Treatyse*, sig. aa4ᵛ–5ʳ.

45 See J. Leclercq, F. Vandenbroucke, L. Bouyer, *The Spirituality of the Middle Ages* (London, 1968), pp. 484–98; H. C. White, *The Tudor Books of Private Devotion* (Wisconsin, 1951).

46 Fisher, *Treatyse*, sig. aa2ᵛ.

47 William Tyndale, *The obedience of a Christen man and how Christen rulers ought to governe* ([Antwerp], 1528), facsimile edn (Menston, 1970), fols. 135ᵛ–6ʳ. Cf. William Tyndale, *Doctrinal Treatises and Introductions to different portions of the Holy Scripture*, ed. H. Walter, Parker Society (Cambridge, 1848), p. 310.

48 Wyatt ostensibly addressed his third satire to Sir Francis Brian on the grounds that Brian appreciated 'how great a grace In writing is to cownsell man the right', see 'A spending hand that alway powreth owte' lines 9–10, *Collected Poems*, ed. Muir & Thomson, p. 95.

49 For Wyatt's epigram and its relation to his 1541 'Defence' and his 'Declaration ... of his Innocence', see ibid., p. 242 and *Sir Thomas Wyatt, Collected Poems*, ed. J. Daalder (Oxford, 1975), p. 209 n. Cf. Muir, *Life and Letters*, pp. 184–5, 193.

50 For Surrey's epigram see *Henry Howard Earl of Surrey, Poems*, ed. E. Jones (Oxford, 1964, repr., 1973), p. 32; cf. Wyatt, *Collected Poems*, ed. Muir & Thomson, p. 242.

51 See ibid., pp. 187–8, for this and subsequent quotations; see further *Collected Poems*, ed. Rebholz, p. 424. The heading and the poem in the Blage manuscript (Dublin, Trinity College, MS D.2.7. parts 2 and 3) are in different hands (see *Collected Poems*, ed. Daalder, p. 185 n.). Sir George Blage was one of Wyatt's closest friends, see *Collected Poems*, ed. Muir & Thomson, pp. xii-xiii, and Muir, *Life and Letters*, pp. 213–14.

52 See *Collected Poems*, ed. Muir & Thomson, pp. 75–7, 328–32, and 240.

53 Ibid., p. 75; cf. 'Frett not thy self at the ungodly, be not thou envious agaynst the evell doers. For they shall soone be cut downe like the grasse, & be wythered even as the grene herbe. Put thou thy trust in the Lorde, & be doinge good: so shalt thou dwell in the londe.'

(Ps. 36[37]:1–3, 1535 Bible.) Cf. Vulgate & Campensis quoted in *Collected Poems*, ed. Muir & Thomson, p. 328.

54 Ibid., p. 240; see further *The Arundel Harington Manuscript of Tudor Poetry*, ed. R. Hughey, 2 vols. (Columbus, Ohio, 1960), ii, 245.

55 *Collected Poems*, ed. Muir & Thomson, p. 240. The address to 'Myne Earle' was probably to Surrey since Surrey's verses to 'My Deny' and 'My Blage', which serve as prologues to his paraphrases of Pss. 88 and 73, appear to be modelled on this argument; cf. *Surrey Poems*, ed. Jones, pp. 32–3. See further above p. 89.

56 See above, n. 21.

57 *Surrey Poems*, ed. Jones, p. 29.

58 Sackville's verses are quoted in *Wyatt: The Critical Heritage*, ed. P. Thomson (London & Boston, 1974), p. 33.

59 The full title of William Baldwin's anthology (*STC²* 1248) is *A Myrrour for Magistrates. Wherein maye be seen by example of other, with howe grevous plages vices are punished: and howe frayle and unstable worldly prosperity is founde, even of those whom Fortune seemeth most highly to favour.* For a view of Wyatt's psalms in the 'Fall of Princes' tradition in which David represents Henry VIII, see E. St Sure Lifschutz, 'David's Lyre & the Renaissance Lyric: A Critical Consideration of the Psalms of Wyatt, Surrey and the Sidneys' (University of California, Berkeley, Ph.D. 1980), pp. 143–55; cf. Greenblatt, n. 10 above.

60 *Surrey Poems*, ed. Jones, p. 29; for a view of Wyatt as a Christian poet and moralist see also the elegies by his friend John Leland in Leland's *Naeniae in mortem Thomae Viati equitis incomparabilis* (London, 1542), esp. sig. A4ᵛ and A6ʳ.

61 See above n. 21.

62 See M. Dewar, *Sir Thomas Smith A Tudor Intellectual in Office* (London, 1964), esp. pp. 56–66.

63 See London, British Library, MS. Royal 17A xvii: 'Certaigne Psalmes or Songues of David translated into Englishe meter by Sir Thomas Smith Knyght, then Prisoner in the Tower of London, with other prayers and songues by him mad to pas the tyme there . 1549.' The manuscript was edited by Bror Danielsson, in *Stockholm Studies in English*, xii (1963), who states (p. 12) that it is in Smith's hand. For Smith's paraphrases and collects see above pp. 98–103.

64 MS Royal 17A xvii, fols. 25ʳ–26ᵛ (all quotations are based on the manuscript).

65 Cf. Ps. 2:1, Ps. 10:1, Ps. 77:9; also Smith's metrical paraphrase of Ps. 119[120]:5 'In prison strong . . . in a cabon of sorowes ure' (fol. 5ʳ).

66 Cf. Ps. 7:4–5.

67 See Ps. 14:1, Ps. 53:1; cf. Ps. 10:4 and 6, Ps. 73:11.

68 Cf. Ps. 73:3–6.

69 Cf. Ps. 73:12–15.

70 Cf. Wyatt's ironic advice to Francis Brian in the third satire 'A spending hand . . . ' (lines 32–4):

who so can seke to plese
Shall pourchase frendes where trowght shall but offend.
Fle therefore trueth: it is boeth welth and ese
(*Collected Poems*, ed. Muir & Thomson, p. 96)

71 For biblical psalmist's representation of God's direct speech cf. Ps. 50:5, 7–23, esp. 19–20. Cf. also God's rebuke to the poet in an anonymous poem 'The secreat flame that made all Troye so hot' in the Arundel Harington MS (ed. Hughey, i, 344–6, esp. lines 61ff.), also printed in the second edition of Tottel's *Songes and Sonettes* (*Tottel's Miscellany (1557–1587)*), ed. H. E. Rollins, 2 vols. (Cambridge, Mass., 1928–9, rev. 1965), no. 279.

72 Cf. Smith's metrical paraphrase of Ps. 145[146]:3–4

Never in Princes, put yow yowr trust
Nor yowr confidence in the sonnes of man
Thei will not help yow, thei will leave yow in the dust.
Thei be not those, that help yow can   (fol. 17ᵛ)

73 Cf. Ps. 73:25–6.

74 Cf. Wyatt's 'Myne owne John Poyntz . . .' lines 3 and 35; 'A spending hand . . .' line 83 in *Collected Poems*, ed. Muir & Thomson, pp. 88–9 and 97.

75 See above n. 43.

3 Particuler prayers of particular persons

1 Anthony Gilby's remarks are from his preface to *The Psalmes of David, Truly Opened and explaned by Paraphrasis . . . by . . . Theodore Beza* (London, 1581), sig. A3ᵛ.

2 From the dedication to Queen Elizabeth, dated 10 Feb. 1559 from Geneva, in *The Booke of Psalmes, wherein are contayned prayers meditations, prayses and thankesgiving to God . . . translated faithfully according to the Ebrewe* (London, 1578), sig. f3ᵛ. Cf. Robert Filles's dedication in his *Godly prayers and Meditations* (London, 1572?), sig. A3ʳ.

3 *The Booke of Psalmes* (1578), sig. f6ʳ.

4 Ibid., sig. f3ᵛ.

5 Calvin's comments are from his address to 'godly Readers', dated 23 July 1557 from Geneva, included in Arthur Golding's translation *The Psalmes of David and others. With M. John Calvins Commentaries* (London, 1571), sig. ⋆⋆2ᵛ.

6 *The Booke of Psalmes* (1578), sig. f3ᵛ.

7 Ibid., sig. f4ʳ.

8 The description of Hooper is by the editor of *Certeine comfortable Expositions of the constant Martyr of Christ, M. John Hooper . . . written in the time of his tribulation and imprisonment, upon the XXIII. LXII. LXXIII. and LXXVII. Psalmes of the Prophet David* (London, 1580), sig. ¶ 4ʳ.

9 Hooper recommended Pss. 77 and 88, also Pss. 6, 22, 30, 31, 38 and 69, in 'An exhortation to patience, sent to his godlye wife Anne Hoper:

wherby all the true members of Christe may take comforte and courage, to suffer trouble and affliction for the profession of his holy Gospell' dated 13 October 1553; see Coverdale's edition of *Certain most godly, fruitful, and comfortable letters of . . . Saintes and holy Martyrs of God . . . written in the tyme of theyr affliction and cruell imprisonment* (London, 1564), pp. 147–57, esp. 152. (Cf. *Later Writings of Bishop Hooper, together with his Letters and other Pieces*, ed. C. Nevinson, Parker Society (Cambridge, 1852), pp. 583–4.)

10 See above notes 4 and 7.

11 For a discussion of the texts and composition of More's 'instruction, meditations and prayers' see G. E. Haupt's introduction to *The Complete Works of St Thomas More*, xiii (New Haven & London, 1976), cxl–cxlvii.

12 For More's Latin prayer 'Imploratio divini auxilii' see ibid., pp. cliii ff., 214–25 and 302–11; see further G. Marc'hadour, *The Bible in the Works of Thomas More*, 5 parts (Nieuwkoop, 1969–72), i, 105–77. For the composition and use of Jerome's Psalter in English Books of Hours or Primers see E. Hoskins, *Horae Beatae Mariae Virginis* (London, 1901), passim; see further C. C. Butterworth, *The English Primers (1529–1545) Their Publication and Connection with the English Bible and the Reformation in England* (Philadelphia, 1953); A. C. Southern, *Elizabethan Recusant Prose 1559–1582* (London, [1950]), pp. 223–6; see also H. C. White, *The Tudor Books of Private Devotion* (Wisconsin, 1951), esp. pp. 48–51 on Fisher's *Psalmi seu precationes*; and cf. Appendix, no. 12.

13 For More's English prayer see *Thomas More's Prayer Book. A Facsimile Reproduction of the Annotated Pages*, ed. L. L. Martz & R. S. Sylvester (New Haven & London, 1969, repr., 1976), pp. 3–21, 185–7; cf. *Complete Works*, xiii, ed. Haupt, 226–7, 314. The title 'A godly meditacion' was used in *The Workes of Sir Thomas More* (London, 1557) edited by More's nephew William Rastell, see p. 1416.

14 For More's Psalter annotations see *More's Prayer Book* ed. Martz & Sylvester, esp. pp. xxxix–xlv, 189–202. I am indebted to the editors' introduction.

15 For Haupt's conjecture that More wrote the 'godly meditacion' on 2 July 1535 see *Complete Works*, xiii, ed. Haupt, cli, n. 1.

16 For the relationships between the Psalter annotations and the two prayers see *More's Prayer Book*, ed. Martz & Sylvester, pp. xxxi–xxxix and *Complete Works*, xiii, ed. Haupt, 302–11.

17 For transcriptions and translations of the Psalter annotations see *More's Prayer Book* ed. Martz & Sylvester, pp. 189–202.

18 Ibid., pp. 59–60, 193.

19 Ibid., pp. 144, 200; for More's other references to imprisonment see his annotations to Pss. 24[25]:15; 68[69]:34; 83[84]:2; ibid., pp. 53, 116, 139.

20 On the relationship of 'the Tower Works and More the Man' see *Complete Works*, xiii, ed. Haupt, clxvii–clxxx; the *Treatise* was probably partly composed before More was imprisoned but Haupt still groups it with the 'Tower Works'.

21 For an analysis of the structure of More's English prayer see ibid., clxv–clxvii; for its structure and significance as a 'psalm' see *More's Prayer Book*, ed. Martz & Sylvester, pp. xxxvi–xxxix.

22 Ibid., p. 4.

23 Ibid., pp. 3–5; and pp. 6–21 for all subsequent quotations from More's prayer.

24 Ibid., pp. 13 and 16; More originally wrote 'my' after 'bere' (p. 13) but crossed it out as he wrote.

25 Ibid., p. 76; for a discussion of the relationship between More's Psalter annotations and his conduct during his trial see ibid., pp. xlii–xliii.

26 Coverdale's comment is from his dedication to the reader of *A Paraphrasis upon all the Psalmes of David, made by Johannes Campensis, reader of the Hebrue lecture in the universite of Lovane* (London, 1539), sig. A2^r, see also above p. 33.

27 *Letters and Papers, Foreign and Domestic, of the Reign Henry VIII*, ed. J. Gairdner & R. H. Brodie (London, 1901), xviii, pt 1, p. 164; pt 2, p. 140. For biographical details of Sternhold see A. B. Emden, *A Biographical Register of the University of Oxford A.D. 1501–1540* (Oxford, 1974), p. 539.

28 For a fuller discussion of Sternhold's psalms see above pp. 113 ff.

29 Sternhold's version of Ps. 120 was included in *Certayne Psalmes chosen out of the Psalter of David, and drawen into Englishe Metre by Thomas Sternhold grome of the kynges Majesties Roobes* (London [1549?]), sig. D5^v–D6^r, all quotations from his Ps. 120 are from this edition.

30 For names of other prisoners in the Fleet see *Letters & Papers*, n. 27 above.

31 For a brief account of the events of 1543 see G. R. Elton, *England under the Tudors* (London, 1955, repr., 1967), pp. 196–200.

32 Thomas Wilcox, *A Right Godly and learned Exposition, upon the whole Booke of Psalmes* (London, 1586), sig. B1^r; Sternhold, *Certayne Psalmes*, sig. D5^v.

33 For texts and notes on Surrey's prison poems see *Henry Howard Earl of Surrey Poems*, ed. E. Jones (Oxford, 1964, repr., 1973), pp. 24–6, 30–1 and 120–1, 127–9. Surrey's 'London, hast thow accused me' related to his imprisonment in the Fleet in the spring of 1543 when he was accused of Protestant sympathies; this was also the period of Sternhold's imprisonment.

34 For Surrey's confession of his rashness, 'folly' and 'heady will' see the apologetic letter he wrote to the Privy Council from the Fleet in 1542 begging them to remit his sentence for striking a man at court, in *The Works of Henry Howard Earl of Surrey*, ed. G. F. Nott (London, 1815), p. 169. Surrey was imprisoned at Windsor Castle in 1537 and 1546, in the Fleet in 1542 and 1543 and finally in the Tower 1546–7; see further E. Casady, *Henry Howard, Earl of Surrey* (New York, 1938).

35 For speculation on the date of Surrey's Pss. 55, 73 and 88 see ibid., pp. 207–9; *Surrey Poems*, ed. Jones, pp. 153, 158–9; H. A. Mason, 'Wyatt and the Psalms', *Times Literary Supplement*, 6 March 1953. G. F. Nott

(*Works of Surrey*, p. 390) suggests that the psalms date from the Windsor imprisonment in 1546. Surrey's version of Ps. 8 is not usually attributed to the same period; see further *The Arundel Harington Manuscript of Tudor Poetry*, ed. R. Hughey, 2 vols. (Columbus, Ohio, 1960), i, 125–7; ii, 99–102, esp. 101. In his forthcoming edition of Surrey's poems for the 'Oxford English Texts' series, W. D. McGaw attributes paraphrases of Pss. 31 and 51 printed in *Certayne Chapters of the proverbes of Salomon* [1549–50], *STC²* 2760, to Surrey; see further Appendix, no. 26.

36 Both contemporary manuscript anthologies of verse containing copies of Surrey's psalms were compiled and formerly owned by successive generations of the Harington family: London, British Library, Additional MS 36529 (also known as the Hill MS or the Phillips MS); Arundel Castle, Harington MS. For texts and notes on Surrey's epistles to Blage and Denny see *Surrey Poems*, ed. Jones, pp. 32–3, 130; *Arundel Harington MS*, ed. Hughey, ii, 102, 104–5.

37 For text and notes on Surrey's Ps. 73 see *Surrey Poems*, ed. Jones, pp. 99–100, 159 (includes Latin text of Campensis paraphrase Ps. 73:1–3, 8–10); *Arundel Harington MS*, ed. Hughey, ii, 105–7 (includes English text (1539) of selections from Campensis for comparison); see further Mason, *TLS*, 6 March 1953.

38 The rivalry between Surrey and Seymour (later Duke of Somerset) dated from 1537 at least, see Casady, *Henry Howard*, pp. 60–3.

39 For text and notes on Surrey's Ecclesiastes see *Arundel Harington MS*, ed. Hughey, i, 133–42; ii, 113–20; *Works of Surrey*, ed. Nott, pp. 66–77 (*Surrey Poems*, ed. Jones, omits Ecclesiastes 5).

40 Most of these similarities between Surrey's versions of Ecclesiastes and Ps. 88 are in the passages where Surrey departed from his biblical sources, so they give no indication which of the paraphrases was written first. (Cf. Eccl. 2, lines 44–56 and Ps. 88, lines 25–30, *Surrey Poems*, ed. Jones, pp. 91, 98–9.) However, the phrase 'sleapes/ that wearied lymbs oppresse' (Eccl. 5, line 39, *Arundel Harington MS*, ed. Hughey, i, 141) echoed in Ps. 88, line 32 as 'sleape my weryd lymes oppresse' (*Surrey Poems*, ed. Jones, p. 99) was derived from the text of Ecclesiastes 5:11 'sweet is the sleep of a labouring man' (contrast, 'and early shall my prayer come before the', Great Bible, Ps. 88:13). G. F. Nott (*Works of Surrey*, p. 377) suggested that the Ecclesiastes paraphrases were written when Surrey returned from France in 1546.

41 For Surrey's epistle to Denny see *Surrey Poems*, ed. Jones, p. 32; for Denny see further Thompson Cooper's article in *DNB*.

42 Cf. 'I am so fast in preson' (1535 and Great Bible, Ps. 88:8), 'Affecerunt me malis tam multis adversarii mei, ut visus sim ipse mihi precipitatum in puteum, aut in carcerem obscurissimum et profundissimum retrusus', Ps. 88:6, J. Campensis, *Psalmorum omnium: iuxta Hebraicam veritatem paraphrastica, interpretatio* (Paris, 1534), sig. N1ʳ.

43 For this and subsequent quotation from Hooper's comments on Ps. 88 see *Certain letters*, ed. Coverdale (1564), p. 152; see above notes 8 and 9.

44 For text and notes on Surrey's Ps. 88 see *Works of Surrey*, ed. Nott, pp. 78–9, 392; *Arundel Harington MS*, ed. Hughey, i, 127–8; ii, 102–4; *Surrey Poems*, ed. Jones, pp. 98–9, 158; my quotations in the following discussion are from Jones's edition.

45 The Arundel Harington MS has 'blazed' (written over an erasure) in line 27; see frontispiece plate of fol. 53ʳ in vol. 1 of Hughey's edition. 'Blazed' in this context would have had connotations of sound rather than sight; cf. Chaucer, *House of Fame* (ed. F. N. Robinson (2nd edn, London, 1970), lines 1801–2)

> And with his blake clarioun
> He gan to blasen out a soun

cf. lines 1865–6

> And tok his blake trumpe faste
> And gan to puffen and to blaste

Blaze was also used by Caxton and Coverdale, see *OED*, blaze, v².1; Gavin Douglas (*Aeneis*, xiii, Prol. line 165) used blaze with the sense of to describe or to celebrate, see *OED*, blaze, v².4.

46 See *OED*, declare: v.1 'It is no nede to declare it, the matter is playne ynoughe' (1530, Palsgrave, 508/2); v. 2 'The cause ... shall be more playnly declared' (1526, *Pilgrimage of Perfection*); v. 4 The 'heavens declare the glory off God' (1535, Coverdale, Ps. 18[19]:1); v. 5 'His name of confort I will declair, Welcom ...' (Dunbar, d.1530).

47 For Surrey's treatment of the theme of the Last Judgement see also his paraphrase of Ecclesiastes 3, lines 44–8 (*Surrey Poems*, ed. Jones, p. 93).

48 Ps. 88, line 37 (cf. Ps. 88:15).

49 Cf. Arthur Golding's description of the Psalms in the preface to his translation of *The Psalmes of David and others*, sig. ★4ᵛ. For discussion of the Protestant's disposition to relate the lyric sections of the Bible to a Protestant paradigm of salvation by assimilating the 'biblical voices' see B. K. Lewalski, *Protestant Poetics and the Seventeenth-Century Religious Lyric* (Princeton, 1979), pp. 13–27 and 234–40.

50 See above pp. 27ff.

51 Ecclesiastes 5, line 8 (*Arundel Harington MS*, ed. Hughey, i, 140).

52 Epistle to Blage, lines 1–2 (*Surrey Poems*, ed. Jones, p. 33).

53 Ps. 55, lines 36–7, 47–8 (ibid., p. 102).

54 According to Surrey's son 'the last thinge that [his father] wrote before his end which made his judgement cleere' was 'The stormes are past, these cloudes are overblowne', see Oxford, Bodleian Library, MS Bodley 903, fol. 6ʳ. This poem was printed in Tottel's *Songes and Sonettes* (London, 1557), sig. D3ᵛ, with the title 'Bonum est mihi quod humiliasti me' (cf. Ps. 118[119]:71); for text see *Surrey Poems*, ed. Jones, p. 33, esp. lines 4–5, and notes pp. 130–1.

55 For Surrey's elegies for Wyatt (d. 1542) see ibid., pp. 27–9 (no. 28, esp. lines 34–5; no. 30, esp. lines 11–12; no. 31, esp. lines 6–14).

56 On the fall of Somerset see W. K. Jordan, *Edward VI: The Young King*

(London, 1968), pp. 494–523; see also Mary Dewar's account in her *Sir Thomas Smith A Tudor Intellectual in Office* (London, 1964), pp. 56–66.

57 London, British Library, MS Royal 17A xvii. Smith's 'Certaigne Psalmes' are Ps. 102[103]:8–18; Pss. 141[142]; 142[143]; 119[120]; 85[86]; 30[31]; 40[41]; 70[71]; 54[55]; 144[145]; 145[146]. This and subsequent quotations are based on the manuscript. (Cf. also Smith's metrical version of the Ten Commandments in *Arundel Harington MS*, ed. Hughey, i, 367–8; ii. 464.)

58 MS Royal 17A xvii, fol. 13^v; on Warwick see W. K. Jordan, *Edward VI: The Threshold of Power* (London, 1970), pp. 32–6, and above n. 56.

59 In September 1549 Warwick was seeking the support of Catholic nobles to depose Somerset who claimed that Warwick was resolved to make Princess Mary the new Regent; see Jordan, *The Young King*, pp. 506–8. On the obsessive fear of public disorders between Oct. 1549 and Oct. 1551 see Jordan, *The Threshold of Power*, pp. 56–63.

60 For Bradford's prose paraphrase of Ps. 79 written 1554–5 see *The Writings of John Bradford ... Martyr 1555*, ed. A. Townsend, 2 vols., Parker Society (Cambridge, 1848), i, 282–91.

61 MS Royal 17A xvii, fols. 17^v and 18^v; B. Danielsson (*Stockholm Studies in English* xii (1963), 13) quotes a letter written by Cecil: 'Our hope cometh slowly forward, having the hindrance of heavy adversaries, but I trust in God, the strength of our friends shall within these few days draw it to his place' (London, Public Record Office, S. P. 10–9–58); Cecil was released 15 January 1550.

62 On Smith's 'other psalme', see above pp. 74–9.

63 Cf. Smith's version of Ps. 119[120] and Sternhold's see above pp. 86–8.

64 London, British Library, MS Stowe 1066, fol. 1^r; see plate in J. N. King, *English Reformation Literature The Tudor Origins of the Protestant Tradition* (Princeton, 1982), fig. 16 at p. 143, and pp. 113–121. Cf. also Somerset's sonnet 'Experience now doth shew/ what god us taught before' in *Arundel Harington MS*, ed. Hughey, i, 343; ii, 439–40 also printed in Tottel's *Songes and Sonettes* (1557), sig. U3^r.

65 On Sternhold and his imitators, see above pp. 113–21 and 124–6.

66 On the fall of Northumberland see D. Mathew, *Lady Jane Grey. The Setting of the Reign* (London, 1972); D. M. Loades, *Two Tudor Conspiracies* (Cambridge, 1965), pp. 89–112; Jordan, *The Threshold of Power*, pp. 520–32.

67 John Dudley became Earl of Warwick in 1551 when his father took the title Duke of Northumberland. For texts and notes of the Dudley brothers' psalms see *Arundel Harington MS*, ed. Hughey, i, 338–41; ii, 433–38. All my quotations are from this edition.

68 Cf. Warwick's 'garded ... withe thye tryumphant shylde' (line 19), 'with speede' (line 22), 'Clokes of truce' (line 23), 'Dischardge my fraughtfull brest of woe/ and poure in heaps of blisse ... send consuming plages' (lines 28–9); Robert Dudley's 'garde ... with his mightie shyeld' (line 26), 'with speede' (line 32), 'cloked faultes' (line 12), 'carefull

thoughtes . . . consume my brest . . . discharg'de/ and fild my soule with rest' (lines 35–6), 'to plague' (line 44).

69 On the identity of the Dudleys' enemies, see *Arundel Harington MS*, ed. Hughey, ii, 435.

70 Warwick, Ps. 55, lines 2–3, 12, 16, 4, 17–18.

71 For Surrey's Ps. 55 see *Surrey Poems*, ed. Jones, pp. 101–2; for comparisons see further above pp. 108–11.

72 See above pp. 30 and 27.

73 *Iulii Caesaris Scaligeri, viri clarissimi, Poetices libri septem* (Lyon, 1561), p. 6, col. 1; see above pp. 8–9.

74 *De tradendis disciplinis, seu de institutione christiana* in *Io. Lodovici Vivis Valentini Opera in duos distincta tomos* (Basle, 1555), i, 494.

75 Vives, *Opera*, (1555), i, 495; see above pp. 15–16.

76 Erasmus, *Dialogus Ciceronianus* (1528), ed. P. Mesnard in *Opera Omnia* (Amsterdam, 1971), I, ii, 647.

4 Holye songes of veritie

The quotations in the half-title are from: Thomas Sternhold, *Certayne Psalmes chosen out of the Psalter of David and drawen into Englishe Metre* (London [1549?]), sig. A3ʳ; William Byrd, *Psalmes, Sonets, & songs of sadnes and pietie* (London, 1588), title page; *Injunctions geven by the Queenes Majestie* (London, 1559), sig. C4ʳ.

1 See above Ch. 1, n. 150 and 154.

2 See title page of Robert Crowley's *The Psalter of David newely translated into Englysh metre* (London, 1949), Appendix no. 22.

3 The holy songs in Coverdale's *Goostly psalmes* (see further Appendix no. 5), were translated from Lutheran models whereas the vogue for English metrical psalms during the reigns of Edward VI and Elizabeth was based on Calvinist models. On Coverdale's *Goostly psalmes* see further E. Althoff, *Myles Coverdales 'Goostly Psalmes and Spirituall Songes' und das deutsche Kirchenlied. Ein Beitrag zum Einfluss der deutschen Literatur auf die englische im 16. Jahrhundert* (Münster, 1935). Althoff concludes that the stanza forms used by Coverdale depend heavily on those of the German models, but that he allowed himself to be influenced by their texts only when his own text was not taken directly from the Bible (p. 143). However writers of holy songs had recourse to Coverdale's two prose translations of the Psalms: the first for the 1535 Bible and the second (based on Münster's *Hebraica Biblia*) for the Great Bible of 1539; see above Ch. 1, n. 163.

4 For 'the names of certen bokes whiche . . . were prohibyted' see *Actes and Monuments of these latter and perillous dayes, touching matters of the Church . . . by John Foxe* (London [1563]), pp. 573–4, esp. 'Item Psalmes and songes, drawen as is pretended out of holy scripture' listed on p. 573.

5 On music at court see J. Stevens, *Music and Poetry in the Early Tudor Court* (London, 1961 and repr., Cambridge, 1979), pp. 265–95 (on

domestic and amateur music at court) and pp. 296–328 (on professional court musicians); cf. L. B. Campbell, *Divine Poetry and Drama in Sixteenth-century England* (Cambridge, Berkeley & Los Angeles, 1959), p. 45; J. N. King, *English Reformation Literature The Tudor Origins of the Protestant Tradition* (Princeton, 1982), pp. 178–84 and 217–26 (for music and poetry in the court of Edward VI).

6 See above Ch. 1, n. 125; for the influence of Catherine on Elizabeth Tudor see J. K. McConica, *English Humanists and Reformation Politics under Henry VIII and Edward VI* (Oxford, 1965), pp. 7–8; see further Oxford, Bodleian Library, MS Cherry 36 for Elizabeth's holograph of her translation into English of Marguerite of Navarre, *Le Miroir de l'âme pecheresse* (Alençon, 1531) presented to Catherine Parr as a new year's gift; and London, British Library, MS Royal 7 D x for Elizabeth's holograph of her translation into Latin, French and Italian of selections from Catherine's *Prayers or Medytacions* presented to Henry VIII.

7 For references to biographical details of Sternhold see above Ch. 3, n. 27.

8 Coverdale, *Goostly psalmes and spirituall songes* [1535?] sig. + i^r; for Becon's view see above p. 4.

9 (My italics.) Sternhold, *Certayne Psalmes*, sig. A3^r; cf. Sternhold's version of Ps. 4:2 'Why wandre ye in vanitie, and folowe after lyes?' (ibid., sig. A7^r).

10 Ibid., sig. A3^r.

11 For a contemporary reference to Sternhold's holy songs being sung at court see William Baldwin's dedication of his *The Canticles or Balades of Salomon* (London, 1549), sig. A3^v where Sternhold is described as the king's 'godly disposed servaunt' who 'brought' the psalms 'in to fine englysh meter'.

12 On the use of popular tunes see Stevens *Music and Poetry*, pp. 40–7 and 123–32. There are indications in the headings to some biblical psalms that they were sung to popular tunes at the time of the Temple in Jerusalem, see Pss. 9, 22, 45, 56, 57, 58, 60, 69, 80, 88.

13 Ibid., pp. 111, 285–9; for Protestant use of plain-song see the musical setting in Crowley's *Psalter of David* (1549) in P. Le Huray, *Music and the Reformation in England 1549–1660* (London, 1967 and repr., Cambridge, 1978), pp. 371–2; and *Grove's Dictionary of Music and Musicians*, ed. E. Blom, 5th edn, 9 vols. (London, 1954), vi, 957–8.

14 (My italics.) Sternhold, *Certayne Psalmes*, sig. A3^r; cf. J. Leclercq's description of the 'literature of reminiscence' in *The Love of Learning and the Desire for God*, tr. C. Misrahi (New York, 1961), pp. 91–2.

15 For Coverdale's warning about paraphrase see above p. 12.

16 Sternhold, *Certayne Psalmes*, sig. A2^v.

17 Ibid., sig. A2^r.

18 Ibid., sig. A2^v–A3^r.

19 Ibid., sig. A2^r.

20 Sternhold was listed with Wyatt, Surrey, Nicholas Vaux and others as a

'courtly maker' 'of much facilitie' in Puttenham's *Arte of English Poesie* (1589), see *Elizabethan Critical Essays*, ed. G. G. Smith, 2 vols. (Oxford, 1904, repr. 1971), ii, 63.

21 Sternhold, *Certayne Psalmes*, sig. A4^{r-v}.

22 (My italics.) Cf. also 'pulvis' (Vulgate, Ps. 1:5) but 'seat of scornful' and 'chaff' in Great Bible.

23 The text of 'The Nutbrown Maid' was printed in Richard Arnold's [*Customs of London*, Antwerp, 1503?] (*STC*² 782), fol. lxxv^{r}ff; see *The Oxford Book of Sixteenth Century Verse*, ed. E. K. Chambers (Oxford, 1932, repr. 1945), pp. 1–14, which prints the text from Richard Hill's commonplace book (Oxford, Balliol College, MS 354, fol. 210^v). On ballad metre see G. H. Gerould, *The Ballad of Tradition* (New York, 1957), pp. 124–30.

24 *Songes and Sonettes*, ed. Richard Tottel (London, 1557), sig. U2^r; cf. Surrey's 'Geve place ye lovers, here before', ibid., sig. C2^r. On John Heywood (1497?–1579?) see *The New Grove Dictionary of Music and Musicians*, ed. S. Sadie, 20 vols. (London, 1980), viii, 545.

25 George Gascoigne considered that 'wordes of many syllables do cloye a verse' and warned his readers to use 'as few wordes of many sillables . . . as may be', see his *Certayne Notes of Instruction concerning the making of verse . . . in English* (1575), note 5, in *Elizabethan Critical Essays*, ed. Smith, i, 51. According to Gascoigne the long verse 'of twelve and foureteene sillables' was 'the commonest sort' used in his day, he recommended it 'for Psalmes and Himpnes' (see ibid., pp. 54–7, notes 16 and 14). Gerould (*Ballad of Tradition*, p. 129) notes the tendency for stresses to 'fall with heavier and lighter weight in strict alternation' in ballads.

26 For Sternhold's use of alliterative doublets see e.g. 'safe & sounde' (Ps. 41:2); 'call and cry' (Ps. 3:4); 'good and godly' (Ps. 4:3); 'fret & fume' (Ps. 2:1); 'pure and perfyt' (Ps. 32:11); cf. 'faultes and frayltie' (Ps. 25:6); 'potentates and prynces' (Ps. 20:1); 'stycke and stande' (Ps. 25:20); 'stayed . . . and stopped' (Ps. 29:9), all from his *Certayne Psalmes*.

27 E.g. redundant phrases: 'prosper . . . *well*' (Ps. 1, line 15); and 'Therefore, *must I say once agayne*' (Ps. 8) 'And more to be embrast of thee, then fyndd golde *I say*' (Ps. 19) in *Al such Psalmes of David as Thomas Sternehold late grome of the kinges Majesties Robes, didde in his life time draw into English metre* (London, 1549), sig. B3^v & C5^v.

28 Ibid., sig. A8^v; cf. Sternhold's taste for alliteration in:

> I waxe wondrous faynt:
> And washe my bed where as I couch,
> with teares . . .
> My beautye fadeth cleane awaye,
> with anguishe of myne hearte:
> For feare of those that be my foes,
> and woulde my soule subverte   (Ps. 6, ibid., sig. B1^r)

Thou makest infantes overcome,
thy myghtye mortall foes   (Ps. 8, ibid., sig. B3^r)

He lyeth hyd in secrete stretes,
to slea the innocent   (Ps. 10, ibid., sig. B6^r)

His lawe ne yet his lore.
My hope, my helpe, my hartes relefe.
Extoll thy flocke with faithfull foode
        (Ps. 28 (misnumbered 27), *Certayne Psalmes*, sig. B4^r)

And beare no yoke upon theyr necke
nor burden on their backe   (Ps. 73, ibid., sig. C3^v)

The flocke therfore of flatterers
doe furnishe up their trayne   (Ps. 73, ibid., sig. C4^r)

29 On the use of doublet forms cf. Cranmer's style in the Book of Common Prayer collects translated from *orationes* in Sarum primers, e.g. 'supplications and prayers', 'vocation and ministry', 'truly and godly' (all from the second collect for Good Friday); and from a random choice of 'Gyrtt in my giltlesse gowne . . .': 'to looke/ and note', 'skill and Conninge', 'to learne and know', 'powre and will', 'truth nor right' in *The Arundel Harington Manuscript of Tudor Poetry*, ed. R. Hughey, 2 vols. (Columbus, Ohio, 1960), i, 117; see also C. S. Lewis, *English Literature in the Sixteenth Century* (Oxford, 1954, repr., 1973), pp. 217–18.

30 Sternhold, *Al such Psalmes*, B1^r; cf. 'oculus meus' (Vulgate); 'my face' (Joye, *The Psalter of David* (1530); 'my sight' (Joye, *Davids Psalter* (1534)); 'my countenance' (Coverdale, 1535 Bible). (On Joye's translations see above Appendix nos. 1 and 2.)

31 Sternhold, *Al such Psalmes*, sig. C6^r.

32 Sternhold, *Certayne Psalmes*, sig. B7^r.

33 Ibid., sig. C3^v.

34 Cf. Campensis: 'admodum vestis totum hominem tegere solet', *Psalmorum omnium: iuxta Hebraicam veritatem paraphrastica interpretatio* (Paris, 1534), sig. K5^v. See also Surrey's Ps. 73, line 12: 'As garments clothe the naked man' (from Campensis), *Henry Howard Earl of Surrey Poems*, ed. E. Jones (Oxford, 1964, repr., 1973), p. 99.

35 Sternhold, *Certayne Psalmes*, sig. D3^v; Campensis, *A Paraphrasis upon all the Psalmes of David*, tr. Coverdale (London, 1539), sig. O6^r.

36 Sternhold, *Certayne Psalmes*, sig. D4^v.

37 Cf. Ps. 102[103]:15 'sicut fenum . . . flos agri florebit' (Vulgate); 'for he florysheth as a floure of the felde' (Great Bible).

38 Campensis, *A Paraphrasis*, sig. O6^v.

39 For a critical edition of Marot's psalms from early manuscripts and printed texts see *Les Psaumes de Clément Marot*, ed. S. J. Lenselink (Assen, 1969). See also P. Leblanc, *La Poésie religieuse de Clément Marot* (Paris, 1955), pp. 301–42.

40 For contemporary references to patronage of Marot by Marguerite and by Charles V see *Le Psautier huguenot du XVIe siècle: Mélodies et documents*,

ed. P. Pidoux, 2 vols. (Basle, 1962), II, viii–ix. On Marguerite de Valois, Queen of Navarre, also known as Marguerite d'Angoulème (1492–1549) see the article by L. Dubois in L. G. Michaud, *Biographie universelle ancienne et moderne*, nouvelle edn, 45 vols. (Paris, 1843–65), xxvi, 552–4; see further I. D. McFarlane, *A Literary History of France: Renaissance France 1470–1589* (London, 1974), pp. 125–8.

41 For Marot's sources including the paraphrases by Campensis (first printed in 1532) and the new translation from Hebrew by Bucer (1529) see *Les Psaumes de Marot*, ed. Lenselink, pp. 32–56.

42 Marot and Sternhold also both wrote versions of Pss. 19, 25, 32, 43, 103 and 128.

43 *Les Psaumes de Marot*, ed. Lenselink, p. 60.

44 See A. L. Prescott, 'The Reputation of Clément Marot in Renaissance England', *Studies in the Renaissance*, xviii (1971), 173–202; and the same author's *French Poets and the English Renaissance: Studies in Fame and Transformation* (New Haven & London, 1978), pp. 1–36.

45 Wyatt's surviving psalm paraphrases are all in *terza rima*. Wyatt visited the French court in 1526, 1532 and 1539, on the last occasion he may have witnessed Marot's presentation of his psalms to Charles V, see above n. 40 and K. Muir, *The Life and Letters of Sir Thomas Wyatt* (Liverpool, 1963), pp. 6, 24, 95. On the French vogue for metrical psalms which M. Jeanneret attributes to Marot's example see Jeanneret's *Poésie et tradition biblique au XVIᵉ siècle: Recherches stylistiques sur les paraphrases des psaumes de Marot à Malherbe* (Paris, 1969) in which he describes and illustrates the work of about sixty metrical psalmists.

46 On Bellemain, see *DNB*; on Denisot's life and works see C. Juge, *Nicolas Denisot du Mans ... Essai sur sa vie et ses oeuvres* (Paris, 1907); Oxford, Keble College MS 33 contains *Cantiques et chansons de Noël* by Denisot who wrote under the pseudonym 'Conte d'Alsinois' (an anagram of his own name).

47 E. Gautier-Desvaux & V. Koechlin-Schwartz, *Noël au Perche, 'Noels' et 'Cantiques' spirituels du XVIᵉ siècle* (Saint-Mard-de-Réno, 1977), pp. 47–70.

48 For Denisot's verses, see London, British Library, MS Royal 12 A vii, fols. 25ff.

49 *Le Tombeau de Marguerite de Valois royne de Navarre. Faict premierement en Disticques Latins par les trois Soeurs Princesses en Angleterre* (Paris, 1551); see E. Gautier-Desvaux & V. Koechlin-Schwartz, *Noël au Perche*, pp. 56–7.

50 On early Tudor court song-books, e.g. London, British Library, Additional MSS 5465 (Fayrfax MS); 31922 (Henry VIII's MS); 5665 (Ritson's MS) see Stevens, *Music and Poetry*, Appendix A (pp. 337–428, for texts) and Appendix B (pp. 429–60, for an index of selected songs), Appendix C (pp. 461–8) contains a list of printed and manuscript sources of songs. On Wyatt's texts in manuscript sources see *Collected Poems of Sir Thomas Wyatt*, ed. K. Muir & P. Thomson (Liverpool, 1969), pp. xi–xvii; on the printed sources see ibid., pp. xvii–xix.

51 The first posthumous edition of Sternhold's psalms is *Al such Psalmes of David as Thomas Sternehold late grome of the kinges Majesties Robes, didde in his life time draw into English Metre*; see above Appendix no. 24.

52 On Sternhold's imprisonment see above p. 85; on connexions between the royal households and printers such as Crowley and Whitchurch see King, *Reformation Literature*, pp. 217–26.

53 Sternhold, *Al such Psalmes*, sig. B4ᵛ; cf. 'O prayse the Lord, which dwelleth in Syon, shewe the people of hys doinges' (Great Bible, Ps. 9:11).

54 Sternhold, *Al such Psalmes*, sig. G2ᵛ. Hopkins took his B.A. in 1544; from 1561 until his death in 1570 he was rector of Great Waldingfield, Suffolk (see *DNB*).

55 On Wyatt's *Certayne psalmes*, see above Appendix no. 25; on *Certayne Psalmes* by Hunnis and by Seagar see above Appendix nos. 28 and 31. Cf. title of Smith's 'Certaigne Psalmes', see above p. 278 n.63. Sternhold's title was used repeatedly by his imitators. A letter from Sir John Harington to Lord Burleigh (1595) states that Harington's father was 'much skilled in musicke ... which he learnt in the fellowship of good Maister Tallis when a young man'. See Harington's *Nugae Antiquae* (1769), p. 133, quoted in *Tudor Church Music* 1st ser., vol. 6, *Thomas Tallis c. 1505–1585* (Oxford, 1928).

56 *Certayne Chapters of the proverbes of Salomon* (London, [1549–50]), sig. A2ʳ; see further Appendix no. 26.

57 John Hall, *Certayn chapters taken out of the Proverbes of Salomon* (London, 1550); see Appendix no. 27.

58 For Surrey's Ecclesiastes see London, British Library, Additional MS 36529 and Arundel Castle, Harington MS; for Surrey's Pss. 31 and 51 see Appendix no. 26.

59 Surrey's name appears on the title page of Tottel's Miscellany (1557) which contains his secular poems: *Songes and Sonettes, written by the ryght honorable Lorde Henry Haward late Earle of Surrey, and other* (*STC²* 13860).

60 For 'Certaigne Psalmes of Davyd in meeatre/ added to maister Sterne-holdis/ and oothers/ by William Forreste, 1551' see London, British Library, MS Royal 17A xxi, esp. fol. 1ᵛ; see further T. von Riese, *Die Englische Psalmdichtung im sechzehnten Jahrhundert* (Münster, 1937), pp. 68–71. Forrest was a Catholic and later served as a chaplain to Queen Mary for whom he wrote his '*History of Grisild the Second': a narrative, in verse, of the divorce of Queen Katherine of Arragon*, ed. W. D. Macray, Roxburgh Club (London, 1875), Macray's preface describes Forrest's other literary works. Anthony Wood described Forrest as 'well skill'd in music and poetry, [he] had a collection of the choicest compositions in music that were then in use' which were given after his death to the University of Oxford: see Wood's *Athenae Oxoniensis* (3rd edn), ed. P. Bliss, 4 vols. (London, 1813), i, cols. 297–300.

61 London, British Library, MS Royal 17A xxi, fol. 3ʳ.

62 Hall, *Proverbes* (1550), sig. A4ʳ⁻ᵛ.

63 Ibid., sig. A5^r; on Sternhold's 'exquisite doynges' cf. Hopkins's epistle 'To the Reader' in *Al such Psalmes*, sig. G2^v.

64 Hall, *Proverbes* (1550), sig. A5^r.

65 On Hall's *Courte of Vertue* see above Appendix no. 40.

66 John Hall, *The Court of Virtue* (1565), ed. R. A. Fraser (London, 1961), p. 15.

67 Ibid., p. 16.

68 Ibid., pp. 169–72.

69 Ibid., pp. 164–9, esp. p. 168.

70 Ibid., p. 9.

71 Ibid., p. 10.

72 Ibid., pp. 10 and 11.

73 Ibid., p. 79.

74 Ibid., p. 61; see further R. Zim, 'The Maidstone Burghmote and John Hall's *Courte of Vertue* (1565)', *Notes & Queries* n.s., xxxiii (1986), 320–7.

75 See *The Lyrics of the Red Book of Ossory*, ed. R. L. Greene (Oxford, 1974); *The Early English Carols*, ed. R. L. Greene, 2nd edn (Oxford, 1977), pp. cxv–vi; *Secular Lyrics of the XIVth and XVth Centuries*, 2nd edn R. H. Robbins (Oxford, 1955), pp. xxxv–vii.

76 Verstegan, *Odes in Imitation of the seaven penitential psalmes, with sundry other Poemes and ditties tending to devotion and pietie* ([Antwerp], 1601), sig. A2^r; see above Appendix no. 85.

77 Ibid., sig. A2^v.

78 Ibid., p. 4; the subsequent quotations from Verstegan's psalms are from this edition in the facsimile series *English Recusant Literature 1558–1640*, ed. D. M. Rogers (Menston, 1970), liii, 1–20.

79 Ibid., p. 14; cf. Ps. 101[102]:18 (Vulgate). Cf. Verstegan's 'Complaint of Church Controversy', ibid., pp. 94–7, esp. p. 96.

80 Ibid., sig. A2^v; cf. Sternhold, *Certayne Psalmes*, sig. A3^r.

81 Verstegan produced a new English translation in prose of the proper psalms for different offices in his parallel text English and Latin Primer published in Antwerp in 1599 and 1604 (*STC^2* 16094 and 16095). Verstegan's *Odes* does not appear to be indebted to his English prose translation of the seven psalms in his Primer.

82 A. Gilby, tr., *The Psalmes of David, Truly Opened and explaned by Paraphrasis* (London, 1581), sig. A5^r.

83 Hall, *Court of Virtue*, ed. Fraser, p. 16.

84 For Patten's psalms printed as broadsides see above Appendix nos. 69 and 83; see also London, British Library, MS Royal 14 B.l. for his version of Ps. 21 (no music). On Patten and his work see B. O'Kill, 'The Printed Works of William Patten (*c.* 1510–*c.* 1600)', *Transactions of the Cambridge Bibliographical Society*, vii (1977), 28–45; B. Hill, 'Trinity College Cambridge MS B.14.52, and William Patten', ibid., iv (1968), 192–200 and the same author's 'William Patten: A Tudor Londoner', *Essays and Studies* (1983), pp. 14–26.

85 See headtitles to Patten's, *The Sallm by the olld Translation called Deus*

Iudicium (*STC*² 2368.3); and *Psal. terseptimus: Domine in virtute tua* (*STC*² 2368.5).

86 *STC*² 2368.5.

87 See above n. 84.

88 *STC*² 2368.3.

89 Ibid. For a different kind of personal compliment see Richard Robinson's version of Ps. 6 in acrostic verses naming Thomas Leigh of Adlington in *A Golden Mirrour. Conteyning certaine Pithie and figurative Visions* (London, 1589), sig. E4ʳ; Appendix no. 76.

90 On Bownell's paraphrases see above Appendix no. 30.

91 On Bentley's psalms see above Appendix no. 63. Cf. Andrew Willet's *Ecclesia Triumphans: that is, The Joy of the English Church, for the happie Coronation of the most vertuous and pious Prince, James ... and for the joyfull continuance of religion and peace by the same. With a briefe Exposition of the 122. Psalme, and fit application to the time* (Cambridge, 1603) which contains twenty meditations linking the situation of England with Israel (in Ps. 122) and the exploits of James VI and David.

92 On Crowley's *Psalter of David* see n. 13 above, and Appendix no. 22.

93 I am grateful to Dr M. B. Parkes and the Rev. Dr D. G. Rowell for advice on the liturgy.

94 For directions to choirs, rectors and soloist ('The Meane') see especially Ps. 107 in Parker's *The whole Psalter translated into English Metre* [1567], see Le Huray, *Music & the Reformation*, p. 309 and pl. 14; for antiphonal singing by choir and rectors of 'The song of the three children' see Parker, *Whole Psalter*, sig. SS3ᵛ. See further above Appendix no. 44; von Riese, *Englische Psalmdichtung*, pp. 71–83; Thomas Warton, *The History of English Poetry, from the Close of the Eleventh Century to the Commencement of the Eighteenth Century*, 4 vols. (London, 1781), iii, 181–7.

95 Parker, *Whole Psalter*, sig. A2ᵛ (cf. Ephesians 5:19); and sig. B4ʳ.

96 Ibid., sig. A4ᵛ & B1ʳ.

97 Ibid., sig. B2ʳ–B3ᵛ.

98 Ibid., sig. B2ᵛ & B3ʳ; the sixteenth-century Hebraists cited by Parker are François Vatable (d. 1547); Konrad Pellican (1478–1556); Sebastian Münster (1489–1552); and Sanctes Pagninus (1470–1536).

99 John Holland, *The Psalmists of Britain: Records Biographical and Literary*, 2 vols. (London, 1843), i, 172.

100 Parker, *Whole Psalter*, sig. G3ʳ.

101 On Buchanan's paraphrases see above p. 31; Parker's 'Prologue' states

> That some in verse: right lately,
>   have strunged Davids harpe:
> They have their laudes: most worthely,
>   their paynes ought no man carpe   (Sig. B2ᵛ)

102 See e.g. Pss. 43, 101, 102, 103.

103 Parker, *Whole Psalter*, sig. B2ᵛ; Parker also quotes Athanasius, Basil,

Chrisostom, Augustine, Josephus, Eusebius, Jerome, Bernard, and the
Earl of Surrey's Ecclesiastes.

104 Ibid., sig. A2^r.

105 For Tallis's eight tunes see ibid., sig. VV4^v–YY4^r; see M. C. Boyd,
Elizabethan Music and Musical Criticism (Philadelphia, 1940, repr.,
1962), pp. 45–52 for the tunes in modern notation.

106 Parker, or the editor of his Psalter, prefaced the music with a note on
'the Conjunction of Psalmes and tunes' (sig. VV2^v–VV3^r) and verses
on 'The nature of the eyght tunes' (sig. VV4^r) as follows:

> The first is meeke: devout to see,
> The second sad: in majesty.
> The third doth rage: and roughly brayth,
> The fourth doth fawne: and flattry playth,
> The fyth deligth: and laugheth the more,
> The sixt bewayleth: it weepeth full sore,
> The seventh tredeth stoute: in froward race,
> The eyghte goeth milde: in modest pace

The first tune is ascribed in the first instance to Ps. 1; the second to
Ps. 68; the third to Ps. 2; the fourth to Ps. 95; the fifth to Ps. 42; the
sixth to Ps. 5; the seventh to Ps. 52; the eighth to Ps. 67.

107 On the eight melodic formulae or 'tones' associated with the Psalms in
Gregorian chant see 'Octo tonorum distinctiones & proprietates',
ibid., sig. E1^v; see further *New Grove Dictionary*, ed. Sadie, xv, 324ff.

108 For Ps. 95 see Parker, *Whole Psalter*, UU1^r and XX4^r.

109 See 'Basilius in Psalmos', ibid., E2^{r-v}.

110 See *The Autobiography of Thomas Whythorne*, ed. J. M. Osborn
(Oxford, 1961), pp. xlviii-xlix, 254–5, 272; for Whythorne's other
psalm paraphrases see ibid., pp. 151–2 (Ps. 51), 161–2 (Ps. 103:1–3 and
Ps. 138), 267 (Ps. 86), 288 (Ps. 71:1–2), 291 (Ps. 96); and above
Appendix nos. 51 and 77.

111 See *Le Psautier huguenot*, ed. Pidoux; in 1553, the year Mary succeeded
to the throne, an edition of eighty-three metrical psalms by Marot and
by Beza was published which included a 'Table pour trouver les
pseaumes selon qu'on les chante en l'Eglise de Genève' see *Le Psautier
huguenot*, ed. Pidoux, ii, 61–2; on the Protestant exiles see further
C. H. Garrett, *The Marian Exiles. A Study in the Origins of Elizabethan
Puritanism* (Cambridge, 1938).

112 Crespin published the metrical psalms with *The forme of prayers and
ministration of the sacraments ... used in the Englishe Congregation at
Geneva: and approved by ... John Calvyn* (*STC*² 16561, title from
*STC*²); cf. *La Forme des prières et chantz ecclesiastiques, avec la manière
d'administrer les Sacremens* (1542) containing metrical psalms by Marot
and by Calvin, see *Le Psautier huguenot*, ed. Pidoux, ii, 15. For the
music published with the English metrical psalms and its sources see
M. Frost, *English & Scottish Psalm & Hymn Tunes c. 1543–1677*
(London & Oxford, 1953), pp. 3–30.

113 On Whittingham see A. B. Emden, *A Biographical Register of the University of Oxford A.D. 1501–1540* (Oxford, 1974), p. 625.

114 *The forme of prayers* (1556), p. 21 (there is no separate preface to the *One and Fiftie Psalmes*).

115 Sternhold, *Certayne Psalmes*, sig. D3ᵛ.

116 *One and Fiftie Psalmes*, p. 135.

117 Ibid., title page, see above n. 114.

118 Cf. Ps. 103:6

עֹשֵׂה צְדָקוֹת יְהוָה
וּמִשְׁפָּטִים לְכָל־עֲשׁוּקִים:

[The] Lord does acts-of-righteousness
and-acts-of justice for-all [the] oppressed   (my translation)

The Lorde executeth ryghteousnesse and judgment
for all them that are oppressed wyth wronge   (Great Bible)

Faciens misericordias Dominus, et judicium
omnibus injuriam patientibus   (Vulgate)

119 Sternhold, *Certayne Psalmes*, sig. D5ʳ; *One and Fiftie Psalmes*, p. 137.

120 Ibid., p. 3; cf. 'The man is blest that hath not bent to wicked rede his eare: nor led his lyf as synners do, nor sate in scorners chayre' (ibid., pp. 1–2) and Sternhold's version of Ps. 1:1 above pp. 116–17. Lines 7–15 of Sternhold's Ps. 120 (see above pp. 86–7) were revised as follows:

> What vantage, or what thinge
> getest thou thus for to stinge,
> thou false and flattering lier?
>
> Thy tongue doth hurt I wene
> no lesse then arrowes kene,
> of whote consumyng fyre.
>
> Alas to longe I slake
> with in these tentes so blake:
> which kedars are by name   (*One and Fiftie Psalmes*, pp. 144–5)

John Hopkins's seven psalms were also revised for the *One and Fiftie Psalmes*.

121 E.g. Ps. 6:8, ibid., p. 16, 'My sight is dymme' with marginal note: 'Hebr. myn eye is eaten, as with wormes'. Head note to Ps. 25, ibid., pp. 57–8: 'The Prophete towched with the consideration of his synnes, and also greaved with the cruel malice of his ennymies, prayeth to god most ferventlie to have his synnes forgeaven, especially, suche as he had committed in his youthe. He begynneth everie verse accordyng to the hebrewe letters .ii. or .iii. except'. (The Hebrew Ps. 25 is based on an alphabetical acrostic with three letters omitted.) Each verse of this English metrical version is headed by the appropriate printed letter from the Hebrew alphabet.

122 I have described London editions of the Genevan metrical psalms as Anglo-Genevan psalms; cf. Frost (*English & Scottish Tunes*) who refers to the 'Anglo-Genevan' psalms for those printed in Geneva, and to the 'English' psalms for those printed in London.

123 See *Foure score and seven Psalmes of David in English mitre by Thomas Sterneholde and others: conferred with the Hebrewe, and in certeine places corrected, as the sense of the Prophet requireth* ([London], 1561), *STC²* 2428; this edition contains three new psalms attributed to Sternhold (d. 1549) i.e. Pss. 18, 22 and 23. Cf. *The residue of all Davids psalmes in metre, made by J. Hopkins and others. Now fyrst imprinted and sette forth in this fourme for such as have bookes alredy, that thei be disposed maye joyne these wyth them: and so to have the whole psalmes* (London, 1562), *STC²* 2429.5 (title from *STC²*).

124 For the title of the first complete metrical psalter see above Appendix no. 38. Cf. *Injunctions* (1559), sig. C4ʳ, 'Continuance of singyng in the Churche'.

125 See Anthony Wood's comments (*c.* 1690) in his *Athenae Oxoniensis* (1813), i, cols. 183–7; and E. Phillips, *Theatrum Poetarum, or a Compleat Collection of the Poets, Especially The Most Eminent, of all Ages* (London, 1675), p. 184. Scottish editions of these metrical psalms were also well known; most of the psalms in Genevan and in Anglo-Genevan editions printed in London were reprinted in the Scottish editions with some few exceptions for which alternative versions were provided, see further J. W. MacMeeken, *History of the Scottish Metrical Psalms* (Glasgow, 1872), and Frost, *English & Scottish Tunes.*

126 On the musical settings East commented: 'And regarding chiefely to help the simple, curiositie is shunned'. He concluded his dedication: 'The profit is theirs that will use this booke, the paynes theirs that have compyled it, the charges his, who setting it foorth, respecteth a publique benefit, not his private gaine' (sig. A2ᵛ). (On the commercial profits in publishing music for psalters see Boyd, *Elizabethan Music*, pp. 62 and 73.) For examples of harmonized settings of the Anglo-Genevan metrical psalms see Le Huray, *Music & the Reformation*, pp. 376–82; see also Frost, *English & Scottish Tunes.*

127 See *New Grove Dictionary*, ed. Sadie, xv, 358.

128 Bale's comments on Sternhold are as follows: '... vir erat, cui benignissimus Deus multa suae gratiae beneficia dedit. Qui, ut amatoriae & obscoenae cantiones aula pellerentur, miro sermonis ornatu & eloquentia in Anglicos rhythmos traduxit, ad eundem regem, *Ex Psalmis selectioribus* 37 ...', *Scriptorum illustrium maioris Brytannie, quam nunc Angliam & Scotiam vocant: Catalogus ... Autore Ioanne Baleo* (Basle, 1557), p. 728.

129 Wood, *Athenae Oxoniensis* (1813), i, col. 183; cf. title-page of John Day's 1563 edn of Anglo-Genevan psalms with music for four voices: 'which may be song to al Musical instrumentes, set forth for the encrease of vertue: and aboleshyng of other vayne and triflyng ballades' (*STC²* 2431).

130 Bliss noted (*Athenae Oxoniensis* (1813), i, col. 187) that Sternhold's texts had 'suffered considerable alteration from the early impressions'. Thomas Tanner (1674–1735) noted in his copy (now Oxford, Bodleian

Library, Tanner 56) of an early edition (1551, STC^2 2422) of Sternhold's psalms with Hopkins's supplement, the distinction between Sternhold's and the Genevan psalms.

131 The *Short Title Catalogue* (STC^1 and STC^2) groups reprints of Sternhold's texts from Edward's reign with London editions of Anglo-Genevan versions under the heading: Bible, Psalms, Sternhold and Hopkins. Genevan versions, i.e. printed in Geneva from 1556, are catalogued separately under Liturgies. (See STC^2 2419ff., and STC^2 16561ff.)

132 For Sternhold's popular image in the twentieth century see William Whittingham's version of Ps. 137 from *The Whole Booke of Psalmes* (1562), STC^2 2430 reprinted as 'By Thomas Sternhold and John Hopkins' in *The Literature of Renaissance England*, ed. J. Hollander & F. Kermode, *The Oxford Anthology of English Literature* (New York, London & Toronto, 1973), p. 37.

133 Surrey's Ps. 88 was printed in *Certayne Chapters of the proverbes* [1549–50]. STC^2 2760, sig. F1ʳ–2ᵛ, see p. 125 above, and Appendix no. 26; for Seagar's *Certayne Psalmes* (1553) see Appendix, no. 31.

134 For these and subsequent quotations from Surrey's Ps. 88 see *Surrey Poems*, ed. Jones, pp. 98–9 (text edited from London, British Library, Additional MS 36529, fol. 63ʳ⁻ᵛ), and *Certayne Chapters of the proverbes* [1549–50], sig. F1ʳ–2ᵛ (hereafter, 1549–50 edn). I am grateful to Mr W. D. McGaw for allowing generous access to material in his forthcoming edition of Surrey's poems. For discussion of Surrey's Ps. 88 see pp. 91–7 above.

135 Puttenham, *Arte of Englishe Poesie* (1589), Bk II, ch. 4, in *Elizabethan Critical Essays*, ed. Smith, ii, 76.

136 For this and subsequent quotations from Seagar's Ps. 88 see his *Certayne Psalmes*, sig. A3ᵛ–A6ʳ. I have transcribed the rhythm from the top part ('the meane') which looks more 'tuneful', although the tune for Seagar's second setting is in the tenor part, as is more usual in this period. I am grateful to Dr J. A. Caldwell for advice on Seagar's music.

137 Ps. 88:8, Coverdale 1535 and 1539 Bibles; see further ch. 3 n. 42 above.

138 For Surrey's Ecclesiastes 4, line 4 see *Surrey Poems*, ed. Jones, p. 94; for similarities between Surrey's Ecclesiastes and his Ps. 88 see further ch. 3 n. 40 above.

139 For Seagar's dedication see his *Certayne Psalmes*, sig. A2ʳ.

140 John Case, *The Praise of Musicke: Wherein besides the antiquitie, dignitie, delectation, & use thereof in civill matters, is also declared the sober and lawfull use of the same in the congregation and Church of God* (Oxford, 1586), p. 66.

141 *Autobiography of Whythorne*, ed. Osborn, p. 250.

142 For Whythorne's settings see his *Songes for three, fower, and five voyces* (London, 1571); Appendix, no. 51.

143 See Calvin's epistle to the reader in *La Forme des prieres et chantz*

ecclesiastiques (Geneva, 1543), repr. in *Le Psautier huguenot*, ed. Pidoux, ii, 21.

144 For Byrd's *Psalmes, Sonets, & songs* (1588), and his *Songs of sundrie natures* (1589), see above Appendix, nos. 74 and 75. (Cf. this secular context of holy-song psalms with secular use of psalm tunes for 'Phillida was a fair maid' from Tottel's *Songs and Sonnets*, see discussion in Stevens, *Music and Poetry*, pp. 126–7.)

145 For Byrd's 'Reasons . . . to learne to sing' see *Psalmes, Sonets & songs*, sig. πiᵛ.

146 See e.g. a short introduction to the 'Science of Musicke' in *The whole Booke of Psalmes* (1562), sig. +2ʳ– 7ʳ.

147 See Aquinas: 'A multiplicity of modes or forms is encountered in the Holy Scriptures . . . whatever is said in other books in the aforesaid modes is fashioned here [in the Psalms] in the mode of praise and prayer . . . ' ('Modus seu forma in sacra Scriptura multiplex invenitur . . . quidquid in aliis libris praedictis modis dicitur, hic ponitur per modum laudis et orationis . . . '), *In Psalmos Davidis expositio*, 'Proemium', printed in *Sancti Thomae Aquinatis opera omnia* (Parma, 1863), xiv, 148. This procedure was described by medieval scholars and critics as the *modus agendi* or *forma tractandi* of the work. For discussion with examples from the twelfth century onwards see A. J. Minnis, 'Literary Theory in Discussions of *Formae Tractandi* by Medieval Theologians', *New Literary History*, xi (1979/80), 133–45; and the same author's *Medieval Theory of Authorship: Scholastic Literary Attitudes in the Later Middle Ages* (London, 1984), esp. ch. 4.

148 From Calvin's epistle to the reader in the 1542 edition of *La Forme des prieres et chantz ecclesiastiques*, repr. in *Le Psautier huguenot*, ed. Pidoux, ii, 17. Cf. Parker's quotation of Basil, see p. 139 above.

149 (My italics.) From Calvin's epistle in the 1543 edition of *La Forme des prieres*, repr. in *Le Psautier huguenot*, ed. Pidoux, ii, 21. Cf. John Donne's sermon on Ps. 90:14 preached at St Paul's (*c.* 1622): '. . . whereas the whole Book of Psalms is called *Sepher Tehillim*, that is, *Liber Laudationum*, The Book is Praise, yet this Psalme, and . . . divers others . . . are called Prayers; The Book is Praise, the parts are Prayer . . . Prayer, and Praise, in the Originall [Hebrew] differs no more then so, *Tehillim*, and *Tephilloth*'. *John Donne's Sermons on the Psalms and Gospels*, ed. E. M. Simpson (Berkeley, Los Angeles, & London, 1963, repr., 1974), p. 47.

5   that Lyricall kind: Sidney

1 For Sidney's praise of English poetry of 'that Lyricall kind of Songs and Sonets', see his *The Defence of Poesie* (William Ponsonby, London, 1595), facsimile edn (Menston, 1973), sig. I2ᵛ (cf. *Sir Philip Sidney, An Apology for Poetry or The Defence of Poesie*, ed. G. Shepherd (Manchester, 1965, repr., 1967), p. 137.

2 *Defence of Poesie*, sig. B4ʳ (cf. *Apology for Poetry*, ed. Shepherd, p. 99).

3 For Sidney's Ps. 34, lines 9-12 see *The Poems of Sir Philip Sidney*, ed. W. A. Ringler, Jr (Oxford, 1962, repr., 1971), p. 319; all subsequent quotations from Sidney's psalms are from this edition (pp. 270-337) based on Oxford, Bodleian Library, MS Rawlinson poet. 25, a 1695 transcript by Samuel Woodford of one of the Countess's working copies of Sidney's and her own psalms.

4 For discussions on the date of Sidney's psalms see *Poems*, ed. Ringler, pp. 500-1, and *Sir Philip Sidney, Selected Poems*, ed. K. Duncan-Jones (Oxford, 1973), p. xv; both these editors suggest that the psalms were late works (*c.* 1585), however, N. L. Rudenstine in an appendix to his *Sidney's Poetic Development* (Cambridge, Mass., 1967), pp. 284-6, argued for an earlier date (*c.* 1580-1) on stylistic grounds. For the date of the Countess's completion of drafts of all the remaining psalms see M. G. Brennan, 'The Date of the Countess of Pembroke's Translations of the Psalms', *Review of English Studies*, n.s., xxxiii (1982), 434-6. On the Countess's imitations see above ch. 6.

5 For a resumé of critical opinion on Sidney's psalms published before 1969 see Coburn Freer, 'The Style of Sidney's Psalms', *Language and Style*, ii (1969), 63; see also further below.

6 T. Spencer, 'The Poetry of Sir Philip Sidney', *ELH: A Journal of English Literary History*, xii (1945), 251-78, esp. 254. Cf. the overt experimentation with quantitative metres in English by Richard Stanyhurst in his Pss. 1-4 (1582), see above Appendix, no. 65.

7 H. Smith, 'English Metrical Psalms in the Sixteenth Century and their Literary Significance', *Huntington Library Quarterly*, ix (1946), 269. For similar views of Sidney's psalms see J. Buxton, *Sir Philip Sidney and the English Renaissance* (London, 1954), pp. 152-5; L. L. Martz, *The Poetry of Meditation: A Study of English Religious Literature of the Seventeenth Century* (New Haven & London, 1954, repr. 1976), pp. 273-8; L. B. Campbell, *Divine Poetry and Drama in Sixteenth-century England* (Cambridge, Berkeley & Los Angeles, 1959), p. 52; D. Kalstone, *Sidney's Poetry: Contexts and Interpretations* (Cambridge, Mass., 1965), p. 4; Rudenstine, *Sidney's Poetic Development*, p. 286; C. Freer, *Music for a King: George Herbert's Style and the Metrical Psalms* (Baltimore & London, 1972), pp. 72ff.; D. Connell, *Sir Philip Sidney: The Maker's Mind* (Oxford, 1977), p. 145; B. K. Lewalski, *Protestant Poetics and the Seventeenth-century Religious Lyric* (Princeton, 1979), pp. 241-4 and 301.

8 For contemporary views of paraphrase see above pp. 12-13 and ch. 1, n. 58.

9 See Ascham's *The Scholemaster Or plaine and perfite way of teachyng children ... the Latin tong* (London, 1570), in *English Works of Roger Ascham*, ed. W. A. Wright (Cambridge, 1904, repr., 1970), pp. 239 and 265.

10 *Defence of Poesie*, sig, I2ᵛ and B4ʳ (cf. *Apology for Poetry*, ed. Shepherd, pp. 137 and 99). For an authoritative study of the *Defence* and its

background see Shepherd's introduction (ibid., esp. pp. 11–46); see also the literature cited (pp. xi–xviii).

11 Ibid., sig. C1^v (cf. p. 101).

12 For Sidney's view of David as a *vates* see *Defence of Poesie*, sig. B3^v–B4^r (cf. *Apology for Poetry*, ed. Shepherd, pp. 98–9).

13 Ibid., sig. E2^r (cf. p. 113).

14 Ibid., sig. C3^r (cf. p. 104). For Scaliger see above p. 19.

15 Ibid., sig. C1^v, B3^r and C2^v (cf. pp. 101, 98 and 103).

16 Ibid., sig. E3^{r-v} (cf. p. 115).

17 For the Countess of Pembroke's 'To the Angell spirit of the most excellent Sir Philip Sidney', see *Poems*, ed. Ringler, pp. 267–9, esp. lines 8–10.

18 See above p. 80.

19 Sidney's sources include Coverdale's translation for the Great Bible (1539) used with the Book of Common Prayer; the Geneva Bible Psalms (1559–60); Theodore Beza's paraphrases *Psalmorum Davidis et aliorum prophetarum, libri quinque. Argumentis & Latina Paraphrasi illustrati, ac etiam vario carminum genere latine expressi* (London, 1580), ded. to Henry Hastings, Earl of Huntingdon; also Anthony Gilby's translation of Beza's prose paraphrases *The Psalmes of David truely opened and explaned by Paraphrasis* (London, 1580; anr edn 1581) ded. to the Countess of Huntingdon (Sidney's aunt); the French metrical psalter by Marot and Beza first published in 1562 in Geneva, Lyons, Paris and other places (see *Le Psautier huguenot du XVIe siècle. Mélodies et documents*, ed. P. Pidoux, 2 vols. (Basle, 1962), ii, 132–7). For a description of Sidney's use of these sources see *Poems*, ed. Ringler, pp. 505–8.

20 For Sidney's definition of 'right poets' as 'they which most properly do imitate to teach & delight' see *Defence of Poesie*, sig. C2^{r-v} (cf. *Apology for Poetry*, ed. Shepherd, p. 102).

21 Ibid., sig. C3^r (cf. p. 103); see further Shepherd's discussion, pp. 81–2.

22 Ibid., sig. C1^r (cf. p. 100).

23 Beza, *Psalmorum Davidis*, 'Paraphrasis', p. 123; *Psalmes of David*, (1581), tr. Gilby, p. 61.

24 *The Bible and Holy Scriptures conteyned in the Olde and Newe Testament* (Geneva, 1560), fol. 241^v.

25 A. Golding, tr. *The Psalmes of David and others. With M. John Calvins Commentaries* (London, 1571), fol. 128^v.

26 *The Bible* (Geneva, 1560), fol. 240^r.

27 *Defence of Poesie*, sig. C1^v (cf. *Apology for Poetry*, ed. Shepherd, p. 101).

28 Beza, *Psalmorum Davidis*, 'Paraphrasis', p. 51; *Psalmes of David* (1581), tr. Gilby, p. 25.

29 *Defence of Poesie*, sig. D1^v (cf. *Apology for Poetry*, ed. Shepherd, p. 107); see further ch. 4, n. 147 above.

30 *The Bible* (Geneva, 1560), fol. 236^r. Cf. ch. 4, n. 121 above; Beza, 'Exedit tineae voracis instar', *Psalmorum Davidis*, p. 18.

31 Cf. 'Thou moth like mak'st his beauty fading be' (Sidney, Ps. 39, line 35).

32 *Psalmes of David* (1581), tr. Gilby, p. 8; cf. Beza, 'Corrosa est prae
    tristitia facies mea', *Psalmorum Davidis*, 'Interpretatio', p. 16.

33 See *OED*, shend v¹, to put to shame or confusion, to disgrace or
    confound. For further examples of Sidney's 'framing of his style to an
    olde rusticke language' (*Defence of Poesie*, sig. H3ᵛ) see: 'wight' (Ps.
    21:35), 'guerdon' (Ps. 28:4), 'burgess' (Ps. 8:8), 'fell' (Ps. 25:22), 'bane'
    (Ps. 31:13) 'bale' (Ps. 40:14), 'orethwart' (Ps. 38:17).

34 Cf. *Arcadia*, Bk. 3, ch. 10, see *Complete Works of Sir Philip Sidney*, ed.
    A. Feuillerat, 4 vols. (Cambridge, 1912–26), i, 403.

35 Cf. Sidney's personification of death in Ps. 30:3; see further Genevan
    gloss on Ps. 30:9, praise of God's 'Name ... is the end of man's
    creation', *The Bible* (Geneva, 1560), fol. 240ᵛ. Cf. also Surrey's Ps. 88,
    lines 23, 29–30:

    > The fleshe that fedeth wormes can not thy love declare.

    > The livelye voyce of them that in thy word delight
    > Must be the trumppe that must resound the glorye of thy might
    >
    > (see above p. 93.)

36 For Sidney's view of the Hebrew Psalms as 'fully written in meeter as all
    learned Hebritians agree, although the rules be not yet fully found' see
    Defence of Poesie, sig. B4ʳ (cf. *Apology for Poetry*, ed. Shepherd, p. 99); see
    further J. L. Kugel, *The Idea of Biblical Poetry: Parallelism and its History*
    (New Haven & London, 1981), pp. 152–6, 167–70, 251–8; see also above
    ch. 1, n. 162.

37 *Defence of Poesie*, sig. C3ʳ (cf. *Apology for Poetry*, ed. Shepherd, p. 103).

38 Cf. Donne's view of the Anglo-Genevan metrical psalter as 'hoarse' and
    'harsh' in his 'Upon the Translation of the Psalmes by Sir Philip Sydney,
    and the Countesse of Pembroke his Sister', line 44, see John Donne, *The
    Divine Poems*, ed. H. Gardner (2nd edn Oxford, 1978), pp. 33–5.

39 For a list of all Sidney's verse forms see *Poems*, ed. Ringler, pp. 569–72.

40 Metrical psalm paraphrases by Buchanan and by Beza were published in
    the same volume (*Psalmorum sacrorum Davidis libri quinque duplici poetica
    metaphrasi, altera alteri è regione opposita vario carminum genere Latinè
    expressi Theodoro Beza Vezelio, & Georgio Buchanano Scoto autoribus*) by
    Jean Le Preux at Morges in 1581. Psalm paraphrases by Buchanan were
    first published by Henri Estienne in Paris 1556, but new, enlarged and
    revised editions were published by several printers until Buchanan's
    death in 1582. Beza had written to Buchanan (12 April 1572) congratu-
    lating him on the publication of a new revised edition and encouraging
    yet further revision ('ex bonis etiam optimos reddas'); see I. D. Mc-
    Farlane, *Buchanan* (London, 1981), pp. 261 and 271.

41 On Sidney's use of the French metrical psalter see *Poems*, ed. Ringler,
    pp. 507–8; 509 *et passim*.

42 *Psalmi Davidici septuaginta quinque, in lyricos versus servata ecclesiasticae
    versionis veritate & Hebraeorum varietate, redacti: Authore Ioanno Ganeio
    Parisino Theologo, Parisiensis ecclesiae atque Academiae Cancellario* (Paris,

1547), sig. *2ᵛ; Jean de Gagnay (Gagnaeius) gave hospitality to Buchanan in the mid 1540s (see McFarlane, *Buchanan*, pp. 280–1). On the relations of these poets with Sidney's circle see J. E. Phillips, 'George Buchanan and the Sidney Circle', *Huntington Library Quarterly*, xi (1948), 23–55.

43 Golding, tr. *Psalmes of David* (1571), sig. *4ᵛ. For the connexion between Golding and Sidney see E. Rosenberg, *Leicester Patron of Letters* (New York, 1955, repr. 1976), pp. 272–4; and L. T. Golding, *An Elizabethan Puritan: Arthur Golding the Translator of Ovid's Metamorphoses and also of John Calvin's Sermons* (New York, 1937).

44 Golding, tr. *Psalmes of David* (1571), sig. *4ᵛ; cf. the similar concerns in Surrey's Ps. 88, lines 25–6 (see above p. 94).

45 Cf. Sidney's conclusions to *Astrophil and Stella* nos. 1, 5, 12, 47, 70, 71, 77, in *Poems*, ed. Ringler, pp. 165–237.

46 Martz, *Poetry of Meditation*, p. 276.

47 See *Defence of Poesie*, sig. C3ʳ (cf. *Apology for Poetry*, ed. Shepherd, p. 103).

48 For the rhetorical figure 'translatio' ('Metaphora') see L. E. Sonnino, *A Handbook to Sixteenth-Century Rhetoric* (London, 1968), pp. 181–3.

49 On the terse qualities of biblical poetry see Kugel, *Idea of Biblical Poetry*, esp. pp. 71, 87–92.

50 For the text of Marot's Ps. 38 see *Les Psaumes de Clément Marot*, ed. S. J. Lenselink (Assen, 1969), pp. 161–71. In printed editions of the French metrical psalter based on the complete edition of 1562, Ps. 38 is prefaced by the 'argument': 'David ayant la peste, ou quelque autre ulcere en la cuisse, se plaind fort à Dieu de la vehemence de son mal, du defaut de ses amis, de la cruauté de ses ennemis: & implore l'aide de Dieu' (ibid., p. 161).

51 For further examples of French literary and devotional sensibilities in penitential prayers and lyrics see 'Poetry of Sin, Sickness and Death', T. C. Cave, *Devotional Poetry in France c. 1570–1613* (Cambridge, 1969), pp. 94–135.

52 Sidney, Ps. 14, line 8.

53 *Defence of Poesie*, sig. C3ʳ (cf. *Apology for Poetry*, ed. Shepherd, p. 104).

54 Golding, tr. *The Psalmes of David* (1571), sig. *5ʳ and fol. 150ᵛ.

55 For Ps. 38:15 cf. 'For on thee, ô Lord, do I waite: thou wilt heare me, my Lord, my God' (Geneva Bible);

> Mais avecques esperance,
>   L'asseurance
> De ton bon secours j'attens:
> Et ainsi, mon Dieu, mon Pere,
>   Que j'espere,
> Tu me respondras à temps   (Marot, stanza 15)
>
> For on thee, Lord, without end
>   I attend,
> My God Thou wilt heare my voice (Sidney, lines 43–5)

56 *Defence of Poesie*, sig. D2ᵛ (cf. *Apology for Poetry*, ed. Shepherd, p. 107).

57 See above, ch. 1, n. 36.

58 See W. S. Pratt, *The Music of the French Psalter of 1562. A Historical Survey and Analysis. With the Music in Modern Notation* (New York, 1939), pp. 25–6; see further C. Ing, *Elizabethan Lyrics. A Study in the development of English metres and their relation to poetic effect* (London, 1951), esp. ch. 5 'Elizabethan Lyrics influenced by Music', pp. 107–150.

59 For the music of the French metrical psalter see *Le Psautier huguenot*, ed. Pidoux, i (Les Mélodies); cf. Pratt's *Music of the French Psalter* which includes some references to Sidney's use of the French metres; see further J. C. A. Rathmell, 'A Critical Edition of the Psalms of Sir Philip Sidney and the Countess of Pembroke' (University of Cambridge, Ph.D., 1964), pp. 530–3.

60 For further discussion see D. Attridge, *The Rhythms of English Poetry* (London & New York, 1982).

61 Sidney's letter to Edward Denny (22 May, 1580) closes with the charge 'remember with your good voyce, to singe my songes for they will one well become an other', see J. M. Osborn, *Young Philip Sidney 1572–1577* (New Haven & London, 1972), p. 540. See further a similar letter to Robert Sidney (18 Oct. 1580) in which Sidney urges his younger brother to continue his education in music and implies that he regrets not doing so himself: 'Now sweete brother take a delight to keepe and increase your musick, yow will not beleive what a want I finde of it in my melancholie times' (*Complete Works*, ed. Feuillerat, iii, 130–3, esp. 132–3).

62 *Defence of Poesie*, sig. B4ʳ (cf. *Apology for Poetry*, ed. Shepherd, p. 99).

63 On Sidney's contrafaction in his 'Certaine Sonnets' see F. J. Fabry, 'Sidney's Verse Adaptations of Two Sixteenth-Century Italian Art Songs', *Renaissance Quarterly*, xxiii (1970), 237–55; and the same author's 'Sidney's Poetry and Italian Song-Form', *English Literary Renaissance*, iii (1973), 232–48. See further D. G. Cardamone, *The 'canzone villanesca alla napolitana' and Related Forms, 1537–1570*, 2 vols. (Ann Arbor, 1981) esp. i, 67–103 on musical and metrical forms.

64 On the Winchester MS (Winchester College, The Fellows' Library, MS 153) see J. Ritterman, 'The Winchester Part Books' (University of London, M. Mus., 1977).

65 For the French tune to Ps. 42 and textual underlay of the first stanza see *Le Psautier huguenot*, ed. Pidoux, i, 51; subsequent quotations and transcription are from this edition. Cf. Pratt, *Music of the French Psalter*, p. 122 (tune only). This tune was first published with Ps. 42 in an edition of eighty-three metrical psalms printed in Geneva, 1551.

66 Cf. *Poems*, ed. Ringler, pp. 507–8.

67 On Byrd's *Songs of sundrie natures* (1589) see above Appendix, no. 75, and *The English Madrigalists*, ed. E. H. Fellowes, xv (rev. P. Brett) (London, 1962). For F. Kindlemarsh's Christmas carol (song no. 35) see *The Paradyse of daynty devises*, ed. R. Edwards (1576), STC² 7516, p. 4.

Sidney's song is no. 33 in Byrd's edition. See also the lyrics of song no. 14 which appears in G. Whitney's *A Choice of Emblemes* (Leiden, 1586), *STC²* 25438, p. 191 and song no. 28, a single stanza from T. Churchyard's 'Shores Wife', in W. Baldwin's *A Myrrour for Magistrates* (1563), *STC²* 1248, sig. Z3ᵛ.

68 For a description of the presentation manuscript (Penshurst, Viscount De L'Isle and Dudley MS) see *Poems*, ed. Ringler, pp. 546–7.

69 Among composers the Countess might have asked to set Sidney's psalms in the 1590s are: William Byrd (d. 1623) whose *Psalmes, Sonets, & songs* (1588) includes settings of elegiac verses for Sidney, see above Appendix, no. 74; Thomas Morley (d. 1602) who published musical arrangements for metrical psalms in the late 1590s (when Byrd's monopoly expired) and dedicated his *Canzonets. Or little short songs to three voyces* (1593) (*STC²* 18121) to the Countess in 'humble devotion', see *The English Madrigalists*, ed. E. H. Fellowes, rev. T. Dart, vol. 1, part ii (London, 1956); and John Danyel (d. 1626), composer of *Songs for the Lute, Viol and Voice* (1606) (*STC²* 6268), the younger brother of Samuel Daniel who enjoyed the Countess's patronage at Wilton. In addition, Robert Jones dedicated his *The First Booke of Songes or Ayres of foure parts* (1600) (*STC²* 14732) to Sir Robert Sidney as brother of Sir Philip. On Danyel and Morley see *The New Grove Dictionary of Music and Musicians*, ed. S. Sadie, 20 vols. (London, 1980), v. 233–4; xii, 579–85. On Danyel and Jones see P. Warlock [i.e. P. Heseltine], *The English Ayre* (London, 1926), pp. 52–63 and 63–81.

70 London, British Library, Additional MS 15117, fols. 4ᵛ and 5ᵛ. For a note of sixteenth- and seventeenth-century settings of Sidney's secular poems see *Poems*, ed. Ringler, pp. 566–8.

71 See n.29 above. J. Buxton (*Sidney and the English Renaissance*, pp. 115–16) quotes a passage from the *Old Arcadia* in an early draft in which Dicus and Lalus discuss quantitative verse and music; Lalus argues that

Dicus did muche abuse the dignitie of Poetrye to applye yt to musicke since rather Musicke is a servante of poetrye, for by thone the eare onelye, by thother the mynde is pleased

i.e. poetry is superior to music in that it has an intellectual appeal as well as a sensual one. Cf. Sir Philip Sidney, *The Countess of Pembroke's Arcadia* (*The Old Arcadia*), ed. J. Robertson (Oxford, 1973), pp. 89–90.

72 *Defence of Poesie*, sig. E2ʳ (cf. *Apology for Poetry*, ed. Shepherd, p. 113). Puttenham states 'Poesie is a skill to speake & write harmonically: and verses or rime be a kind of Musicall utterance'; cf. 'speech by meeter is ... as a kind of Musicke', see *Arte of English Poesie* in *Elizabethan Critical Essays*, ed. G. G. Smith, 2 vols. (Oxford, 1904, repr., 1971), ii, 67, cf. ii, 8.

73 Ibid., ii, 88.

74 Ibid.

75 Ibid., ii, 90–1.

76 Ibid., ii, 95.
77 Horace, *On Poetry: The 'Ars Poetica'*, ed. C. O. Brink (Cambridge, 1971), p. 67, lines 343–4; tr. D. A. Russell in *Ancient Literary Criticism The Principal Texts in New Translations*, ed. D. A. Russell & M. Winterbottom (Oxford, 1972, repr., 1978), pp. 288–9; cf. Ben Jonson's translation:

> But he hath every suffrage, can apply
> Sweet mix'd with sowre, to his Reader, so
> As doctrine, and delight together go

in *Ben Jonson*, ed. C. H. Herford, P. & E. Simpson, 11 vols. (Oxford, 1925–52), viii (1947), 329, lines 514–16.
78 *L'Art poëtique de Jacques Peletier du Mans (1555)*, ed. A. Boulanger (Paris, 1930), p. 97.
79 Countess of Pembroke, 'To the Angell spirit of . . . Sidney', *Poems*, ed. Ringler, p. 269, lines 74–5, 71.
80 Cf. Lodge, Puttenham, Harington, see above ch. 1, n. 22.

6 that Lyricall kind: Pembroke

1 *The Complete Poems of Sir Philip Sidney*, ed. A. B. Grosart, 2 vols. (London, 1873), ii, 207.
2 For the Countess of Pembroke's 'To the Angell spirit of the most excellent Sir Philip Sidney', see *The Poems of Sir Philip Sidney*, ed. W. A. Ringler, Jr (Oxford, 1962, repr. 1971), pp. 267–9, lines 27–8, 30, 71–2, 77, 78–9, 82.
3 Ibid., lines 37–40.
4 G. F. Waller, 'The Text and Manuscript Variants of The Countess of Pembroke's Psalms', *Review of English Studies*, n.s., xxvi (1975), 1–18, esp. 1–3 for the stemma based on J. C. A. Rathmell's in 'A Critical Edition of the Psalms of Sir Philip Sidney and the Countess of Pembroke' (University of Cambridge, Ph.D., 1964).
5 See above ch. 5, n. 3 and *Poems*, ed. Ringler, pp. 547–8.
6 Ibid., p. 502; cf. Waller, *RES*, xxvi (1975), 2.
7 For the texts of Pss. 1–43 in Oxford, Bodleian Library, MS Rawlinson poet. 25 (Woodford's transcript) see *Poems*, ed. Ringler; for those in the Penshurst MS see Rathmell, 'Critical Edition' (1964) and the same editor's *The Psalms of Sir Philip Sidney and the Countess of Pembroke* (New York, 1963). See further *The Triumph of Death and other Unpublished and Uncollected Poems by Mary Sidney, Countess of Pembroke (1561–1621)*, ed. G. F. Waller (Salzburg, 1977) for early drafts of twenty-two psalms by the Countess from Woodford's transcript.
8 Rathmell ('Critical Edition' (1964), p. 530) notes the following correspondences between the Countess's stanza forms and those of the French metrical psalter (some may be fortuitous): Ps. 44 & Marot's (M) Ps. 25; Ps. 45 & Beza's (B) Ps. 85; Ps. 47 & (B) Ps. 132; Ps. 50 & (B) Ps. 85; Ps. 51 & (M) Ps. 10; Pss. 58, 78, 94, 98, 104 cf. (B) Ps. 85; Ps. 71 & (M) Ps.

36; Ps. 97 & (B) Ps. 97; Ps. 105 & (B) Ps. 49; Ps. 111 & (B) Ps. 93; Ps. 118 & (M) Ps. 9; Ps. 119F & (B) Ps. 136; Ps. 119I & (B) Ps. 75; Ps. 129 & (B) Ps. 75; Ps. 136 & (B) Ps. 100; Ps. 138 & (M) Ps. 137.

9 *Poems*, ed. Ringler, p. 267, lines 2–4; cf. Donne's description of 'A Brother and a Sister', 'Two by their bloods' but made 'one' by God, in his 'Upon the Translation of the Psalmes by Sir Philip Sydney, and the Countesse of Pembroke his Sister', lines 14–15, see John Donne, *The Divine Poems*, ed. H. Gardner (2nd edn, Oxford, 1978), pp. 33–5.

10 For Sidney's views of the Psalms and English verse see above ch. 5, n. 1 and 10.

11 For Vives on imitation see above pp. 15–16.

12 Daniel's tribute to the Countess, contained in the dedication to his *Cleopatra* (1594) STC² 6243.4, formerly 6254, is quoted by Rathmell in his introduction to *Psalms of Sidney and the Countess of Pembroke* (1963), p. xxvi.

13 Ibid., p. xx.

14 Waller, *RES*, xxvi (1975), 6–8, 10–11.

15 For this and subsequent quotations from the Countess's psalms see *Psalms of Sidney and the Countess of Pembroke*, ed. Rathmell (1963); I am also indebted to Dr Rathmell's thesis (see above n. 4).

16 (My italics.) A. Golding, tr., *The Psalmes of David and others. With M. John Calvins Commentaries* (London, 1571), fol. 171^r.

17 Waller, *RES*, xxvi (1975), 12–13.

18 (My italics.) T. Beza, *The Psalmes of David Truly opened and explaned by Paraphrasis*, tr. A. Gilby (London, 1581), p. 335.

19 C. Freer, *Music for a King: George Herbert's Style and the Metrical Psalms* (Baltimore & London, 1972), p. 74.

20 *Psalmes of David*, tr. Gilby, p. 335.

21 Golding, tr., *Psalmes of David* (1571), pt 2, fol. 231^v.

22 *Psalmes of David*, tr. Gilby, p. 336.

23 Golding, tr., *Psalmes of David* (1571), pt 2, fol. 231^v.

24 *Psalmes of David*, tr. Gilby, p. 340.

25 For Puttenham's description of epizeuxis see *The Arte of English Poesie*, ed. G. D. Willcock & A. Walker (Cambridge, 1936), p. 201. For mimetic qualities in the Countess's use of syntax see also

> my other self, my inward frend:
> *Whom unto me, me unto whom* did bind
> Exchanged secrets   (Ps. 55, lines 39–41; my italics)

> *Stay* would I not, till I in rest might *stay*   (Ps. 55, line 15)

Cf. also,

> Nay ev'n within my self, my self did say:
> In vain my hart I purge, my hands in vain   (Ps. 88, lines 37–8)

For figures of repetition (such as Sidney had used) involving variants on a single word, see e.g.

the grave of graves
Where lightning of thy wrath
Upon me lighted hath (Ps. 88, lines 25, 28–9)
Where earth doth end with endless ending (Ps. 65, line 25)

Compare Sidney's Ps. 24, lines 9–10:

Who shunning vanity and works of vaineness leaving,
Vainly doth not puff up his mind

26 For Sidney's comment from his *Defence of Poesie* see above p. 159.

27 *Psalmes of David*, tr. Gilby, p. 164; cf. also Sternhold's Ps. 73:6, see above p. 119.

28 Golding, tr., *Psalmes of David* (1571), pt 1, fol. 275ʳ.

29 See *Henry Howard Earl of Surrey Poems*, ed. E. Jones (Oxford, 1964, repr., 1973), pp. 99–101, for this and subsequent quotations from Surrey's Ps. 73.

30 For Professor Jones's comment on Surrey's sonnet see ibid., p. 127; cf. also *The Arundel Harington Manuscript of Tudor Poetry*, ed. R. Hughey, 2 vols. (Columbus, Ohio, 1960), ii, 106.

31 For Coverdale's translation see J. Campensis, *A Paraphrasis upon all the Psalmes of David*, (London, 1539), sig. K2ᵛ.

32 *Psalmes of David*, tr. Gilby, p. 165.

33 Freer, *Music for a King*, pp. 74–5, 105–6.

34 Cf. 'Sing ye … Knowe ye …' (Geneva Bible, Ps. 100:1 and 3); 'Be ye joyfull … Be ye sure …' (Bishops' Bible, Ps. 100: 1 & 2); see also *Astrophil and Stella* 6, lines 1 and 5; sonnet 15, lines 1 and 5; sonnet 42, lines 1 and 5.

35 *Psalmes of David*, tr. Gilby, p. 202; cf. 'My lovers and frendes hast thou put away fro me and hyd myne acquayntaunce out of my syght' (Great Bible/BCP Ps. 88:18); 'and mine acquaintance hid them selves' (Geneva Bible, Ps. 88:18). For Surrey's imitation of this verse see above p. 92.

36 Cf. The Countess's Ps. 90, line 37: 'Our daies of life make seaventy yeares'. For Surrey's image of '… them whose fatall threde' is 'cut in twayne' see his Ps. 88, line 7, in *Surrey Poems*, ed. Jones, p. 98.

37 For David as a celestial Orpheus see above p. 34; for Urania as the new muse of Christian poetry see L. B. Campbell's discussion of Saluste Du Bartas, *La Muse chrestiene* (1574), translated into English by King James VI (1584), in her *Divine Poetry and Drama in Sixteenth-century England* (Cambridge, Berkeley & Los Angeles, 1959), pp. 74–83. George Buchanan had made pointed allusions to the work of pagan poets in his Latin metrical psalm paraphrases, see I. D. McFarlane, *Buchanan* (London, 1981), pp. 285–6.

38 See *Poems*, ed. Ringler, pp. 165–237 (esp. p. 167) for this and all subsequent quotations from *Astrophil and Stella*.

39 Cf. Sidney's Ps. 14:1 (my italics),

The foolish man by flesh and fancy led
His *guiltie heart* with this fond *thought* hath fed,
There is no God

('The foole hath sayed in his hert there is no God.' Great Bible/BCP Ps. 14:1.) The 'inward light' corresponds to the 'reasonable parte of youre sowle', see *Poems*, ed. Ringler, p. 461 for discussion of this concept.

40 Golding, tr., *Psalmes of David* (1571), pt 1, fol. 203^v.

41 See 'To the Angell spirit ...', lines 5–6, in *Poems*, ed. Ringler, p. 267.

42 *The Defence of Poesie* (William Ponsonby, London, 1595) facsimile edn (Menston, 1973), sig. B4^r.

43 See Donne's 'Upon the translation ... by Sydney, and the Countesse of Pembroke', lines 38, 50, 46, 34, 31–2 in *Divine Poems*, ed. Gardner, pp. 33–5.

44 See 'To the Angell spirit ...', lines 13–14, 62–3, in *Poems*, ed. Ringler, pp. 267–8.

45 Ibid., line 7.

7 Epilogue

1 G. Pico della Mirandola, 'Oration on the Dignity of Man', tr. E. L. Forbes, in *The Renaissance Philosophy of Man*, eds. E. Cassirer, P. O. Kristeller & J. H. Randall, Jr (Chicago, 1948, repr. 1971), p. 225.

2 See *Astrophil and Stella* 45, line 14, in *The Poems of Sir Philip Sidney*, ed. W. A. Ringler, Jr (Oxford, 1962, repr., 1971), p. 187; subsequent quotations of Sidney's poetry are from this edition.

3 See 'Jordan I' from *The Temple* in *The Works of George Herbert*, ed. F. E. Hutchinson (Oxford, 1945), p. 56; subsequent quotations of Herbert's poetry are from this edition.

4 B. K. Lewalski, *Protestant Poetics and the Seventeenth-Century Religious Lyric* (Princeton, 1979, repr., 1984), p. 241.

5 From Coverdale's address to the reader in his translation *A Paraphrasis upon all the Psalmes of David, made by Johannes Campensis* (London, 1539), sig. A2^r; see above p. 33.

6 For a select list of metrical psalm versions by Sir John Harington, Joseph Hall, George Chapman, Sir Edwin Sandys, George Wither, Thomas Carew, Sir John Davies, Francis Bacon, Richard Crashaw and Henry King amongst others, see *The New Cambridge Bibliography of English Literature*, ed. G. Watson, vol. 1 (Cambridge, 1974), cols. 1906–14: see further P. von Rohr-Sauer, *English Metrical Psalms from 1600 to 1660. A Study in the Religious and Aesthetic Tendencies of that Period* (Freiburg, 1938); D. S. Greenwood, 'The Seventeenth-Century English Poetic Biblical Paraphrase: Practitioners, Texts and Contexts' (University of Cambridge, Ph.D., 1985).

7 For discussion of Sidney's influence on *The Temple* see L. L. Martz, *The Poetry of Meditation A Study in English Religious Literature* (New Haven & London, 1954, repr. 1976), pp. 261–79; *The Psalms of Sir Philip Sidney and the Countess of Pembroke*, ed. J. C. A. Rathmell (New York, 1963), pp. xviii–xix; C. Freer, *Music for a King George Herbert's Style and the Metrical Psalms* (Baltimore & London, 1972), p. 75 *et passim*; Lewalski,

Protestant Poetics, pp. 243–4; see further H. Fisch, *Jerusalem and Albion: the Hebraic Factor in Seventeenth-Century Literature* (London, 1964), pp. 56–62; and C. Bloch, *Spelling the Word: George Herbert and the Bible* (Berkeley, Los Angeles & London, 1985), pp. 231–305, for discussion of the direct influence of the Psalms on Herbert's poetry.

8 T. Wilcox, *A Right Godly and learned Exposition, upon the whole Booke of Psalmes* (London, 1586), sig. B1ʳ; see above p. 27.

9 For this and subsequent quotations from Milton's psalms see *John Milton, Complete Shorter Poems*, ed. J. Carey (London, 1968, repr., 1971), p. 318; also pp. 6–10, 304–19, 400–6 and literature cited; see further M. Studley, 'Milton and his Paraphrases of the Psalms', *Philological Quarterly*, iv (1925), 364–72.

10 M. Hope Nicolson, *John Milton A Reader's Guide to his Poetry* (London, 1964, repr., 1970), p. 24.

SELECT BIBLIOGRAPHY

Manuscripts cited or mentioned
(excluding theses)

Arundel Castle:
  Harington MS
London, British Library:

Additional MS	5465	
Additional MS	5565	
Additional MS	12047	
Additional MS	12048	
Additional MS	15117	
Additional MS	30981	
Additional MS	31922	
Additional MS	36529	('Hill' or 'Phillips' MS)
Additional MS	46372	
Egerton	2711	
Harley	2252	
Harley	6930	
Royal	7 D x	
Royal	12 A vii	
Royal	14 B l	
Royal	17 A xvii	
Royal	17 A xxi	
Royal	18 B xvi	
Stowe	1066	

Public Record Office:
  S.P. 10–9–58
New Haven, Yale, Beinecke Library:
'The Prayer Book of St Thomas More'
Oxford, Bodleian Library:

Bodley	903	
Cherry	36	
Don.d.	152	
Douce	361	
Rawlinson Poet.	24	
Rawlinson Poet.	25	
Balliol College	354	(Richard Hill's book)
Keble College	33	
Keble College	39	

Penshurst, Penshurst Place:
Viscount De L'Isle and Dudley MS

Select list of printed works cited
(excluding English metrical psalm versions printed 1530–1601)

TEXTS

Modern editions of sixteenth-century texts are listed under author. For collections see first under title.

Ancient Literary Criticism. *See* Russell and Winterbottom.

Aquinas, T. *Opera omnia* (Parma, 1852–63).

Aretino, P. *I sette salmi de la Penitentia de David* (Venice, 1536).

Paraphrase upon the Seaven Penitentiall Psalmes of the Kingly Prophet, tr. J. Hawkins (Douai, 1635).

The Arundel Harington Manuscript of Tudor Poetry, ed. R. Hughey, 2 vols. (Columbus, Ohio, 1960).

Ascham, R. *English Works*, ed. W. A. Wright (Cambridge, 1904, repr. 1970).

Baldwin, W. *The Canticles or Balades of Salomon* (London, 1549).

A Treatise of Moral Phylosophye (London, 1550).

A Myrrour for Magistrates. Wherein maye be seen by example of other, with howe grevous plages vices are punished: and howe frayle and unstable worldly prosperity is founde, even of those whom Fortune seemeth most highly to favour (London, 1563).

Bale, J. *Scriptorum illustrium maioris Brytannie, quam nunc Angliam & Scotiam vocant: Catalogus* (Basle, 1557).

Becon, T. *A Potacion or drinkynge for this holi time of lent very comfortable for all penitent synners* (London, 1542).

Early Works, ed. J. Ayre, Parker Society (Cambridge, 1843).

Beza, T. *See Psalmorum Davidis.*

Bible *Hebraica Biblia Latina planeque nova Sebast. Munsteri tralatione*, 2 vols. (Basle, 1534–5).

The newe testament both Latine and Englyshe ech correspondent to the other after the vulgare texte, communely called S. Jeroms. Faythfully translated by Myles Coverdale (Southwark, 1538).

The Byble in Englyshe ... *after the veryte of the Hebrue and Greke textes* (London, 1539).

The Bible and Holy Scriptures Conteyned in the Olde and Newe Testament. Translated according to the Ebrue and Greke, and conferred With the best translations in divers langages (Geneva, 1560).

The. holie. Bible. conteyning the olde Testament and the newe (London, 1568).

The Second Tome of the Holie Bible Faithfully Translated into English, out of the Authentical Latin. Diligently conferred with the Hebrewe, Greeke, and other Editions in divers languages (Douai, 1610).

See also Psalms/Psalters; *Records of the English Bible.*

The Writings of John Bradford ... Martyr 1555, ed. A. Townsend, 2 vols., Parker Society (Cambridge, 1848).

Buchanan, G.   See *Psalmorum sacrorum*.

Cajetan, T. de Vio   See *Psalmi Davidici*.

Calvin, J.   *The Institution of Christian Religion, written in Latine by M. John Calvine, and translated into English according to the authors last edition, by Thomas Norton* (London, 1578).

Campensis, J.   See *Psalmorum omnium*.

Case, J.   *The Praise of Musicke: Wherein besides the antiquitie, dignitie, delectation, & use therof in civill matters, is also declared the sober and lawfull use of the same in the congregation and Church of God* (Oxford, 1586).

The Works of Geoffrey Chaucer, ed. F. N. Robinson, 2nd edn (London, 1957, repr. 1970).

Marcus Tullius Ciceroes thre bookes of duties, to Marcus his sonne, turned out of latine into english, by Nicolas Grimalde. Wherunto the latine is adjoyned (London, 1558).

Coverdale, M. (ed.)   *Certain most godly, fruitful, and comfortable letters of ... Saintes and holy Martyrs of God ... written in the tyme of theyr affliction and cruell imprisonment* (London, 1564).

Remains, ed. G. Pearson, Parker Society (Cambridge, 1846).

Daniel, S.   *Delia and Rosamond augmented. Cleopatra* (London, 1594).

The Complete Works in Verse and Prose, ed. A. B. Grosart, 5 vols. (London, 1885–96).

Danyel, J.   *Songs for the Lute, Viol and Voice* (London, 1606).

Donne, J.   *The Divine Poems*, ed. H. Gardner, 2nd edn (Oxford, 1978).

Sermons on the Psalms and Gospels, ed. E. M. Simpson (Berkeley, Los Angeles and London, 1963, repr. 1974).

Drant, T.   See *Horace*.

Drayton, M.   *The Harmonie of the Church. Containing, The Spirituall Songes and holy Hymnes, of godly men, Patriarkes and Prophetes* (London, 1591).

Du Bartas, G. du Salluste,   *La Muse chrestiene* (Paris, 1574).

Du Bellay, J.   *La Defense et illustration de la langue francoise* (Paris, 1561).

The Early English Carols, ed. R. L. Greene, 2nd edn (Oxford, 1977).

Elizabethan Critical Essays, ed. G. G. Smith, 2 vols. (Oxford, 1904, repr. 1971).

England, Church of   *The Booke of Common Prayer and administracion of the sacramentes, and other rites and ceremonies of the Churche: after the use of the Churche of England* (London, 1549) (STC^2 16269.5).

Injunctions geven by the Queenes Majestie (London, 1559).

The English Madrigalists, ed. E. H. Fellowes, revised series ed. T. Dart (London, 1956–); vol. i, rev. edn, T. Dart (1956); vol. xiv, rev. edn, P. Brett (1965); vol. xv, rev. edn, P. Brett (1962); vol. xxxv[B], rev. edn, P. Brett (1961).

Erasmus, D.   *Opera omnia* (Amsterdam, 1969–).

Estienne, R.   *Dictionarium, seu Latinae linguae Thesaurus* (Paris, 1531); 3 vols. (Paris, 1543).

Fisher, J.   *This treatyse concernynge the fruytfull saynges of Davyd the kynge &*

prophete in the seven penytencyall psalmes (London, 1509). Facsimile edn (Amsterdam and Norwood N.J., 1979).

Forrest, W. *'History of Grisild the Second': a narrative, in verse, of the divorce of Queen Katherine of Arragon*, ed. W. D. Macray, Roxburgh Club (London, 1875).

Foxe, J. *Actes and Monuments of these latter and perillous dayes, touching matters of the Church* (London, [1563]).

Fraunce, A. *The Countesse of Pembrokes Ivychurch* (London, 1591).

Gagnay, J. de (Gagnaeius). See *Psalmi Davidici.*

Gascoigne, G. *Works*, ed. J. W. Cunliffe, 2 vols. (Cambridge, 1907–10). *A Hundreth Sundrie Flowres from the Original Edition*, ed. B. M. Ward (London, 1926).

Golding, A. *See* Ovid.

A Gorgeous Gallery of Gallant Inventions (1578). ed. H. E. Rollins (Cambridge, Mass., 1926).

[Gude and Godlie Ballatis] *A Compendious Book of Godly and Spiritual Songs commonly known as the Gude and Godlie Ballatis*, ed. A. F. Mitchell, Scottish Text Society, xxxix (Edinburgh, 1897).

Hall, J. *The Court of Virtue* (1565), ed. R. A. Fraser (London, 1961).

Hawkins, J. *See* Aretino.

Herbert, G. *The Works of George Herbert*, ed. F. E. Hutchinson (Oxford, 1945).

Herbert, M., Countess of Pembroke, *The Triumph of Death and other Unpublished and Uncollected Poems by Mary Sidney, Countess of Pembroke (1561–1621)*, ed. G. F. Waller, *Elizabethan & Renaissance Studies*, ed. J. Hogg, lxv, Salzburg Studies in English Literature (Salzburg, 1977).

Hilsey, J. (ed.) *See* Primer.

Hooker, R. *Of the Lawes of Ecclesiasticall Politie The fift Booke* (London, 1597).

Later Writings of Bishop Hooper, together with his Letters and other Pieces, ed. C. Nevinson, Parker Society (Cambridge, 1852).

Horace his arte of poetrie, pistles, and satyrs Englished, tr. T. Drant (London, 1567).

Horace, *On Poetry: The 'Ars Poetica'*, ed. C. O. Brink (Cambridge, 1971).

Howard, H., Earl of Surrey, *The Works*, ed. G. F. Nott (London, 1815). *Poems*, ed. E. Jones (Oxford, 1964, repr. 1973).

Humfrey, L. *Interpretatio linguarum: seu de ratione convertendi & explicandi autores tam sacros quam prophanos* (Basle, 1559).

James VI. *The Poems of King James VI of Scotland*, ed. J. Craigie, 2 vols., Scottish Text Society, ser. 3, xxii, xxvi (Edinburgh, 1955–8).

Jewel, J. *Works*, ed. J. Ayre, 4 vols., Parker Society (Cambridge, 1845–50).

Jones, R. *The First Booke of Songes or Ayres of foure parts with tableture for the lute* (London, 1600).

Ben Jonson, ed. C. H. Herford, P. and E. Simpson, 11 vols. (Oxford, 1925–52).

SELECT BIBLIOGRAPHY

Leland, J.   *Naeniae in mortem Thomae Viati equitis incomparabilis* (London, 1542).

Letters and Papers, Foreign and Domestic, of the Reign Henry VIII, xviii, ed. J. Gairdner and R. H. Brodie (London, 1901).

Lily, W. and Colet, J.   *A Shorte Introduction of Grammar, generally to be used in the Kynges Majesties dominions* (London, 1549).

Marguerite of Navarre,   *Le Miroir de l'âme pecheresse* (Alençon, 1531).

Le Tombeau de Marguerite de Valois royne de Navarre. Faict premierement en Disticques Latins par les trois Soeurs Princesses en Angleterre (Paris, 1551).

Les Psaumes de Clément Marot, ed. S. J. Lenselink (Assen, 1969).

Milton, J.   *Complete Shorter Poems*, ed. J. Carey (London, 1968, repr. 1971).

More, T.   *The Workes of Sir Thomas More*, ed. W. Rastell (London, 1557).

Thomas More's Prayer Book: A Facsimile Reproduction of the Annotated Pages, ed. L. L. Martz and R. S. Sylvester (New Haven and London, 1969).

The Complete Works of St Thomas More, xiii, ed. G. E. Haupt (New Haven and London, 1976).

Morley, T.   *Canzonets. Or little short songs to three voyces* (London, 1593).

Mulcaster, R.   *The first part of the Elementarie* (London, 1582).

Münster, S.   *See* Bible.

North, T.   *See* Plutarch.

Norton, T.   *See* Calvin.

Ovid   *The Fyrst Fower Bookes of P. Ovidius Nasos worke, intitled Metamorphosis, translated oute of Latin into Englishe meter by Arthur Golding Gent. A woorke very pleasaunt and delectable* (London, 1565).

The Paradyse of daynty devises, ed. R. Edwards (London, 1576).

Parr, C.   *Prayers or Medytacions, wherein the mynd is stirred, paciently to suffre all afflictions here, to set at nought the vayne prosperitee of this worlde, and alwaie to longe for the everlastynge felicitee: Collected out of holy woorkes* (London, 1545).

The lamentacion of a sinner, made by the most vertuous Lady Quene Caterin (London, 1547).

L'Art poëtique de Jacques Peletier du Mans (1555), ed. A. Boulanger (Paris, 1930).

Pembroke, Countess of   *See* Herbert, M.

Petrarch, F.   *Epistolae Selectae*, ed. A. F. Johnson (Oxford, 1923).

La Familiari Libri I-IV, ed. U. Dotti (Urbino, 1970).

Petrarch The First Modern Scholar and Man of Letters: A Selection from his Correspondence, tr. J. H. Robinson and H. W. Rolfe (New York and London, 1898).

Phaer, T.   *See* Virgil.

Plutarch   *The Lives of the Noble Grecians and Romanes, Compared together by that grave learned Philosopher and Historiographer, Plutarke of Chaeronea: Translated out of Greeke into French by James Amyot . . . and out of French into English, by Thomas North* (London, 1579).

Primer   *A Manual of prayers or the prymer in Englysh & Laten set out at length ... by Jhon by Goddes grace, & the Kynges callyng, Bysshoppe of Rochester* (London, 1539).

Psalmi Davidici ad Hebraicam veritatem castigati ... per ... Thomam de Vio Caietanum (Venice, 1530).

Psalmi Davidici septuaginta quinque, in lyricos versus servata ecclesiasticae versionis veritate & Hebraeorum varietate, redacti: Authore Ioanno Ganeio Parisino Theologo, Parisiensis ecclesiae atque Academiae Cancellario (Paris, 1547).

Psalmorum Davidis et aliorum prophetarum, libri quinque. Argumentis & Latina Paraphrasi illustrati, ac etiam vario carminum genere latine expressi ... T. Beza auctore (London, 1580).

Psalmorum omnium: iuxta Hebraicam veritatem paraphrastica, interpretatio J. Campensi (Paris, 1534).

Psalmorum sacrorum Davidis libri quinque duplici poetica metaphrasi, altera alteri e regione opposita vario carminum genere Latine expressi Theodoro Beza Vezelio, & Georgio Buchanano Scoto autoribus (Morges, 1581).

Our Prayer Book Psalter, ed. E. Clapton (London, 1934).

Le Psautier huguenot du xvie siècle. Mélodies et documents, ed. P. Pidoux, 2 vols. (Basle, 1962).

Puttenham, G.   *The Arte of English Poesie*, ed. G. D. Willcock and A. Walker (Cambridge, 1936).

Quintilian.   *Institutio oratoria*, tr. H. E. Butler, Loeb Classical Library, 4 vols. (London and Cambridge, Mass., 1922, repr. 1961).

Rastell, W. (ed.)   *See under* More.

Records of the English Bible, ed. A. W. Pollard (Oxford, 1911).

Russell, D. A. and Winterbottom, M. (tr.),   *Ancient Literary Criticism The Principal Texts in New Translations* (Oxford, 1972, repr. 1978).

Iulii Caesaris Scaligeri, viri clarissimi, Poetices libri septem (Lyon, 1561).

Select Translations from Scaliger's Poetics, tr. F. M. Padelford, *Yale Studies in English*, xxvi (New York, 1905).

Sebillet, T.   *Art poetique françois. Pour l'instruction des jeunes studieux, & encor' peu avancez en la Poësie Françoise* (Paris, 1573).

Secular Lyrics of the XIVth and XVth Centuries, ed. R. H. Robbins, 2nd edn (Oxford, 1955, repr. 1961).

Seneca   *Ad Lucilium Epistulae Morales*, tr. R. M. Gummere, Loeb Classical Library, 3 vols. (London, and Cambridge, Mass., 1920, repr. 1962).

Shakespeare, W. *The First Folio. The Norton Facsimile*, ed. C. Hinman (London and New York, 1968).

Sidney, M.   *See* Herbert, M.

Sidney, P.   *The Complete Poems*, ed. A. B. Grosart, 2 vols. (London, 1873).

Complete Works of Sir Philip Sidney, ed. A. Feuillerat, 4 vols. (Cambridge, 1912–26).

The Countess of Pembroke's Arcadia (The Old Arcadia), ed. J. Robertson (Oxford, 1973).

The Defence of Poesie. By Sir Phillip Sidney, Knight (William Ponsonby, London, 1595), facsimile edn (Menston, 1973).

An Apology for Poetry or the Defence of Poesy ed. G. Shepherd (Manchester, 1965, repr. 1967).

The Poems of Sir Philip Sidney, ed. W. A. Ringler (Oxford, 1962).

Selected Poems, ed. K. Duncan-Jones (Oxford, 1973).

The Psalms of Sir Philip Sidney and the Countess of Pembroke, ed. J. C. A. Rathmell (New York, 1963).

'A Critical Edition of the Psalms of Sir Philip Sidney and the Countess of Pembroke', ed. J. C. A. Rathmell (unpublished Ph.D. thesis, University of Cambridge, 1964).

Smith, T.   *Literary and Linguistic Works, 1542, 1549, 1568*, ed. B. Danielsson, Stockholm Studies in English (1963–83).

Songes and Sonettes, ed. R. Tottel (London, 1557).

Tottel's Miscellany (1557–1587), ed. H. E. Rollins, 2 vols. (Cambridge, Mass., 1928–9, rev. 1965).

Surrey, Earl of   See Howard.

Tottel, R. (ed.)   See *Songes and Sonettes*.

Tudor Church Music, Thomas Tallis c. 1505–1585, 1st series (Oxford, 1928).

Tyndale, W.   *The obedience of a Christen man and how Christen rulers ought to governe* ([Antwerp], 1528), facsimile edn (Menston, 1970).

Doctrinal Treatises and Introductions to different portions of the Holy Scripture, ed. H. Walter, Parker Society (Cambridge, 1848).

Virgil   *The seven first bookes of the Eneidos of Virgill, converted in English meter by Thomas Phaer* (London, 1558).

Vives, J. L.   *Opera in duos distincta tomos* (Basle, 1555).

Vives on Education. A Translation of the 'De Tradendis Disciplinis' of Juan Luis Vives, tr. F. Watson (Cambridge, 1913).

Webb, W.   *A Discourse of English Poetrie* (London, 1586).

Whitney, G.   *A Choice of Emblemes* (Leiden, 1586).

The Autobiography of Thomas Whythorne, ed. J. M. Osborn (Oxford, 1961).

Willet, A.   *Ecclesia Triumphans: that is, The Joy of the English Church, for the happie Coronation of the most vertuous and pious Prince James* (Cambridge, 1603).

Wilson, T.   *The arte of Rhetorique* (1560), ed. G. H. Mair (Oxford, 1909).

Wyatt, T.   *Collected Poems of Sir Thomas Wyatt*, ed. K. Muir and P. Thomson (Liverpool, 1969).

The Complete Poems, ed. R. A. Rebholz (Harmondsworth, 1978)

REFERENCE AND SECONDARY WORKS

Althoff, E.   *Myles Coverdales 'Goostly Psalmes and Spirituall Songes' und das deutsche Kirchenlied. Ein Beitrag zum Einfluss der deutschen Literatur auf die englische im 16. Jahrhundert* (Münster, 1935).

Amos, F. R.   *Early Theories of Translation* (New York, 1920).

ap Roberts, R. 'Old Testament Poetry: The Translatable Structure', *Publications of the Modern Language Association of America*, xcii (1977).

Attridge, D. *The Rhythms of English Poetry* (London and New York, 1982).

Baldwin, T. W. *William Shakspere's Petty School* (Urbana, 1943).
William Shakspere's Small Latine and Lesse Greek, 2 vols. (Urbana, 1944).

Baron, H. V. 'Sir Thomas Wyatt's Seven Penitential Psalms: A study of textual and source materials' (unpublished Ph.D. thesis, University of Cambridge, 1977).

Baroway, I. 'The Bible as Poetry in the English Renaissance: An Introduction', *Journal of English and Germanic Philology*, xxxii (1933), 447–80.
'Tremellius, Sidney, and Biblical Verse', *Modern Language Notes*, xlix (1934), 145–9.

Baumgartner, A. J. *De l'enseignement de l'hébreu chez les protestants à partir de l'époque de la Réformation* (Lausanne, 1889).

Bloch, C. *Spelling the Word: George Herbert and the Bible* (Berkeley, Los Angeles and London, 1985).

Boyd, M. C. *Elizabethan Music and Musical Criticism* (Philadelphia, 1940, repr. 1962).

Brennan, M. G. 'The Date of the Countess of Pembroke's Translations of the Psalms', *Review of English Studies*, n.s., xxxiii (1982), 434–6.

Brod, M. *Johannes Reuchlin und sein Kampf eine historische Monographie* (Stuttgart, 1965).

Brook, V. J. K. *A Life of Archbishop Parker* (Oxford, 1962, repr. 1965).

Bruce, F. F. *The English Bible: A History of Translations*, 2nd edn (London, 1970).

Butterworth, C. C. *The Literary Lineage of the King James Bible* (Philadelphia, 1941).
The English Primers (1529–1545) Their Publication and Connection with the English Bible and the Reformation in England (Philadelphia, 1953).

Butterworth, C. C. & Chester, A. G. *George Joye 1495?–1553* (Philadelphia, 1962).

Buxton, J. *Sir Philip Sidney and the English Renaissance* (London, 1954).

The Cambridge History of the Bible, ii. *The West from the Fathers to the Reformation*, ed. G. W. H. Lampe (Cambridge, 1969); iii, *The West from the Reformation to the Present Day*, ed. S. L. Greenslade (Cambridge, 1963).

Campbell, L. B. *Divine Poetry and Drama in Sixteenth-Century England* (Cambridge, Berkeley and Los Angeles, 1959).

Cardamone, D. G. *The 'canzone villanesca alla napolitana' and Related Forms, 1537–1570*, 2 vols. (Ann Arbor, 1981).

Casady, E. *Henry Howard, Earl of Surrey* (New York, 1938).

Cassirer, E., Kristeller, P. O., Randall, J. H. (ed.) *The Renaissance Philosophy of Man* (Chicago, 1948, repr. 1971).

Cave, T. C. *Devotional Poetry in France c. 1570–1613* (Cambridge, 1969).
The Cornucopian Text: Problems of Writing in the French Renaissance (Oxford, 1979).

SELECT BIBLIOGRAPHY

Chatterjee, K. K. *In Praise of Learning: John Colet and Literary Humanism in Education* (New Delhi, 1974).

Colie, R. L. *The Resources of Kind: Genre-Theory in the Renaissance*, ed. B. K. Lewalski (Berkeley, 1973).

Conley, C. H. *The First English Translators of the Classics* (New Haven, 1927).

Connell, D. *Sir Philip Sidney: The Maker's Mind* (Oxford, 1977).

Cowan, W. 'A Bibliography of the Book of Common Order and Psalm Book of the Church of Scotland: 1556–1644', *Papers of the Edinburgh Bibliographical Society*, x (1913), 71–98.

Curtius, E. R. *European Literature and the Latin Middle Ages*, tr. W. R. Trask (London, 1953, repr. 1979).

Daiches, D. *The King James Version of the English Bible: An Account of the Development and Sources of the English Bible of 1611 with Special Reference to the Hebrew Tradition* (Chicago, 1941).

Darlow, T. H. and Moule, A. F., rev. Herbert, A. S., *Historical Catalogue of Printed Editions of the English Bible 1525–1961* (London and New York, 1968).

de Vocht, H. *History of the Foundation and the Rise of the Collegium Trilingue Lovaniense 1517–1550* (Louvain, 1951).

Dewar, M. *Sir Thomas Smith, A Tudor Intellectual in Office* (London, 1964).

d'Ors, E. *Vivès humaniste espagnol* (Paris, 1941).

Elton, G. R. *England under the Tudors* (London, 1955, repr. 1967).

Emden, A. B. *A Biographical Register of the University of Oxford A. D. 1501–1540* (Oxford, 1974).

Ewbank, I.-S. 'The House of David in Renaissance Drama', *Renaissance Drama*, vii (1965), 3–40.

Fabry, F. J. 'Sidney's Verse Adaptations of Two Sixteenth-Century Italian Art Songs', *Renaissance Quarterly*, xxiii (1970), 237–55.

'Sidney's Poetry and Italian Song-Form', *English Literary Renaissance*, iii (1973), 232–48.

Fisch, H. *Jerusalem and Albion: the Hebraic Factor in Seventeenth-Century Literature* (London, 1964).

Fowler, A. *Kinds of Literature: An Introduction to the Theory of Genres and Modes* (Oxford, 1982).

Freer, C. 'The Style of Sidney's Psalms', *Language and Style*, ii (1969).

Music for a King: George Herbert's Style and the Metrical Psalms (Baltimore and London, 1972).

Friedman, D. M. 'The "Thing" in Wyatt's Mind', *Essays in Criticism*, xvi (1966), 375–81.

Frost, M. *English & Scottish Psalm & Hymn Tunes c. 1543–1677* (London and Oxford, 1953).

Froude, J. A. *Life and Letters of Erasmus* (London, 1894).

Garrett, C. H. *The Marian Exiles: A Study in the Origins of Elizabethan Puritanism* (Cambridge, 1938).

Gautier-Desvaux, E., Koechlin-Schwarz, V. *Nöel au Perche, 'Noels' et 'Cantiques' spirituels du XVIᵉ siècle* (Saint-Mard-de-Réno, 1977).

Geiger, L. *Johann Reuchlin: sein Leben und seine Werke* (Leipzig, 1871, repr. 1964).

Gerould, G. H. *The Ballad of Tradition* (New York, 1957).

Golding, L. T. *An Elizabethan Puritan: Arthur Golding the Translator of Ovid's Metamorphoses and also of John Calvin's Sermons* (New York, 1937).

Gosselin, E. A. *The King's Progress to Jerusalem: Some Interpretations of David during the Reformation Period* (Los Angeles, 1976).

Greenblatt, S. *Renaissance Self-Fashioning: From More to Shakespeare* (Chicago and London, 1980).

Greene, T. M. *The Light in Troy: Imitation and Discovery in Renaissance Poetry* (New Haven and London, 1982).

Greenwood, D. S. 'The Seventeenth-Century English Poetic Biblical Paraphrase: Practitioners, Texts and Contexts' (unpublished Ph.D. thesis, University of Cambridge, 1985).

Grove's Dictionary of Music and Musicians, ed. E. Blom, 5th edn, 9 vols. (London, 1954).

The New Grove Dictionary of Music and Musicians, ed. S. Sadie, 20 vols. (London, 1980).

Hailperin, H. *Rashi and the Christian Scholars* (Pittsburg, 1963).

Hammond, G. *The Making of the English Bible* (Manchester, 1982).

Hatcher, O. L. 'Aims and Methods of Elizabethan Translators', *Englische Studien*, xliv (1912), 174–92.

Haugaard W. P. 'Katherine Parr: the Religious Convictions of a Renaissance Queen', *Renaissance Quarterly*, xxii (1969), 346–59.

Herrick, M. T. *The Fusion of Horatian and Aristotelian Literary Criticism, 1531–1555* (Urbana, 1946).

Hill, B. 'Trinity College Cambridge MS B.14.52, and William Patten', *Transactions of the Cambridge Bibliographical Society*, iv (1968), 192–200.
'William Patten: A Tudor Londoner', *Essays & Studies* (1983), 14–26.

Hodnett, E. *English Woodcuts, 1480–1535* (London, 1935).

Holland, J. *The Psalmists of Britain: Records Biographical and Literary*, 2 vols. (London, 1843).

Hope Nicolson, M. *John Milton A Reader's Guide to his Poetry* (London, 1964, repr. 1970).

Hopf, C. *Martin Bucer and the English Reformation* (Oxford, 1946).

Hoskins, E. *Horae Beatae Mariae Virginis* (London, 1901).

Howell, W. S. *Logic and Rhetoric in England, 1500–1700* (New York, 1961).

Huttar, C. A. 'Poems by Surrey and Others in a Printed Miscellany Circa 1550', *English Miscellany*, xvi (1965), 9–18.

Ing. C. *Elizabethan Lyrics: A Study in the Development of English Metres and their Relation to Poetic Effect* (London, 1951).

Jarrott, C. A. L. 'Erasmus' Biblical Humanism', *Studies in the Renaissance*, xvii (1970), 119–52.

Jayne, S. *Library Catalogues of the English Renaissance* (Berkeley and Los Angeles, 1956).

Jeanneret, M. *Poésie et tradition biblique au XVIᵉ siècle: Recherches stylistiques sur les paraphrases des psaumes de Marot à Malherbe* (Paris, 1969).

Jentoft, C. W. *Sir Thomas Wyatt and Henry Howard, Earl of Surrey a Reference Guide* (Boston, 1980).

Joiner, M. B.M. Add. MS 15117: An Index, Commentary & Bibliography', *Royal Musical Association Research Chronicle*, vii (1969), 51–109; viii (1970), 102.

Jones, G. L. 'The Influence of Medieval Jewish Exegetes on Biblical Scholarship in Sixteenth-Century England: with Special Reference to the Book of Daniel' (unpublished Ph.D. thesis, University of London, 1975).

  The Discovery of Hebrew in Tudor England: A Third Language (Manchester, 1983).

Jordan, W. K. *Edward VI: The Young King* (London, 1968).

  Edward VI: The Threshold of Power (London, 1970).

Juge, C. *Nicolas Denisot du Mans . . . Essai sur sa vie et ses oeuvres* (Paris, 1907).

Kalstone, D. *Sidney's Poetry: Contexts and Interpretations* (Cambridge, Mass., 1965).

Kastan, D. S. 'An Early English Metrical Psalm: Elizabeth's or John Bale's?', *Notes & Queries*, n.s., xxi (1974), 404–5.

Kelly, L. G. *The True Interpreter: A History of Translation Theory and Practice in the West* (Oxford, 1979).

Ker, N. R. 'Oxford College Libraries in the Sixteenth Century', *Bodleian Library Record*, vi (1959), 459–515.

King, J. N. *English Reformation Literature: The Tudor Origins of the Protestant Tradition* (Princeton, 1982).

Krebs, M., ed. *Johannes Reuchlin 1455–1522 Festgabe seine Vaterstadt Pforzheim* (Pforzheim, 1955).

Kugel, J. L. *The Idea of Biblical Poetry: Parallelism and its History* (New Haven and London, 1981).

Kukenheim, L. *Contributions à l'histoire de la grammaire Grecque, Latine et Hebraïque à l'époque de la Renaissance* (Leiden, 1951).

Kunoth-Leifels, E. *Uber die Darstellungen der 'Bathseba im Bade': Studien zur Geschichte des Bildthemas 4. bis 17. Jahrhundert* (Essen, 1962).

Leblanc, P. *La Poésie religieuse de Clément Marot* (Paris, 1955).

Leclercq, J. *The Love of Learning and the Desire for God* (New York, 1961).

Le Huray, P. *Music and the Reformation in England 1549–1660* (London, 1967, repr. Cambridge, 1978).

Leroquais, V. *Les Livres d'heures manuscrits de la Bibliothèque Nationale* (Paris, 1927–43).

Lewalski, B. K. *Protestant Poetics and the Seventeenth-Century Religious Lyric* (Princeton, 1979).

Lifschutz, E. St Sure 'David's Lyre & the Renaissance Lyric: A Critical Consideration of the Psalms of Wyatt, Surrey and the Sidneys' (unpublished Ph.D. thesis, University of California, Berkeley, 1980).

Lupton, J. H. *A Life of John Colet, D. D.* (London, 1887).

McConica, J. K. *English Humanists and Reformation Politics under Henry VIII and Edward VI* (Oxford, 1965).

McFarlane, I. D. *A Literary History of France: Renaissance France 1470–1589* (London, 1974).

Buchanan (London, 1981).

MacMeeken, J. W. *History of the Scottish Metrical Psalms* (Glasgow, 1872).

Marc'hadour, G. *The Bible in the Works of Thomas More,* 5 parts (Nieuwkoop, 1969–72).

Martz, L. L. *The Poetry of Meditation: A Study of English Religious Literature of the Seventeenth Century* (New Haven and London, 1954, repr. 1976).

Mason, H. A. 'Wyatt and the Psalms', *The Times Literary Supplement,* 27 Feb. and 6 March 1953.

Humanism and Poetry in the Early Tudor Period (London, 1959, repr. 1980).

Matthiessen, F. O. *Translation: An Elizabethan Art* (Cambridge, Mass., 1931, repr. New York, 1965).

Maunsell, A. *The First Part of the Catalogue of English Printed Bookes* (London, 1595).

Michaud, L. G. *Biographie universelle ancienne et moderne ... Nouvelle édition,* 45 vols. (Paris, 1843–[65]).

Miles, L. *John Colet and the Platonic Tradition* (London, 1962).

Minnis, A. J. 'Literary Theory in Discussions of *Formae Tractandi* by Medieval Theologians', *New Literary History,* xi (1979/80), 133–45.

Medieval Theory of Authorship: Scholastic Literary Attitudes in the Later Middle Ages (London, 1984).

Montgomery, R. L. *Symmetry and Sense: The Poetry of Sir Philip Sidney* (Austin, 1961).

Mozley, J. F. *Coverdale and his Bibles* (London, 1953).

Muir, K. *Life and Letters of Sir Thomas Wyatt* (Liverpool, 1963).

Namèche, A-J. *Mémoire sur la vie et les écrits de Jean-Louis Vivès* (Brussels, 1841).

Noble, R. *Shakespeare's Biblical Knowledge and Use of the Book of Common Prayer as Exemplified in the Plays of the First Folio* (London, 1935).

Norton, G. P. 'Translation Theory in Renaissance France: Etienne Dolet and the Rhetorical Tradition', *Renaissance and Reformation,* x (1974), 1–13.

'Translation Theory in Renaissance France: The Poetic Controversy', *Renaissance and Reformation,* xi (1975), 30–44.

The Ideology and Language of Translation in Renaissance France and their Humanist Antecedents, Travaux d'Humanisme et Renaissance, cci (Geneva, 1984).

O'Kill, B. 'The Printed Works of William Patten (*c.* 1510–*c.* 1600)', *Transactions of the Cambridge Bibliographical Society,* vii (1977), 28–45.

O'Rourke Boyle, M. *Christening Pagan Mysteries: Erasmus in Pursuit of Wisdom* (Toronto, 1981).

Osborn, J. M.   *Young Philip Sidney 1572–1577* (New Haven and London, 1972).

Pafort, E.   'A Group of Early Tudor School Books', *The Library*, 4th ser., xxvi (1946), 255–60.

Peterson, R. S.   *Imitation and Praise in the Poems of Ben Jonson* (New Haven and London, 1971).

Pfeiffer, R.   *History of Classical Scholarship from 1300–1850* (Oxford, 1976).

Phillips, E.   *Theatrum Poetarum, or a Compleat Collection of the Poets, Especially the Most Eminent, of all Ages* (London, 1675).

Phillips, J. E.   'George Buchanan and the Sidney Circle', *Huntington Library Quarterly*, xi (1948), 23–55.

Phillips, M. M.   *Erasmus and the Northern Renaissance* (London, 1949, repr. Woodbridge, 1981).

Pratt, W. S.   *The Music of the French Psalter of 1562. A Historical Survey and Analysis. With the Music in Modern Notation* (New York, 1939).

Prescott, A. L.   'The Reputation of Clément Marot in Renaissance England', *Studies in the Renaissance*, xviii (1971), 173–202.
   French Poets and the English Renaissance: Studies in Fame and Transformation (New Haven and London, 1978).

Prothero, R. E.   *The Psalms in Human Life* (London, [1903]).

Rabil, A.   *Erasmus and the New Testament: The Mind of a Christian Humanist* (San Antonio, 1972).

Réau, L.   *Iconographie de l'art chrétien* (Paris, 1955–9).

Ritterman, J.   'The Winchester Part Books' (University of London, M. Mus., 1977).

Robinson, F. G.   *The Shape of Things Known: Sidney's Apology in its Philosophical Tradition* (Cambridge, Mass., 1972).

Rohr-Sauer, P. von   *English Metrical Psalms from 1600 to 1660. A Study in the Religious and Aesthetic Tendencies of that Period* (Freiburg, 1938).

Rosenberg, E.   *Leicester Patron of Letters* (New York, 1955, repr. 1976).

Rosenthal, F.   'The Rise of Christian Hebraism in the Sixteenth Century', *Historia Judaica*, vii (1945), 167–91.

Rudenstine, N. L.   *Sidney's Poetic Development* (Cambridge, Mass., 1967).

Rudick, M.   'Two Notes on Surrey's Psalms', *Notes & Queries*, n.s. xxii (1975), 291–4.

Schwarz, W.   *Principles and Problems of Biblical Translation: Some Reformation Controversies and their Background* (Cambridge, 1955).

Smalley, B.   *The Study of the Bible in the Middle Ages*, 3rd edn (Oxford, 1984).

Smith, H. 'English Metrical Psalms in the Sixteenth Century and their Literary Significance', *Huntington Library Quarterly*, ix (1946), 249–71.
   Elizabethan Poetry: A Study in Conventions, Meaning, and Expression (Cambridge, Mass., 1952, repr. 1964).

Sonnino, L. E.   *A Handbook to Sixteenth-Century Rhetoric* (London, 1968).

Southall, R.   *The Courtly Maker: An Essay on the Poetry of Wyatt and his Contemporaries* (Oxford and New York, 1964).

321

Southern, A. C. *Elizabethan Recusant Prose 1559–1582* (London, [1950]).

Spencer, T. 'The Poetry of Sir Philip Sidney', *A Journal of English Literary History*, xii (1945), 251–78.

Steiner, G. *After Babel: Aspects of Language and Translation* (Oxford, 1975, repr. 1977).

Stevens, J. *Music and Poetry in the Early Tudor Court* (London, 1961, repr. Cambridge, 1979).

Studley, M. 'Milton and his Paraphrases of the Psalms', *Philological Quarterly*, iv (1925), 364–72.

Sweeting, E. J. *Early Tudor Criticism: Linguistic and Literary* (Oxford, 1940).

Tentler, T. N. *Sin and Confession on the Eve of the Reformation* (Princeton, 1977).

Thomson, P. (ed.) *Wyatt: The Critical Heritage* (London and Boston, 1974).

Twombly, R. G. 'Thomas Wyatt's Paraphrase of the Penitential Psalms of David', *Texas Studies in Literature and Language*, xii (1970), 345–80.

von Riese, T. *Die englische Psalmdictung im sechzehnten Jahrhundert* (Münster, 1937).

Waller, G. F. ' "This matching of contraries": Calvinism and Courtly Philosophy in the Sidney Psalms', *English Studies*, lv (1974), 22–31.

'The Text and Manuscript Variants of the Countess of Pembroke's Psalms', *Review of English Studies*, n.s., xxvi (1975), 1–18.

Warton, T. *The History of English Poetry, from the Close of the Eleventh Century to the Commencement of the Eighteenth Century*, 4 vols. (London, 1781).

Watson, F. *Luis Vives El Gran Valenciano 1492–1540* (Oxford, 1922).

White, H. C. *Social Criticism in Popular Religious Literature of the Sixteenth Century* (New York, 1944).

The Tudor Books of Private Devotion (Wisconsin, 1951).

Williams, F. B. 'Lost Books of Tudor England', *The Library*, 5th ser., xxxiii (1978), 1–14.

Wolfley, L. S. 'Sidney's visual-didactic poetic: some complexities and limitations', *The Journal of Medieval and Renaissance Studies*, vi (1976), 217–41.

Wood, A. *Athenae Oxoniensis An Exact History of all the Writers and Bishops who have had their education in the University of Oxford*, 3rd edn, ed. P. Bliss (London, 1813).

Wortham, J. 'Arthur Golding and the Translation of Prose', *Huntington Library Quarterly*, xii (1949), 339–67.

Wright, L. B. 'Translations for the Elizabethan Middle Class', *The Library*, 4th ser., xiii (1932), 312–31.

Middle Class Culture in Elizabethan England (1935, repr. London, 1964).

Zim, R. 'The Maidstone Burghmote and John Hall's *Courte of Vertue* (1565)', *Notes & Queries*, n.s., xxxiii (1986), 320–7.

INDEX

Figures in bold refer to items in the Appendix; all other references are to page numbers.

INDEX

imitatio/imitation
  definitions of: 8, 13–15; as
    'continuity-in-change' 26; in
    traditional metaphors (anabolic) 16,
    19–20, (legal) 18–19, 20, 267 n.88
    practice of, in meditation 80–1; in
    poetry 18–19, 23, 164
    views of 8–24; see also *paraphrasis*;
    poetry; translation
    and eloquence 24, 32
    and emulation 12–13
    and originality 9, 15, 23, 107–11,
    144–9; see also style
imprisonment 81–111 *passim*
instruction, religious 3, 30–4, 41, 74,
  79, 115, 135, 150

James VI, king of Scotland **70**, and
  David 292 n.91
Jewel, John 28
Jonson, Ben 18–19, 207, 304 n.77
Joye, George 1–2, 63, 115, **1, 2**
Juda, Leo 223

Kethe, William 232
kinds of literature 6, 8, 79, 150–1
  English metrical psalms 2, 40, 41,
  206, 207
Knox, John **33**

Learned and . . . profitable exposition, A
  [Ps. 111] **60**
Lefèvre d'Etaples, Jacques 30
Leland, John 278 n.60
Lewalski, Barbara K. 3, 46, 206
liturgy 24, 29, 37, 114, 134–5; metrical
  psalms in, 139, 142–3, 207
London, Tower of
  prisoners in 104, 107; Dudley
  brothers 183; More 81, 82; Somerset
  74, 103; Smith 74, 98; Surrey 89;
  Wyatt 45, 71–2
Lok, Henry **82**
Lumsden, Charles **84**
Luther, Martin 37, 121, 150, 217, 240,
  see also Coverdale, M.

Manual of Prayers, A **67**
Mardley, John 232
Marguerite d'Angoulème, queen of
  Navarre 121, 123, 221, 237
Marot, Clément 121–2, 123, 139 see also
  Beza T.; and Sidney's psalms 165,
  (Ps. 38) 172–6, 178

Marlorat, Augustine **89**
Marshall, William **3**
Martinius, Petrus 255
Martyr, Peter see Vermigli, P. M.
Martz, L. L. 3, 169
Mary I, queen of England 101, 117,
  134, 135, 139, 284 n.59, 290 n.60
Mason, H. A. 3, 44–6
Maunsell, Andrew 259
meditation 29–30, 80
  More 82–3, 85
  Surrey 90, 92–7
  Somerset 103
  see also devotion, personal
metre and verse forms
  common measure 130, 145–6, 152,
  209; fourteeners 114; octosyllabics
  130, 139; *ottava rima* 47; pentameters
  130; poulters measure 130, 145, 146;
  septenaries 134, 209; *terza rima* 47
  regularity of, in ballads and holy
  songs 117, 149, 165
  variety of: in French psalms 122, 172;
  in neo-Latin psalms 137, 165; in
  Parker's psalms 137, 138; in Sidney's
  psalms 152–3, 164–5
  and music 146–8, 178–81, 182
Milton, John 206, 207–8, 209, 210
More, Sir Thomas 82–5, 88, 91, 97, 98,
  104, 107, 248
Muir, K. 45
Muir K. and Thomson, P. 3, 44
Mulcaster, Richard 32
Mundy, John **80**
Münster, Sebastian 35, 136
  Hebraica biblia 37, 271 nn.156–7 and
  159–60, 272 n.161, 285 n.3
Musculus, Wolfgang **41, 90**
music 34, 150, 295 n.126
  improvisation and adaptation 114,
  117, 129
  musical settings 41, 128, 133, 134,
  137–9, 140, 142, 143, (Seagar's
  Ps. 88) 145–8, 149, (Sidney) 178–82,
  240, 273 n.172, (Tallis) 293 n.106,
  295 n.129, 297 n.144
  psalms printed with musical settings
  **5, 22, 30, 31, 34, 38, 39, 40, 44, 51,
  68, 69, 74, 75, 77, 80**
  see also Byrd. W.; Dowland, J.;
  East, T.; Farnaby, G.; Tallis, T.;
  Whythorne, T.
Myrror for Magistrates, A 74